Gleim Publications, Inc., offers five university-level study systems:

Auditing & Systems Exam Questions and Explanations with Test Prep Software
Business Law/Legal Studies Exam Questions and Explanations with Test Prep Software
Federal Tax Exam Questions and Explanations with Test Prep Software
Financial Accounting Exam Questions and Explanations with Test Prep Software
Cost/Managerial Accounting Exam Questions and Explanations with Test Prep Software

The following is a list of Gleim examination review systems:

CIA Review: Part 1, The Internal Audit Activity's Role in Governance, Risk, and Control
CIA Review: Part 2, Conducting the Internal Audit Engagement
CIA Review: Part 3, Business Analysis and Information Technology
CIA Review: Part 4, Business Management Skills
CIA Review: A System for Success

CMA Review: Part 1, Financial Planning, Performance, and Control
CMA Review: Part 2, Financial Decision Making
CMA Review: A System for Success

CPA Review: Financial
CPA Review: Auditing
CPA Review: Business
CPA Review: Regulation
CPA Review: A System for Success

EA Review: Part 1, Individuals
EA Review: Part 2, Businesses
EA Review: Part 3, Representation, Practices, and Procedures
EA Review: A System for Success

An order form is provided at the back of this book or contact us at www.gleim.com or (800) 874-5346.

Groundwood Paper and Highlighters — All Gleim books are printed on high quality groundwood paper. We recommend you use a non-bleed-through (dry) highlighter (ask for it at your local office supply store) when highlighting items within these books.

REVIEWERS AND CONTRIBUTORS

Garrett W. Gleim, B.S., CPA (not in public practice), is a graduate of The Wharton School at the University of Pennsylvania. Mr. Gleim coordinated the production staff, reviewed the manuscript, and provided production assistance throughout the project.

Grady M. Irwin, J.D., is a graduate of the University of Florida College of Law and has taught in the University of Florida College of Business. Mr. Irwin provided substantial editorial assistance throughout the project.

John F. Rebstock, B.S.A., is a graduate of the Fisher School of Accounting at the University of Florida. He has passed the CIA and CPA exams. Mr. Rebstock reviewed portions of the manuscript.

Kristina M. Rivet, CPA, graduated *cum laude* from Florida International University. She has extensive public accounting experience in the areas of financial accounting, tax, and consulting. Ms. Rivet provided substantial editorial assistance throughout the project.

Stewart B. White, B.M., *cum laude*, University of Richmond, B.S., Virginia Commonwealth University, has passed the CPA, CIA, and CISA exams and has worked in the fields of retail management, financial audit, IT audit, COBOL programming, and data warehouse management. Mr. White provided substantial editorial assistance throughout the project.

A PERSONAL THANKS

This manual would not have been possible without the extraordinary effort and dedication of Jacob Brunny, Julie Cutlip, Kate Devine, Eileen Nickl, Teresa Soard, Joanne Strong, and Candace Van Doren, who typed the entire manuscript and all revisions, and drafted and laid out the diagrams and illustrations in this book.

The author also appreciates the production and editorial assistance of Katie Anderson, Ryan Cianciolo, Katie Larson, Cary Marcous, Jean Marzullo, Shane Rapp, Drew Sheppard, Katie Wassink, and Martha Willis.

The author also appreciates the critical reading assistance of Brett Babir, Ellen Buhl, Lauren Bull, Reed Daines, Lawrence Lipp, and Andrew Stargel.

Finally, we appreciate the encouragement, support, and tolerance of our families throughout this project.

SIXTEENTH EDITION

PART 4

BUSINESS MANAGEMENT SKILLS

by

Irvin N. Gleim, Ph.D., CPA, CIA, CMA, CFM

with the assistance of
Stewart B. White, CIA

ABOUT THE AUTHOR

Irvin N. Gleim is Professor Emeritus in the Fisher School of Accounting at the University of Florida and is a member of the American Accounting Association, Academy of Legal Studies in Business, American Institute of Certified Public Accountants, Association of Government Accountants, Florida Institute of Certified Public Accountants, The Institute of Internal Auditors, and the Institute of Management Accountants. He has had articles published in the *Journal of Accountancy*, *The Accounting Review*, and *The American Business Law Journal* and is author/coauthor of numerous accounting and aviation books and CPE courses.

Gleim Publications, Inc.
P.O. Box 12848
University Station
Gainesville, Florida 32604
(800) 87-GLEIM or (800) 874-5346
(352) 375-0772
Fax: (352) 375-6940
Internet: www.gleim.com
Email: admin@gleim.com

For updates to the first printing of the sixteenth edition of *CIA Review: Part 4*

Go To:	www.gleim.com/updates
Or:	Scan code with your mobile device
Or:	Email update@gleim.com with **CIA 4 16-1** in the subject line. You will receive our current update as a reply.

Updates are available until the next edition is published.

ISSN: 1547-8076

ISBN: 978-1-58194-020-6 *CIA Review: Part 1*
ISBN: 978-1-58194-021-3 *CIA Review: Part 2*
ISBN: 978-1-58194-022-0 *CIA Review: Part 3*
ISBN: 978-1-58194-023-7 *CIA Review: Part 4*
ISBN: 978-1-58194-041-1 *CIA Review: A System for Success*

ACKNOWLEDGMENTS FOR PART 4

The author is grateful for permission to reproduce the following materials copyrighted by The Institute of Internal Auditors: Certified Internal Auditor Examination Questions and Suggested Solutions (copyright © 1980 - 2008), excerpts from *The Practice of Modern Internal Auditing* (2nd ed.), excerpts from *Sawyer's Internal Auditing* (5th ed.), parts of the 2012 *Certification Candidate Handbook*, The IIA Code of Ethics, *International Standards for the Professional Practice of Internal Auditing*, Practice Advisories, and parts of Practice Guides.

This publication is designed to provide accurate and authoritative information with regard to the subject matter covered. It is sold with the understanding that the publisher is not engaged in rendering legal, accounting, or other professional service.

If legal advice or other expert assistance is required, the services of a competent professional person should be sought.

(From a declaration of principles jointly adopted by a Committee of the American Bar Association and a Committee of Publishers.)

TABLE OF CONTENTS

GLEIM® CIA Review System

PREFACE

The purpose of this book is to help **you** prepare to pass Part 4 of the CIA exam. Our overriding consideration is to provide an inexpensive, effective, and easy-to-use study program. This book

1. Explains how to optimize your grade by focusing on Part 4 of the CIA exam.

2. Defines the subject matter tested on Part 4 of the CIA exam.

3. Outlines all of the subject matter tested on Part 4 in 10 easy-to-use-and-complete study units, including all relevant authoritative pronouncements.

4. Presents multiple-choice questions from past CIA examinations to prepare you for questions in future CIA exams. Our answer explanations are presented to the immediate right of each question for your convenience. Use a piece of paper to cover our explanations as you study the questions.

5. Suggests exam-taking and question-answering techniques to help you maximize your exam score.

The outline format, the spacing, and the question-and-answer formats in this book are designed to facilitate readability, learning, understanding, and success on the CIA exam. Our most successful candidates use the Gleim CIA Review System*, which includes books, Test Prep Software, Audio Review, Gleim Online, FREE Practice Exams, and access to a Personal Counselor; or a group study CIA review program. (Check our website for live courses we recommend.) This review book and all Gleim *CIA Review* materials are compatible with other CIA review materials and courses that are based on The IIA's exam content outlines.

To maximize the efficiency and effectiveness of your CIA review program, augment your studying with *CIA Review: A System for Success*. This booklet has been carefully written and organized to provide important information to assist you in passing the CIA examination.

Thank you for your interest in our materials. We deeply appreciate the thousands of letters and suggestions we have received from CIA, CMA, CPA, and EA candidates and accounting students and faculty during the past 5 decades.

If you use Gleim materials, we want YOUR feedback immediately after the exam and as soon as you have received your grades. The CIA exam is NONDISCLOSED, and you must maintain the confidentiality and agree not to divulge the nature or content of any CIA question or answer under any circumstances. We ask only for information about our materials, i.e., the topics that need to be added, expanded, etc.

Please go to www.gleim.com/feedbackCIA4 to share your suggestions on how we can improve this edition.

Good Luck on the Exam,

Irvin N. Gleim

April 2012

PREPARING FOR AND TAKING THE CIA EXAM

Follow These Steps to PASS the Exam 2
About the CIA Exam 3
   Introduction 3
   Overview of the CIA Examination 3
   Subject Matter for Part 4 4
   Nondisclosed Exam 4
   The Institute of Internal Auditors (The IIA) 4
   CIA Program 5
   The IIA's Professional Certifications Department 5
   The IIA's Requirements for CIA Designations 6
   How to (1) Apply to the CIA Certification Program, (2) Register for an Exam Part, and
     (3) Schedule Your Appointment at Pearson VUE 6
   Education and Experience Requirements 8
   Professional Recognition Credit for Part 4 9
   How Many Parts to Take 9
   CIA Exam Fees 9
   Special Professor and Student Examination Fee 10
   Maintaining Your CIA Designation 10
   Examination Sites 10
   Eligibility Period 11
   If You Failed One or More Parts 11
Preparing to Pass the CIA Exam 11
   Gleim Study Unit Listing 12
   Study Plan, Time Budget, and Calendar 12
   How to Study a Study Unit Using the Gleim CIA Review System 12
   CIA Gleim Online 13
   Gleim Books 13
   CIA Test Prep Software 14
   Studying with Books and Software 14
   Gleim Audio Reviews 15
   Time-Budgeting and Question-Answering Techniques for the Exam 15
If You Have Questions about Gleim Materials 17
Taking the CIA Exam 17
   Control: How To Be In 17
   Exam Psychology 18
   Computer-Based Testing (CBT) Preparation 18
   Examination Tactics Emphasized by Gleim 18
   CIA Testing Procedures at Pearson VUE 19

Notice to CIA Candidates

In the fall of 2011, The IIA announced the following changes to the CIA exam, effective January 1, 2012:

1. The reduction of the amount of pretest questions for each part from 20 to 10 (which reduces the total amount of questions from 100 to 90)

2. The removal of the Pearson VUE tutorial from the beginning of the exam, and the subsequent availability of the tutorial on The IIA's website

3. The reduction of total seat time for each part from 3 hours (2 hours and 45 minutes for 100 questions plus 15 minutes for tutorial and survey) to 2 hours and 30 minutes (2 hours and 25 minutes for 90 questions plus 5 minutes for survey)

NOTE: There is no change to the total number of scored questions per part (80), nor does the time allocable to each question change.

FOLLOW THESE STEPS TO PASS THE EXAM

1. Read this **Introduction** to familiarize yourself with the content and structure of Part 4 of the CIA exam. In the following pages, you will find

    a. An **overview of Part 4** and what it generally tests, including The IIA's exam content outlines

    b. A detailed plan with **steps to obtain your CIA certification**, including

        1) The order in which you should apply, register, schedule your exam, and buy your study materials
        2) The studying tactics on which you should focus
        3) How to organize your study schedule to make the most out of each resource in the Gleim CIA Review System (i.e., books, Test Prep Software, Audio Review, Gleim Online, etc.)

    c. Tactics for your **actual test day**, including

        1) Time budgeting, so you complete all questions with time to review
        2) Question-answering techniques to obtain every point you can
        3) An explanation of how to be in control of your CIA exam

2. Scan the Gleim *CIA Review: A System for Success* booklet and note where to revisit later in your studying process to obtain a deeper understanding of the CIA exam.

    a. *CIA Review: A System for Success* has six study units:

        Study Unit 1: The CIA Examination: An Overview and Preparation Introduction
        Study Unit 2: CIA Exam Content Outlines
        Study Unit 3: Content Preparation, Test Administration, and Performance Grading
        Study Unit 4: Multiple-Choice Questions
        Study Unit 5: Preparing to Pass the CIA Exam
        Study Unit 6: How to Take the CIA Exam

    b. If you feel that you need even more details on the test-taking experience, access Pearson VUE's **Testing Tutorial and Practice Exam** at www.vue.com/athena. You should also view The IIA's **CBT Exam Tutorial** at www.globaliia.org/certification. It is available in all languages in which the exam is offered.

        1) These tutorials are most useful to candidates who have little or no experience with computerized exams and have anxiety about performing well in unfamiliar circumstances.

3. Before you begin studying, take a **Diagnostic Quiz** at www.gleim.com/ciadiagnosticquiz.php or use our **Gleim Diagnostic Quiz App** for iPhone, iPod Touch, and Android.

    a. The Diagnostic Quiz includes a representative sample of 40 multiple-choice questions and will determine your weakest areas in Part 4.

    b. When you are finished, one of our **Personal Counselors** will consult with you to better focus your review on any areas in which you have less confidence.

4. Follow the steps outlined beginning on page 12, "How to Study a Study Unit Using the Gleim CIA Review System." This is the **study plan** that our most successful candidates adhere to. Study until you have reached your **desired proficiency level** (e.g., 75%) for each study unit in Part 4.

    a. As you proceed, be sure to check any **Updates** that may have been released.

        1) Gleim Online is updated automatically.

    2)   Test Prep Software is updated by the Online Library Updates system in the Tools menu of your Test Prep. You can (and should) set your Test Prep to automatically update at least once a month.

    3)   Book updates can be viewed at www.gleim.com/updates/, or you can have them emailed to you. See the information box in the top right corner of page iv for details.

  b. **Review the *CIA Review: A System for Success* booklet** and become completely comfortable with what will be expected from you on test day.

5.   Shortly before your test date, take a **Practice Exam** (FREE with the purchase of the complete Gleim CIA Review System) at www.gleim.com/ciapracticeexam.

  a. This timed and scored exam emulates the actual CIA exam and tests you not only on the content you have studied, but also on the question-answering and time-management techniques you have learned throughout the Gleim study process.

  b. When you have completed the exam, study your results to discover where you should **focus your review during the final days before your exam**.

6.   **Take and PASS** Part 4 of the CIA exam!

  a. When you have completed the exam, please contact Gleim with your **suggestions, comments, and corrections**. We want to know how well we prepared you for your testing experience.

ABOUT THE CIA EXAM

Introduction

CIA is the acronym for Certified Internal Auditor. The CIA designation is international, with the examination administered in numerous countries. The CIA exam has been administered by The Institute of Internal Auditors (The IIA) since 1974.

The exam tests a candidate's knowledge and ability regarding the current practice of internal auditing. It enables candidates and prospective managers to adapt to professional changes and challenges by

- Addressing nearly all management skills
- Focusing on the principles of management control
- Measuring a candidate's understanding of risk management and internal controls

Overview of the CIA Examination

The total exam is 10 hours of testing (including 5 minutes per part for a survey). It is divided into four parts, as follows:

Part 1 – The Internal Audit Activity's Role in Governance, Risk, and Control
Part 2 – Conducting the Internal Audit Engagement
Part 3 – Business Analysis and Information Technology
Part 4 – Business Management Skills

Each part consists of 90 questions, and testing lasts 2 hours and 25 minutes plus 5 minutes for a survey. The exam is offered continually throughout the year.

The CIA exam is computerized to facilitate easier testing. Pearson VUE, the testing company that The IIA contracts to proctor the exams, has over 400 testing centers worldwide. The Gleim Test Prep Software and Gleim Online provide tutorials and exact exam emulations of the Pearson VUE computer screens and procedures to prepare you to PASS.

Subject Matter for Part 4

The IIA's abbreviated exam content outline for Part 4 is provided here along with corresponding study units/subunits of the Gleim CIA Review. The percentage coverage of each topic is indicated to its right. (Note that The IIA "percentage coverage" is given in ranges, e.g., 15-25%, as presented in Appendix A. Below, we present the midpoint of each range to simplify and provide more relevant information to CIA candidates, e.g., 20% instead of 15-25%. In other words, the percentages listed are plus or minus 5% of the percentage coverages you can expect to encounter during the actual exam.) We adjust the content of our materials to any changes in The IIA's content outlines.

Part 4: Business Management Skills

A.	Strategic Management	25%
B.	Global Business Environments	20%
C.	Organizational Behavior	20%
D.	Management Skills	25%
E.	Negotiating	10%

Appendix A contains the content outlines in their entirety as well as cross-references to the subunits in our text where topics are covered. Remember that we have studied and restudied the content outlines in developing our CIA Review materials. Accordingly, you do not need to spend time with Appendix A. Rather, it should give you confidence that Gleim CIA Review is the best review source available to help you PASS the CIA exam.

Nondisclosed Exam

The CIA exam is a **nondisclosed** exam. **Nondisclosed** means that exam questions and solutions are NOT released after each examination.

As part of The IIA's nondisclosure policy and to prove each candidate's willingness to adhere to this policy, a confidentiality and nondisclosure statement must be accepted by each candidate before each part is taken. This statement is reproduced here to remind all CIA candidates about The IIA's strict policy of nondisclosure, which Gleim consistently supports and upholds.

> *This exam is confidential and is protected by law. It is made available to you, the examinee, solely for the purpose of becoming certified. You are expressly prohibited from disclosing, publishing, reproducing, or transmitting this exam, in whole or in part, in any form or by any means, verbal or written, electronic or mechanical, for any purpose, without the prior written permission of The Institute of Internal Auditors (IIA).*

> *The IIA requires all exam candidates to read and accept the above Non-Disclosure Agreement and General Terms of Use for IIA exams prior to taking an IIA Exam.*

> *If you do not accept the exam non-disclosure agreement, your exam will be terminated. If this occurs, your registration will be voided, you will forfeit your exam registration fee, and you will be required to register and pay for that exam again in order to sit for it in the future.*

The Institute of Internal Auditors (The IIA)

The IIA is an international professional association that was organized in 1941 to develop the professional status of internal auditing. The organization's international headquarters is in Altamonte Springs, about 5 miles north of Orlando, Florida.

The IIA has over 170,000 members in more than 165 countries working in the fields of internal auditing, risk management, governance, internal control, IT audit, education, and security. Presently, over 70,000 individuals have attained The IIA's CIA designation. The approximately 250 chapters and affiliated institutes around the world hold regular meetings, seminars, and conferences that encourage members to network with peers, develop professional contacts, and stay informed about current issues and practices in internal auditing.

The IIA's mission is to be the global voice of the internal audit profession and to provide dynamic leadership. The IIA is committed to

- Advocating and promoting the value that internal audit professionals add to their organizations
- Providing comprehensive professional educational and development opportunities, standards and other professional practice guidance, and certification programs
- Researching, disseminating, and promoting to practitioners and stakeholders knowledge concerning internal auditing and its appropriate role in control, risk management, and governance
- Educating practitioners and other relevant audiences on best practices in internal auditing
- Bringing together internal auditors from all countries to share information and experiences

Following are The IIA's annual dues in the United States, Canada, and Caribbean nations:

1.	Regular Member*			3.	Educational Member	US $120
	U.S. and Caribbean	US $215		4.	Life Member	US $2,100
	Canada	US $235		5.	Retired Member	US $70
2.	Government Audit Program	US $120		6.	Student Member	US $70

Specialty (gaming audit and financial services auditor) and group (government audit and standard audit) memberships are also available. Visit www.theiia.org/membership for details.

Individuals outside the United States, Canada, and Caribbean nations may become members of The IIA by joining the nearest IIA institute. Institutes charge their own membership fees and offer local programs and services. Contact the institute directly to obtain specific information regarding fees and membership conditions. Visit www.globaliia.org/Pages/Institutes.aspx to find the nearest IIA institute.

CIA Program

The following is the official statement of The IIA Board of Directors regarding the CIA program:

Professional Qualifications

To assist in achieving the goals and objectives of The Institute, the Certified Internal Auditor (CIA) Program was established. The Board of Directors will develop, approve and modify as necessary, such policies and procedures as may be required to stimulate and encourage this program.

While "Certified Internal Auditor" is intended to be the worldwide designation of qualified internal audit professionals, it is recognized for various reasons other professional organizations of internal auditors may develop similar designations. The Board of Directors will develop, approve and modify as necessary, such procedures as may be deemed desirable to recognize those designations.

The Board may also approve additional certifications as appropriate.

The IIA's Professional Certifications Department

The Professional Certifications Department is comprised of the Professional Certifications Board (PCB) and the Exam Development Committee (EDC).

According to The IIA, The PCB's mission is "to govern and promote The IIA's global certification programs." This includes responsibility for the CIA program's strategic plans, policies, and achievement of objectives. In addition, the PCB develops and administers the CIA program's disciplinary policies and defines the continuing professional education requirements.

The EDC is a subcommittee of the PCB. Its specific responsibilities include defining the common body of knowledge that will be tested on the CIA exam and managing the exam content outlines, questions, and structure.

*New Regular Members must also pay a one-time membership application fee of US $25.

The IIA's Requirements for CIA Designations

The CIA designation is granted only by The IIA. Candidates must complete the following steps to become a CIA:

1. Complete the appropriate certification application form online and register for the part(s) you are going to take. See the following pages for concise instructions on the application and registration process. The *CIA Review: A System for Success* booklet also contains a useful worksheet to help you keep track of your process and organize what you need for exam day.

2. Pass all four parts of the CIA exam or pass Parts 1, 2, and 3 and gain approval for Professional Recognition Credit for Part 4 (see page 9).

3. Fulfill or expect to fulfill the education and experience requirements beginning on page 8.

4. Provide a character reference proving you are of good moral character.

5. Comply with The IIA's Code of Ethics.

Credits can be retained as long as the requirements are fulfilled. Once a designation is earned, the CIA must comply with the program's CPE requirement (see "Maintaining Your CIA Designation" on page 10). Contact Gleim for all of your CPE needs.

How to (1) Apply to the CIA Certification Program, (2) Register for an Exam Part, and (3) Schedule Your Appointment at Pearson VUE

Detailed instructions and screenshots for every step of the application and registration program can be found at www.gleim.com/accounting/cia/steps. You can track your progress and organize your documentation with the help of our CIA Exam Worksheet in the *CIA Review: A System for Success* booklet.

1. Apply to the CIA Certification Program

   a. First, create a profile in The IIA's Certification Candidate Management System (CCMS). To do so, go to The IIA's website (www.theiia.org/certification/certified-internal-auditor/) and click on the link to the CCMS at the bottom of the page. Then, follow the instructions and provide all requested information. You will receive an email within 5 business days with your IIA ID number and instructions to activate your CCMS account using the authorization code provided in the email. Remember, **your account activation capabilities expire 1 month from receipt of email**.

   b. Click on the link provided in your confirmation email (see 1.a. above) and activate your account by entering the authorization code from the confirmation email. The system will then prompt you to choose a username and password for the CCMS. Once entered and verified, you will be directed to your Candidate Landing page, where you can view the status of any IIA certifications in which you are involved.

   c. Click on the "Complete a Form" link and choose the correct application (CIA Application or CIA Application-Student/Professor) from the New Forms tab (the default). Once you have begun filling out an application, you can save it by clicking the "Save for Later" button and return to it later by choosing the In-Process Forms tab. Once you have completed and submitted an application, you can review it by choosing the Completed Forms tab.

   d. Complete your application process by filling out your payment information and submitting your order. Paying by credit card will ensure the quickest processing time.

   e. Receive an email (within 5 business days) confirming your order.

2. Register for an Exam Part

   a. Once you have received the email confirming your application to the CIA program, log in to the CCMS by going to www.theiia.org/certification/certified-internal-auditor/ and clicking on the link at the bottom of the page. Then click on the Complete a Form link. From the New Forms tab (the default), choose the registration form for the exam part you wish to take (e.g., CIA - Part 4 Registration). Once you have begun filling out a registration, you can save it and return to it later by choosing the In-Process Forms tab. Once you have completed and submitted a registration, you can review it by choosing the Completed Forms tab.

   b. Agree to the Pricing Provisions and Conditions statement. On the next screen, fill out the payment information and submit your order. Paying by credit card will ensure the quickest processing time.

   c. Receive an "Authorization to Test" email authorizing you to schedule the part you registered for. **You must print out this email and bring it to the testing center with you when you take your exam.** The email advises that you need to wait at least 48 hours for your information to be processed, and then you can log in to the Pearson VUE website (www.pearsonvue.com/iia) to schedule your appointment to sit for the exam. You have 180 days from the day you registered for the exam to sit for it.

3. Schedule Your Exam at Pearson VUE (You must wait 48 hours after Authorization.)

   a. First, create a profile at Pearson VUE. To do so, go to Pearson VUE's website (www.pearsonvue.com/iia) and click on the "Schedule a Test" link. Then, follow the instructions and provide all requested information. You will receive an email confirming your new account at Pearson VUE and providing you with your password.

   b. Go to Pearson VUE's website (www.pearsonvue.com/iia) and click on the "Schedule a Test" link in the menu on the right. You will need to log in to your account with the username you chose and the password provided to you in your Pearson VUE account confirmation email. When you sign in to your account for the first time, you will be required to change your password from the automatically generated one that is provided in the email.

   c. Proceed through a series of screens to schedule your exam appointment specifics. On these screens, you will

      1) Select the exam part you want to schedule and the language in which you will take it.

      2) Find a test center based on your home address.

      3) Choose the test center you want to schedule your exam for. You can search for appointment availability in up to four test centers near you before you choose. Once you choose the test center you want, be sure to print out and save the Test Center Information for that center so you will have directions and instructions for exam day.

      4) Choose the month and year in which you will sit for the exam, and Pearson VUE will show all available dates for your test center within that month. Select a date on the calendar to show the appointment times available on that date at your test center. Once you have chosen a satisfactory date and time, click Select Appointment.

      5) Review your contact information and appointment details to ensure that you have the correct phone number and address for yourself and the correct time, date, and location for your test. Print out the policies document and save it so you are prepared for the check-in procedures and cancelation policies of Pearson VUE.

   d. Receive an email confirming your payment and restating your appointment details. The email also contains the rules and procedures of your testing center as well as directions to get there. Print out this email and bring it with you to the testing center on exam day.

Education and Experience Requirements

Anyone who satisfies these character, educational, and professional requirements may sit for the examination.

1. **Bachelor's degree or equivalent.** Candidates must have an undergraduate (4-year) degree or its equivalent from an accredited college-level institution.

    a. Educational programs outside the United States and the qualifications of candidates who have completed most but not all of a degree program are evaluated by The IIA to determine equivalency.

    b. The IIA's affiliates have been given the authority to recommend educational and experience criteria for their countries to ensure adequate consideration of cultural and societal differences around the world. In addition, certain international professional designations (such as Chartered Accountant) may be accepted as equivalent to a bachelor's degree.

    c. Full-time university students who are in their senior (final) year may sit for the CIA exam before completing their education requirement as long as they complete the Student/Professor Application Form and submit the Full-Time Student Status Form.

2. **Character reference.** CIA candidates must exhibit high moral and professional character and must submit a character reference from a responsible person, such as a CIA, supervisor, manager, or educator. The character reference must accompany the candidate's exam application.

3. **Work experience.** Candidates are required to have 24 months of internal auditing experience (or the equivalent) prior to receiving the CIA certificate. A candidate may sit for the exam before completing the work experience requirements, but (s)he will not be certified until the experience requirement is met.

    a. An advanced academic degree beyond the Bachelor's (e.g., a Master's degree) or work experience in related business professions (such as accounting, law, finance) can be substituted for 1 year of work experience (1-year maximum).

    b. Equivalent work experience means experience in audit/assessment disciplines, including external auditing, quality assurance, compliance, and internal control.

    c. Full-time college- or university-level teaching in the subject matter of the examination is considered equivalent to work experience. Two years of teaching equals 1 year of internal auditing work experience.

    d. Work experience must be verified by a CIA or the candidate's supervisor. An Experience Verification Form is available on The IIA's website and in the CIA *Candidate Handbook* for use in verifying professional experience. This may accompany the candidate's application or be submitted later when criteria have been met.

If you have questions about the acceptability of your work experience, contact The IIA Certification Department at certification@theiia.org or by fax at (407) 937-1108. If you do not possess a Bachelor's degree and are unsure whether your educational achievements or professional designation qualify as equivalents to a Bachelor's degree, you should check "Other" in the Education section of the application and submit required documentation with the application. Include a complete description of your situation. Submit documentation as an attachment to your application via email at certification@theiia.org or by fax at (407) 937-1108.

The IIA will typically review all submitted documents within 5 business days of receipt. You may confirm approval of a document through your online CCMS (Certification Candidate Management System) account. Applicants for equivalency may be registered for the exam pending review but should expect a separate letter regarding the outcome of the review. Applicants who do not receive an equivalency status letter within 4 weeks of submission of the application and equivalency request should contact The IIA.

Professional Recognition Credit for Part 4

The IIA offers a Part 4 Professional Recognition Credit for qualified professional certifications. Registered candidates and new CIA candidates who have successfully completed the examination requirements for many designations are eligible to receive credit for Part 4 of the CIA exam. Hence, candidates who attain the credit for Part 4 and pass Parts 1, 2, and 3 satisfy the examination requirement for the CIA designation.

In the U.S., the designations that qualify for the credit include

CBA	CCSA	CFIRS	CISA	CPEA
CBM	CDFM	CGAP	CISSP	CPA
NCCO	CFSA	CGFM	CIDA	CRCM
CCBIA	CFE	CHFP	CMA	CRP

Please visit The IIA's website [www.theiia.org/certification/certified-internal-auditor; click on Professional Recognition Credit (Exam Part 4 Exemption)] for a complete list of certifications approved for credit in other countries. See Study Unit 1 in the *CIA Review: A System for Success* booklet for detailed instructions.

How Many Parts to Take

As previously discussed, the CIA examination consists of four parts: Parts 1 and 2 cover internal auditing subject matter, whereas Part 3, Business Analysis and Information Technology, and Part 4, Business Management Skills, cover a wide variety of material.

According to The IIA, you may choose to take only one part at each sitting, which is what Gleim recommends. Unless you have a strong preference to do otherwise, it is best to take the parts in numerical order, from Part 1 to Part 4. Also, be sure to investigate whether you qualify to receive the Professional Recognition Credit for Part 4 and, if you do, submit your application and documentation for it immediately.

CIA Exam Fees

Fees	IIA Members	Nonmembers	Professors/ Full-Time Students
Exam Application (initial nonrefundable fee)	US $75	US $100	US $50
Exam Parts Registration (per part/per sitting)	US $150	US $200	US $105
Deferrals/Cancelations/Changes			
...at least 2 days prior to your appointment*	US $50	US $50	US $50

*If you have not made any necessary changes or cancelations at least 2 days prior to your appointment, you will forfeit your exam fee and must pay to register again.

Special Professor and Student Examination Fee

The exam application fee is the charge for enrolling candidates in the CIA program. The CIA examination is available to professors and full-time students at reduced fees. For them, the exam application fee is US $50 (instead of US $75), plus an exam registration fee of US $105 (instead of US $150) per part. Professors and students may sit for each part at this special rate one time only.

1. To be eligible for the reduced rate, a student must
    a. Be enrolled as a senior in an undergraduate program or as a graduate student
    b. Be a full-time student as defined by the institution in which the student is enrolled (a minimum of 12 semester hours or its equivalent for senior-level undergraduate students and 9 semester hours for graduate students)
    c. Register for and take the CIA exam while enrolled in school
2. To be eligible for the reduced rate, a professor must
    a. Work full-time as a professor with an accredited educational institution
    b. Provide a letter from the local IIA chapter verifying his/her eligibility for professor status for pricing
3. In addition to the requirements on page 8, the following items should be submitted to the Certification Department of The Institute of Internal Auditors:
    a. A Certified Internal Auditor Examination Registration/Application-Student/Professor Form
    b. A completed and signed Full-Time Student/Professor Status Form
    c. A completed and signed Character Reference Form
    d. Payment for the US $50 exam application fee and the US $105 exam registration fee for each part
4. IIA approval of full-time student or professor status is valid for 180 days. Exam parts must be completed within that time period for candidates to use the discounted prices.

Maintaining Your CIA Designation

After certification, CIAs are required to maintain and update their knowledge and skills. As of January 1, 2012, practicing CIAs must complete and report 40 hours of Continuing Professional Education (CPE) every year. The reporting deadline is December 31. See The IIA's website (www.globaliia.org/certification) or the 2012 *Certification Candidate Handbook* for information on how to report your CPE hours during the transition from pre-2012 reporting requirements. Complete your CPE Reporting Form through the online Certification Candidate Management System. Nonmembers must submit a US $100 processing fee with their report. Contact Gleim for all of your CPE needs.

Examination Sites

The CIA examinations are administered at Pearson VUE testing centers, which are located in over 165 countries across the world. A complete list of these test centers, addresses, and driving directions can be found at www.pearsonvue.com. Click on the "locate - Find a test center" link at the right of the screen, choose the CIA testing program (Institute of Internal Auditors), and then choose the country and region in which you would like to take your exam.

If you require testing accommodations because of a special need, call a Pearson VUE agent at the time of registration for assistance.

Eligibility Period

Candidates must complete the program certification process within 4 years of application approval. If a candidate has not completed the certification process within 4 years, all fees and exam parts will be forfeited.

If You Failed One or More Parts

The pass rate on each part of the CIA exam averages 44%. Thus, you may not pass all parts attempted. If you failed a part, you must wait at least 90 days to retake it.

1. Once you have put the reaction to the bad news behind you, you should regroup and begin implementing the suggestions in this introduction. The Gleim system really works! Avoid thinking "I knew that" or "I don't have to study that again." What you knew and how you took the exam last time did NOT work. Develop new and improved perspectives.

2. Avoid failure on the next exam by **identifying**, **correcting**, and **understanding** your mistakes as you practice answering multiple-choice questions during your study sessions. Use the Gleim system as described on the following pages. This methodology applies to all CIA candidates. Understand your mistakes while you study so you can avoid them on the exam.

PREPARING TO PASS THE CIA EXAM

1. Decide when you are going to take the CIA exam (the sooner, the better).

2. Acquire the Gleim CIA Review System (including books, Test Prep Software Download, Audio Review, and Gleim Online with your Personal Counselor) to thoroughly prepare for the CIA exam. Commit to systematic preparation for the exam as described in our review materials, including *CIA Review: A System for Success*.

3. Communicate with your Personal Counselor to design a study plan that meets your needs. Call (800) 874-5346 or email CIAOnline@gleim.com.

4. Apply for membership in The IIA (suggested but not required).

5. Register online to take the desired part of the exam. You will receive authorization to take the exam from The IIA and will then have 180 days to take that exam part.

6. Schedule your test with Pearson VUE (online or call center).

7. Work systematically through each study unit in the Gleim CIA Review System.

8. Sit for and PASS the CIA exam while you are in control, as described in Study Unit 6 of *CIA Review: A System for Success*. Gleim will make it easy.

9. Email, fax, or call Gleim with your comments on our study materials and how well they prepared you for the exam. Alternatively, go to www.gleim.com/feedbackCIA4.

10. Enjoy your career, pursue multiple certifications (CMA, CPA, EA, etc.), and recommend Gleim to others who are also taking these exams.

Gleim Study Unit Listing

We believe our 10 study unit titles better describe the content of each part of the CIA exam. Our study unit titles and content also reflect feedback from CIA candidates. Please go to www.gleim.com/feedbackCIA4 to give us feedback after each exam. Thank you.

LISTING OF GLEIM STUDY UNITS	
Part 1: The Internal Audit Activity's Role in Governance, Risk, and Control 1. Overview of Internal Auditing 2. Internal Audit Proficiency, Due Care, and Quality Assurance 3. Internal Audit Ethics 4. Managing the Internal Audit Activity 5. Nature of Internal Audit Work 6. Control Knowledge Elements 7. Specific Controls 8. Control Aspects of Management 9. Planning and Supervising the Engagement 10. Internal Audit Responsibilities for Fraud	**Part 3: Business Analysis and Information Technology** 1. Business Processes 2. Managing Business Resources 3. Financial Accounting -- Basic 4. Financial Accounting -- Advanced 5. Finance 6. Managerial Accounting 7. Regulatory, Legal, and Economic Issues 8. IT Controls, Networks, and Business Applications 9. IT Roles, Software, and Application Development 10. IT Contingency Planning, Systems Security, and Databases
Part 2: Conducting the Internal Audit Engagement 1. Engagement Information 2. Procedures and Working Papers 3. Internal Audit Ethics 4. Communicating Results 5. Fraud Investigation 6. Conducting Assurance Engagements 7. Compliance, Consulting, and Other Engagements 8. Information Technology 9. Engagement Tools -- Statistical 10. Engagement Tools -- Others	**Part 4: Business Management Skills** 1. Structural Analysis and Strategies 2. Industry and Market Analysis 3. Industry Environments 4. Strategic Decisions 5. Global Business Issues 6. Motivation and Communications 7. Organizational Structure and Effectiveness 8. Managing Groups 9. Influence and Leadership 10. Time Management, Conflict, and Negotiation

Study Plan, Time Budget, and Calendar

Communicate with your Personal Counselor to design a study plan. Each week, you should evaluate your progress and review your preparation plans for the time remaining prior to the exam. Marking a calendar will facilitate your planning. Note the exam dates and the weeks to go before the exam. Review your commitments, e.g., out-of-town assignments, personal responsibilities, etc., and note them on your calendar to assist you in keeping to your schedule.

How to Study a Study Unit Using the Gleim CIA Review System

To ensure that you are using your time effectively, we recommend that you follow the steps listed below and on the next page when using all of the CIA Review System materials together (books, Test Prep Software, Audio Review, and Gleim Online):

1. (25 minutes, plus 10 minutes for review) In the CIA Gleim Online course, complete Multiple-Choice Quiz #1 in 30 minutes. It is expected that your scores will be lower on the first quiz than on subsequent quizzes.

    a. Immediately following the quiz, you will be prompted to review the questions you flagged and/or answered incorrectly. For each question, analyze and understand why you flagged it or answered it incorrectly. This step is an essential learning activity.

2.   (30 minutes) Use the audiovisual presentation for an overview of the study unit. CIA Audio Review can be substituted for audiovisual presentations and can be used while driving to work, exercising, etc.

3.   (45 minutes) Complete the 30-question True/False quiz. It is interactive and most effective if used prior to studying the Knowledge Transfer Outline.

4.   (60 minutes) Study the Knowledge Transfer Outline, specifically the troublesome areas identified from the multiple-choice questions in the Gleim Online course. The Knowledge Transfer Outlines can be studied either online or from the books.

5.   (25 minutes, plus 10 minutes for review) Complete Multiple-Choice Quiz #2 in the Gleim Online course.

   a.   Immediately following the quiz, you will be prompted to review the questions you flagged and/or answered incorrectly. For each question, analyze and understand why you flagged it or answered it incorrectly. This step is an essential learning activity.

6.   (50 minutes) Complete two 20-question quizzes while in Test Mode from the CIA Test Prep Software. Review as needed.

When following these steps, you will complete all 10 units in about 45 hours. Then spend about 5-10 hours using the CIA Test Prep Software to create customized tests for the problem areas that you identified. When you are ready, create 20-question quizzes that draw questions from all 10 study units. Continue taking 20-question quizzes until you approach your desired proficiency level, e.g., 75%+.

The times mentioned above are recommendations based on prior candidate feedback and how long you will have to answer questions on the actual exam. Each candidate's time spent in any area will vary depending on proficiency and familiarity with the subject matter.

CIA Gleim Online

CIA Gleim Online is a versatile, interactive, self-study review program delivered via the Internet. It is divided into four courses (one for each part of the CIA exam) and emulates the CIA exam.

Each course is broken down into 10 individual, manageable study units. Completion time per study unit will be about 4 hours. Each study unit in the course contains an audiovisual presentation, 30 true/false study questions, Knowledge Transfer Outlines, and two 20-question multiple-choice quizzes.

CIA Gleim Online provides you with access to a Personal Counselor, a real person who will provide support to ensure your competitive edge. CIA Gleim Online is a great way to get confidence as you prepare with Gleim. This confidence will continue during and after the exam.

Gleim Books

This edition of the Gleim CIA Review books has the following features to make studying easier:

1.   **Gleim Success Tips:** These tips supplement the core exam material by suggesting how certain topics might be presented on the exam or how you should prepare for an issue.

Candidates for the CIA exam should understand that an organization uses one set of analytical tools to choose the industries in which it will compete and another to determine what competitive moves are appropriate in those industries.

2.   **Core Concepts:** Core concepts are included at the end of each subunit. The core concepts provide an overview of the key points of each subunit that serve as the foundation for learning. In many cases, the core concepts are concise statements of attribute, performance, and implementation standards. As part of your review, you should make sure that you understand each of them.

Core Concepts

- Strategic management focuses on long-term planning. While senior management typically oversees strategy, all employees should also understand the organization's strategy.

- Strategic management is a process that includes development of a grand strategy, strategic planning, implementation, and control.

- A grand strategy describes how an organization's mission is to be achieved. This is based on situational analysis, called SWOT analysis. In SWOT analysis, strengths and weaknesses of the firm (internal environment) are identified, along with opportunities and threats (external environment).

CIA Test Prep Software

Twenty-question tests in the **CIA Test Prep** Software will help you focus on your weaker areas. Make it a game: How much can you improve?

Our CIA Test Prep (in test mode) forces you to commit to your answer choice before looking at answer explanations; thus, you are preparing under true exam conditions. It also keeps track of your time and performance history for each study unit, which is available in either a table or graphical format.

Studying with Books and Software

Simplify the exam preparation process by following our suggested steps listed below and on the next page. DO NOT omit the step in which you diagnose the reasons for answering questions incorrectly; i.e., learn from your mistakes while studying so you avoid making similar mistakes on the CIA exam.

1.   In test mode, answer a 20-question diagnostic test before studying any other information.

2.   Study the Knowledge Transfer Outline for the corresponding study unit in your Gleim book.

   a.   Place special emphasis on the weaker areas that you identified with the initial diagnostic quiz in Step 1.

3.   Take two or three 20-question tests in test mode after you have studied the Knowledge Transfer Outline.

4.   Immediately following each test, you will be prompted to review the questions you flagged and/or answered incorrectly. For each question, analyze and understand why you answered it incorrectly. This step is an essential learning activity.

5.   Continue this process until you approach a predetermined proficiency level, e.g., 75%+.

6.   Modify this process to suit your individual learning process.

   a.   Learning from questions you answer incorrectly is very important. Each question you answer incorrectly is an **opportunity** to avoid missing actual test questions on your CIA exam. Thus, you should carefully study the answer explanations provided to understand why you chose the incorrect answer so you can avoid similar errors on your exam. This study technique is clearly the difference between passing and failing for many CIA candidates.

b.   Also, you **must** determine why you answered questions incorrectly and learn how to avoid the same error in the future. Reasons for missing questions include

1)   Misreading the requirement (stem)
2)   Not understanding what is required
3)   Making a math error
4)   Applying the wrong rule or concept
5)   Being distracted by one or more of the answers
6)   Incorrectly eliminating answers from consideration
7)   Not having any knowledge of the topic tested
8)   Employing bad intuition when guessing

c.   It is also important to verify that you answered correctly for the right reasons (i.e., read the discussion provided for the correct answers). Otherwise, if the material is tested on the CIA exam in a different manner, you may not answer it correctly.

d.   It is imperative that you complete your predetermined number of study units per week so you can review your progress and realize how attainable a comprehensive CIA review program is when using the Gleim CIA Review System. Remember to meet or beat your schedule to give yourself confidence.

Avoid studying Gleim questions to learn the correct answers. Use Gleim questions to help you learn how to answer CIA questions under exam conditions. Expect the unexpected and be prepared to deal with it. Become an educated guesser when you encounter questions in doubt; you will outperform the inexperienced exam taker.

Gleim Audio Reviews

Gleim CIA Audio Reviews provide an average of 30 minutes of quality review for each study unit. Each review provides an overview of the Knowledge Transfer Outline in the *CIA Review* book. The purpose is to get candidates "started" so they can relate to the questions they will answer before reading the study outlines in each study unit.

The audios get to the point, as does the entire Gleim System for Success. We are working to get you through the CIA exam with minimum time, cost, and frustration. You can listen to sample audio reviews on our website at www.gleim.com/accounting/demos.

Time-Budgeting and Question-Answering Techniques for the Exam

The following suggestions are to assist you in maximizing your score on each part of the CIA exam. Remember, knowing how to take the exam and how to answer individual questions is as important as studying/reviewing the subject matter tested on the exam.

1.   **Budget your time.**

a.   We make this point with emphasis. Just as you would fill up your gas tank prior to reaching empty, so too should you finish your exam before time expires.

b.   You have 145 minutes to answer 90 questions, i.e., 1.61 minutes per question. We suggest you attempt to answer eight questions every 10 minutes, which is 1.25 minutes per question. This would result in completing 90 questions in 112.5 minutes to give you just over 30 minutes to review questions that you have flagged.

c.   Use the wipeboard provided by Pearson VUE for your Gleim Time Management System at the exam. List the question numbers for every 15 questions (i.e., 1, 16, 31, etc.) in a column on the left side of the wipeboard. The right side of the wipeboard will have your start time at the top and will be used for you to fill in the time you have remaining at each question checkpoint. Stay consistent with 1.25 minutes per question.

2.   **Answer the items in consecutive order.**

   a.   Do **not** agonize over any one item. Stay within your time budget.

   b.   Note any items you are unsure of by clicking the "Flag for Review" button in the upper-right corner of your screen, and return to them later if time allows. Plan on going back to all the questions you flagged.

   c.   Never leave a question unanswered. Make your best guess in the time allowed. Your score is based on the number of correct responses out of the 80 total scored questions, and you will not be penalized for guessing incorrectly.

3.   **For each multiple-choice question,**

   a.   **Try to ignore the answer choices.** Do not allow the answer choices to affect your reading of the question.

   1)   If four answer choices are presented, three of them are incorrect. These incorrect answers are called **distractors** for good reason. Often, distractors are written to appear correct at first glance until further analysis.

   2)   In computational items, distractors are carefully calculated such that they are the result of making common mistakes. Be careful, and double-check your computations if time permits.

   b.   **Read the question carefully** to determine the precise requirement.

   1)   Focusing on what is required enables you to ignore extraneous information and to proceed directly to determining the correct answer.

   a)   Be especially careful to note when the requirement is an **exception**; e.g., "Which of the following is **not** an indication of fraud?"

   c.   **Determine the correct answer** before looking at the answer choices.

   1)   However, some multiple-choice questions are structured so that the answer cannot be determined from the stem alone. See the stem in b.1)a) above.

   d.   **Read the answer choices carefully.**

   1)   Even if the first answer appears to be the correct choice, do not skip the remaining answer choices. Questions often ask for the "best" of the choices provided. Thus, each choice requires your consideration.

   2)   Treat each answer choice as a true/false question as you analyze it.

   e.   **Click on the best answer.**

   1)   If you are uncertain, guess intelligently (see "If you don't know the answer" below). Improve on your 25% chance of getting the correct answer with blind guessing.

   2)   For many of the multiple-choice questions, two answer choices can be eliminated with minimal effort, thereby increasing your educated guess to a 50-50 proposition.

4.   After you have answered all 90 questions, return to the questions that you flagged.

5.   **If you don't know the answer.**

   a.   Again, guess; but make it an educated guess, which means select the best possible answer. First, rule out answers that you think are incorrect. Second, speculate on what The IIA is looking for and/or the rationale behind the question. Third, select the best answer, or guess between equally appealing answers. Your first guess is usually the most intuitive. If you cannot make an educated guess, read the stem and each answer and pick the best or most intuitive answer. It's just a guess!

   b.   Make sure you accomplish this step within your predetermined time budget per checkpoint.

IF YOU HAVE QUESTIONS ABOUT GLEIM MATERIALS

Content-specific questions about our materials will be answered most rapidly if they are sent to us via email to accounting@gleim.com. Our team of accounting experts will give your correspondence thorough consideration and a prompt response.

Questions regarding the information in this Introduction (study suggestions, studying plans, exam specifics) should be emailed to personalcounselor@gleim.com.

Questions concerning orders, prices, shipments, or payments should be sent via email to customerservice@gleim.com and will be promptly handled by our competent and courteous customer service staff.

For technical support, you may use our automated technical support service at www.gleim.com/support, email us at support@gleim.com, or call us at (800) 874-5346.

TAKING THE CIA EXAM

Control: How To Be In

You have to be in control to be successful during exam preparation and execution. Control can also contribute greatly to your personal and other professional goals. The objective is to be confident that the best possible performance is being generated. Control is a process whereby you

1. Develop expectations, standards, budgets, and plans
2. Undertake activity, production, study, and learning
3. Measure the activity, production, output, and knowledge
4. Compare actual activity with expected and budgeted activity
5. Modify the activity, behavior, or study to better achieve the desired outcome
6. Revise expectations and standards in light of actual experience
7. Continue the process or restart the process in the future

Every day you rely on control systems implicitly. For example, when you groom your hair, you use a control system. You have expectations about the desired appearance of your hair and the time required to style it. You monitor your progress and make adjustments as appropriate. The control process, however, is applicable to all of your endeavors, both professional and personal. You should refine your personal control processes specifically toward passing the CIA exam.

In the *CIA Review: A System for Success* booklet, we suggest explicit control systems for

1. Preparing to take the CIA exam
2. Studying an individual Gleim study unit
3. Answering individual multiple-choice questions

Most endeavors will improve with explicit control. This is particularly true of the CIA examination. Use the *CIA Review: A System for Success* booklet to (1) develop an explicit control system over your study process and (2) prepare a detailed plan of steps you will take at the CIA exam. Then, practice your question-answering techniques (and develop control) as you answer recent CIA questions during your study program.

Exam Psychology

Plan ahead for the exam and systematically prepare for it. Go to the exam and give it your best. Neither you nor anyone else can expect more. If you have undertaken a systematic preparation program, you will do well.

Maintain a positive attitude and do not become anxious or depressed if you encounter difficulties before or during the exam. An optimist will usually do better than an equally well-prepared pessimist. Remember, you are not in a position to be objective about your results during the exam. Many well-prepared examination candidates have been pleasantly surprised by their scores. Indeed, you should be confident because you are competing with many less-qualified persons who have not prepared as well as you. Optimism and a fighting spirit are worth points on every exam; fear, anxiety, and depression tend to impair performance.

Proper exercise, diet, and rest during the weeks before the exam are very important. High energy levels, reduced tension, and a positive attitude are among the benefits. A good aerobic fitness program, a nutritious and well-balanced diet, and a regular sleep pattern will promote your long-term emotional and physical well-being as well as contribute significantly to a favorable exam result. Of course, the use of health-undermining substances should be avoided.

Computer-Based Testing (CBT) Preparation

Your examination will be taken on a computer at the Pearson VUE testing center. You do not need any computer experience or typing skills to take your examination. If you have used the Gleim CIA Test Prep Software and Gleim Online, you will be completely familiar and comfortable with the computer-based testing format. You can also access a tutorial/demo on the testing experience at Pearson VUE on their website (www.vue.com/athena) or on The IIA's website, where it is available in every language in which the exam is offered.

Examination Tactics Emphasized by Gleim

1. Dressing for exam success means emphasizing comfort, not appearance. Be prepared to adjust for changes in temperature, e.g., remove a sweater or put on a coat. Do not bring notes, this text, other books, etc., to the exam. You will only make yourself nervous and confused by trying to cram during the last 5 minutes before the exam. Books are not allowed in the exam room, and there is limited on-site storage space anyway.

2. Arrive 30 minutes before your scheduled appointment. If you arrive less than 30 minutes before your scheduled time, you may be denied the ability to take your exam on that day and forfeit your registration fee. This early check-in allows time for you to sign in and for staff to verify your identification.

3. Bring your Authorization to Test notification from The IIA, your appointment confirmation letter from Pearson VUE, and at least one valid form of identification with you.

4. Read the exam instructions carefully.

5. Answer the 90 questions in chronological order. Flag any questions that you are leaving for later or you wish to review.

6. You have 145 minutes (2 hours 25 minutes) to answer 90 questions. If you allocate 1.25 minutes per question, you will use only 112.5 minutes, leaving about 30 minutes to complete Step 7. If you use the Gleim Time Management System (see Study Unit 4 of *CIA Review: A System for Success*) to pace yourself during the exam, you will have adequate time to complete each part.

7. After you worked through all 90 questions, you should return to the questions you flagged and make a final selection, i.e., your best answer.

    a. Review each question carefully. If you made an obvious mistake, e.g., misread the question, make the correction. **Do not**, however, begin changing answers and second-guessing yourself. Your first answer to each question should be based on the systematic question-answering technique that you have practiced throughout your preparation program.

8. Upon exiting the testing room, you will receive a printout of your unofficial exam results. Your score will become official once The IIA publishes the score to the CCMS within a few days.

9. As soon as you return home from your exam, please go to www.gleim.com/feedbackCIA4 and give us your comments on our materials. We are particularly interested in which topics need to be added or expanded. We are **not** asking about specific CIA questions. Rather, we are asking for feedback on our materials. This approach is approved by The IIA.

10. When you are ready to take another part of the exam, re-review this tactics list and be confident in maximizing your score.

CIA Testing Procedures at Pearson VUE

The following procedures for taking the CIA exam at Pearson VUE were adapted from The IIA's 2011 *Candidate Handbook*.

1. Arrive 30 minutes early and bring your Authorization to Test notification, your appointment confirmation letter, and your identification (see below).

2. The test center administrator will show you where to store your personal items. You must place all personal belongings, including purses, wallets, watches, jewelry, cell phone, etc., in the storage lockers (or other secured location) provided by the test center. You will be given the key to your locker, which must be returned to the test center staff when you leave. The lockers are very small and are not intended to hold large items. Do not bring anything to the test center unless it is absolutely necessary. Neither test center personnel, Pearson VUE, nor The IIA will be responsible for lost or stolen items.

3. The administrator will provide you with a copy of the Candidate Rules Agreement. You must accept the terms of this agreement in order to take an exam at a Pearson VUE testing center.

4. You must provide one form of acceptable identification (e.g., driver's license, passport, military identification, etc.). The administrator will verify that the name on the identification matches the name on the exam registration. You must keep this identification with you at all times during the exam. If you leave the testing room for any reason, you will be required to show your identification to be re-admitted.

    a. Identification must contain your name exactly as you provided it during your registration process, have a permanently affixed photo of your face, and be current (non-expired). Employee or student IDs will not be accepted.

5. The administrator will capture your signature (digital or pen) and verify that your signature matches that on your identification (if any).

6. Your fingerprint and/or palm vein image will be captured, and a digital photograph of your face will be made. According to The IIA, the fingerprint is optional, but the photograph is mandatory.

7. If you have brought a translation dictionary, the administrator will check it to be certain that it is acceptable and does not contain any markings or inserted material.

    (Please note that the only item that a candidate may bring to the test that is allowed in the testing room is a non-electronic language translation dictionary. This dictionary may not contain definitions of terms. It cannot have anything written or highlighted in the book nor can it contain any added notes or documents inserted into the book.)

8. You will be offered an erasable note board and pen on which you can take notes during the exam. You must return this to the administrator prior to leaving the test center. You cannot take any notes from the test center.

9. An onscreen calculator will be available during the exam. If you prefer a hand-held calculator and the test center has one available, you may request to be provided with one. You will not be allowed to bring a personal calculator or any other such device with you into the testing room.

10. You will be required to sign the test center log prior to being admitted to the test. Your test will start within 30 minutes of the scheduled start time. If circumstances arise, other than candidate error, that delay your session more than 30 minutes, you will be given the choice of continuing to wait or rescheduling your appointment.

11. If you leave the testing room for any reason, you will be required to sign the test center log and show your identification.

12. You will not be allowed to bring any food or drink into the testing room.

13. You will be escorted to a workstation by the exam proctor. You must remain in your seat during the exam, except when authorized to leave the testing room.

14. After you are logged into your exam, proceed through the introductory screens without delay.

15. If you encounter ANY computer problem, report it immediately to the exam proctor.

16. When you finish the exam, leave the testing room quietly, turn in your note board, and sign the test center log. The test center staff will provide you with a printed "unofficial" score report and dismiss you after completing all necessary procedures.

    NOTE: Your score will become official once The IIA publishes the score to The IIA Certification Candidate Management System. This normally takes a few days. Exam scores may be suspended, voided, or otherwise invalidated after becoming official if The IIA discovers errors or evidence of cheating or other improper activity.

STUDY UNIT ONE
STRUCTURAL ANALYSIS AND STRATEGIES

(17 pages of outline)

This study unit begins with an overview of the strategic management process, including development of a grand strategy, planning, implementation, and control. The next two subunits address Porter's model for analyzing the structure of industries and competition. This model is based on five competitive forces and four generic competitive strategies. The fourth subunit considers an alternative model of competitive strategies that, like Porter's, has a marketing perspective.

1.1 STRATEGIC MANAGEMENT

 Candidates for the CIA exam should understand that an organization uses one set of analytical tools to choose the industries in which it will compete and another to determine what competitive moves are appropriate in those industries.

Strategic Management and Strategic Planning

1. Strategic management has a **long-term planning horizon**. Thus, a strategic orientation is traditionally associated with senior management. However, all employees should have this orientation because it encourages foresight. Strategic thinking also helps employees understand and implement managerial decisions. Moreover, it is consistent with the modern trend toward cooperation and teamwork and away from authoritarian managerial styles.

2. Strategic management includes developing a grand strategy, strategic planning, implementation, and control.

   a. A **grand strategy** describes how the organization's mission is to be achieved. This strategy is based on a **situational analysis** that considers organizational **strengths** and **weaknesses** (a capability profile) and their interactions with environmental **opportunities** and **threats**. Such an evaluation is also called a **SWOT analysis**.

      1) Strengths and weaknesses (the **internal environment**) are usually identified by considering the firm's capabilities and resources. What the firm does particularly well or has in greater abundance are **core competencies**.

         a) Core competencies are the source of competitive advantages that in turn are the basis for an overall strategy.

      2) Opportunities and threats (the **external environment**) are identified by considering

         a) **Macroenvironment factors** (economic, demographic, political, legal, social, cultural, and technical) and

         b) **Microenvironment factors** (suppliers, customers, distributors, competitors, and other competitive factors in the industry).

      3) For example, speed in reacting to environmental changes, introducing new products, etc., is an important competitive advantage. To achieve it, the organization may have to reengineer its processes.

b. **Strategic planning** formulates specific and measurable objectives, plans, policies, and budgets.

1) Thus, strategic planning involves

   a) **Portfolio management** of the organization's businesses,

   b) Determining the strength of each business with respect to the potential of markets and the position of businesses in their markets, and

   c) Creating a strategy for each business.

2) At the highest level, a firm's strategic planning function involves (a) formulating its **mission** (ultimate firm purposes and directions), (b) determining its **strategic business units (SBUs)**, (c) allocating resources to SBUs, (d) planning to start new businesses, and (e) downsizing or divesting old businesses.

   a) A mission statement should address reasonably limited **objectives**, define the firm's major **policies and values**, and state its primary **competitive scopes**. These scopes may extend to

      i) Industries,
      ii) Products and services,
      iii) Applications,
      iv) Core competencies,
      v) Market segments,
      vi) Degree of vertical integration, and
      vii) Geographic markets.

   b) Businesses should be defined in market terms, that is, in terms of needs and customer groups. Moreover, a distinction should be made between a **target market definition** and a **strategic market definition**.

      i) For example, a target market for a railroad might be freight hauling, but a strategic market might be transportation of any goods and people.

   c) A business also may be defined with respect to customer groups and their needs and the technology required to satisfy those needs.

   d) A large firm has multiple businesses. Thus, the concept of the **strategic business unit** is useful for strategic planning by large firms.

      i) An SBU is a business (or a group) for which separate planning is possible. It also has its own competitors and a manager who engages in strategic planning and is responsible for the major determinants of profit.

c. **Implementation.** Strategic plans must be passed down the organizational structure through development of plans at each lower level. This process is most likely to succeed if

1) The structure is compatible with strategic planning,
2) Personnel have the necessary abilities,
3) The organizational culture is favorable or can be changed, and
4) Controls exist to facilitate implementation.

d. **Control.** Strategic controls should be established to monitor progress, isolate problems, identify invalid assumptions, and take prompt corrective action.

1) As plans are executed at each organizational level, control measurements are made to determine whether objectives have been achieved. Thus, objectives flow down the organizational hierarchy, and control measures flow up.

2) One category of strategic control measures relates to **external effectiveness**.

    a) At the **business-unit level**, these measures concern performance in the marketplace (market share, etc.).

    b) At the **business-operating-system level**, these measures concern customer satisfaction and flexibility.

    c) At the **departmental or work-center level**, these measures concern quality and delivery.

3) A second category of strategic control measures relates to **internal efficiency**.

    a) At the **business-unit level**, these measures concern financial results.

    b) At the **business-operating-system level**, these measures concern flexibility (both an external effectiveness and internal efficiency issue).

    c) At the **departmental or work-center level**, these measures concern cycle time (time to change raw materials into a finished product) and waste.

Strategic Management

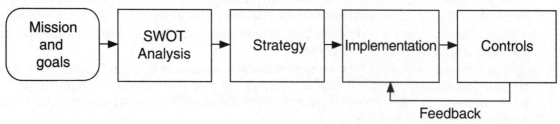

Figure 1-1

3. Strategic management is dependent on **forecasts** of outcomes of events, their timing, and their future values.

Synergies and Strategies

4. Strategic management is facilitated when managers think synergistically. **Synergy** occurs when the combination of formerly separate elements has a greater effect than the sum of their individual effects. The following are types of synergy observed in business:

    a. **Market synergy** arises when products or services have positive complementary effects. Shopping malls reflect this type of synergy.

    b. **Cost synergy** results in cost reduction. It occurs in many ways, for example, in recycling of by-products or in the design, production, marketing, and sales of a line of products by the same enterprise.

    c. **Technological synergy** is the transfer of technology among applications. For example, technology developed for military purposes often has civilian uses.

    d. **Management synergy** also involves knowledge transfer. For example, a firm may hire a manager with skills that it lacks.

5. An **operations strategy** formulates a long-term plan for using resources to reach strategic objectives. The following are five operations strategies:

    a. A **cost** strategy is successful when the enterprise is the low-cost producer. However,

        1) The product (e.g., a commodity) tends to be undifferentiated in these cases,

        2) The market is often very large, and

        3) The competition tends to be intense because of the possibility of high-volume sales.

      b.   A **quality** strategy involves competition based on product quality or process quality.

         1)   Product quality relates to design, for example, the difference between a luxury car and a subcompact car.

         2)   Process quality concerns the degree of freedom from defects.

      c.   A **delivery** strategy may permit an enterprise to charge a higher price when the product is consistently delivered rapidly and on time. An example firm is UPS.

      d.   A **flexibility** strategy involves offering many different products or an ability to shift rapidly from one product line to another.

         1)   An example firm is a publisher that can write, edit, print, and distribute a book within days to exploit the public's short-term interest in a sensational event.

      e.   A **service** strategy seeks to gain a competitive advantage and maximize customer value by providing services, especially post-purchase services, such as warranties on automobiles and home appliances.

Core Concepts

- Strategic management focuses on long-term planning. While senior management typically oversees strategy, all employees should also understand the organization's strategy.
- Strategic management is a process that includes development of a grand strategy, strategic planning, implementation, and control.
- A grand strategy describes how an organization's mission is to be achieved. This is based on situational analysis, called SWOT analysis. In SWOT analysis, strengths and weaknesses of the firm (internal environment) are identified, along with opportunities and threats (external environment).
- Strategic planning formulates specific objectives, plans, policies, and budgets. This involves portfolio management of each of the organization's businesses. Furthermore, strategic planning involves (1) formulating a mission, (2) determining strategic business units (SBUs), (3) allocating resources, and (4) defining target and strategic markets.
- Implementation passes the strategy of the organization down to mid- and lower-level employees, who then carry out the organization's strategy.
- Strategic control should be established to monitor the implementation of the organization's strategy. Controls should measure external effectiveness and internal efficiency.
- Strategic management looks for synergies. Synergy occurs when the combination of formerly separate elements has a greater effect than the sum of their individual effects. Types of synergy include (1) market synergy, (2) cost synergy, (3) technological synergy, and (4) management synergy.
- An operations strategy formulates a long-term plan for using enterprise resources to reach strategic objectives. Examples of operations strategies include (1) cost strategy, (2) quality strategy, (3) delivery strategy, (4) flexibility strategy, and (5) service strategy.

Stop and review! You have completed the outline for this subunit. Study multiple-choice questions 1 through 4 beginning on page 37.

1.2 STRUCTURAL ANALYSIS OF INDUSTRIES

Overview

1. An economy as a whole can be subdivided into **sectors, industries**, and **segments**.

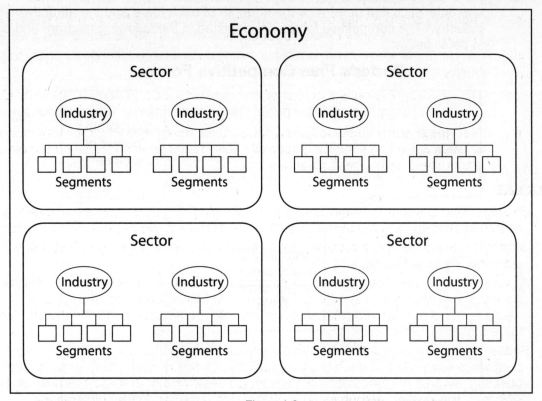

Figure 1-2

2. Economists speak of, for example, the healthcare sector or the transportation sector of the economy. Within each sector are multiple industries. Hill and Jones (*Strategic Management*, 6th ed., 2004) define an industry as "a group of companies offering products or services that are close substitutes for each other – that is, products or services that satisfy the same basic customer needs."

   a. Thus, the transportation sector has an automobile industry, an airline industry, and a passenger rail industry. Each provides its own way of moving people from one place to another.

   b. Hill and Jones define market segments as groups of customers with "distinct attributes and specific demands."

      1) Thus, the automobile industry serves one market segment with sedans, another with sport utility vehicles, another with minivans, etc.

         a) Segments consist of customers, not firms.
         b) One firm in an industry may attempt to serve multiple segments.

3. **Michael E. Porter** has developed a model of the structure of industries and competition. It includes an analysis of the **five competitive forces** that determine long-term profitability as measured by long-term return on investment.

    a. This analysis includes an evaluation of the basic economic and technical characteristics that determine the strength of each force and the attractiveness of the industry. The competitive forces are depicted in the following diagram and discussed in detail below:

Porter's Five Competitive Forces

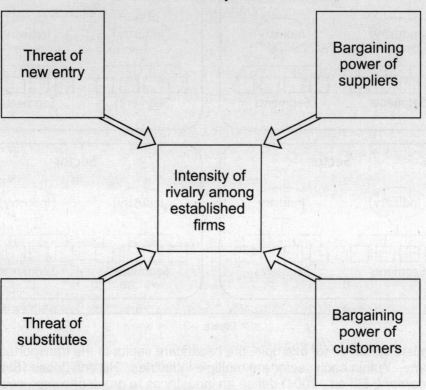

Figure 1-3

4. **Rivalry** among existing firms will be intense when an industry contains many strong competitors. Price-cutting, large advertising budgets, and frequent introduction of new products are typical. The intensity of rivalry and the threat of entry vary with the following factors:

    a. The stage of the **industry life cycle**, e.g., rapid growth, growth, maturity, decline, or rapid decline.

        1) Thus, growth is preferable to decline. In a declining or even a stable industry, a firm's growth must come from winning other firms' customers, thereby strengthening competition.

    b. The distinctions among products **(product differentiation)** and the **costs of switching** from one competitor's product to another.

        1) Less differentiation tends to heighten competition based on price, with price cutting leading to lower profits. But high costs of switching suppliers weaken competition.

c. Whether **fixed costs** are high in relation to variable costs.

   1) High fixed costs indicate that rivalry will be intense. The greater the cost to generate a given amount of sales revenues, the greater the **investment intensity** and the greater the need to operate at or near capacity. Hence, price cutting to sustain demand is typical.

d. **Capacity expansion.**

   1) If the size of the expansion must be large to achieve economies of scale, competition will be more intense. The need for large-scale expansion to achieve production efficiency may result in an excess of industry capacity over demand.

e. **Concentration and balance.**

   1) If an industry has many firms or a few equal competitors with no leader or leaders, the situation tends to be unstable and the rivalry intense.

f. The extent of **exit barriers**.

   1) Low exit costs make an industry more attractive.

g. **Competitors' incentives** to remain in the industry.

   1) When incentives are low, competitors are less likely to incur the costs and risks of intense rivalry.

Four Threats

5. **Threats of, and barriers to, entry.** The prospects of long-term profitability depend on the industry's exit and entry barriers.

   a. Factors that **increase the threat of entry** are the following:

      1) **Economies of scale** (and learning curve effects) are not significant.
      2) **Brand identity** of existing products is weak.
      3) Costs of switching suppliers are low.
      4) Existing firms do not have the cost advantages of vertical integration.
      5) Product differences are few.
      6) Access to existing suppliers is not blocked, and distribution channels are willing to accept new products.
      7) Capital requirements are low.
      8) Existing firms are unlikely to retaliate against a new firm.
      9) The government's policy is to encourage new entrants.

   b. The most favorable industry condition is one in which entry barriers are high and exit barriers are low. The following grid reflects Porter's view of the relationship of **returns, entry barriers, and exit barriers**:

		Exit Barriers	
		Low	High
Entry Barriers:	Low	Low, stable returns	Low, risky returns
	High	High, stable returns	High, risky returns

      1) When the threat of new entrants is minimal and exit is not difficult, returns are high, and risk is reduced in the event of poor performance.
      2) Low entry barriers keep long-term profitability low because new firms can enter the industry, increasing competition and lowering prices and the market shares of existing firms.

3)   **Exit barriers** are reasons for a firm to remain in an industry despite poor (or negative) profits. They include the following:

a)   Assets with a low residual value because of obsolescence or specialization

b)   Legal or ethical duties to stakeholders, such as employees, creditors, suppliers, or customers

c)   Governmental regulations

d)   Lack of favorable alternative investments

e)   Substantial vertical integration

f)   Emotional factors, such as history and tradition

6.   The **threat of substitutes** limits price increases and profit margins. The greater the threat, the less attractive the industry is to potential entrants.

a.   **Substitutes** are types (not brands) of goods and services that have the same purposes, for example, plastic and metal or minivans and SUVs. Hence, a change in the price of one such product (service) causes a change in the demand for its substitutes.

b.   The **price elasticity of demand** is a measure of the threat posed by substitutes. It is the ratio of the percentage change in the quantity of a product (service) demanded to the percentage change in the price causing the change in the quantity.

1)   Demand is **elastic** when the ratio exceeds 1.0 (ignoring the minus sign that results if the price and demand changes are in opposite directions). If demand is elastic, the effect of a price change on a firm's **total revenue** will be in the opposite direction of the change.

a)   If demand is **inelastic** (the ratio is less than 1.0), the price effect on total revenue is greater than the quantity effect. Thus, a firm could increase total revenue by raising its prices.

2)   The better the substitutes for a product (service), the more likely that demand is elastic and the greater the threat of substitutes.

c.   **Structural considerations** affecting the threat of substitutes are

1)   Relative prices,

2)   Costs of switching to a substitute, and

3)   Customers' inclination to substitute.

7.   As the **threat of buyers' bargaining power** increases, the appeal of an industry to potential entrants decreases. Buyers seek lower prices, better quality, and more services. Moreover, they use their purchasing power to obtain better terms, possibly through a bidding process. Thus, buyers affect competition.

a.   **Buyers' bargaining power** varies with the following factors:

1)   When purchasing power is **concentrated** in a few buyers or when buyers are well organized, their bargaining power is greater. This effect is reinforced when sellers are in a capital-intensive industry.

2)   High (low) **switching costs** decrease (increase) buyers' bargaining power.

3)   The threat of **backward (upstream) vertical integration**, that is, the acquisition of a supply capacity, increases buyers' bargaining power.

4)   Buyers are most likely to bargain aggressively when their profit margins are low and a supplier's product accounts for a substantial amount of their costs.

5)   Buyers are in a stronger position when the supplier's product is **undifferentiated**.

6)   The more important the supplier's product is to buyers, the less bargaining power they have.

b. A supplier may seek to limit buyers' power by choosing those with the least ability to bargain or switch to other suppliers. However, a preferable response is to make offers that are difficult to reject.

8. As the **threat of suppliers' bargaining power** increases, the appeal of an industry to potential entrants decreases. Accordingly, suppliers affect competition through pricing and the manipulation of the quantity supplied.

 a. **Suppliers' bargaining power** is greater when

 1) Switching costs are substantial.
 2) Prices of substitutes are high.
 3) They can threaten forward (downstream) vertical integration.
 4) They provide something that is a significant input to the value added by the buyer.
 5) Their industry is concentrated, or they are organized.

 b. Buyers' best responses are to develop favorable, mutually beneficial relationships with suppliers or to diversify their sources of supply.

Core Concepts

- Porter's five competitive forces that determine long-term profitability of an industry include (1) rivalry among existing firms, (2) entry and exit barriers, (3) threat of substitutes, (4) buyer's bargaining power, and (5) supplier's bargaining power.
- Rivalry among existing competitors is intense when an industry contains many strong competitors. The intensity of the rivalry varies with (1) the stage of the industry life cycle, (2) the degree of product differentiation and costs of switching, (3) fixed costs, (4) the size of the necessary capacity expansion, (5) market concentration, (6) exit barriers, and (7) competitors' incentives.
- Entry and exit barriers affect an industry's long-term profitability. The most favorable industry condition is one in which entry barriers are high and exit barriers are low.
- Some factors that affect entry barriers include economies of scale, brand identity of existing products, product differences, and capital requirements. Some factors that affect exit barriers include obsolescence of assets, governmental regulations, and substantial vertical integration.
- The threat of substitutes limits potential price increases and profitability. Substitutes are goods and services that have the same purpose as the good or service being sold.
- High bargaining power of buyers decreases an industry's appeal. Buyers can seek lower prices, higher quality, and more services. Some of the factors that affect buyers' bargaining power include concentration of purchasing power, switching costs, and differentiation of products.
- High supplier bargaining power also decreases an industry's appeal. High supplier bargaining power gives suppliers the ability to manipulate price and quantity of supplied products and services. Some of the factors that affect bargaining power of suppliers include switching costs, prices of substitutes, threat of vertical integration, and supplier industry concentration. Buyers' best responses are to develop favorable, mutually beneficial relationships with suppliers or to diversify supply sources.

Stop and review! You have completed the outline for this subunit. Study multiple-choice questions 5 through 15 beginning on page 38.

1.3 GENERIC COMPETITIVE STRATEGIES

Four Strategies

1. Although profitability is substantially determined by the industry in which the firm functions, its relative position in the industry is also important. That position is influenced by its choice of competitive strategy.

2. Porter's **generic strategies model** is based on the concept that each of a firm's **competitive advantages** ultimately may be either a **cost** advantage or a **differentiation** advantage.

   a. The firm's advantages should be used within the firm's **competitive (target) scope** to achieve its objectives. This scope may be **broad** (e.g., industry wide) or **narrow** (e.g., a market segment).

3. Using the variables of **competitive advantage** (cost and differentiation) and **competitive scope** (broad and narrow), Porter described four generic strategies to be applied by business units.

Competitive Advantage

Competitive Scope	Low Cost	Product Uniqueness
Broad (Industry wide)	Cost Leadership Strategy	Differentiation Strategy
Narrow (Market segment)	Focused Strategy: Cost	Focused Strategy: Differentiation

Figure 1-4

   a. **Cost leadership** is the generic strategy of a firm that seeks competitive advantage through **lower costs**. It has a **broad competitive scope**. Such a firm can earn higher profits than its competitors at the industry average price or charge a lower price to increase market share.

      1) A firm **acquires a cost advantage** over its competitors by the following:

         a) Vertical integration
         b) Exclusive access to low-cost materials
         c) Economies of scale or other efficiencies resulting in low unit cost
         d) Outsourcing

      2) **Strengths of cost leaders.** The typical firm that follows a cost leadership strategy has low profit margins, a high volume of sales, and a substantial market share. Such a firm

         a) Has efficient supply and distribution channels;
         b) Is capable of large capital investment;
         c) If it is a manufacturer, has strengths in product design and process engineering; and
         d) Closely supervises its labor force.

3) The **risks** of this strategy include the possibility that advances in technology or successful imitation may eliminate the cost leader's advantage.

    a) Furthermore, multiple firms following a strategy with a **narrow focus on cost** may achieve advantages in their market segments.

    b) Still another risk is that the emphasis on cost may cause managers to overlook product and marketing changes. For example, the cost advantage must outweigh the differentiation advantages held by others.

4) **Organization.** A cost leader is ordinarily highly structured to achieve close control of costs. Detailed reports are provided with great frequency, and benefits are tied to numerical goals.

b. **Differentiation** is the generic strategy of a firm that seeks competitive advantage through providing a **unique product or service**. This strategy has a **broad competitive scope**. Such a firm may earn higher profits because consumers are willing to pay a price higher than that charged by competitors. However, that price difference must exceed the additional cost of the differentiated product or service.

1) A successful differentiation strategy creates a buyer perception that few, if any, **substitutes** are available. Thus, the firm may have the additional advantage of being able to pass supplier **cost increases** to buyers.

    a) Uniqueness may be based on, for example, massive promotion, excellence of design, superior service, technical leadership, or brand identification.

    b) A differentiation strategy does not signify a disregard for cost control, but simply a greater emphasis on creating a perception of the uniqueness of the product or service.

2) The following are typical **strengths** of successful broad-scope differentiators:

    a) An effective R&D function

    b) Creative product development

    c) A strong marketing function that communicates (or helps to create) the perceived uniqueness of the product or service

    d) A reputation for quality or technical leadership

    e) A tradition reaching back for decades

    f) Effective coordination with suppliers and distributors

    g) An ability to apply the expertise of other enterprises

3) The **risks** of a differentiation strategy include the following:

    a) The maturing of the industry produces successful imitation by competitors.

    b) Consumer tastes change as they become more sophisticated buyers or as they have less need for the differentiating factor.

    c) Multiple firms following a strategy with a narrow focus on differentiation can achieve advantages in their market segments.

    d) The differentiating factor may no longer justify its premium price. Brand loyalty may decrease as lower-cost competitors improve the quality and image of their products or services.

4) An **organization** adopting a differentiation strategy usually has close cooperation among its R&D and marketing functions. Incentive compensation is often based on relatively subjective performance measures, and the firm must succeed in attracting highly skilled or creative individuals.

    c. **Cost focus** is the generic strategy of a firm that seeks competitive advantage through **lower costs** but with a **narrow competitive scope** (e.g., a regional market or a specialized product line). The reason for a cost-focus strategy is that the narrower market can be better served because the firm knows it well.

        1) Firms that successfully adopt a cost-focus strategy achieve very strong **customer loyalty**, a disincentive to potential competitors.

        2) The **strengths** of successful firms employing a cost-focus strategy are similar to those of broad-target firms.

        3) The **risks** of a cost-focus strategy include the following:

            a) A narrow focus means lower purchasing volume and therefore a weaker position relative to suppliers.

            b) The cost (or differentiation) advantage of serving a narrow target may be more than offset by the cost advantage achieved by broad-target competitors through economies of scale and other factors.

            c) Even more narrowly focused competitors may serve their niches better.

            d) A firm following a broad-target strategy may, by imitation or otherwise, change its product or service to compete more effectively in the narrower market.

            e) The narrower market itself may change.

        4) The **organizational attributes** of firms employing a cost-focus strategy are similar to those of broad-target firms.

    d. **Focused differentiation** is the generic strategy of a firm that seeks competitive advantage through providing a **unique product or service** but with a **narrow competitive scope**, e.g., a regional market or a specialized product line.

        1) The analysis of these firms is similar to that for cost-focus firms.

4. According to Porter, using a **combination of generic strategies** may leave the firm **stuck in the middle**, that is, unable to create or sustain a competitive advantage. The danger is that attempting to follow more than one generic strategy will prevent the firm from achieving a competitive advantage.

    a. Thus, pursuit of, for example, both cost leadership and differentiation may interfere with reaching either objective. Furthermore, even if the firm could succeed by following multiple generic strategies, the result might be an ambiguous public image.

    b. In Porter's view, a firm that pursues multiple generic strategies may be more likely to succeed if it creates a separate **strategic business unit** to implement each strategy.

        1) However, some writers disagree with Porter's advice not to pursue a combination of strategies. They argue that following a single strategy may not serve the needs of customers who want the best combination of product attributes, e.g., price, service, and quality.

    c. A firm also may need to adapt as a result of the changes that occur as the firm, its products or services, and the industry proceed through their **life cycles**.

        1) For example, an appropriate and successful focus strategy may need to be changed to a cost leadership strategy as the firm matures.

Five Forces

5. **Porter's generic strategies** are responses to the **five competitive forces**.

    a. **Rivalry Among Existing Firms**

        1) Cost leadership permits a firm to compete by charging lower prices.

        2) Differentiation strengthens brand loyalty.

        3) Focus strategies provide superior attention to customer needs, whether for quality, price, or other product attributes.

b. **Threats of, and Barriers to, Entry**

1) Cost leadership permits a firm to reduce prices as a deterrent to potential entrants.
2) Differentiation creates brand loyalty that a new entrant may not be able to overcome.
3) Focus strategies develop core competencies in a narrow market that potential entrants may not be able to match.

c. **Threat of Substitutes**

1) Cost leadership may result in low prices that substitutes cannot match.
2) Differentiation may create unique product (service) attributes not found in substitutes.
3) Focus strategies are efforts to develop core competencies or unique product attributes that may protect against substitutes as well as potential entrants.

d. **Buyers' Bargaining Power**

1) Cost leadership may enable a firm to remain profitable while charging the lower prices required by strong buyers.
2) Differentiation may reduce the power enjoyed by strong buyers because of the uniqueness of the product and the resulting lack of close substitutes.
3) Focus strategies also may reduce buyers' ability to negotiate in a narrow market. Substitutes may not be able to compete on price, quality, etc.

e. **Threat of Suppliers' Bargaining Power**

1) Cost leadership provides protection from strong suppliers.
2) Differentiation may permit a firm to increase its price in response to suppliers' price increases.
3) Focus strategies must allow for the superior bargaining power of suppliers when sellers operate in a narrow, low-volume market. For example, focused differentiation may permit the firm to pass along suppliers' price increases.

Core Concepts

- Competitive advantages are cost advantages or differentiation advantages. The competitive scope is where a firm uses its advantages. A company may have a broad scope (e.g., industry wide) or narrow scope (e.g., market segment).
- Cost leadership is the generic strategy of a firm that seeks competitive advantage through lower costs. It has a broad competitive scope. Such a firm can earn higher profits than its competitors at the industry average price or charge a lower price to increase market share.
- Differentiation is the generic strategy of a firm that seeks competitive advantage through providing a unique product or service. This strategy has a broad competitive scope. Such a firm may earn higher profits because consumers are willing to pay a price higher than that charged by competitors.
- Cost focus is the generic strategy of a firm that seeks competitive advantage through lower costs but with a narrow competitive scope (e.g., a regional market or a specialized product line). The reason for a cost-focus strategy is that the narrower market can be better served because the firm knows it well.
- Focused differentiation is the generic strategy of a firm that seeks competitive advantage through providing a unique product or service but with a narrow competitive scope, e.g., a regional market or a specialized product line.
- A firm that pursues multiple generic strategies may be more likely to succeed if it creates a separate strategic business unit to implement each strategy.

Stop and review! You have completed the outline for this subunit. Study multiple-choice question 16 on page 41.

1.4 MARKET-BASED COMPETITIVE STRATEGIES

<u>**Market Leader**</u>

1.   The dominant firm in a market pursues a **market-leader strategy**.

    a.   The leader should attempt to **increase total demand** in the market because the market leader will gain the most. Demand will increase if the firm

        1)   Attracts **new users**.

            a)   A **market-penetration strategy** focuses on customers who might use the product or service.

            b)   A **new-market segment strategy** pursues customers who have never used the product or service.

            c)   A **geographical expansion strategy** targets users in previously unserved localities.

        2)   Encourages **new uses** of the product or service.

        3)   Promotes **increased use**, for example, by planned obsolescence.

    b.   Moreover, the leader must **defend market share** through offensive and defensive actions.

        1)   Constant innovation to improve products and services, control costs, and increase distribution effectiveness is the basis for a good **offensive strategy**. The leader must continuously improve the value offered to customers.

        2)   Kotler and Singh have identified six **defense strategies**:

            a)   A **position defense** strengthens the firm's **brand power.**

            b)   A **flank defense** creates outposts that protect the leader's position. For example, a firm might respond to a competitor's price attack on one of its major products by introducing new brands. One of these might be sold at the same price as the attacker's brand and a second at a lower price, in effect outflanking the attacker.

            c)   A **preemptive defense** anticipates an attack. It may (1) target particular competitors before they can launch assaults, (2) flood the market with products for every segment and niche, or (3) send **market signals** indicating ways in which the leader intends to anticipate attacks.

            d)   A **counteroffensive defense** is a counterattack. For example, the leader may meet an attacker's price cuts in one market by slashing prices in another market that is more important to the attacker.

            e)   A **mobile defense** may involve **market broadening**, a reorientation from a specific product to the underlying need. An example is the repositioning of oil companies as energy companies. An alternative is **market diversification**, an effect of conglomerate mergers of firms in wholly different industries.

            f)   A **contraction defense** is planned contraction or strategic withdrawal. This defense involves concentrating resources in the areas of greatest strength rather than defending all of the firm's positions.

    c.   The leader also may attempt to obtain a **greater market share**. In general, a firm that increases its market share in its **served (target) market**, as opposed to the total market, will increase profits if it adopts an appropriate strategy.

        1)   This strategy must avoid the risk of **antitrust** suits.

2) The **economic cost** of the strategy must be acceptable. Beyond a certain **optimal market share**, profits may decline.

   a) The incremental market share may not provide economies of scale and experience,

   b) Costs borne by the market leader (e.g., legal and lobbying costs) may increase, and

   c) Customers may want more than one supplier.

3) The leader must adopt the right **marketing mix** (the marketing methods used). For example, market share should be earned, not bought by lower profit margins.

   a) Most firms that gain market share ordinarily are leaders in introducing new products, product quality, and marketing outlays.

Market Challenger

2. Trailing (runner-up) firms may choose a **market challenger strategy**.

   a. A challenger must determine its strategic objective (such as leadership or a larger market share) and specific targets.

   1) The challenger may attack the leader, for example, by across-the-board innovation or by better serving the market.

   2) The attack may be directed at firms of similar size that are not serving the market, e.g., by failing to introduce new products or by overpricing.

   3) The challenger may seek to grow by absorbing small firms.

   b. Kotler suggests five general **attack strategies** by a challenger:

   1) A **frontal attack** directly pits the firm's products, prices, promotions, and methods of distribution against the target's.

   a) An example of a modified frontal attack is price cutting, a strategy that may succeed if there is no retaliation, and the perception is that the product's quality equals that of the target.

   2) A **flank attack** may be directed at a geographic or segmental weakness of the target (an underserved market) or an unmet need (such as the desire for more healthful fast food).

   a) A flank attack succeeds when market segments shift. The result is a gap in need fulfillment that the attacker can convert into a strong position in a profitable segment.

   3) An **encirclement attack** is used by a challenger with an advantage in resources. It is an assault on multiple marketing fronts.

   4) The **bypass attack** directs the assault against markets other than those where the competitive target is strong. It may involve diversification of products or geographic markets. It also may entail developing next-generation technology so as to move the competition to an arena where the challenger is in a stronger position.

   5) **Guerrilla warfare** consists of numerous small attacks designed to reduce the strength of the target, e.g., by ad campaigns, carefully chosen price decreases, and lawsuits. Such warfare ordinarily must be followed by a different (and stronger) type of attack if the challenge is to succeed.

     c.   The market challenger also must devise combinations of strategies that are more specific than the general strategies.

        1) **Price discounting** tends to succeed if buyers are price sensitive, the product or service is similar to the market leader's, and the discounts are not matched.

        2) **Lower-priced goods** of average quality may substantially outsell higher quality goods if the price is much lower.

        3) **Prestige goods** are high-quality items sold at a high price.

        4) **Product proliferation** is a strategy based on better product variety.

        5) Other specific strategies emphasize improved service, development of a new distribution channel, increased marketing expenditures, or manufacturing efficiencies.

Market Follower

3.   **Market-follower strategies** are adopted by firms that do not wish to challenge the leader.

     a.   These firms may adhere to the view that **product imitation** may be preferable to **product innovation**. Because the innovator has already incurred the expenses of bringing the new product to market, the imitator that introduces a similar product may be profitable without being the leader.

     b.   Some industries are characterized by **conscious parallelism**. These industries (e.g., fertilizers and chemicals) tend to have high fixed costs and little product and image differentiation. Market followers tend to imitate the leader because competing for a greater market share provokes painful retaliation.

     c.   A market follower requires a strategy to maintain its share of current and new customers, fend off challengers, protect its advantages (e.g., service or location), lower its costs, and improve the quality of its products and services.

        1) A **counterfeiter** operates illegally by selling copies on the black market.

        2) A **cloner** sells cheap variations of a product with sufficient differentiation to avoid liability for counterfeiting.

        3) An **imitator** sells a product that is significantly differentiated, e.g., with respect to price, promotion, location, and packaging.

        4) An **adapter** improves products and may operate in different markets or evolve into a market challenger.

     d.   Market followers ordinarily have lower percentage returns than market leaders.

Market Niche

4.   **Market-nicher strategies** are followed by small or mid-size firms that compete in small (niche) markets that may be overlooked by large firms.

     a.   Successful niche marketers often have higher rates of return than firms in large markets. They often sell high-quality products at premium prices and have low manufacturing costs.

        1) These firms excel in need satisfaction because they know their markets well.

     b.   Successful niche marketers have high profit margins. By contrast, mass marketers sell in high volume.

     c.   Niche marketers must create, expand, and protect their niches. The risk is that a niche may evaporate or be entered by a large firm.

     d.   The essence of niche marketing is **specialization**. However, success often depends on **multiple niching**. Creating new niches diversifies risk and increases the firm's probability of survival.

5.   Choosing and implementing an effective market-based competitive strategy should never be at the expense of maintaining a **customer orientation**. Firms with this orientation are more likely to be alert to customer-related needs, threats, and opportunities than firms that are competitor oriented.

Core Concepts

- The dominant firm in a market pursues a market-leader strategy. The leader should attempt to increase total demand in the market because the market leader will gain the most. Demand will increase if the firm attracts new users, encourages new uses of its product or service, and promotes increased use.

- The leader must defend market share through offensive and defensive actions. Constant innovation to improve products and services, control costs, and increase distribution effectiveness is the basis for a good offensive strategy. The leader must continuously improve the value offered to customers. The leader also may attempt to obtain a greater market share. In general, a firm that increases its market share in its served (target) market, as opposed to the total market, will increase profits if it adopts an appropriate strategy.

- Trailing (runner-up) firms may choose a market challenger strategy. A challenger must determine its strategic objective (such as leadership or a larger market share) and specific targets. The challenger may attack the leader, for example, by across-the-board innovation or by better serving the market. The attack may be directed at firms of similar size that are not serving the market, e.g., by failing to introduce new products or by overpricing. The challenger may seek to grow by absorbing small firms.

- Market-follower strategies are adopted by firms that do not wish to challenge the leader. These firms may adhere to the view that product imitation may be preferable to product innovation. Because the innovator has already incurred the expenses of bringing the new product to market, the imitator that introduces a similar product may be profitable without being the leader. A market follower requires a strategy to maintain its share of current and new customers, fend off challengers, protect its advantages (e.g., service or location), lower its costs, and improve the quality of its products and services.

- Small or mid-sized firms follow market-nicher strategies and operate in niches often overlooked by large firms. These firms excel in need satisfaction and know their markets well. These marketers must create, expand, and protect the niches. Specialization is imperative.

Stop and review! You have completed the outline for this subunit. Study multiple-choice questions 17 through 19 on page 42.

QUESTIONS

1.1 Strategic Management

1. Which of the following is **least** likely to be an example of synergy?

A. A shopping mall with several businesses providing different products and performing different services.

B. A car dealership providing warranties on automobile parts to maximize customer value.

C. A manufacturing company hiring a new manager with technological experience lacking in the company.

D. Military Humvees being converted into sports utility vehicles for sale to civilians.

Answer (B) is correct. *(Publisher, adapted)*
   REQUIRED: The least likely example of synergy.
   DISCUSSION: Synergy occurs when the combination of formerly separate elements has a greater effect than the sum of their individual effects. However, a car dealership's provision of warranties reflects an operational strategy designed to provide post-purchase services to gain a competitive advantage and maximize customer value. It does not reflect the complementary sharing of resources, technology, or competencies. In contrast, synergy arises from selling a line of cars that share some components or a brand identification.
   Answer (A) is incorrect. A shopping mall with several businesses providing different products and performing different services is an example of market synergy. Answer (C) is incorrect. Hiring a manager with needed skills is an example of management synergy. Answer (D) is incorrect. Conversion of Humvees to SUVs is an example of technological synergy.

2. Which of the following **best** describes a market synergy?

    A. Technology transfer from one product to another.

    B. Bundling of products distributed through the same channels.

    C. Production of multiple products at one facility.

    D. Use of complementary management skills to achieve entry into a new market.

Answer (B) is correct. *(CIA, adapted)*
    REQUIRED: The best description of market synergy.
    DISCUSSION: Market synergy arises when products or services have positive complementary effects. Shopping malls reflect this type of synergy. Also, bundling of products, distribution through the same distribution channels, and use of the same sales force are other examples of market synergies.
    Answer (A) is incorrect. Technology transfer constitutes technology synergy. Answer (C) is incorrect. The production of multiple products at one production facility is an example of cost synergy. Answer (D) is incorrect. Using complementary management skills is an example of management synergy.

3. Which of the following is a market-oriented definition of a business versus a product-oriented definition of a business?

    A. Making air conditioners and furnaces.

    B. Supplying energy.

    C. Producing movies.

    D. Selling men's shirts and pants.

Answer (B) is correct. *(CIA, adapted)*
    REQUIRED: The market-oriented business definition.
    DISCUSSION: Businesses should be defined in market terms, that is, in terms of needs and customer groups. Moreover, a distinction should be made between a target market definition and a strategic market definition. For example, a target market for a railroad might be freight hauling, but a strategic market might be transportation of any goods and people. Accordingly, stating that a business supplies energy is a market-oriented definition as opposed to the product-oriented definition. Moreover, it is also a strategic market definition.
    Answer (A) is incorrect. Air conditioners and furnaces are products, not customer needs. Answer (C) is incorrect. Movies are products, not a customer need (e.g., entertainment). Answer (D) is incorrect. Shirts and pants are products, not an underlying need.

4. Which one of the following is a social trend affecting the organization?

    A. Changes in labor markets.

    B. Tougher legislation to protect the environment.

    C. Rising inflation.

    D. Replacements for steel in cars and appliances.

Answer (A) is correct. *(CIA, adapted)*
    REQUIRED: The social trend that affects organizations.
    DISCUSSION: Social trends, such as changes in labor markets, reflect social, cultural, and demographic factors in the organization's macroenvironment that may constitute opportunities or threats (identified in a SWOT analysis). The attributes of people (age, education, income, ethnicity, family status, etc.) and their beliefs, attitudes, and values shape and are shaped by social trends that in turn affect the organization. Thus, changes in the characteristics, sources, locations, and costs of labor resources supplied (a basic factor of production) have great effects on an organization's strategic position.
    Answer (B) is incorrect. Tougher legislation to protect the environment is a political trend. Answer (C) is incorrect. Rising inflation is an economic trend. Answer (D) is incorrect. Replacements for steel in cars and appliances represent a technological trend.

1.2 Structural Analysis of Industries

5. Which of the following factors is **least** typical of an industry that faces intense competitive rivalry?

    A. Price-cutting.

    B. Large advertising budgets.

    C. Frequent introduction of new products.

    D. A high threat of substitutes.

Answer (D) is correct. *(Publisher, adapted)*
    REQUIRED: The situation least typical of an industry facing intense rivalry.
    DISCUSSION: A high threat of substitutes reduces the attractiveness of an industry. It tends to increase the price elasticity of demand and therefore limits price increases and profit margins. If other factors are constant, fewer entrants result in less intense competition.
    Answer (A) is incorrect. Price-cutting is typical of an industry with intense competitive rivalry. Answer (B) is incorrect. A large advertising budget is typical of an industry with intense competitive rivalry. Answer (C) is incorrect. Frequent introduction of new products is typical of an industry with intense competitive rivalry.

6. Intensity of rivalry among existing firms in an industry increases when

I. Products are relatively undifferentiated.
II. Consumer switching costs are low.

    A. I only.

    B. II only.

    C. Both I and II.

    D. Neither I nor II.

Answer (C) is correct. *(Publisher, adapted)*
REQUIRED: The condition(s), if any, that increase(s) the intensity of rivalry in an industry.
DISCUSSION: The degree of product differentiation and the costs of switching from one competitor's product to another increase the intensity of rivalry and competition in an industry. Less differentiation tends to heighten competition based on price, with price cutting leading to lower profits. Low costs of switching products also increase competition.
Answer (A) is incorrect. Low consumer switching costs also increase rivalry. Answer (B) is incorrect. A low degree of product differentiation also increases rivalry. Answer (D) is incorrect. Both low consumer switching costs and a low degree of product differentiation increase rivalry.

7. The prospect for the long-term profitability of an existing firm is greater when

    A. The firm operates in an industry in which learning curve effects are significant.

    B. The costs of switching suppliers are low.

    C. New entrants are encouraged by government policy.

    D. Distribution channels are willing to accept new products.

Answer (A) is correct. *(Publisher, adapted)*
REQUIRED: The circumstance improving the prospect of long-term profitability.
DISCUSSION: The prospects of long-term profitability depend upon the industry's entry barriers. The entry of new firms in a market decreases the prospect for long-term profitability. When economies of scale (and learning curve effects) in an industry are significant, it is more difficult for new firms to enter. Thus, the prospects of long-term profitability are greater for an existing firm.
Answer (B) is incorrect. When the costs of switching suppliers are low, the threat of entry by new firms is increased. Answer (C) is incorrect. When new entrants are encouraged by government policy, the threat of entry by new firms is increased. Answer (D) is incorrect. When distribution channels are willing to accept new products, the threat of entry by new firms is increased.

8. Structural considerations affecting the threat of substitutes include all of the following **except**

    A. Relative prices.

    B. Brand identity.

    C. Cost of switching to substitutes.

    D. Customers' inclination to use a substitute.

Answer (B) is correct. *(Publisher, adapted)*
REQUIRED: The structural consideration that does not affect the threat of substitutes.
DISCUSSION: Substitutes are types of goods and services that serve the same purpose. All products that can replace a good or service should be considered substitutes. For example, bicycles and cars are substitutes for public transportation. Structural considerations determine the effect substitutes have on one another. However, because substitutes are types (not brands) of goods and services that have the same purposes, brand identity is not a structural consideration affecting the threat of substitutes.
Answer (A) is incorrect. Relative price is a structural consideration affecting the threat of substitutes. Answer (C) is incorrect. The cost of switching is a structural consideration affecting the threat of substitutes. Answer (D) is incorrect. Customers' inclination to use a substitute is a structural consideration affecting the threat of substitutes.

9. A corporation is performing research to determine the feasibility of entering the truck rental industry. The decision to enter the market is **most** likely to be deterred if

    A. Buyer switching costs are high.

    B. Buyers view the product as differentiated.

    C. The market is dominated by a small consortium of buyers.

    D. Buyers enjoy large profit margins.

Answer (C) is correct. *(Publisher, adapted)*
REQUIRED: The deterrent to market entry.
DISCUSSION: When purchasing power is concentrated in a few buyers or when buyers are well organized, their bargaining power is greater. This effect is reinforced when sellers are in a capital-intensive industry, such as trucking.
Answer (A) is incorrect. High switching costs decrease buyers' bargaining power. Answer (B) is incorrect. Buyers are in a weaker position when the supplier's product is differentiated. Answer (D) is incorrect. Buyers are most likely to bargain aggressively when their profit margins are low, especially if the supplier's product accounts for a substantial amount of their costs.

10. Which industry factor does **not** contribute to competitive rivalry?

- A. Price-cutting, large advertising budgets, and frequent introduction of new products.
- B. A firm's growth must come from winning other firms' customers.
- C. High costs of customers switching suppliers.
- D. High fixed costs relative to variable costs.

Answer (C) is correct. *(Publisher, adapted)*
REQUIRED: The industry factor that does not contribute to competitive rivalry.
DISCUSSION: If it is expensive to switch suppliers, customers will be less motivated to respond to competitor advances.
Answer (A) is incorrect. Price-cutting, large advertising budgets, and frequent introduction of new products are characteristic of intense competitive rivalry. Answer (B) is incorrect. The need to win other firms' customers to grow strengthens competition. Answer (D) is incorrect. The greater the fixed costs needed to generate a given amount of sales revenues, the greater the incentive to compete on price, service, etc., to maintain and increase sales levels.

11. Which condition does **not** increase the threat of new competitor entry into the industry?

- A. Strong brand identity.
- B. Existing firms do not enjoy the cost advantages of vertical integration.
- C. Few proprietary product differences.
- D. Low capital requirements.

Answer (A) is correct. *(Publisher, adapted)*
REQUIRED: The condition that decreases the threat of new competition.
DISCUSSION: Strong brand identity decreases the threat that new competitors will enter an industry. New competitors have difficulty because potential customers are loyal to established firms in the industry.
Answer (B) is incorrect. Cost advantages of existing firms make entry difficult for new competitors. Answer (C) is incorrect. Proprietary product differences make entry more difficult. Answer (D) is incorrect. High capital requirements make entry more difficult.

12. The concurrent action of basic competitive forces as defined by Porter's model determines the

- A. Long-term profitability and the competitive intensity of the industry.
- B. Entrance barriers that potential players must face to get into the industry.
- C. Rivalry inside the industry.
- D. Strategy that a firm should follow to achieve its objectives.

Answer (A) is correct. *(CIA, adapted)*
REQUIRED: The industry factors determined by the basic competitive forces in Porter's model.
DISCUSSION: Porter developed a model of the structure of industries and competition. It includes an analysis of the five competitive forces that determine long-term profitability measured by long-term return on investment. This analysis results in an evaluation of the attractiveness of an industry.
Answer (B) is incorrect. Potential profitability depends on threats of, and barriers to, entry. Answer (C) is incorrect. Intensity of rivalry is one of the five competitive forces. Answer (D) is incorrect. The analysis of the effects of the five forces is only the first step in the development of a strategy.

13. Which factor **most** likely encourages entry into an existing market?

- A. Governmental subsidies for new investors.
- B. High product differentiation, principally produced by trademarks.
- C. Knowledge of the industry, with high investments in development.
- D. Low fixed exit costs.

Answer (A) is correct. *(CIA, adapted)*
REQUIRED: The factor likely to encourage market entry.
DISCUSSION: Subsidies for new firms lower entry barriers. Thus, new firms may enter the industry and intensify competition. Government policy also may affect competition by means of regulations that encourage or discourage substitutes or affect costs, that govern competitive behavior, or that limit growth. Government also may be a buyer or supplier.
Answer (B) is incorrect. Product differentiation is an entry barrier. New firms may be incapable of offering a comparable product, so the industry's profitability is protected. Answer (C) is incorrect. Knowledge of the industry is an asset that new firms must acquire. This cost in some cases becomes extremely high and may discourage new firms from entering the industry. Answer (D) is incorrect. Low fixed exit costs facilitate exit when firms decide to leave the industry. They mildly encourage entry because they make investment less risky.

14. Which of the following is a favorable condition for a firm competing in a profitable, expanding industry?

    A. The firm does not have a strong customer base.

    B. A few suppliers who can restrict supply.

    C. Competitors find it difficult to acquire the firm's customers.

    D. The firm has high costs relative to other firms in the industry.

Answer (C) is correct. *(CIA, adapted)*
    REQUIRED: The favorable condition for a firm competing in a profitable, expanding industry.
    DISCUSSION: A firm that has successfully differentiated its products through developing a desirable image, better services, cost leadership, the features of the product, or other means is in a favorable competitive position. Competitors find it difficult to acquire the firm's customers, for example, by price cutting. The reason is that the firm's products are perceived to have few substitutes, and brand loyalty is high. Furthermore, barriers to entry are favorable to the firm. These barriers deter competitors from entering the market. Existing firms can increase market share and emphasize cutting costs and increasing value.
    Answer (A) is incorrect. Without brand loyalty, growth or even survival is difficult. Answer (B) is incorrect. These few suppliers can bid up the prices at the expense of the firm. Answer (D) is incorrect. The firm will not be able to reap economies of scale and lower their production costs.

15. Which basic force(s) drive(s) industry competition and the ultimate profit potential of the industry?

    I. Threat of new entrants
    II. Bargaining power of suppliers
    III. Favorable access to raw materials and labor
    IV. Product differentiation

    A. I only.

    B. I and II only.

    C. III and IV.

    D. I, II, III, and IV.

Answer (B) is correct. *(CIA, adapted)*
    REQUIRED: The factor(s) driving industry competition and the profit potential in the industry.
    DISCUSSION: Threat of new entrants and bargaining power of suppliers are among the five basic forces that drive industry competition and the ultimate profit potential in the industry. This potential is measured in terms of long-term return on invested capital. The other three forces are rivalry among existing firms, threat of substitutes, and threat of buyers' bargaining power.
    Answer (A) is incorrect. The bargaining power of suppliers also drives industry competition and ultimate profit potential. Answer (C) is incorrect. Labor unrest and material shortages are short-run factors that may affect competition and profitability but are not among the five basic forces driving competition. Answer (D) is incorrect. Product differentiation is a competitive strategy, not one of the five basic forces.

1.3 Generic Competitive Strategies

16. A manufacturing company produces plastic utensils for a particular segment at the lowest possible cost. The company is pursuing a cost

    A. Leadership strategy.

    B. Focus strategy.

    C. Differentiation strategy.

    D. Containment strategy.

Answer (B) is correct. *(CIA, adapted)*
    REQUIRED: The cost strategy pursued by the manufacturing company.
    DISCUSSION: Cost focus is the generic strategy that seeks competitive advantage through lower costs but with a narrow competitive scope (e.g., a regional market or a specialized product line). The reason for a cost-focus strategy is that the narrower market can be better served because the firm knows it well.
    Answer (A) is incorrect. A cost leader is the lowest cost producer in the industry as a whole. Answer (C) is incorrect. Cost differentiation aims at providing a product at different costs in different market segments. Answer (D) is incorrect. Cost containment aims at controlling costs related to a particular product/market but not necessarily producing at the lowest possible cost.

1.4 Market-Based Competitive Strategies

17. A runner-up firm in a market may choose a market-challenger strategy. Which general attack strategy adopted by a market challenger is directed at a gap in customer need fulfillment?

- A. Guerrilla warfare.
- B. Bypass attack.
- C. Frontal attack.
- D. Flank attack.

Answer (D) is correct. *(Publisher, adapted)*
REQUIRED: The general attack strategy adopted by a market challenger to exploit a need-fulfillment gap.
DISCUSSION: A flank attack may be directed at a geographic or segmental weakness of the target (an underserved market) or an unmet need (such as the desire for more healthful fast food). A flank attack succeeds when market segments shift. The result is a gap in need fulfillment that the attacker can convert into a strong position in a profitable segment.
Answer (A) is incorrect. Guerrilla warfare consists of numerous small attacks designed to reduce the strength of the target, e.g., by ad campaigns, carefully chosen price decreases, and lawsuits. Such warfare ordinarily must be followed by a different (and stronger) type of attack if the challenge is to succeed. Answer (B) is incorrect. The bypass attack directs the assault against markets other than those where the competitive target is strong. It may involve diversification of products or geographic markets. It also may entail developing next-generation technology so as to move the competition to an arena where the challenger is in a stronger position. Answer (C) is incorrect. A frontal attack directly pits the firm's products, prices, promotions, and methods of distribution against the target's.

18. What strategy seeks to gain a larger share of a current market for a current product?

- A. Market penetration.
- B. Market development.
- C. Product development.
- D. Diversification.

Answer (A) is correct. *(CIA, adapted)*
REQUIRED: The strategy to gain market share for a current product in current market.
DISCUSSION: Market penetration is the percentage of potential users of a product in a current market who buy the product. A firm's market penetration strategy may be to (1) convince its current customers to increase their usage frequency, (2) convince other firms' customers to switch, or (3) convert nonusers in the target market.
Answer (B) is incorrect. Market development seeks new markets for current products. Answer (C) is incorrect. Product development is launching new products in existing markets. Answer (D) is incorrect. Diversification is launching new products for new markets.

19. The dominant firm in a market pursues a market-leader strategy. This strategy may involve

- A. Holding the market stable to avoid attracting new competitors.
- B. A flank defense to strengthen the firm's brand.
- C. Sending market signals as a mobile defense.
- D. Innovation as an offensive strategy.

Answer (D) is correct. *(Publisher, adapted)*
REQUIRED: The action taken by a market leader.
DISCUSSION: Constant innovation to improve products and services, control costs, and increase distribution effectiveness is the basis for a good offensive strategy. The leader must continuously improve the value offered to customers.
Answer (A) is incorrect. As the firm most likely to gain, the leader should attempt to increase total demand, for example, by attracting new users, encouraging new uses, and promoting increased use. Answer (B) is incorrect. A position defense strengthens the firm's brand power. Answer (C) is incorrect. A preemptive defense anticipates an attack, such as by targeting particular competitors before they can launch assaults, flooding the market with products for every segment and niche, or by sending market signals indicating ways in which the leader intends to anticipate attacks.

Use the additional questions in Gleim *CIA Test Prep* Software to create Test Sessions that emulate Pearson VUE!

STUDY UNIT TWO
INDUSTRY AND MARKET ANALYSIS

(19 pages of outline)

This study unit begins with the broad subject of competitive intelligence, including customer value analysis. Without accurate intelligence, effective competitive analysis is not feasible. The next subunit addresses methods for determining how diversification should be used to achieve the firm's objectives. These methods include the growth-share matrix and General Electric's multifactor portfolio matrix. The third subunit covers the evaluation of competitors' indirect market communications, or market signals. The following subunit extends the analysis of an industry as a whole in Study Unit 1. It considers strategic groups in an industry and competitor analysis. The final subunit builds on the concepts of competitive forces and the product life cycle. The outline shows how evolutionary processes move an industry from its initial structure to its potential structure.

2.1 COMPETITIVE INTELLIGENCE

The internal audit activity is management's partner in improving risk management, control, and governance processes. To fulfill this role effectively, internal auditors must be familiar with the standard tools for analyzing the competitive environment in which the organization operates.

1. Leonard Fuld defines competitor intelligence as "highly specific and timely information about a corporation" (*Competitor Intelligence*, Wiley, 1985).

Competitive Intelligence System

2. A competitive intelligence system should be established to

   a. Identify competitor strategies,
   b. Monitor their new-product introductions,
   c. Analyze markets for the firm's own new-product introductions and acquisitions,
   d. Obtain information about nonpublic firms,
   e. Evaluate competitor R&D activity,
   f. Learn about competitors' senior executives, and
   g. Perform other necessary information-gathering tasks.

3. **Setting up the system** involves determining the kinds of information to be collected, sources, and persons responsible.

4. **Data collection** should be continuous. Field sources include the firm's own sales agents, distributors, and suppliers. Trade associations and market researchers are also useful sources.

   a. Other information may come from competitors' customers and suppliers and observation of competitors.

   b. An enormous amount of published information is publicly available from various services (Dun & Bradstreet, Moody's, Standard & Poor's, and others), newspapers, general business periodicals, special business publications, government data, reports submitted to government regulators, and much more.

c.   The Internet, e.g., websites of competitors, trade associations, and governments, is a fertile source of business intelligence. Patent applications, help wanted ads, licensing agreements, and many other activities may be revealing.

5.   **Data analysis** validates and processes the intelligence gathered.

6.   **Information dissemination.** The system should be able to transmit timely information to decision makers and respond to queries.

Customer Value Analysis

7.   Competitive intelligence permits a firm to create effective competitive strategies that target the appropriate competitors.

a.   A starting point is **customer value analysis (CVA)**. The premise of CVA is that customers choose from competitors' products or services the brands that provide the greatest customer value.

1)   Customer value equals **customer benefits** (product, service, personnel, and image benefits) minus **customer costs** (price and the costs of acquisition, use, maintenance, ownership, and disposal).

2)   The **steps in a CVA** are

a)   Determine what customers value.

b)   Assign quantitative amounts to the elements of customer value and have customers rank their relative significance.

c)   Evaluate how well the firm and its competitors perform relative to each element.

d)   Focus on performance with respect to each element compared with an important competitor in a given market segment. For example, if the firm outperforms the competitor in every way, it may be able to raise its price.

e)   Repeat the foregoing steps as circumstances change.

8.   Using the results of the CVA, the firm may then target a given **class of competitors**.

a.   Targeting **weak competitors** may be the cheapest way to gain market share. However, targeting **strong competitors** also may be appropriate because this strategy forces the firm to improve. Moreover, a strong competitor may have an exploitable weakness.

b.   **Close competitors**, that is, firms that are similar, are the usual targets. Nevertheless, **distant competitors** are also threats. For example, any beverage may be a competitor of soft drink makers.

c.   **Bad competitors** should be targeted because they disturb the competitive equilibrium, e.g., by excessive expansion of capacity or overly risky behavior.

1)   **Good competitors** make sound business decisions that promote the long-term health of the industry, e.g., about prices, entry into new segments, and pursuit of market share.

Core Concepts

■   A competitive intelligence system should identify competitor strategies, monitor competitors' new products and R&D, analyze markets for the firm's own new products, obtain information about nonpublic firms, learn about competitors' key executives, and perform other information-gathering tasks.

■   Customer value analysis (CVA) is useful in targeting a given class of competitors. Customer value equals the customer benefits (product, service, image, etc.) minus the customer costs (price, use, maintenance, etc.).

■   Targeting weak competitors may be the least expensive way for a firm to gain market share. However, targeting strong competitors may be appropriate because the competitor may have an exploitable weakness, and it forces the firm to improve to compete.

Stop and review! You have completed the outline for this subunit. Study multiple-choice questions 1 through 3 on page 62.

2.2 PORTFOLIO TECHNIQUES OF COMPETITIVE ANALYSIS

Integration and Diversification

1. Firms use **diversification** to grow, improve profitability, and manage risk.

    a. **Vertical integration** occurs upstream (backward) by acquiring suppliers or downstream (forward) by acquiring wholesalers and retailers.

    b. **Horizontal integration** is the acquisition of competitors.

    c. **Concentric diversification** results from developing or acquiring related businesses that do not have products, services, or customers in common with current businesses. However, they offer **internal synergies**, e.g., through common use of brands, R&D, plant facilities, or marketing expertise.

    d. **Horizontal diversification** is the acquisition of businesses making products unrelated to current offerings but that might be demanded by the firm's current customers.

    e. **Conglomerate diversification** is the acquisition of wholly unrelated businesses. The objectives of such an acquisition are financial, not operational, because of the absence of common products, customers, facilities, expertise, or other synergies.

The Growth-Share Matrix

2. A large firm may be viewed as a portfolio of investments in the form of strategic business units (SBUs). Hence, **techniques of portfolio analysis** have been developed to aid management in making decisions about resource allocation, new business startups and acquisitions, downsizing, and divestitures.

    a. One of the two portfolio models most frequently used for competitive analysis was created by the **Boston Consulting Group (BCG)**. This model, the **growth-share matrix**, has two variables. The **market growth rate** (MGR) is on the vertical axis, and the firm's **relative market share** (RMS) is on the horizontal axis.

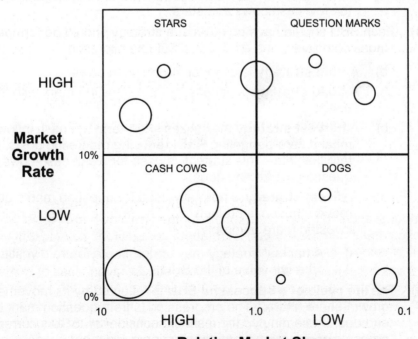

Boston Consulting Group
Growth – Share Matrix

Relative Market Share

Figure 2-1

1) The annual MGR is stated in constant units of the currency used in the measurement. It reflects the maturity and attractiveness of the market and the relative need for cash to finance expansion.

   a) An MGR of **10% or more** is generally regarded as high.

2) The RMS reflects the SBU's competitive position in the market segment. It equals the SBU's absolute market share divided by that of its leading competitor.

   a) An RMS of **1.0 or more** signifies that the SBU has a strong competitive position.

3) The growth-share matrix has four quadrants. The firm's SBUs are commonly represented in their appropriate quadrants by circles. The size of a circle is directly proportional to the SBU's sales volume.

   a) **Dogs** (low RMS, low MGR) are weak competitors in low-growth markets. Their net cash flow (plus/minus) is modest.

   b) **Question marks** (low RMS, high MGR) are weak competitors and poor cash generators in high-growth markets. They need large amounts of cash not only to finance growth and compete in the market, but also to increase RMS. If RMS increases significantly, a question mark may become a star. If not, it becomes a dog.

   c) **Cash cows** (high RMS, low MGR) are strong competitors and cash generators. A cash cow ordinarily enjoys high profit margins and economies of scale. Financing for expansion is not needed, so the SBU's excess cash can be used for investments in other SBUs. However, marketing and R&D expenses should not necessarily be slashed excessively. Maximizing net cash inflow might precipitate a premature decline from cash cow to dog.

   d) **Stars** (high RMS, high MGR) are strong competitors in high growth markets. Such an SBU is profitable but needs large amounts of cash for expansion, R&D, and meeting competitors' attacks. Net cash flow (plus/minus) is modest.

   e) A portfolio of SBUs should not have too many dogs and question marks or too few cash cows and stars.

4) Each SBU should have objectives, a strategy should be formulated to achieve those objectives, and a budget should be allocated.

   a) A **hold strategy** is used for strong cash cows.

   b) A **build strategy** is necessary for a question mark with the potential to be a star.

   c) A **harvest strategy** maximizes short-term net cash inflow. Harvesting means zero-budgeting R&D, reducing marketing costs, not replacing facilities, etc. This strategy is used for weak cash cows and possibly question marks and dogs.

   d) A **divest strategy** is normally used for question marks and dogs that reduce the firm's profitability. The proceeds of sale or liquidation are then invested more favorably.

      i) A harvest strategy may undermine a future divestiture by decreasing the fair value of the SBU.

5) The **life cycle of a successful SBU** is reflected by its movement within the growth-share matrix. The progression is from question mark to star, cash cow, and dog. Accordingly, a firm should consider an SBU's current status and its probable progression when formulating a strategy.

6) A serious **mistake** is not to tailor objectives (e.g., rates of return or growth) to the circumstances of each SBU.

    a) Cash cows should not be underfunded. The risk is premature decline. However, overfunding cash cows means less investment in SBUs with greater growth prospects.

    b) A large investment in a dog with little likelihood of a turnaround is also a typical mistake.

    c) A firm should not have too many question marks. Results are excess risk and underfunded SBUs.

The GE Matrix

b. The other most frequently used (and more detailed) portfolio model for competitive analysis was developed by **General Electric**. Shell, McKinsey and Company, and Arthur D. Little have also developed portfolio models. The GE model is a multifactor portfolio matrix with two variables. **Business strength or competitive position** (BUS) is on one axis, and **market attractiveness** (MAT) is on the other.

GE Portfolio Matrix

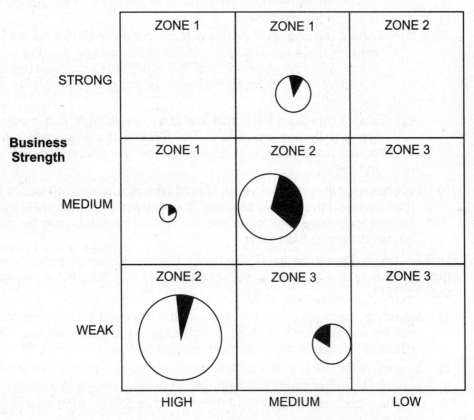

Market Attractiveness
Figure 2-2

1) BUS is classified as strong, medium, or weak, and MAT is classified as high, medium, or low. Thus, the matrix in this model is 3 × 3 and has **nine cells**.

2) SBUs are shown in the matrix as **circles**. Circle size is directly proportional to the size of the related market, with a shaded portion in the circle that represents the SBU's market share.

3) To **measure BUS and MAT**, the firm must isolate the multiple factors affecting each, quantify them, and create an index. Factors will vary with each business. The measurements will provide the values on the axes of the matrix.

    a) Typical **BUS factors** are the SBU's size, market share, growth rate, customer loyalty, profit margins, distribution network, technology position, and marketing skills.

    b) Typical **MAT factors** are market size, growth rate, competitive intensity, price levels, profit margins, technology requirements, and degree of regulation.

    c) One approach to the computation of BUS or MAT is to rate each factor on a scale from 1 to 5 (the highest ranking), weight each ranking by the factor's relative significance (0 to 1.0 each for a total of 1.0), and add the results.

4) The nine cells in the matrix may be classified into **three zones**.

    a) **Zone 1 (strong BUS and high MAT, medium BUS and high MAT, strong BUS and medium MAT).** The SBUs in the three cells in the upper left corner have strong overall attractiveness. Investment and growth are indicated.

    b) **Zone 2 (strong BUS and low MAT, medium BUS and MAT, weak BUS and high MAT).** The SBUs in the three cells on the diagonal from the lower left to the upper right of the matrix have medium overall attractiveness. Selective investment and management for earnings are indicated.

    c) **Zone 3 (medium BUS and low MAT, weak BUS and medium MAT, weak BUS and low MAT).** The SBUs in the three cells in the lower right corner have low overall attractiveness. A harvest or divest strategy is indicated.

5) Forecasts for the next 3-5 years should be made to estimate each SBU's position given the current strategy, the stage of the product life cycle, competitor actions, and other events. These forecasts may be indicated by arrows drawn on the matrix.

  c. Portfolio models should be used with care. They may over-emphasize entry into high growth markets and increasing market share and may lead to inadequate attention to current SBUs.

1) Moreover, because averages and weights are used in many models, they are subject to manipulation. Also, businesses in the same cell may have very different ratings for the multiple analytical factors.

2) Strategies for SBUs in the middle positions may be hard to determine.

3) Synergies among SBUs are ignored. Thus, divesting a low-rated SBU may be a mistake because of benefits it offers to other SBUs, such as a vital core competency.

Core Concepts

- A large firm can be viewed as a portfolio investment in the form of strategic business units (SBUs). The techniques of portfolio analysis have been developed to help management in making decisions about resource allocation, new business startups, and acquisition, downsizing, and divestitures.

- In the growth-share matrix, the market growth rate (MGR) is on the vertical axis, and the firm's relative market share (RMS) is on the horizontal axis.

- An MGR of 10% or more is generally regarded as high, while an RMS of 1.0 or more signifies that the SBU has a strong competitive advantage. The growth-share matrix has four quadrants: dogs, question marks, cash cows, and stars.

- A strategy should be formulated to achieve the SBU's objectives. The strategy may be to hold, build, harvest, or divest and is directly related to the quadrant in which the SBU is located in the growth-share matrix.

- The other most frequently used portfolio model for competitive analysis was developed by General Electric. It is a multifactor portfolio matrix with two variables: business strength or competitive position (BUS) on the vertical axis and market attractiveness (MAT) on the horizontal axis.

- BUS is classified as strong, medium, or weak and is typically based on factors such as the SBU's size, market share, growth rate, and profit margin. MAT is classified as high, medium, or low and is based on factors such as market size, growth rate, and competitive intensity.

- The nine cells in the matrix can be classified into three zones: Zone 1 consists of the three cells in the upper left corner. SBUs in this zone have strong overall attractiveness, and investment and growth are indicated. Zone 2 consists of the three cells in the diagonal from lower left to upper right. SBUs in this zone have medium overall attractiveness, and selective investment and management for earnings are indicated. Zone 3 consists of the three cells in the lower right corner. SBUs in this zone have low overall attractiveness, and a harvest or divest strategy is indicated.

Stop and review! You have completed the outline for this subunit. Study multiple-choice questions 4 and 5 on page 63.

2.3 MARKET SIGNALS

Introduction

1. Porter defines a **market signal** as "any action by a competitor that provides a direct or indirect indication of its intentions, motives, goals, or internal situation." These indirect communications are helpful in **competitive analysis** and the design of **competitive strategies**.

    a. However, signals may be sent to warn or mislead rather than to indicate a genuine intention to execute a planned action. Accordingly, the firm must understand competitors so as not to ignore, or be deceived by, their signals.

Types of Signals

2. Market signals may be classified as **true signals** or **bluffs**. The types of signals vary with the nature of the competitor's signaling behavior and the media used.

    a. **Prior announcements of moves**, that is, to do or not do something, have value as signals in part because an announced move need not actually occur. A competitive battle may be fought entirely with announcements, thus avoiding the negative effects of, for example, a price war.

        1) Prior announcements of moves may

            a) Preempt competition, such as by inducing customers to wait for the introduction of the firm's new product.

            b) Threaten action, for example, by declaring that the firm will substantially undercut a competitor's intended price reduction.

            c) Test competitor sentiment, as when the firm proposes a new customer warranty program. The reaction then determines whether the firm continues with, modifies, or withdraws the program.

            d) Express pleasure or displeasure with a competitor's action. Announcement of a move has greater force than simply communicating pleasure or displeasure in an interview or speech.

e)   Minimize the provocation caused by a future strategic adjustment, e.g., a price cut. Such a move may be a genuine attempt to realign prices with changes in costs, not an aggressive grab for market share. However, the move also may be an attempt to mislead.

f)   Avoid costly simultaneous moves, such as capacity expansions that might result in overcapacity.

g)   Be intended to influence the financial community. The firm may wish to raise its share price or improve its reputation, but such announcements may be misread by competitors.

h)   Be a means of ending internal debate.

2)   A firm must examine the competitor's possible motives for a prior announcement to determine whether it is preemptive or conciliatory. Conciliation is more likely if preemptive benefits are few, the announced action is less damaging than it could have been, or the announcement is made far in advance.

3)   A **bluff** is an announcement of an action not intended to be executed. For example, a firm may issue a threat in an effort to prevent a competitor action even though following through would not be beneficial.

a)   Bluffs may cause loss of credibility for future announcements.

4)   Prior announcements may be in many media. Examples are interviews with journalists, news conferences, meetings with securities analysts, updates of website content, and regulatory disclosures.

a)   The medium and the breadth of the audience chosen have signaling value. Thus, an announcement that is widely disseminated may represent a greater commitment.

b.   **Announcements of results or actions after the fact**, especially of information difficult to obtain or that is surprising, ensure competitor awareness. Misleading announcements of this kind may be intended to preempt action or affirm commitment.

1)   However, a firm's discovery that an announcement is misleading (or wrong) may be a source of useful inferences about the competitor's purposes and strengths.

c.   **Competitors' public discussions of the industry** address such matters as cost increases and forecasts of demand, prices, and capacity. These discussions may signal, perhaps unintentionally, the firm's assumptions underlying its strategy. Thus, they may be sincere efforts to clarify motives, prevent conflict, and promote cooperation.

1)   The discussions also may be ways for the firm to seek an advantage, for example, to portray competitors' prices as excessive. Hence, other firms must evaluate the firm's true intent by determining whether and how the firm's position may be improved by its interpretation of industry conditions.

2)   Direct commentary on a competitor's moves likewise may be subject to different interpretations of its motives.

d.   **Competitors' discussions of their own moves** may be in public or private forums (e.g., with customers or suppliers) with the intent of signaling to competitors. One motive is to persuade others that a move is appropriate and not provocative. A second motive is preemption. A third motive is to express commitment.

e.   **Competitors' tactics** may have signaling content if they differ from the feasible alternative conduct. A conciliatory (aggressive) signal is conveyed by a move within the range of options that is the least (most) harmful to competitors.

f. The **manner of initially implementing a strategic change** may signal aggressive intent or a cooperative attitude, or it may be a bluff. For example, initial price cutting on a competitor's key products rather than in secondary markets, introducing a new product targeted to a competitor's most important customers, or undertaking a move at an unusual time during the year may signal aggressive if not punitive intent.

g. A firm's **divergence from prior strategic objectives** suggests that other firms should be alert to profound changes in its objectives and assumptions.

h. A firm's **divergence from industry precedent**, e.g., discounting of never-before-discounted items, implies aggressive intent.

i. The **cross-parry** is a response to a competitor's move in one area with a move in another. For example, firm X, which is well established in region A, may move to compete with firm Y in its stronghold in region B. Firm Y's cross-parry is to enter the market in region A.

    1) A cross-parry is an indirect response by the defending firm that potentially avoids destructive conflict in the newly penetrated market. However, it also signals the possibility of retaliation, especially if it occurs in one of the initiating firm's key markets. For example, price cutting as a cross-parry may be very effective against a firm with a large share of the market where the parry is made. This firm has more to lose in a price war in that market. Consequently, maintenance of a presence in a cross market deters the large-share firm from attacking elsewhere.

j. **Introduction of a fighting brand** by a firm threatened or potentially threatened by a competitor is a tactic similar to the cross-parry. The brand may threaten or deter the rival, or it may bear the burden of competition. Thus, a competitor's product that is gaining market share could be countered by introduction of a very similar product in the competitor's key markets.

k. A **private antitrust suit**, which can be dismissed by the plaintiff at any time, may simply indicate displeasure without incurring the risks of a more serious signal, e.g., a price cut. Suits also may be harassing or delaying tactics.

    1) A suit by a large firm against a small firm is a way to punish the defendant regardless of the outcome. The legal costs of the small firm may be high, and the suit may prove a distraction over a long period.

3. One aspect of competitor analysis is the study of the relationship between a firm's signals and later moves or other events. This study may reveal unconscious signals (what poker players call "tells") that help to interpret and react to the firm's actions.

a. However, an effective competitor analysis should discover any economic and organizational factors that might cause a firm to behave in a manner inconsistent with its prior patterns.

Core Concepts

- Porter defines a market signal as "any action by a competitor that provides a direct or indirect indication of its intentions, motives, goals, or internal situation." Signals are helpful in competitive analysis and the design of competitive strategies.

- Market signals may be true signals or bluffs. Types of signals are (1) prior announcements of moves, (2) announcements of results or actions after the fact, (3) competitors' public discussion of the industry and their own moves and tactics, (4) the manner of initially implementing strategic changes, (5) divergence from prior strategic objectives and industry precedent, (6) the cross-parry, (7) introduction of a fighting brand, and (8) a private antitrust suit.

Stop and review! You have completed the outline for this subunit. Study multiple-choice questions 6 through 8 beginning on page 63.

2.4 STRUCTURAL ANALYSIS WITHIN AN INDUSTRY

Aspects of Industries

1.   An **industry** consists of firms selling products or services that are substitutes.

    a.   One way to describe an industry considers the number of sellers and the extent of differentiation of products and services.

        1)   **Pure competition** is rare, but the model is instructive. It illustrates in simple form processes that exist in certain real-world markets. A purely competitive market (a price-taker market) consists of so many buyers and sellers that none can affect the price of the product.

            a)   The product is homogeneous or standardized (undifferentiated). Accordingly, the product of one firm is a perfect substitute for that of any other firm. Because products are undifferentiated, the only basis for competition is price. Barriers to entry by new competitors or to exit by existing competitors are negligible. Examples are the stock market and agricultural markets.

        2)   In a **monopoly**, the entire industry consists of a single firm. The firm's product has no close substitutes.

            a)   Because it is the sole supplier of the product, the firm can strongly influence price. Entry by other firms is effectively blocked. For example, a monopoly may be created by a government. A natural monopoly results when economic or technical conditions permit only one efficient supplier (e.g., a local utility).

        3)   In **monopolistic competition**, an industry has numerous buyers and sellers. The industry has a large number of firms, fewer than in pure competition, but enough that firms cannot combine to fix prices and output.

            a)   Products are differentiated, so competition is based on nonprice factors, such as quality, styles, or after-market services. A firm attempts to create a mini-monopoly in its own product. This approach is reflected in the advertising slogan, "Only Cadillac makes a Cadillac." Because differentiation is crucial, advertising costs are high. Few barriers to entry and exit exist, but some existing firms may have exclusive patents, trademarks, trade names, etc., that make entry more difficult for new firms. An example is the carbonated drink market.

        4)   An **oligopoly** consists of a few large firms. Products can be differentiated (e.g., autos) or standardized (e.g., steel).

            a)   Competitors are mutually interdependent. Thus, their decisions, for example, about price and advertising, are dependent on the actions of the other firms. Prices tend to be rigid ("sticky") because of the interdependence among firms. A firm that raises prices loses market share without increasing profits. A firm that lowers prices loses profits and does not gain market share. The other firms match its lower prices.

    b.   Another way to describe an industry considers its **entry, exit, or mobility barriers**.

        1)   **Entry barriers** may be high or low. Industries vary as to the necessary capital investment, economies of scale, intellectual property, materials, locations, distribution channels, and other factors.

        2)   **Exit barriers** may consist of legal and moral obligations, regulatory requirements, lack of alternative investments, vertical integration, low residual value of assets, and tradition.

        3)   **Mobility barriers** restrict movement within an industry's segments. They are similar to industry entry barriers.

4) In general, high entry and mobility barriers and low exit barriers promote profitability.

c. The **cost structure** of an industry affects its competitive strategy. For example, the physical plant and distribution costs of oil refineries are much greater than those of restaurants. Other industries may have especially high R&D costs (pharmaceutical industry) or marketing costs (the brewery industry).

d. The degree of backward or forward **vertical integration** along the value chain varies with the industry. For example, a manufacturer that has acquired suppliers is **backward integrated**, and a movie producer that has acquired a chain of theaters is **forward integrated**.

1) Integration may reduce costs, and a firm may be able to choose where in the value chain to earn profits and pay the lowest taxes.

2) However, an integrated firm may be inflexible and face high exit barriers.

e. The extent of **globalization** varies with the industry. For example, restaurants are in a local industry, and manufacturers of large passenger aircraft are in a global industry, one that requires large R&D outlays and economies of scale.

Strategic Groups

2. To analyze competition within an industry, its **strategic groups** should be evaluated. Hence, a potential entrant must consider which strategic group to target. This choice and a firm's ability to implement its competitive strategy will determine profitability.

a. A strategic group consists of firms in an industry that have adopted **similar competitive strategies**. The analysis of strategic groups addresses such issues as

1) Their composition, number, and size.

2) Mobility barriers, i.e., barriers to movement among groups. The ability to move depends on the firm's current strategic group and its targeted group.

3) The bargaining power of a group.

4) The degree of the threat of substitutes.

5) Intergroup competition.

a) The level of competition primarily depends on

i) **Market interdependence**, i.e., the extent to which groups pursue the same customers. The greater the interdependence, the stronger the competition.

ii) Product differentiation or substitutability. Lower substitutability means less competition.

iii) Number and size of groups. The greater the number and the more equal their size, the greater the competition.

b. The **dimensions of the competitive strategies** adopted by the firms in a strategic group include the following:

1) Specialization

2) Brand identification (e.g., within the distribution channels or with ultimate consumers)

3) Selection of channels

4) Product or service quality

5) Technical leadership

6) Cost, service, and price

7) Degree of integration and leverage

8) Relationships with regulators and the parent firm

    c.   An **overall industry analysis** considers the following:

       1)   The characteristics of the industry (growth, demand, technology, strength of suppliers and buyers, and other factors)

       2)   The industry's strategic groups in relation to the five competitive forces

       3)   How the firm compares with the competitors within the chosen strategic group, e.g., on the basis of its scale of operations, the intensity of group rivalry, and the differences in the ability of the group members to implement their strategies

    d.   A **strategic group analysis**

       1)   Determines what mobility barriers exist and which groups are weak.

       2)   Forecasts future group actions and trends.

       3)   Predicts reaction patterns to events, such as competitive attacks.

       4)   Addresses the risks confronting the firms in the group. Risks include those that

          a)   Lower mobility barriers,
          b)   Arise from the investments needed to raise protective mobility barriers, and
          c)   Result from entering a new strategic group.

       5)   Helps the firm to make competitive choices. These include whether to

          a)   Move to another strategic group,
          b)   Improve the strategic group's structural position or the firm's relative position within the group, or
          c)   Establish its own strategic group.

Analysis of Competitors

3.   **Analysis of competitors** begins with determining the firm's actual and potential competitors. Accordingly, a firm must consider which other firms attempt to satisfy the same **customer needs** (a market approach). Moreover, a firm may be more threatened by new entrants or the evolution of technology than by existing competition.

    a.   Each **competitor's characteristics** should be considered, e.g., revenues, profits, market share, financial position, and relations with its parent firm.

       1)   Moreover, the SBU and product-market sales and market share are especially interesting. They are measures of the effectiveness of a competitor's strategy.

    b.   Each **competitor's objectives** also should be considered.

       1)   The organizational structure suggests the significance of given functions, where decisions are made, and the status of the competitor within a larger entity.

       2)   Tradeoffs may be made among financial and market position goals, in particular in the short run. For example, some firms emphasize short-run profits, but others may concentrate on market-share growth and long-run profits.

       3)   The competitor may believe itself to be the overall market leader or a leader in price or technology. An issue is what the competitor will do to remain in that position.

          a)   The competitor's assumptions about its products, its position, and other firms in its strategic group may reveal probable objectives and possible misjudgments.

       4)   The incentive and control systems of the competitor affect its ability to react to competitive pressures.

       5)   The experience, background, and attitudes of senior managers and directors may be clues to the competitor's objectives and its corporate culture.

       6)   Various commitments (e.g., debt or joint ventures) may limit a competitor's flexibility.

7) Regulatory restraints, e.g., on price, also may limit a competitor's options.

8) Recent setbacks or successes are often predictors of future behavior.

9) The analysis of the parent of a competitor may indicate, for example,

a) The reasons for the parent's entry into the competitor firm's business,

b) Its significance to the parent,

c) The parent's use of generic strategies with other businesses it controls,

d) The parent's corporate strategies, and

e) The parent's results.

10) The competitor's portfolio of businesses should be assessed to determine which are successful.

11) A crucial question about a competitor's objectives is whether it plans to expand.

c. The **competitor's history** may be revealing. Its current and past performance, record in relevant markets, successful and unsuccessful actions, and past reactions to strategic moves by rivals are factors identifying past and current **competitor strategies**.

d. A competitor's **strengths and weaknesses** indicate whether and how it may be attacked.

1) Areas to be addressed are

a) **Innovation** (ability to develop new products and technologies);

b) **Manufacturing** (capacity, efficiency, workforce, access to materials, degree of integration);

c) Access to **financing** at low cost;

d) **Product** quality and availability;

e) **Marketing and selling** (brands, distribution, advertising, customer orientation, diversity of products, relations with retailers);

f) **Service**;

g) **Management** skills at all levels (quality of decisions, loyalty);

h) The firm's **portfolio** (investments, degree of diversification); and

i) The **organizational structure**.

2) A firm should identify a competitor's **core competencies** and assess its growth potential, ability to respond quickly to threats and opportunities, and staying power in the industry.

3) Evaluating a competitor's market position is necessary to judge how and whether to challenge it. According to Arthur D. Little, an organization of consultants, a competitor firm may hold one of the following **competitive positions**:

a) A **dominant firm** has a choice of strategies. It controls other firm's actions.

b) A **strong firm** can act independently and sustain its long-term status regardless of the behavior of others.

c) A firm in a **favorable position** has strengths that give it a better-than-average chance to improve its status.

d) The performance of a firm in a **tenable position** justifies continuation of the business, but its chance for improvement is below average.

e) The performance of a firm in a **weak position** must change, or it must withdraw from the business.

f) A **nonviable firm** is a poor performer with no chance of improvement.

4)   Arthur D. Little also suggests a three-factor model for assessing a competitor's current and future market share.

a)   **Market share** is the share of the target market.

b)   **Mind share** is the percentage of customers who name the firm as the first "that comes to mind" in the industry.

c)   **Heart share** is the percentage of customers who name the firm as the one from which they "would prefer to buy."

d)   A competitor that improves its mind share and heart share will ultimately increase its market share and profits.

5)   Bruce Henderson has analyzed firms' **reaction patterns** when confronted with competitive attacks. A key to the analysis is **competitive equilibrium**.

a)   Almost **identical competitors** have an unstable equilibrium because differentiation cannot be sustained. Price wars are common.

b)   When one major factor is the **critical factor**, the equilibrium is unstable. A cost advantage obtained through economies of scale, technology gains, or experience allows a firm to gain market share.

c)   Given **multiple critical factors** (quality, service, price, convenience, etc.), differentiation is more likely. More competitors can secure an advantage with respect to a critical factor in a market segment or niche.

d)   The **number of competitors** is directly related to the number of critical factors.

e)   When one competitor has approximately twice the **market share** of a second competitor, equilibrium exists. The costs of gaining market share outweigh the benefits to either party.

4.   A competitor analysis may be used to assess a firm's best strategy for countering a competitor.

a.   The **offensive ability** of a firm to make a competitive move depends on

1)   Its satisfaction with the status quo
2)   Its probable competitive moves
3)   The strength and seriousness of its competitive moves

b.   A firm's **defensive ability** to respond to a competitive move depends on

1)   Its vulnerability to environmental threats
2)   The extent of the provocation, that is, the moves that cause a reaction
3)   The effectiveness of retaliation

a)   A competitor may be unable to respond quickly to some events.

Core Concepts

- An industry consists of firms selling products or services that are substitutes. One way to describe an industry is to consider the number of sellers and differentiation of products and services. The industry may be classified as (1) a monopoly, (2) an oligopoly, (3) monopolistic competition, or (4) pure competition. Another way to describe an industry is to consider its entry, exit, or mobility barriers.

- A strategic group consists of firms within an industry that have adopted similar competitive strategies. To analyze competition within an industry, its strategic groups should be evaluated. The analysis of strategic groups addresses such issues as mobility barriers, the degree of the threat of substitutes, and intergroup competition.

- Analysis of competitors begins with determining the firm's actual and potential competitors (the firms that try to satisfy the same customers' needs). Analysis of competitors considers each competitor's (1) characteristics, (2) objectives, (3) history, (4) strengths, and (5) weaknesses. The analysis of strengths and weaknesses includes evaluation of the competitor's core competencies, its competitive position, and its current and future market share.

- A competitor analysis may be used to assess the firm's best strategy for countering a competitor. The offensive ability of a firm to make a competitive move depends on its satisfaction with the status quo, its probable competitive moves, and the strength and seriousness of its competitive moves. The defensive ability to respond to a competitive move depends on its vulnerability to environmental threats, the extent of the provocation that causes a reaction, and the effectiveness of retaliation.

Stop and review! You have completed the outline for this subunit. Study multiple-choice questions 9 through 13 beginning on page 64.

2.5 INDUSTRY EVOLUTION

1. The **five competitive forces** within an industry or market are a basis for analyzing its structure. However, that structure and the firm's competitive strategies will evolve. Early recognition of change and prompt adjustment of strategies are essential to maintaining a competitive advantage. The costs of adjustments will be lower and their benefits greater the sooner they are made.

   a. The analysis of industry evolution should begin with how it affects each competitive force (see Study Unit 1, Subunit 2).

Product Life Cycle

2. Another concept useful in analysis of industry evolution is the **product life cycle**. It has the following stages:

   a. **Precommercialization** (product development). The strategy in this stage is to innovate by conducting R&D, marketing research, and production tests. During product development, the firm has no sales, but it has high investment costs.

   b. In the **introduction stage**, sales and profit growth are slow because of the high expenses of promotion and selective distribution to generate awareness of the product and encourage customers to try it. Thus, the per-customer cost is high.

      1) Competitors are few, basic versions of the product are produced, and higher-income customers (innovators) are usually targeted.

      2) Cost-plus prices are charged. They may initially be high to permit cost recovery when unit sales are low.

      3) The strategy is to infiltrate the market, plan for financing to cope with losses, build supplier relations, increase production and marketing efforts, and plan for competition.

   c. In the **growth stage**, sales and profits increase rapidly, cost per customer decreases, customers are early adopters, new competitors enter an expanding market, new product models and features are introduced, and promotion spending declines or remains stable.

      1) The firm enters new market segments and distribution channels and attempts to build brand loyalty and achieve the maximum share of the market.

         a) Thus, prices are set to penetrate the market, distribution channels are extended, and the mass market is targeted through advertising.

      2) The strategy is to advance by these means and by achieving economies of productive scale.

d.   In the **maturity stage**, sales peak but growth declines, competitors are most numerous but may begin to decline in number, and per-customer cost is low.

   1)   Profits are high for large market-share firms. For others, profits may fall because of competitive price-cutting and increased R&D spending to develop improved versions of the product.

   2)   The strategy is to defend market share and maximize profits through (a) diversification of brands and models to enter new market segments, (b) still more intensive distribution, (c) cost cutting, (d) advertising and promotions to encourage brand switching, and (e) emphasizing customer service.

   3)   Some writers identify a separate stage between growth and maturity. During the **shakeout period**, the overall growth rate falls, price cutting occurs, and weaker firms leave the market.

e.   The sales of most product types and brands eventually decrease permanently. This **decline stage** may be slow or rapid. This first symptom of the decline stage of a product's life cycle triggers such other effects as price cutting, narrowing of the product line, and reduction in promotion budgets.

   1)   Sales and profits drop as prices are cut, and some firms leave the market. Customers include late adopters (laggards), and per-customer cost is low. Weak products and unprofitable distribution media are eliminated, and advertising budgets are reduced to the level needed to retain the most loyal customers.

   2)   The strategy is to withdraw by reducing production, promotion, and inventory.

Industry Evolution

3.   According to Porter, **evolutionary processes** are the incentives or pressures that cause structural change in an industry.

a.   These processes operate to move an industry from its **initial structure** (technology, entry and exit barriers, power of suppliers and buyers, product traits, beginning size constraints, etc.) to its **potential structure**. The nature of that structure and the speed at which it will be achieved are unlikely to be known.

   1)   They depend on numerous factors that are hard to predict, such as

      a)   Innovations in technology and marketing,

      b)   Resources and skills of firms,

      c)   Favorable or unfavorable random events, and

      d)   Judgments about investments (e.g., which marketing or technology approaches to follow).

4.   The major evolutionary processes described by Porter are interacting and dynamic factors common to all industries, although their speed and direction vary.

a.   **Long-run changes in the industry growth rate** affect rivalry, entry, expansion, and supply.

   1)   These changes occur because of changes in five external factors:

      a)   Demographic traits (such as consumer ages and income levels),

      b)   Trends in needs of buyers (caused by changes in regulation, tastes, and lifestyles),

      c)   Relative positions of substitute products,

      d)   Relative positions of complementary products, and

      e)   Sales to new customers (market penetration).

   2)   Product innovation, an internal factor, alters the industry's position regarding the external factors.

b. **Changes in buyer segments served** occur when new segments are created (e.g., sale of computers to scientists, then to business, and finally to consumers), existing segments are subdivided, and old segments are no longer served.

  1) Consequently, industry structure evolves to meet the requirements of new customers.

c. **Learning by buyers** who become more sophisticated and better informed causes a decrease in product differentiation. These buyers tend increasingly to demand similar product characteristics (quality, service, etc.).

  1) Thus, products may become more like commodities.

    a) This effect may be offset by changes in the product or its marketing and by attracting new, inexperienced customers.

d. **Reduction of uncertainty** about such factors as the potential market size, resolution of technical problems, possible buyers, and marketing methods occurs as a result of experimentation. Successful strategies will be imitated and unsuccessful strategies will be discarded.

  1) Moreover, the reduction in risk will attract new and often larger competitors, especially if the potential market is large.

e. **Proprietary knowledge** (knowledge held only by one firm) may become more available to potential competitors as the industry evolves.

  1) This diffusion may result from

    a) Reverse engineering (a form of imitation) or another form of competitive intelligence (e.g., that obtained from suppliers, distributors, or customers),

    b) Expiration of patents,

    c) Purchase,

    d) Migration of personnel to new firms, and

    e) Spinoffs of operating segments.

  2) Thus, because barriers created by proprietary knowledge and specialized personnel tend to disappear, new competitors may emerge, and vertical integration becomes more likely.

    a) However, if further technological advances are feasible, economies of scale in R&D may create a protective barrier against new competition. The problem of diffusion may be met by creation of a substantial capacity to develop new proprietary knowledge.

f. **Accumulation of experience** (the learning curve effect) permits unit costs of manufacturers to decrease. This lead may not be sustainable because of diffusion of proprietary knowledge.

  1) A one-time leader may then be at a disadvantage because it has incurred costs not borne by its competitor-imitators.

g. **Expansion** of industry scale and firm scale permits a broader group of strategies to be implemented. The results are potentially greater economies of scale, capital needs, and desirability and feasibility of vertical integration.

  1) Also, suppliers and customers in an expanding industry will gain bargaining power.

  2) All these factors raise entry barriers.

  3) An increase in the scale of the industry may attract new, large firms once the scale has reached a level that provides sufficient opportunity to justify the necessary investment.

  4) Contraction of an industry has effects opposite to those of expansion.

h. **Changes in input costs** (of labor, materials, capital, communication, and transportation) most directly affect the cost and price of the product and the demand for it.

    1) These changes affect the existence of economies of scale and may promote substitution of inputs, reorganization of production, and use of different marketing media.

    2) Distribution channels and geographic market boundaries also may be altered.

    3) Exchange rate changes have similar effects on competition.

i. **Product innovation** may broaden markets or increase product differentiation.

    1) Furthermore, barriers are affected because innovation may involve high costs to market new products. Other changes are to marketing, distribution, and manufacturing methods and the related economies of scale.

    2) Innovation cancels buyer experience and therefore changes purchasing behavior.

    3) Product innovation may come from external sources and from suppliers and buyers.

j. **Marketing innovation** (e.g., in media, channels, or themes) may increase demand by differentiating the product, appealing to new buyers, or lowering costs.

    1) Indirect effects may include changes in economies of scale, e.g., as a result of changing to a wider-scope but more expensive medium.

k. **Process innovation** in manufacturing may affect the degree to which it is more or less capital intensive, economies of scale, vertical integration, the proportions of fixed and variable costs, and the gaining of experience, among other things.

    1) Technology changes may occur outside the industry, so a firm must extend its awareness of such developments.

l. **Structural changes in suppliers' and customers' industries** affect their bargaining power.

    1) For example, as concentration of customers' industries increases, the tendency is for sellers' industries to become more concentrated so as to counter their greater power.

m. **Government policies** affect industry evolution by explicit regulation of entry, competitive practices, licensing, and pricing. Moreover, strong government regulation has profound effects on foreign trade and global competition.

    1) Governments also regulate such matters as product quality and safety, worker safety and compensation, environmental quality, and investor protection.

        a) The social benefits must be weighed against the costs of regulation, which increase capital requirements and entry barriers and lessen competition.

n. **Entry** changes industry structure, especially when strong outsiders with special skills and large resources are the entrants. Entry occurs when outside firms believe that potential growth and profits justify the costs of entry.

o. **Exit** is motivated by diminished returns on investment. It is impeded by **exit barriers**. Exit improves the position of the remaining firms, but exit barriers weaken those firms.

p. Firms should consider how each evolutionary process may affect industry structure, their strategic position, and the ways of coping with the resulting change.

    1) Thus, firms must monitor the environment for the **strategic signals** relative to each evolutionary process.

    2) Moreover, firms must be aware that some processes (e.g., learning) may be operating without the occurrence of obvious external events.

5. **Key Relationships**

   a. An industry is a **system**. Hence, a change in one subsystem (e.g., marketing) tends to cause other changes elsewhere (e.g., in manufacturing methods leading to greater economies of scale and backward vertical integration that reduces suppliers' power).

   b. **Industry concentration and mobility barriers** are directly correlated. Thus, increasing barriers normally predict increasing concentration.

   c. **Low or decreasing barriers** generally signify an absence of concentration because unsuccessful exiting firms will likely be replaced.

   d. **Exit barriers** keep unsuccessful firms in the industry and therefore limit concentration to the detriment of successful firms.

   e. **Potential for above-average long-term profits** for the remaining firms depends on an industry's structure in its maturity stage, i.e., the presence of high mobility barriers.

   f. **Industry boundaries** change, for example, when refrigeration and genetic engineering allowed perishables to be transported long distances.

   g. Firms may **influence industry structure** by initiating changes (e.g., product, marketing, or process innovation) or responding to changes (e.g., by influencing regulation or licensing externally developed technology to control its diffusion).

Core Concepts

- The five competitive forces within an industry or market are a way of analyzing the structure of the industry. A firm's early recognition of change and prompt adjustment of its strategies are essential to maintaining a competitive advantage. The costs of adjustment will be lower and their benefits greater the sooner they are made.

- The five stages of the product life cycle are precommercialization, introduction, growth, maturity, and decline.

- Evolutionary processes are the incentives or pressures that cause a structural change in an industry. These processes move an industry from its initial structure (state of technology, entry and exit barriers, power of suppliers and buyers, product traits, etc.) to its potential structure.

- The major evolutionary processes are interacting and dynamic factors common to all industries. These factors include (1) long-run changes in the industry growth rate; (2) changes in buyer segments served; (3) learning by buyers; (4) reduction of uncertainty; (5) proprietary knowledge; (6) accumulation of experience; (7) expansion of industry scale; (8) changes in input costs; (9) product, marketing, and process innovation; (10) structural changes in suppliers' and customers' industries; (11) governmental policies; and (12) entries to and exits from the industry.

- An industry is a system, and a change in one subsystem tends to cause changes in other subsystems.

- Industry concentrations and mobility barriers are directly correlated. Low or decreasing barriers generally signify an absence of concentration, and unsuccessful exiting firms will be replaced. But exit barriers keep unsuccessful firms in the industry and limit concentration to the detriment of successful firms.

Stop and review! You have completed the outline for this subunit. Study multiple-choice questions 14 through 20 beginning on page 66.

QUESTIONS

2.1 Competitive Intelligence

1. Which of the following is **not** a step in the establishment of a competitive intelligence system?

- A. Data analysis.
- B. Data collection.
- C. Information dissemination.
- D. Classification of competitors.

Answer (D) is correct. *(Publisher, adapted)*
REQUIRED: The choice not a step in the establishment of a competitive intelligence system.
DISCUSSION: A competitive intelligence system is established to identify competitor strategies, monitor their new-product introductions, analyze markets for the firm's own new-product introductions and acquisitions, obtain information about nonpublic firms, evaluate competitor R&D activity, learn about competitors' senior executives, and perform other necessary information gathering tasks. Its establishment consists of setting up the system, collecting data, analyzing the data, and disseminating the information. Classification of competitors, however, is not a step in this process. Competitors are classified and targeted by a firm based on that classification following the results of a customer value analysis (CVA).
Answer (A) is incorrect. The data analysis phase of the establishment of a competitive intelligence system follows the data collection phase. Answer (B) is incorrect. The data collection phase of the establishment of a competitive intelligence system follows the system setup phase. Answer (C) is incorrect. The information dissemination phase of the establishment of a competitive intelligence system follows the data analysis phase.

2. Which of the following are steps in a customer value analysis (CVA)?

- I. Determining what customers value
- II. Having customers rank the relative significance of the elements of customer value
- III. Evaluating how well the firm and its competitors perform relative to the elements of customer value
- IV. Focusing on performance with respect to each element of customer value

- A. I, III, and IV only.
- B. I, II, and III only.
- C. I, II, and IV only.
- D. I, II, III, and IV.

Answer (D) is correct. *(Publisher, adapted)*
REQUIRED: The steps that are part of a customer value analysis (CVA).
DISCUSSION: The steps in a CVA are to

- Determine what customers value.
- Assign quantitative amounts to the elements of customer value and have customers rank their relative significance.
- Evaluate how well the firm and its competitors perform relative to each element.
- Focus on performance with respect to each element, compared with an important competitor in a given market segment.
- Repeat the foregoing steps as circumstances change.

3. Usually, the cheapest way to gain market share is by targeting what class of competitors?

- A. Close competitors.
- B. Distant competitors.
- C. Weak competitors.
- D. Bad competitors.

Answer (C) is correct. *(Publisher, adapted)*
REQUIRED: The class of competitors to target to gain market share cheaply.
DISCUSSION: Using the results of a customer value analysis, a firm may target a given class of competitors in order to gain market share. Although there are various methods, targeting weak competitors is usually the cheapest way to gain market share because weak competitors generally do not offer much resistance.
Answer (A) is incorrect. Close competitors are firms that are similar and are the usual targets, but it is not necessarily easy or cheap to take away market share from them. Answer (B) is incorrect. Distant competitors are not direct competitors. They are indirect competitors that pose a "distant" threat. Thus, taking away market share from them may not necessarily guarantee your firm the entire share taken. Moreover, such a taking may be costly. Answer (D) is incorrect. Bad competitors are ones that disturb the competitive equilibrium by engaging in such activities as excessive expansion of capacity or overly risky behavior. Although targeting a bad competitor would be a good move by the firm because it would be the healthiest thing for the industry, it may not necessarily be cheap to topple such an erratic foe.

2.2 Portfolio Techniques of Competitive Analysis

4. A company sells a diverse line of cookies. Its acquisition of another company, a maker of cake mixes, is **most** likely an example of

- A. Vertical integration.
- B. Horizontal diversification.
- C. Concentric diversification.
- D. Conglomerate diversification.

Answer (B) is correct. *(Publisher, adapted)*
REQUIRED: The nature of the acquisition.
DISCUSSION: Horizontal diversification is the acquisition of businesses making products unrelated to current offerings but that might appeal to the firm's current customers. Cookies and cake mixes are based on different technologies but may be demanded by the same customers.
Answer (A) is incorrect. Vertical integration occurs when suppliers, wholesalers, or retailers are acquired. Answer (C) is incorrect. Concentric diversification results from developing or acquiring related businesses that do not have products, services, or customers in common with current businesses but that offer internal synergies. Thus, the new products or services may be demanded by customers different from those currently served by the company. Answer (D) is incorrect. Conglomerate diversification is the acquisition of wholly unrelated businesses.

5. A strategic business unit (SBU) has a relative market share (RMS) of 2.0 and a market growth rate (MGR) of 9.5%. According to the growth-share matrix for competitive analysis created by the Boston Consulting Group, such an SBU is considered a

- A. Star.
- B. Question mark.
- C. Cash cow.
- D. Dog.

Answer (C) is correct. *(Publisher, adapted)*
REQUIRED: The characterization by the growth-share matrix of an SBU.
DISCUSSION: The annual MGR reflects the maturity and attractiveness of the market and the relative need for cash to finance expansion. An MGR of 10% or more is generally regarded as high. The RMS reflects an SBU's competitive position in the market segment. An RMS of 1.0 or more signifies that the SBU has a strong competitive position. Cash cows have high RMS and low MGR. They are strong competitors and cash generators in low-growth markets.
Answer (A) is incorrect. Stars have both high RMS and high MGR because they are strong competitors in high growth markets. Answer (B) is incorrect. Question marks are weak competitors in high-growth markets, meaning they have a low RMS and a high MGR. Answer (D) is incorrect. Dogs have both low RMS and low MGR, meaning they are weak competitors in low-growth markets.

2.3 Market Signals

6. When firms compete in different geographical locations or have multiple product lines that do not necessarily overlap, the **most** effective way of responding to an aggressive move by a competitor without directly triggering destructive moves and countermoves is to

- A. Mislead the competitor into taking or not taking an action.
- B. Make a prior announcement of intended moves.
- C. Initiate a move in the market where the competitor is strong.
- D. Initiate direct aggressive moves.

Answer (C) is correct. *(CIA, adapted)*
REQUIRED: The most effective response to an aggressive move by a competitor.
DISCUSSION: Initiating a move in the market where the competitor is strong is a cross-parry. A cross-parry is an effective way to signal displeasure and raise the threat of more serious retribution without directly triggering destructive moves and countermoves.
Answer (A) is incorrect. Misleading other firms into taking or not taking an action to benefit the firm is a bluff. A bluff is a form of market signal that is not intended to be carried out.
Answer (B) is incorrect. A market signal by a competitor that provides a direct or indirect indication of its intentions, motives, goals, or internal situation is a means of communicating in the market place and an essential input in competitor analysis. A prior announcement may therefore incite countermoves.
Answer (D) is incorrect. Direct aggressive moves are aimed at reducing the performance of significant competitors or threaten their goals. They are likely to cause a countermove.

7. Prior announcements of moves have value as market signals in part because an announced move need not actually occur. Which of the following is true regarding the effects of prior announcements of moves on the market?

I. The effects may preempt competition

II. The effects may express pleasure or displeasure with a competitor's action

III. The effects may be a means of ending all external debate

IV. The effects may test competitor sentiment

   A. I, II, and III only.

   B. I, II, and IV only.

   C. II, III, and IV only.

   D. I, II, III, and IV.

Answer (B) is correct. *(Publisher, adapted)*
REQUIRED: The true statements about the effects of prior announcements of moves.
DISCUSSION: Among other things, prior announcements of moves may preempt competition, threaten action, test competitor sentiment, express pleasure or displeasure with a competitor's action, and act as a means of ending internal debate. Moreover, prior announcements of moves may be a means of ending some external debate (i.e., if the announcement was aimed at the financial community in order to answer questions about the firm's liquidity). However, all external debate would be impossible to end, even by means of prior announcements of moves.
Answer (A) is incorrect. All external debate would be impossible to end, even by means of prior announcements of moves. Moreover, prior announcements of moves may be used to test competitor sentiment regarding a new firm proposal. Answer (C) is incorrect. All external debate would be impossible to end, even by means of prior announcements of moves. Furthermore, prior announcements of moves may preempt competition, such as by inducing customers to wait for the introduction of the firm's new product. Answer (D) is incorrect. All external debate would be impossible to end, even by means of prior announcements of moves.

8. A firm discounts never-before-discounted items. This action is an example of a

   A. Divergence from industry precedent.

   B. Cross-parry.

   C. Divergence from prior strategic objectives.

   D. Bluff.

Answer (A) is correct. *(Publisher, adapted)*
REQUIRED: The nature of a firm's discounting of never-before-discounted items.
DISCUSSION: The discounting of never-before-discounted items implies aggressive intent. It is an example of a divergence from industry precedent.
Answer (B) is incorrect. A cross-parry is a response to a competitor's move in one area with a move in another. Answer (C) is incorrect. A firm's divergence from prior strategic objectives suggests that other firms should be alert to profound changes in its objectives and assumptions. Answer (D) is incorrect. A bluff is an announcement of an action not intended to be executed. The discounts have already been executed; thus, they are considered true signals, not bluffs.

2.4 Structural Analysis within an Industry

9. In which industry structure is differentiation absent, and all sellers charge the same price?

   A. Monopoly.

   B. Monopolistic competition.

   C. Oligopoly.

   D. Pure competition.

Answer (D) is correct. *(Publisher, adapted)*
REQUIRED: The industry structure in which differentiation is absent and the same prices are charged by all sellers.
DISCUSSION: An industry consists of firms selling products or services that are substitutes. One way to describe an industry considers the number of sellers and the extent of differentiation of products and services. In pure competition, differentiation is absent, and the same prices are charged by all sellers.
Answer (A) is incorrect. A monopoly consists of a single seller of a product or service in an area. Answer (B) is incorrect. In monopolistic competition, an industry has numerous sellers who offer differentiated products and services. Answer (C) is incorrect. An oligopoly consists of a few large firms whose products may be standardized. In that case, competition may be based solely on price.

10. Which of the following statements is true with regard to a vertically integrated acquisition?

   A. A grocery store chain that purchases a dairy and begins to make milk-based products under its own brand is forward integrated.

   B. A movie producer that acquires a chain of theaters is backward integrated.

   C. A clothing manufacturer that acquires a chain of clothing stores is forward integrated.

   D. A soda maker that purchases its leading competitor is backward integrated.

Answer (C) is correct. *(Publisher, adapted)*
REQUIRED: The true statement regarding a vertically integrated acquisition.
DISCUSSION: Vertical integration occurs upstream (backward) by acquiring suppliers or downstream (forward) by acquiring wholesalers and retailers. An example of forward integration is a clothing manufacturer's acquisition of a chain of clothing stores in which to sell its products.
Answer (A) is incorrect. A grocery store chain that begins to make its own brand of dairy products is backward integrated. It acquired a supplier. Answer (B) is incorrect. A movie producer that acquires a chain of theaters is forward integrated. Answer (D) is incorrect. The acquisition of a leading competitor is not vertical integration. The competitor by definition is in the same stage of the value chain.

11. A strategic group analysis does all but which of the following?

   A. Determines what mobility barriers exist.

   B. Forecasts future group actions and trends.

   C. Considers how the firm compares with the competitors within the chosen strategic group.

   D. Predicts reaction patterns to events such as competitive attacks.

Answer (C) is correct. *(Publisher, adapted)*
REQUIRED: The false statement regarding a strategic group analysis.
DISCUSSION: An overall industry analysis, not a strategic group analysis, considers how the firm compares with the competitors within the chosen strategic group, e.g., on the basis of its scale of operations, the intensity of group rivalry, and the differences in the ability of the group members to implement their strategies.
Answer (A) is incorrect. A strategic group analysis determines what mobility barriers exist. Answer (B) is incorrect. A strategic group analysis forecasts future group actions and trends. Answer (D) is incorrect. A strategic group analysis predicts reaction patterns to events such as competitive attacks.

12. According to Arthur D. Little, a competitor firm that can act independently and sustain its long-term status regardless of the behavior of others holds which of the following competitive positions?

   A. A dominant position.

   B. A strong position.

   C. A favorable position.

   D. A tenable position.

Answer (B) is correct. *(Publisher, adapted)*
REQUIRED: The competitive position held by a competitor firm that can act independently and sustain its long-term status regardless of the behavior of others.
DISCUSSION: Evaluating a competitor's market position is necessary to judge how and whether to challenge it. A firm in a strong competitive position can act independently and sustain its long-term status irrespective of the behavior of others.
Answer (A) is incorrect. A competitor firm in a dominant position has a choice of strategies, and it controls other firm's actions. Answer (C) is incorrect. A firm in a favorable position has strengths that give it a better-than-average chance to improve its status. Answer (D) is incorrect. The performance of a firm in a tenable position justifies continuation of the business, but its chance for improvement is below average.

13. The retail petroleum industry consists of a few large firms that sell a standardized product. Which of the following **best** describes this industry?

   A. Monopoly.

   B. Oligopoly.

   C. Monopolistic competition.

   D. Pure competition.

Answer (B) is correct. *(Publisher, adapted)*
REQUIRED: The nature of the retail petroleum industry.
DISCUSSION: An oligopoly consists of a few large firms. If products are standardized, competition may be based solely on price. If products are partially differentiated, each firm may attempt to lead the industry regarding a given attribute, e.g., price, quality, service, or features. The retail petroleum industry is dominated by a small number of firms that control a vast majority of the market. Furthermore, it is an example of an industry that sells a standardized product, with competition based primarily on price.
Answer (A) is incorrect. A monopoly consists of a single seller of a product or service in an area, such as a utility. Answer (C) is incorrect. In monopolistic competition, numerous sellers offer differentiated products and services. Answer (D) is incorrect. In pure competition, numerous sellers offer undifferentiated products.

2.5 Industry Evolution

14. Of the major processes affecting the evolution of an industry, which one affects rivalry, entry, expansion, and supply?

- A. Long-run changes in the industry growth rate.
- B. Changes in input costs.
- C. Structural changes in suppliers' and customers' industries.
- D. Government policies.

Answer (A) is correct. *(Publisher, adapted)*
REQUIRED: The evolutionary process that affects rivalry, entry, expansion, and supply.
DISCUSSION: Long-run changes in the industry growth rate affect rivalry, entry, expansion, and supply. These changes occur because of changes in five external factors: demographic traits (such as consumer ages and income levels), trends in needs of buyers (caused by changes in regulation, tastes, lifestyles), relative positions of substitute and complementary products, sales to new customers (market penetration), and product innovation, an internal factor, alters the industry's position regarding the external factors.
Answer (B) is incorrect. Changes in input costs most directly affect the cost and price of the product and the demand for it. Answer (C) is incorrect. Structural changes in suppliers' and customers' industries affect their bargaining power. Answer (D) is incorrect. Government policies affect industry evolution by explicit regulation of entry, competitive practices, licensing, and pricing.

15. During the growth stage of a product's life cycle,

- A. The quality of products is poor.
- B. New product models and features are introduced.
- C. There is little difference between competing products.
- D. The quality of the products becomes more variable and products are less differentiated.

Answer (B) is correct. *(CIA, adapted)*
REQUIRED: The true statement regarding the growth stage of a product's life cycle.
DISCUSSION: In the growth stage, sales and profits increase rapidly, cost per customer decreases, customers are early adopters, new competitors enter an expanding market, new product models and features are introduced, and promotion spending declines or remains stable. The firm enters new market segments and distribution channels and attempts to build brand loyalty and achieve the maximum share of the market. Thus, prices are set to penetrate the market, distribution channels are extended, and the mass market is targeted through advertising. The strategy is to advance by these means and by achieving economies of productive scale.
Answer (A) is incorrect. Poor product quality is evident during the introduction stage of the product life cycle. Answer (C) is incorrect. Competitors are most numerous and products become less differentiated during the maturity stage of the product life cycle. In this stage, imitators have entered the market and competitors have learned which technologies and features are successful. Answer (D) is incorrect. The quality of the products becomes more variable, and products are less differentiated during the decline stage of the product life cycle.

16. In a product's life cycle, the first symptom of the decline stage is a decline in the

- A. Firm's inventory levels.
- B. Product's sales.
- C. Product's production cost.
- D. Product's prices.

Answer (B) is correct. *(CIA, adapted)*
REQUIRED: The initial symptom of the decline stage in a product's life cycle.
DISCUSSION: The sales of most product types and brands eventually decrease permanently. This decline may be slow or rapid. This first symptom of the decline stage of a product's life cycle triggers such other effects as price cutting, narrowing of the product line, and reduction in promotion budgets.
Answer (A) is incorrect. A decline in the firm's purchases, resulting in a decline in the firm's inventory levels, is not the first symptom. It will occur only when production declines as a result of a drop in sales. Answer (C) is incorrect. A decline in production costs may be due to many factors, e.g., new plant technology or the increased availability of raw materials. Moreover, production costs may decrease in any stage of a product's life cycle and not specifically in the decline stage. Answer (D) is incorrect. A change in prices is a marketing decision. It is an action that may be taken in the maturity stage to compete in the market. Moreover, a decrease in the product's prices is a response to a permanent decline in sales.

17. At the introduction stage of an innovative product, the profit growth is normally slow due to

- A. Expensive sales promotion.
- B. High competition.
- C. A mass market.
- D. Available alternatives.

Answer (A) is correct. *(CIA, adapted)*
REQUIRED: The reason for slow profit growth during the introduction stage of an innovative product.
DISCUSSION: The introduction stage is characterized by slow sales growth and lack of profits because of the high expenses of promotion and selective distribution to generate awareness of the product and encourage customers to try it. Thus, the per-customer cost is high. Competitors are few, basic versions of the product are produced, and higher-income customers (innovators) are usually targeted. Cost-plus prices are charged. They may initially be high to permit cost recovery when unit sales are low. The strategy is to infiltrate the market, plan for financing to cope with losses, build supplier relations, increase production and marketing efforts, and plan for competition.
Answer (B) is incorrect. During the introduction stage, little competition exists. Competitors tend not to enter the market until they have greater assurance of profits. Answer (C) is incorrect. No mass market is available during the introduction stage. Answer (D) is incorrect. By definition, not many alternatives are available during the introduction stage of an innovative product.

18. While auditing a marketing department, the internal auditor discovered that the product life cycle model was used to structure the marketing mix. Under such a philosophy, the price charged on a consistent basis for a specific product would probably be lowest during which life cycle stage?

- A. Introduction stage.
- B. Growth stage.
- C. Maturity stage.
- D. Decline stage.

Answer (C) is correct. *(CIA, adapted)*
REQUIRED: The product life cycle stage during which the price charged on a consistent basis for a specific product is likely to be the lowest.
DISCUSSION: During the maturity stage, competition is at its greatest and costs are at their lowest. Moreover, firms are engaged in competitive price-cutting measures, resulting in some of the lowest prices seen during a product's life cycle.
Answer (A) is incorrect. During the introduction stage, per-unit costs of production are high and little competition exists. Hence, prices are at their highest. Answer (B) is incorrect. During the growth stage, prices will be lower than during the introduction stage, but not as low as during the maturity stage. In the growth stage, costs are dropping and competitors are being added, but costs are not at their minimum and competitors are not at their maximum. Answer (D) is incorrect. During the decline stage, price-cutting predominates as firms struggle to maintain sales volume in the face of a permanent decrease in demand. However, late in the decline stage, there are few competitors, so prices can be raised. In addition, per-unit costs are on the rise because volume is declining, resulting in higher prices.

19. While auditing a marketing department, the internal auditor discovered that the product life cycle model was used to structure the marketing mix. Under such a philosophy, the opportunity for cost reductions would be greatest in which stage of the life cycle?

- A. Introduction stage.
- B. Growth stage.
- C. Maturity stage.
- D. Decline stage.

Answer (B) is correct. *(CIA, adapted)*
REQUIRED: The product life cycle stage during which the opportunity for cost reductions is greatest.
DISCUSSION: During the growth stage, the opportunity for cost reductions is at its maximum because production volume is increasing at a high rate. Thus, fixed costs are being spread over more units of production, and the benefits of the learning curve are being realized.
Answer (A) is incorrect. Production volume is low during the introduction stage. Although costs are also high during this period, low volume reduces the opportunities for cost reductions. Answer (C) is incorrect. Production volume changes little during the maturity stage. The result is less opportunity for cost reductions. Answer (D) is incorrect. Costs per unit typically rise during the decline stage as production volume declines.

20. While auditing a marketing department, the internal auditor discovered that the product life cycle model was used to structure the marketing mix. The manager has asked the auditor for advice about increasing advertising of various products. During which stage of the life cycle would it be appropriate to advertise that the company's product is the lowest price and **best** quality of all competitors?

A. Introduction stage.

B. Growth stage.

C. Maturity stage.

D. Decline stage.

Answer (C) is correct. *(CIA, adapted)*
REQUIRED: The product life cycle stage during which it is appropriate to advertise that the firm's product is lower-priced and of better quality than competing products.
DISCUSSION: The maturity stage is the ideal time for advertising lower prices and superior quality because this is the period during a product's life when competition is greatest. Due to the availability of many substitutes, a firm has reasons to set itself apart. Because price and quality are both concerns of customers during the maturity stage, it is an ideal time for the firm to differentiate its product by advertising low prices and higher quality.
Answer (A) is incorrect. Few competitors exist during the introduction stage, and quality is sometimes poor. Answer (B) is incorrect. Buyers are less concerned with price and quality during the growth stage than in the maturity stage. Answer (D) is incorrect. Few competitors exist during the decline stage. Moreover, prices may rise late in the decline stage for the remaining firms as per-unit costs increase.

Use the additional questions in Gleim *CIA Test Prep* Software to create Test Sessions that emulate Pearson VUE!

STUDY UNIT THREE
INDUSTRY ENVIRONMENTS

(17 pages of outline)

This study unit addresses the content specification outline's coverage of competitive strategies in three stages of the industry life cycle: fragmentation, emergence, and decline. It continues with an analysis of the unique characteristics of competition in global industries.

 While internal auditors cannot make management decisions, expectations about the financial condition and competitive outlook for the organization's lines of business can be formed depending on the development stage of the particular industry.

3.1 FRAGMENTED INDUSTRIES

1. According to Michael E. Porter, individual firms in a **fragmented industry** have insignificant market shares and little influence on industry outcomes. This situation approximates in theory what economists call pure competition and in practice **monopolistic competition**.

    a. The industry has many small- or medium-sized firms with no market leader, products may or may not be significantly differentiated, and the technology may or may not be sophisticated.

    b. Examples are agriculture, grocery retailing, and fitness clubs.

Economic Causes of Fragmentation

2. Although industries may be fragmented for purely historical reasons, economic causes for fragmentation exist in other situations.

    a. **Low entry barriers** are a necessary but not a sufficient condition for fragmentation.

    b. **Economies of scale and a learning curve (experience) effect** usually do not exist in fragmented industries. For example, operations may be simple or labor-intensive.

    c. **High transportation costs** may outweigh economies of scale, for example, when customers must come to a service provider or vice versa.

    d. **High inventory carrying costs or sharp and unpredictable changes in sales volume** also may affect a large producer's advantage in economies of scale. A smaller firm's greater flexibility in adapting to demand changes may be a decisive competitive advantage.

    e. **Buyers or suppliers** may have such strong bargaining power that size offers little additional advantage in dealing with them.

    f. **Important diseconomies of scale** may favor fragmentation. For example, small, flexible firms have an advantage when the following needs are important:

        1) Quick responses to style changes,

        2) The maintenance of low overhead,

        3) Customization of a diverse product line to the special requirements of particular customers,

        4) Substantial creative content in the product,

        5) Individualized personal service, and

        6) Local contacts and image.

g.   **Diverse market needs** resulting from fragmentation of buyers' tastes may prevent the product standardization needed to prevent fragmentation.

h.   High product differentiation based on an **image of exclusivity** also promotes fragmentation. Buyers may wish to have their own brands, and suppliers (e.g., performing artists) may wish to deal with firms that create a unique image.

i.   **Exit barriers** keep firms in the industry and minimize concentration.

j.   **Local regulations** that vary from community to community impede concentration even when other conditions are not present.

k.   **Government antitrust laws** may prohibit significant concentration.

l.   **Newness** is a reason for fragmentation. New firms may not yet have the resources and abilities to achieve concentration.

Overcoming Fragmentation

3.   Overcoming fragmentation has significant strategic payoffs given that entry is not costly and competitors are weak. If the factor(s) preventing consolidation can be eliminated, industry structure will change.

a.   One method is to use technology to create **economies of scale** in production, marketing, distribution, service, etc. For example, television marketing has led to consolidation of many industries.

b.   **Standardizing diverse market needs** may result from introducing a new product, e.g., one that appeals to most buyers in a market.

1)   Another possibility is developing a new product design, e.g., to facilitate mass production of modularized components that may be assembled in different ways.

2)   Standardizing products means to maintain the same product or to standardize the production, operations, and facilities in different locations or markets. Franchises all use standardized products to reduce costs.

c.   **Isolating factors responsible for fragmentation** has been achieved in, for example, the fast food industry. The need to have numerous local operations under tight control and near customers has been isolated or neutralized by franchising to local owners. The franchisor provides national advertising, centralized purchasing, and other services, which result in economies of scale and industry consolidation. In effect, the service or production function is separated from the rest of the business.

1)   Another approach when diverse market needs exist is for a firm to use multiple brands to appeal to the tastes of different customers.

d.   **Acquisitions** (horizontal mergers) that enable a firm to expand when competing with local firms might be difficult because of their contacts and image.

e.   **Early recognition of trends** may permit a firm to exploit them. For example, if the fragmentation is the result of industry newness, the firm may recognize the early signs of industry evolution.

1)   Early awareness of external factors, such as technology changes, that negate the causes of fragmentation also provide an opportunity for the firm.

f.   Industries may be **stuck** in a fragmented state for reasons other than underlying economic factors.

1)   Firms in the industry lack the resources, skills, awareness, or ambition to make the strategic moves needed for consolidation.

2)   Outside firms do not recognize the opportunity offered by an industry stuck in a fragmented state, for example, because it is new, small, or obscure.

Coping with Fragmentation

4.   Coping with fragmentation requires strategic positioning.

   a.   When local management, close control, and personal service are critical success factors, **tightly managed decentralization** may be the appropriate strategy. Local operations remain small scale and autonomous, but managers are held to high standards with performance-based compensation.

   b.   Developing **formula facilities** for use in numerous localities reduces construction and operating costs via standardization.

   c.   When products or services cannot be significantly differentiated, the best strategy may be to **increase the value added**, for example, by adding services or by forward integration.

   d.   **Specialization by product type or segment** is a focus strategy. This focus may enhance bargaining power with suppliers. It also may increase differentiation because of the perceived expertise and image. The downside is reduced growth opportunities.

   e.   Specialization by **customer type** (e.g., small customers or those who are not price sensitive), **type of order** (e.g., small orders for quick delivery or custom orders), or **geographic areas** are other focus strategies.

   f.   A cost strategy is to adopt a **bare bones, no frills** approach by emphasizing tight control of costs, low overhead, and low payroll.

   g.   **Backward integration** is the selective acquisition of suppliers to reduce costs.

5.   The following are **strategic traps** in a fragmented industry:

   a.   Barring basic change in the industry's structure, **seeking dominance** is usually a losing strategy.

   b.   **Lack of strategic discipline** means straying from a focus on an appropriate strategy for a fragmented industry, assuming that the structure cannot be altered.

   c.   **Overcentralization** of the organizational structure is often a mistake. In the intense competition of a fragmented industry, quick response times, local contacts, personal service, and tight operating control are essential.

   d.   Assuming that competitors have similar costs and objectives is frequently wrong. Small, privately held firms in the industry may be content with much lower rates of return, use family members in the business, and avoid some costs of regulation.

   e.   **Overreaction to new products** results when investments are made to respond to new product demand that are inconsistent with the industry structure. As the product enters maturity, price competition from many rivals will become intense, and the profit margins needed to pay for the investments will vanish.

6.   The following is Porter's framework for developing a **competitive strategy in a fragmented industry**:

   a.   Determine the industry's structure and the circumstances of major competitors.

   b.   Create a full list of the reasons for (causes of) fragmentation, if any, and their connection with the industry's economics.

   c.   Analyze whether the causes of fragmentation can be overcome by innovation, strategic changes, additional resources, or a new perspective.

      1)   Determine the effects of trends.

   d.   Assuming fragmentation can be overcome, evaluate whether the new structure will yield acceptable returns and what position the firm should occupy to earn those returns. This step requires repeating the first step above given the new structural equilibrium.

   e.   If fragmentation cannot be overcome, select the best strategy for operating in a fragmented environment.

<u>Core Concepts</u>

■ Individual firms in a fragmented industry have insignificant market shares and little influence on industry outcomes. Examples are retailing, agriculture, and creative enterprises. Thus, the situation approximates what economists call pure competition.

■ Although industries may be fragmented for purely historical reasons, economic causes for fragmentation exist in other situations, such as low entry or high exit barriers, diseconomies of scale, or suppliers or buyers with strong bargaining power.

■ Overcoming fragmentation has significant strategic payoffs given that entry is not costly and competitors are weak. If the factor(s) preventing consolidation can be eliminated, industry structure will change, for example, by (1) achieving economies of scale, (2) standardizing market needs, (3) horizontal mergers, (4) early recognition of trends, and (5) isolating factors responsible for fragmentation (such as in the fast-food industry).

■ Coping with fragmentation requires strategic positioning. When local management, close control, and personal service are critical success factors, tightly-managed decentralization may be the appropriate strategy. Developing formula facilities or increasing the value added are other means of coping with fragmentation.

■ Specialization by product type or segment, customer type, type of order, or geographic areas are examples of focus strategies in coping with fragmentation.

■ Backward integration is the selective acquisition of suppliers to reduce costs.

■ Strategic traps in a fragmented industry include (1) seeking dominance, (2) a lack of strategic discipline, (3) overcentralization, (4) assuming that competitors have similar costs and objectives, and (5) overreaction to new products.

Stop and review! You have completed the outline for this subunit. Study multiple-choice questions 1 through 4 beginning on page 86.

3.2 EMERGING INDUSTRIES

1. An **emerging industry** is new or newly formed and is small in size initially. It results from innovation, changes in cost structures, new customer needs, or another factor that creates an attractive opportunity for selling a product or service.

    a. The competitive issues in emerging industries also are confronted by established firms that must cope with the foregoing changes in environmental factors.

    b. Porter observes that no rules exist for an emerging industry, a condition that creates risks and opportunities.

    c. Examples include electronic calculators in the 1970s, long-distance telephone service in the 1980s, cellular phone service in the 1990s, and Web-based retailing in the 2000s.

<u>Structural Characteristics</u>

2. The following are structural characteristics of emerging industries:

    a. An emerging industry is characterized by **technological uncertainty** regarding products and production methods.

    b. **Strategic uncertainty** arises because effective strategies have not yet been identified. Hence, firms are experimenting with product features, production methods, marketing approaches, etc.

        1) Moreover, competitive intelligence is necessarily poor because competitors have not been identified and industry sales and other data are not available.

    c. **Initial costs** are high, but the **learning curve** is steep. When the efficiency gains from experience combine with economies of scale achieved by growth, cost decreases are dramatic.

d. **Embryonic companies** (firms newly formed and not new units of established entities) are most numerous in the emerging phase of industry evolution. Entry is not discouraged by the presence of economies of scale or strategic certainty.

   1) **Spin-offs** from existing firms are common. Given the uncertainties described on the previous page and the lure of equity interests, employees have incentives to create new firms. Their motive is often to exploit ideas that may not have received a favorable reception by their former employers.

e. By definition, customers are **first-time buyers**. The marketing problem is to convince these customers that the benefits of substituting the product or service for something else exceed the risks.

f. The **short time horizon** for product and customer development means that policies may evolve for reasons other than well-researched decision making.

g. **Subsidy** of early entrants by government or others may occur when the technology is radically new or societal concern is strong. Subsidies create instability because they result from political decisions and interference in the market.

   1) Subsidies are a structural characteristic of an emerging market. If a subsidy is given by the government or other party, it usually assists the growth of the new industry instead of hindering it. Subsidies tend to focus on radically new technology or technology in which societal concern is strong.

h. **Early mobility barriers** tend to consist of willingness to accept risk, proprietary technology, access to resource supplies, and the lower costs of more experienced firms.

   1) Barriers tend not to be branding, economies of scale, or capital intensity.

Limits on Development

3. **Limits on emerging industry development** arise because it is new, depends on external entities for growth, and must persuade customers to substitute its product or service for another.

   a. **Raw materials and components** may be scarce because new suppliers must be found or existing suppliers must expand or modify their output.

   b. **Raw materials prices** may increase rapidly as suppliers struggle to keep pace with demand during the early phase of industry development.

   c. **Infrastructure** (e.g., distribution channels, service centers, skilled labor, and complementary products or services) may not be available.

   d. **Standardization** lags because of product and technology uncertainty.

   e. Customers' belief that product **obsolescence** will occur rapidly may cause slow growth.

   f. **Customer confusion** is created by technological uncertainty, absence of standardization, and the proliferation of competing products. Confusion increases the risk of purchase.

   g. **Product quality** may be uneven because of the presence of many new firms and technological uncertainty (and the consequent lack of agreed-upon technical standards).

   h. Because of the foregoing factors, the industry's **image and financial credibility** may suffer. Thus, lenders may be unwilling to provide debt capital at favorable rates, and customers may have difficulty in securing credit.

   i. **Regulatory approval** may be hard to obtain, especially if customer needs are already served by an established regulated industry.

      1) However, favorable government policy may jump-start an industry, for example, when use of a safety product becomes mandatory.

         a) Moreover, further growth of an industry may be slowed when it attracts first-time regulation.

j.   Initially **high unit costs** may require below-cost pricing or slow industry growth.

k.   **Threatened entities** (e.g., makers of substitutes, unions, or distributors with established relationships with old suppliers) may respond.

1)   For example, the responses may be in the form of political pressure, lobbying of regulators, collective bargaining, lower prices, or greater investment designed to reduce costs.

2)   Entities threatened by substitution are more likely to adopt a price or investment strategy when **exit barriers** are high.

Forecasting Markets

4.   Forecasting **early and late markets** is necessary to guide product development and marketing efforts and to predict structural evolution. Markets, market segments, and customers within a segment may vary in how quickly they accept a new industry's product or service. The following are factors affecting acceptance:

a.   The **nature of the benefit** is the most significant factor. At one extreme, the benefit may consist of a **performance advantage** unattainable by other methods. At the other extreme, the benefit may be a pure **cost advantage**. Ordinarily, early markets purchase a product because it offers a performance advantage. Early markets tend to be suspicious of a product offering a cost advantage.

1)   With respect to a performance advantage, the receptivity of the buyer depends on (a) the magnitude of the advantage, (b) how obvious it is, (c) the buyer's need for it, (d) whether it improves the buyer's competitiveness, (e) the competitive pressures felt by the buyer, and (f) the buyer's price or cost sensitivity.

2)   With respect to a cost advantage, the receptivity of the buyer depends on (a) the magnitude of the advantage, (b) how obvious it is, (c) whether lowered cost will result in a lasting competitive benefit, (d) the competitive pressure to effect a change, and (e) the degree to which the buyer's strategy is cost-based.

b.   Early adoption depends on the **technical performance** buyers require. To obtain significant benefits, different buyers may require different levels of product development.

c.   A higher **cost of product failure** for a buyer leads to later adoption. For example, a buyer that will use the product as part of an integrated system or pay a high price for interrupted service has a high cost of failure.

d.   Buyers vary in the **switching costs** they face, e.g., (1) retraining, (2) additional equipment purchases, (3) disposal of old equipment, (4) requirements for support services (repair, engineering, and R&D), (5) capital needs, and (6) modification of related processes or business elements.

e.   The **cost of obsolescence** will be less for emerging technology if an initial version will meet later buyer needs even though upgrades appear periodically.

f.   Different buyers face different **regulatory, governmental, or union** constraints.

g.   Buyer **resource availability** affects the decision to change.

h.   The **perception of technological change** will be less daunting to a technically sophisticated buyer. Moreover, change may be a threat to some but an opportunity to others.

i.   The greater the **personal risk to the decision maker**, the less the likelihood of early adoption.

Strategic Choices

5. The following are strategic choices in emerging industries:

    a. The firm is best able to **shape the industry structure** when the industry is emerging. It is best able to influence to its advantage industry approaches on such matters as pricing, marketing, and product policy.

    b. A firm in an emerging industry needs to consider **externalities in industry development**. It should balance its self interest with the need to promote the image and credibility of the industry.

        1) Thus, to appeal to first-time buyers and encourage substitution, the firm's enlightened self-interest ordinarily requires **industry cooperation**, improved quality, and standardization. However, as the industry matures, the firm should be less industry-oriented.

        2) An initial industry orientation also may require the firm to follow a strategy and enter market segments on a temporary basis.

    c. A firm benefits by early awareness and exploitation of the **changing role of suppliers and distribution channels**, which may become more cooperative as the industry strengthens.

    d. **Early mobility barriers** may disappear as the industry grows and technology improves. Hence, the firm may no longer be able to rely on early advantages, such as proprietary technology. The necessary response may be a large capital investment.

    e. The **nature of entrants** may change to include larger firms attracted by the proven and less risky industry. Firms must predict when such entry is likely given existing and probable future barriers and the costs of surmounting them.

        1) Firms need to predict how new entrants will compete, e.g., on the basis of marketing power or economies of scale. Furthermore, new entrants may emerge through vertical integration.

    f. **Timing of entry** is a critical choice. Pioneering firms face high risk but low barriers and may earn high returns.

        1) Factors favoring early entry: (a) Pioneering improves the firm's reputation, (b) the learning curve (experience) advantage is important and will persist, (c) customer loyalty will be high, and (d) cost advantages (through early commitment to suppliers or distributors) can be secured.

        2) Factors not favoring early entry: (a) The bases of competition and market segments will change significantly; (b) costs of opening the market are high, and the benefits cannot be retained by the firm; (c) early competition will be expensive, and larger and stronger competitors will emerge later; and (d) early products and processes will become obsolete.

        3) **Tactical moves** that may be beneficial include early commitment to suppliers and taking advantage of lower capital costs if investors are attracted to the industry.

    g. **Responding to competitors** during the emerging phase of industry development is often a poor strategic choice. A firm is frequently best served by reinforcing its strengths and by developing the industry, perhaps through encouraging new entrants (e.g., by licensing) who will sell the industry's products and expedite its technological evolution.

Core Concepts

- An emerging industry is characterized by technological uncertainty regarding products and production methods. Strategic uncertainty arises because effective strategies have not yet been identified.

- By definition, customers of an emerging industry are first-time buyers. The marketing problem is to convince these customers that the benefits of substituting the product or service for something else exceed the risks.

- Limits on an industry's development arise because it is new, depends on external entities for growth, and must persuade customers to substitute its product or service for another.

- Forecasting early and late markets is necessary to guide product development and marketing efforts and to predict structural evolution. Markets, market segments, and customers within a segment may vary in how quickly they accept a new industry's product or service. The most significant factor affecting acceptance is the nature of the benefit, e.g., a performance advantage, cost advantage, or some combination.

- Timing of entry is a critical choice. Pioneering firms face high risks but low barriers and may earn high returns.

Stop and review! You have completed the outline for this subunit. Study multiple-choice questions 5 and 6 on page 87.

3.3 DECLINING INDUSTRIES

1. A **declining industry** is not simply at a low point in the business cycle but has sustained a permanent decrease in unit sales over the long run. However, this phase of the industry life cycle does not correspond exactly to the decline stage in the product life cycle.

    a. Furthermore, the nature of the competition and the range of strategic choices in the decline phase are diverse and vary widely from industry to industry. The result is that some industries may be able to negotiate decline without intense rivalry, long-term overcapacity, and ruinous losses.

    b. Social and technological changes can play a major role in industry decline. Examples include tobacco, passenger rail service, and film developing.

Structural Characteristics

2. **Structure and competition** in the decline phase are determined by the decreased profits resulting from lower unit sales and more intense competition. However, various factors affect the degree of the damage suffered.

    a. The **conditions of demand** and the nature of market segments determine competition in this phase.

        1) **Perceived uncertainty about demand** by competitors is a major influence on the competitive intensity. Rivalry will likely be strong if demand is expected to increase. However, if all firms expect demand to decrease, the weaker firms may plan early withdrawal and a reduction of capacity.

            a) The stronger the firm and the higher its exit barriers, the more likely that its demand perception will be optimistic.

2) The **rate and pattern of decline** affect uncertainty, which stimulates competitive volatility. Thus, a slow decline creates uncertainty, but a rapid decline tends to reduce uncertainty and unjustified optimism. Moreover, the rapid decline makes wholesale decreases in capacity more probable.

   a) The pattern of decline may not be readily distinguishable from the normal seasonal or other variability of sales. In this case, uncertainty is heightened.

   b) The rate of decline in demand is influenced by the pattern of withdrawal. For example, the departure of some suppliers may encourage customers to switch to substitutes so as to guarantee the availability of inputs.

   c) The rate of decline also tends to increase as withdrawals decrease sales volume and increase costs and prices.

3) The **structure of the remaining pockets of demand** determines whether the surviving firms can be profitable. Prospects are favorable if the pockets include price-insensitive buyers of highly differentiated products.

   a) Prospects also are favorable if buyers have little bargaining power because of high switching costs or other factors, such as the need to replace the equipment of the suppliers that have withdrawn from the industry.

   b) Furthermore, firms operating in remaining pockets may thrive if mobility barriers are high (preventing firms in other segments from competing) and if substitute products or strong suppliers are not threats.

4) The **causes of decline** in industry demand include innovation or shifts in costs or quality that make attractive substitutes available.

   a) Other causes are a reduction in the size of a demographic customer group and changes in the needs or tastes of customers.

   b) A firm should consider these causes when evaluating the uncertainty of future demand and potential profits from remaining in particular market segments.

b. High **exit barriers** may restrain firms from leaving the industry even though their returns are poor.

   1) **Specialized assets** and inventory in a declining industry may have a low liquidation value. Few purchasers who wish to operate in the same industry may be available.

      a) **Durable assets** may have a carrying amount far greater than the liquidation value. Hence, liquidation may result in a loss that the firm may not wish to recognize.

      b) Furthermore, a low liquidation value means that the future discounted cash flows from remaining in the industry may exceed the **opportunity cost** of the capital invested in the declining industry.

      c) Thus, the returns from the proceeds of liquidation may be less than the returns from keeping those assets in the business.

   2) Net liquidation value is reduced when the **fixed costs of exit** are high, e.g., the costs of (a) labor settlements, (b) payments to professionals involved in the divestiture (CPAs, attorneys, etc.), (c) cancelation of contracts (with distributors, suppliers, managers, etc.), and (d) resettlement or retraining.

      a) Moreover, announcement of exit may have such effects as reduced employee productivity, loss of customers, and a decline in supplier reliability.

      b) However, some required investments, such as in environmental safeguards, may be avoided.

3) One type of **strategic exit barrier** exists when a business is part of a group executing an overall strategy. Divesting the business may undermine the strategy. For example, it may be important to the parent's image, relations with distributors, or bargaining power with suppliers. Thus, the **relatedness** of the divested business with other components always should be considered.

    a) Exit may harm the **financial standing** of a firm. For example, the financial markets may react by lowering the firm's share price and raising its cost of capital. Recognition of a single large loss from liquidation may subsequently be worse than a succession of small losses from operating the business.

    b) **Vertical integration** of a business may require exit of the entire chain when the reasons for decline affect all its parts. But when only one part of the vertically integrated business is in a declining industry, integration is an argument for exit of the affected part.

4) **Information barriers** exist when one business is closely related to others in the firm. Its actual performance may be unclear in these circumstances, and the information needed to identify the business as an exit candidate may be hard to isolate.

5) **Management and emotional barriers** to exit arise from human nature. Managers may be committed to the business because of their personal involvement in it or the role it played in the firm's history.

    a) Managers also may not wish to admit failure, and they may be concerned about their future employment.

6) **Government and social barriers** reflect opposition to the negative effects of exit: unemployment and harm to local communities.

7) High exit barriers tend to keep capacity in a declining industry, intensifying rivalry and harming even healthy firms.

c. The method of **asset disposition** affects the health of the declining industry. For example, sale of a firm's assets within the industry but at a discount provides the buyer with a lower investment base than the remaining firms. Thus, the buyer may be able to take financially rational actions (e.g., concerning prices) that damage those firms.

1) Discounted sales of assets to employee groups and government subsidies to failing firms have similar negative effects.

d. **Price wars** are more likely in the decline phase.

1) Rivalry is more volatile (intense) when

    a) The product is viewed as a commodity,

    b) Fixed costs are high,

    c) Exit barriers are high,

    d) Firms have strategic reasons for remaining and the resources to do so,

    e) Firms are relatively equally strong, and

    f) Firms are tempted to take ill-advised competitive actions because of uncertainty about their positions.

2) The greater power of suppliers and distributors in the decline phase means higher prices and worse service for industry firms and more intense rivalry.

Strategic Choices

3. The following are strategic choices in declining industries:

   a. A **leadership strategy** is adopted by a firm that believes it can achieve market share gains to become the dominant firm. One assumption is that additional investment can be recovered. A second assumption is that success will allow the firm to maintain its position or subsequently to follow a harvest strategy.

      1) This strategy may involve

         a) Aggressive pricing, marketing, or other investments that raise the stakes for competitors;

         b) Reducing competitors' exit barriers by acquisitions of their capacity or products, assuming their contracts, and producing spare parts and generic versions of goods for them;

         c) Demonstrations of strength and resolve to remain in the industry; and

         d) Publicizing accurate data about the reality of future decline so as to dispel competitors' uncertainty.

   b. A **niche strategy** seeks a market segment (pocket of demand) with stable or slowly decreasing demand with the potential for above-average returns. Some of the moves undertaken when following a leadership strategy may be appropriate.

      1) The firm may eventually change to a harvest or divest strategy.

   c. A **harvest strategy** is in effect a controlled, gradual liquidation. It maximizes cash flow by minimizing new investment, R&D, advertising, service, maintenance, etc., and by exploiting the firm's remaining strengths (e.g., goodwill) to increase prices or maintain sales volume.

      1) To be successful, the strategy assumes that the firm has certain strengths and intense competition is absent. The strengths permit the firm to maintain sales for a time despite price increases, reduced advertising, etc.

         a) Absence of intense competition means that other firms will be less likely to gain market share or lower prices.

         b) However, a firm must be capable of cost reductions that do not cause immediate failure.

      2) Actions to implement a harvest strategy may be **visible** to customers (less advertising or higher prices) or **invisible**. A firm without strength may be limited to invisible actions.

   d. A **quick divestment strategy** assumes that the highest net recovery is obtained by sale early in the decline phase. It is then that uncertainty about the industry's future is greatest and other markets for the assets are most favorable.

      1) Divestiture may be indicated during the maturity phase prior to decline. But the firm risks being wrong about the onset of the decline phase.

4. **Choice of Strategy**

   a. One factor in the choice is whether the declining industry is likely to yield profits to the firm, that is, whether **industry structure** is favorable (e.g., with regard to uncertainty, competitor exit barriers, conditions of demand, etc.).

   b. A second factor is the firm's relative position, or **strengths and weaknesses**.

   c. Given a **favorable industry structure**, a firm with strengths in the remaining pockets of demand is most likely to follow a leadership or niche strategy. Lacking such strengths, it will most likely adopt a harvest or quick divestment strategy.

    d.   Given an **unfavorable industry structure**, a firm with strengths in the remaining pockets of demand is most likely to follow a niche or harvest strategy. Lacking such strengths, it will most likely adopt a quick divestment strategy.

    e.   However, the firm's **strategic needs** may affect the choice. For example, a need for cash flow may override other considerations and prompt an early sale.

    f.   A crucial element of a strategy in the decline phase is to discover methods for influencing competitors to exit.

    g.   **Potential mistakes** made by firms in a declining industry are not recognizing the onset of decline, engaging in wars of attrition with competitors having high exit barriers, and adopting a harvest strategy in the absence of strengths.

    h.   **Preparing for decline** during the maturity phase may be possible given accurate forecasts, e.g., by avoidance of actions creating exit barriers, focusing on market segments that will be profitable in the decline phase, and increasing the customers' costs of switching in those segments.

Core Concepts

- A declining industry is not simply at a low point in the business cycle but has sustained a permanent decrease in unit sales over the long run. However, this phase of the industry life cycle does not correspond exactly to the decline stage in the product life cycle.

- Structure and competition in the decline phase are determined by the decreased profits resulting from lower unit sales and more intense competition. However, various factors affect the degree of the damage suffered. The conditions of demand and the nature of market segments determine competition in this phase.

- High exit barriers may restrain firms from leaving the industry even though their returns are poor. These include (1) specialized or durable assets with low liquidation value, (2) high fixed costs of exit, (3) strategic exit barriers (e.g., the relation of a divested business to other businesses in a group), (4) information barriers, (5) management and emotional barriers, and (6) government and social barriers.

- Strategies in declining industries include (1) a leadership strategy, (2) a niche strategy, (3) a harvest strategy, and (4) a quick divestment strategy.

Stop and review! You have completed the outline for this subunit. Study multiple-choice questions 7 through 9 beginning on page 88.

3.4 COMPETITION IN GLOBAL INDUSTRIES

1.   Analysis of the competition in an industry requires consideration of the economics of the industry and the characteristics of competitors. However, in a global industry, the analysis is not limited to one market, but extends to all markets (geographic or national).

    a.   Porter defines a **global industry** as "one in which the strategic positions of competitors in major geographic or national markets are fundamentally affected by their overall global positions." The proliferation of global industries **(globalization)** has great significance. Competitive analysis must now often address issues of global competition.

    b.   A true global industry is one that requires a firm to compete internationally. Accordingly, an **industry is not global** simply because some or all competitors are multinational. When nonmultinationals can compete in a geographic or national market, the industry is not global.

    c.   Global competition obviously differs in important ways from national competition. For example, costs, market characteristics, and the roles of governments vary among countries. Available resources, competitive monitoring, and objectives also vary.

        1)   Nevertheless, the **five competitive forces** and the basic, underlying **structural factors** are the same as in national competition.

a)   The structural analysis of the forces and factors must still address

i)   Foreign competitors,

ii)   A larger group of possible entrants,

iii) A wider range of substitute products, and

iv)   An even higher probability that firms will vary in their strategic objectives and corporate cultures.

b)   Competitiveness of firms is greatest, and the competitive environment is most intense, when the benefits of global integration and coordination and the benefits of localization (flexibility, proximity, and quick response time) are achieved.

d.   The primary issues are whether a firm should compete and the extent of the threat to the firm from global competition.

Sources of Global Competitive Advantage

2.   An industry becomes global because it perceives a net strategic advantage to competing, as Porter says, "in a coordinated way in many national markets." Thus, the sources of competitive advantage must have greater weight than the impediments.

a.   A firm should consider the materiality of the source of advantage to total cost. Moreover, it also should consider the element of the business where the firm has a global competitive advantage.

1)   Still another consideration is that the sources of advantage reflect the implied presence of **mobility barriers**.

b.   Participation in foreign markets is usually by **licensing; export**; or, after the firm has obtained experience, **direct investment**. A genuinely global industry will have significant export activity or direct investment.

1)   Nevertheless, direct investment does not necessarily signal the existence of global competition. Direct investment also may occur when purely national factors determine a subsidiary's competitive position.

c.   The **competitive advantage** of a nation regarding the cost or quality of a product means that it will produce and export the product. Consequently, a global firm's position in that nation is vital.

d.   **Economies of scale in centralized production** may yield a cost advantage achievable only when output exceeds the demand in one country and exports are feasible. Vertical integration may provide the necessary scale.

e.   **Global experience** may result in more rapid movement along the learning curve when similar products are sold in multiple national markets. Thus, the global firm may be first to achieve the maximum cost advantage from experience. Its cumulative production volume grows more rapidly than that of a purely national firm.

f.   **Logistical economies of scale** may be attained by a global firm that spreads its fixed costs by supplying multiple national markets. A logistical cost advantage also may result because a global firm uses specialized logistical systems.

g.   **Marketing economies of scale** may exceed the volume achievable in a national market even though much marketing is necessarily local. For example, one sales force may be employed globally when buyers are few and technical considerations are complex. Furthermore, some brands require no incremental investment to have international strength. Also, some advertising campaigns may be effective across national borders.

h.   **Purchasing economies of scale** may confer a cost advantage. A global firm will make larger purchases than a purely national firm. One result may be longer and therefore more economical production runs. Another result may be greater bargaining power versus suppliers.

i.   **Product differentiation** through enhanced image and reputation may be achieved in national markets by operating globally.

j.   **Proprietary technology** may be applicable in multiple national markets, thereby creating a global competitive advantage. Furthermore, achieving such an advantage may only be feasible in a global industry. Economies of scale for R&D may only be attainable when the market is global. Also, global operation may help a firm to stay in touch with new developments.

k.   **Mobility of production** allows a global firm to more readily achieve economies of scale and share proprietary technology among operating activities in multiple national markets.

   1)   For example, a construction firm may have a larger organization than would be feasible in a national market. The fixed costs of that organization and of developing its technology will be lower relative to revenues because the global market is greater. Global operation is more likely to be profitable when construction crews and equipment are mobile.

Impediments to Global Competition

3.   Impediments to global competition may (a) increase direct costs, (b) make management more difficult, (c) be imposed by governments or institutions, or (d) consist of perceptual or resource limitations. Impediments that do not block global competition may still create niches for national firms.

a.   **High transportation and storage costs** may require construction of plants in each market.

b.   **Product needs** may differ from country to country because of culture, climate, degree of economic development, income, legal requirements, technical standards, and other factors.

   1)   This barrier limits global procurement and achievement of economies of scale and experience. The height of the barrier depends on the costs of product modifications.

   2)   **Complex segmentation within geographic markets** has similar effects.

c.   Access to **established distribution channels** may be difficult, especially when large volumes of low-cost items are sold. Concessions required to persuade a channel to substitute the product for a domestic producer's may be too great. Chances are better if channels are not established or are few and high-volume.

d.   The need for a **direct sales force** creates a barrier based on a diseconomy of scale, especially if local competitors' sales agents market wide product lines. The need for **local repair** is similar.

e.   **Sensitivity to lead times** means that global firms may not respond quickly to changes in fashion, technology, etc., in a national market. Centralized functions may be at too great a distance from that market to meet quickly evolving customer needs, especially when local needs vary.

   1)   The relevant lead times include those for physical transportation at an economically acceptable cost.

f.   **Lack of world demand** may derive from the product's lack of appeal except in a few markets or its early position in the **product life cycle of world trade**.

   1)   Initial introduction of the product is in a few markets where the product has the greatest appeal. Demand then builds elsewhere by product imitation and technology diffusion, resulting in exports and foreign investment by the pioneer firms.

   2)   Greater demand and diffusion also may result in production in other markets by foreign firms.

3) During the maturity stage, the product is standardized, price competition increases, and local firms enter the market.

4) Thus, global competition may require some industry maturity, but the level of maturity is lower when experienced global competitors can rapidly spread the product to new markets.

g. **Differing marketing tasks** are required in different national markets. Hence, local firms with superior marketing experience in their countries may have the advantage. A possible solution is to have a local marketing function.

h. Local firms tend to be more responsive than global firms when **intensive local services** or other customer contacts are necessary. Accordingly, the local firm's advantages in marketing and other services could outweigh the global firm's advantages.

i. **Rapid changes in technology** that require product and process modifications for a local market also favor the local firm.

j. **Governmental impediments** to global competition are generally imposed for the stated purpose of protecting local firms and jobs and developing new industries. These impediments are most likely when industries are viewed as crucial.

1) They also may have the effect of raising revenue in the short run, but tax revenues ultimately will decline because of reduced trade.

2) Examples of governmental impediments are

a) Tariffs;
b) Duties;
c) Quotas;
d) Domestic content rules;
e) Preferences for local firms regarding procurement, taxes, R&D, labor regulations, and other operating rules; and
f) Laws (e.g., antibribery or tax) enacted by a national government that impede national firms from competing globally.

k. **Perceptual impediments** arise because the complexities of global competition may impair the firm's ability to identify global opportunities.

l. **Resource impediments** consist of information and search costs, the costs of large-scale facilities construction, and the investments needed to penetrate new markets.

Evolution of Global Markets

4. The **triggers** of global market evolution establish or exploit the **sources** of global competitive advantage. They also may negate the **impediments** to global competition.

a. However, negating impediments will not result in globalization unless the firm has sufficient strategic advantages. Moreover, a **strategic innovation** is always necessary for the industry to become global.

1) **Access to the largest markets** also may be critical to successful globalization of an industry.

5. **Environmental triggers** include

a. An increase in any of the types of economies of scale,
b. Lower transportation or storage costs,
c. Changes in distribution channels that facilitate access by foreign firms,
d. Changes in the costs of the factors of production,
e. Increased similarity of economic and social conditions in other nations, and
f. Reduction of governmental limitations.

6. **Strategic innovations** may begin globalization even if environmental triggers are not present.

    a. **Product redefinition** may take the form of a reduction in national product differences resulting from industry maturity and product standardization.

        1) However, a marketing innovation that redefines the product's concept or image may make it more acceptable in global markets.

    b. **Identification of common market segments** among countries that are badly served by national firms is possible even if national product differences persist.

    c. Despite national product differences, **reducing the costs of adapting the product**, for example, by modularization or increasing the product's range of compatibility, may permit global competition.

        1) **Design changes** may have the same effect when they result in standardization of components.

    d. Combining centralized production with local assembly (deintegration of production) may satisfy governmental requirements while creating sufficient economies of scale to trigger global competition.

    e. **Elimination of resource or perceptual constraints** may result from entry of new firms with greater resources or with a fresher perspective that is helpful in developing new strategies and identifying new opportunities.

Strategic Choices

7. The following are strategic choices in global industries:

    a. **Broad line global competition** is competition over the full product line of the firm based on differentiation or low cost. The firm needs large resources for this long-term strategy.

        1) Governmental relations should emphasize impediment reduction.

    b. A **global focus strategy** is limited to an industry segment with low impediments where the firm can compete effectively on a global basis against broad line firms.

        1) The focus of competition is low cost or product differentiation.

    c. A **national focus strategy** is limited to a national market or the segments with the greatest economic impediments to global competitors.

        1) Low cost or product differentiation is the focus of competition.

    d. A **protected niche strategy** is applied in nations where global competitors are discouraged by governmental impediments, such as domestic content rules or tariffs.

        1) The strategy is designed to be effective in markets with governmental constraints and requires close attention to the national government.

    e. **Transnational coalitions** may be created to help the firms overcome impediments to executing the broader strategies, for example, market access or technology barriers.

Trends

8. Trends in Global Competition

    a. **Economic differences** among developed and newly developed countries have narrowed.

    b. Some countries are pursuing more **aggressive industrial policies** by providing resources to stimulate industries to achieve global status.

    c.   **Governmental protection of distinctive national assets**, such as natural assets, is reflected in direct ownership or joint ventures with private firms. A large labor pool is another asset increasingly recognized by some governments.

    d.   The **freer flow of technology** allows many firms, including those in newly developed countries, to invest in world-class facilities.

    e.   **New large scale markets** have emerged, e.g., China, Russia, and India.

    f.   **Newly developed countries**, e.g., Brazil, Taiwan, and South Korea, have emerged as global competitors because of their greater ability to make large investments, acquire new technology, and accept high risks.

Core Concepts

- Porter defines a global industry as "one in which the strategic positions of competitors in major geographic or national markets are fundamentally affected by their overall global positions."

  - The five competitive forces and the basic, underlying structural factors are the same as in national competition.

  - The primary issues are whether a firm should compete and the extent of the threat to the firm from global competition.

- Participation in foreign markets is usually by licensing; export; or, after the firm has obtained experience, direct investment. A genuinely global industry will have significant export activity or direct investment.

  - Among the sources of competitive advantage in a global industry are (1) global experience; (2) a differential product; (3) proprietary technology; (4) mobility of production; and (5) economies of scale in centralized production, logistics, marketing, or purchasing.

- Impediments to global competition may (1) increase direct costs, (2) make management more difficult, (3) be imposed by governments or institutions, or (4) consist of perceptual or resource limitations. Impediments that do not block global competition may still create niches for national firms.

- The triggers of global market evolution establish or exploit the sources of global competitive advantage. They also may negate the impediments to global competition. However, negating impediments will not result in globalization unless the firm has sufficient strategic advantages. Moreover, a strategic innovation is always necessary for the industry to become global. Access to the largest markets also may be critical to successful globalization of an industry.

- Strategic choices in global industries include (1) broadline global competition, (2) a global focus strategy, (3) a national focus strategy, (4) a protected niche strategy, and (5) transnational coalitions.

- Economic differences among developed and newly developed countries have narrowed. Some countries are pursuing more aggressive industrial policies by providing resources to stimulate industries to achieve global status.

Stop and review! You have completed the outline for this subunit. Study multiple-choice questions 10 through 13 beginning on page 89.

QUESTIONS

3.1 Fragmented Industries

1. Firms in a fragmented industry have insignificant market shares and little influence on such matters as market price and total output. A likely economic cause of this fragmentation is the existence of

    A. A learning curve effect.

    B. Diseconomies of scale.

    C. High entry barriers.

    D. Low exit barriers.

Answer (B) is correct. *(Publisher, adapted)*
    REQUIRED: The likely economic cause of fragmentation.
    DISCUSSION: Important diseconomies of scale may favor fragmentation. For example, small, flexible firms have an advantage when the following needs are important: quick responses to style changes, the maintenance of low overhead, customization of a diverse product line to the special requirements of particular customers, substantial creative content in the product, individualized personal service, and local contacts and image.
    Answer (A) is incorrect. Economies of scale or a learning curve effect provide cost advantages to larger or older firms, respectively. However, economies of scale and a learning curve (experience) effect usually do not exist in fragmented industries, for example, because operations are simple or labor-intensive. Answer (C) is incorrect. Low entry barriers, not high entry barriers, constitute a necessary but not a sufficient condition for fragmentation. Answer (D) is incorrect. High exit barriers, not low exit barriers, keep firms in the industry and minimize concentration.

2. The opportunity for franchising comes from the ability to

    A. Develop products.

    B. Differentiate products.

    C. Standardize products.

    D. Diversify products.

Answer (C) is correct. *(CIA, adapted)*
    REQUIRED: The opportunities for franchising.
    DISCUSSION: Standardizing products means to maintain the same product or to standardize the production, operations, and facilities in different locations or markets. Franchises all use standardized products to reduce costs.
    Answer (A) is incorrect. Developing products means adding more value or features to the existing product. Answer (B) is incorrect. Differentiating products implies that the products are to be different in different markets. Answer (D) is incorrect. Diversifying products means to deal in different products, although they may be related (part of the same line).

3. In which of the following industry environments would an internal auditor be **most** likely to recommend strategies such as franchising and horizontal mergers?

    A. Emerging industries.

    B. Declining industries.

    C. Fragmented industries.

    D. Mature industries.

Answer (C) is correct. *(CIA, adapted)*
    REQUIRED: The industries in which franchising and horizontal mergers are most likely.
    DISCUSSION: Strategies such as franchising and horizontal mergers are commonly used in fragmented industries. Overcoming fragmentation has significant strategic payoffs given that entry is not costly and competitors are weak. If the factor(s) preventing consolidation can be eliminated, industry structure will change. Isolating factors responsible for fragmentation has been achieved in, for example, the fast food industry. The need to have numerous local operations under tight control and near customers has been isolated or neutralized by franchising to local owners. The franchisor provides national advertising, centralized purchasing, and other services, which result in economies of scale and industry consolidation. In effect, the service or production function is separated from the rest of the business. Also, acquisitions (horizontal mergers) that enable a firm to expand when competing with local firms might be difficult because of their contacts and image.
    Answer (A) is incorrect. Emerging industries are new and initially small in size. Moreover, they are characterized by great strategic uncertainty. Thus, it is unclear that a franchising or merger strategy is indicated. Answer (B) is incorrect. Declining industries have high exit barriers and are not seeking to acquire competitors. Answer (D) is incorrect. Mature industries have consistent sales and do not need to acquire competitors and franchise to gain market share.

4. A firm in a fragmented industry must position itself by adopting a competitive strategy appropriate to the industry. Which of the following is **most** clearly a focus strategy?

A. Specialization by product type.

B. Backward integration.

C. An emphasis on low overhead and low payroll.

D. Development of formula facilities.

Answer (A) is correct. *(Publisher, adapted)*
   REQUIRED: The focus strategy.
   DISCUSSION: A focus strategy is directed at a buyer group, segment of the product line, or geographic area. Thus, the strategic target is narrow compared with an industrywide strategy designed to achieve cost leadership or product differentiation. Specialization by product type or segment is a focus strategy. This focus may enhance bargaining power with suppliers. It may also increase differentiation because of the perceived expertise and image. The downside is reduced growth opportunities.
   Answer (B) is incorrect. Backward integration is the selective acquisition of suppliers to reduce costs. Answer (C) is incorrect. A cost strategy is to adopt a bare-bones, no-frills approach by emphasizing tight control of costs, low overhead, and low payroll. Answer (D) is incorrect. Developing formula facilities for use in numerous localities reduces construction and operating costs via standardization.

3.2 Emerging Industries

5. An emerging industry is new or newly formed and is small in size initially. An emerging industry results from innovation, changes in cost structures, new customer needs, or another factor that creates an attractive opportunity for selling a product or service. Which of the following is a structural characteristic of an emerging industry?

A. A long time horizon for product development.

B. Low initial costs and a shallow learning curve.

C. Mobility barriers include economies of scale and brand identification.

D. The presence of embryonic companies and spinoffs.

Answer (D) is correct. *(Publisher, adapted)*
   REQUIRED: The characteristic of an emerging industry.
   DISCUSSION: Embryonic companies (firms newly formed and not new units of established entities) are numerous in the emerging phase of industry evolution. Entry is not discouraged by the presence of economies of scale or strategic certainty. Spin-offs from existing firms also are common. Given the strategic uncertainties and the lure of equity interests, employees of these firms may have the incentive, and be well-placed, to create new firms. Their motive is to exploit ideas that may not have received a favorable reception by their former employers.
   Answer (A) is incorrect. The time horizon for product and customer development is short. Thus, policies may evolve for reasons other than well-researched decision making. Answer (B) is incorrect. Initial costs are high, but the learning curve is steep. When the efficiency gains from experience combine with economies of scale achieved by growth, cost decreases are dramatic. Answer (C) is incorrect. Early mobility barriers tend to consist of willingness to accept risk, proprietary technology, access to resource supplies, and the lower costs of experienced firms. Branding, economies of scale, and the need for capital tend not to be barriers.

6. Strategic choices in an emerging industry are inherently subject to great uncertainty and risk with regard to competitors, industry structure, and competitive rules. Accordingly, a firm considering entry into an emerging industry

A. Has little need to be concerned with industry cooperation.

B. Is least likely to be able to shape the industry structure at this stage.

C. May enjoy such benefits of pioneering as experience advantages and early commitment to suppliers.

D. Must be prepared for responding vigorously to competitors' moves.

Answer (C) is correct. *(Publisher, adapted)*
   REQUIRED: The true statement about strategic considerations by a potential entrant into an emerging industry.
   DISCUSSION: Timing of entry is a critical choice. Pioneering firms face high risk but low barriers and may earn high returns. The following are factors favoring early entry: pioneering improves the firm's reputation, the learning curve (experience) advantage is important and will persist, customer loyalty will be high, and cost advantages (through early commitment to suppliers or distributors) can be secured.
   Answer (A) is incorrect. A firm in an emerging industry needs to consider externalities in industry development. It should balance its self interest with the need to promote the image and credibility of the industry. Thus, to appeal to first-time buyers and encourage substitution, the firm's enlightened self-interest ordinarily resides in industry cooperation, improved quality, and standardization. However, as the industry matures, the firm should be less industry-oriented. Answer (B) is incorrect. The firm is best able to shape the industry structure when the industry is emerging. It is best able to influence to its advantage industry approaches on such matters as pricing, marketing, and product policy. Answer (D) is incorrect. Responding to competitors during the emerging phase of industry development is often a poor strategic choice. A firm is frequently best served by reinforcing its strengths and by developing the industry, perhaps through encouraging new entrants (e.g., by licensing) who will sell the industry's product and expedite its technological evolution.

3.3 Declining Industries

7. Industry structure and competition during the decline phase may result in intense and destructive competition. Which factor is **most** likely to contribute to this condition?

- A. Firms do not expect demand to rebound.
- B. The decline is rapid.
- C. Attractive substitutes are not available.
- D. Specialized assets used in the industry have low liquidation values.

Answer (D) is correct. *(Publisher, adapted)*
REQUIRED: The factor most likely to contribute to destructive competition in a declining industry.
DISCUSSION: High exit barriers may restrain firms from leaving the industry even though their returns are poor. For example, specialized assets and inventory in a declining industry may have a low liquidation value. Few purchasers who wish to operate in the same industry may be available. Durable assets may have a carrying amount far greater than the liquidation value. Hence, liquidation may result in a loss that the firm may not wish to recognize. Furthermore, a low liquidation value means that the future discounted cash flows from remaining in the industry may exceed the opportunity cost of the capital invested in the declining industry. Thus, the returns from the proceeds of liquidation may be less than the returns from keeping those assets in the business.
Answer (A) is incorrect. Perceived uncertainty about demand by competitors is a major influence on the competitive intensity. Rivalry will likely be bitter if demand is expected to rebound. However, if all firms expect demand to decrease, the weaker firms may plan early withdrawal and a graceful reduction of capacity. Answer (B) is incorrect. The rate and pattern of decline affect uncertainty, which stimulates competitive volatility. Thus, a slow decline creates uncertainty, but a rapid decline tends to reduce uncertainty and unjustified optimism. Moreover, a rapid decline makes wholesale decreases in capacity more probable. Answer (C) is incorrect. The causes of decline in industry demand include innovation or shifts in costs or quality that make attractive substitutes available.

8. A firm in a declining industry ordinarily adopts one of four strategies. A firm that follows a

- A. Quick divestment strategy should have divested during the maturity phase.
- B. Leadership strategy may assume that success will enable the firm to subsequently pursue a harvest strategy.
- C. Harvest strategy seeks a pocket of stable demand.
- D. Niche strategy is engaged in a gradual liquidation.

Answer (B) is correct. *(Publisher, adapted)*
REQUIRED: The true statement about a strategy followed by a firm in a declining industry.
DISCUSSION: A leadership strategy is pursued by a firm that believes it can achieve market share gains to become the dominant firm. An assumption is that additional investment can be recovered. A second assumption is that success will put the firm in a better position to hold its ground or subsequently to follow a harvest strategy. This strategy may entail aggressive pricing, marketing, or other investments that raise the stakes for competitors; reducing competitors' exit barriers by acquisitions of their capacity or products, assuming their contracts, and producing spare parts and generic versions of goods for them; demonstrations of strength and resolve to remain in the industry; and publicizing accurate data about the reality of future decline so as to dispel competitors' uncertainty.
Answer (A) is incorrect. A quick divestment strategy assumes that the highest net recovery is obtained by sale early in the decline phase. It is then that uncertainty about the industry's future is greatest and other markets for the assets are most favorable. Indeed, divestiture may be indicated. Answer (C) is incorrect. A niche strategy seeks a market segment (pocket of demand) with stable or slowly decreasing demand with the potential for above-average returns. Some of the moves undertaken when following a leadership strategy may be appropriate. The firm may eventually change to a harvest or divest strategy. Answer (D) is incorrect. A harvest strategy is, in effect, a controlled, gradual liquidation. It maximizes cash flow by minimizing new investment, R&D, advertising, service, maintenance, etc., and by exploiting the firm's remaining strengths (e.g., goodwill) to increase prices or maintain sales volume.

9. Which of the following is **not** characteristic of a mature industry environment?

    A. Consolidation.

    B. Competitive interdependence.

    C. Falling demand.

    D. Strategic focus on deterring entry of new competitors into the marketplace.

Answer (C) is correct. *(CIA, adapted)*
    REQUIRED: The characteristic of a mature industry environment.
    DISCUSSION: Falling demand is characteristic of declining industries. These industries have sustained a permanent decrease in unit sales over the long run.
    Answer (A) is incorrect. Consolidation is characteristic of a mature industry environment. Answer (B) is incorrect. Competitive interdependence is characteristic of a mature environment. Answer (D) is incorrect. Strategic focus on deterring entry of new competitors into the marketplace is competitive of a mature industry environment.

3.4 Competition in Global Industries

10. Which strategy in a global industry is **most** likely to be facilitated by a transnational coalition?

    A. A protected niche strategy.

    B. A national focus strategy.

    C. A national segment strategy.

    D. Broad line global competition.

Answer (D) is correct. *(Publisher, adapted)*
    REQUIRED: The strategy in a global industry most likely to be facilitated by a transnational coalition.
    DISCUSSION: Broad line global competition is competition over the full product line of the firm based on differentiation or low cost. The firm needs large resources for this long-term strategy. Governmental relations should emphasize impediment reduction. Transnational coalitions may be created to help the firms overcome impediments to executing the broader strategies, for example, market access or technology barriers.
    Answer (A) is incorrect. A protected niche strategy is applied in nations where global competitors are discouraged by governmental impediments. The strategy is designed to be effective in markets with governmental constraints and requires close attention to the national government. Answer (B) is incorrect. A national focus strategy is limited to a national market or the segments with the greatest economic impediments to global competitors. Low cost or differentiation is sought. Answer (C) is incorrect. A national focus strategy may be limited to national segments with the greatest economic impediments to global competitors. Low cost or differentiation is sought.

11. A global industry is one that

    A. Contains competitors that are multinationals.

    B. Has secured a competitive advantage based on economies of scale in centralized production.

    C. Has a strategic advantage by establishing coordinated competition in many national markets.

    D. Has made large direct investments abroad.

Answer (C) is correct. *(Publisher, adapted)*
    REQUIRED: The nature of a global industry.
    DISCUSSION: Analysis of the competition in an industry requires consideration of the economics of the industry and the characteristics of competitors. However, in a global industry, the analysis is not limited to one market, but extends to all markets (geographic or national) taken together. Michael E. Porter defines a global industry as "one in which the strategic positions of competitors in major geographic or national markets are fundamentally affected by their overall global positions." Thus, an industry becomes global because it perceives a net strategic advantage to competing, as Porter says, "in a coordinated way in many national markets."
    Answer (A) is incorrect. A true global industry is one that requires a firm to compete internationally. Accordingly, an industry is not global simply because some or all competitors are multinational. When nonmultinationals can compete in a geographic or national market, the industry is not global. Answer (B) is incorrect. Economies of scale in centralized production may yield a cost advantage achievable only when output exceeds the demand in one country and exports are feasible. Vertical integration may provide the necessary scale. However, a global competitive advantage may be based on other factors, such as other economies of scale (purchasing, marketing, or logistical), proprietary technology, product differentiation, or mobility of production. Answer (D) is incorrect. Participation in foreign markets is usually by licensing; export; or, after the firm has obtained experience, direct investment. A genuinely global industry will have significant export activity or direct investment, but the presence of the latter does not necessarily signal the existence of global competition. Direct investment also may occur when national factors only determine a subsidiary's competitive position.

12. Which of the following is a source of global competitive advantage?

    A. Low fixed costs.

    B. Production economies of scale.

    C. Weak copyright protection.

    D. Intensive local service requirements.

Answer (B) is correct. *(CIA, adapted)*
    REQUIRED: The source of global competitive advantage.
    DISCUSSION: Production economies of scale exist when a firm can produce and sell the output at which the average total cost of production is minimized. (The archetypal example is oil refining.) In other words, economies of scale in centralized production may yield a cost advantage achievable only when output exceeds the demand in one country, and exports are feasible.
    Answer (A) is incorrect. Low fixed costs generally imply weak barriers to entry and the consequent ability of local firms to compete effectively against a larger global firm. Answer (C) is incorrect. Weak intellectual property rights enforcement enables small local competitors to produce efficiently, if illicitly, in the short term. Answer (D) is incorrect. Intensive local service requirements dilute the advantage of a large and efficient global competitor.

13. The reason(s) governments **most** likely restrict trade include

I. To help foster new industries.
II. To protect declining industries.
III. To increase tax revenues.
IV. To foster national security.

    A. I only.

    B. I and II only.

    C. II and III only.

    D. I, II, and IV only.

Answer (D) is correct. *(CIA, adapted)*
    REQUIRED: The reason(s) governments restrict trade in the long run.
    DISCUSSION: Governmental impediments to global competition are generally imposed for the announced purpose of protecting local firms and jobs, developing new industries, and fostering national security. They also may have the effect of raising revenue in the short run. In the long run, tax and revenues will decline because of reduced trade. Examples of governmental impediments are tariffs; duties; quotas; domestic content rules; preferences for local firms regarding procurement, taxes, R&D, labor regulations, and other operating rules; and laws (e.g., anti-bribery or tax) enacted by a national government that impede national firms from competing globally. These impediments are most likely when industries are viewed as crucial.
    Answer (A) is incorrect. Governments often impose impediments to global competition to protect declining industries. Answer (B) is incorrect. Increasing tax revenues would not be an impetus for governments to restrict trade, since tax revenues would decrease with lessened trade. Answer (C) is incorrect. Restrictions on global trade, e.g., tariffs, may increase tax revenues in the short run. However, in the long run, the effect of reduced trade is to decrease tax revenues.

Use the additional questions in Gleim *CIA Test Prep* Software to create Test Sessions that emulate Pearson VUE!

STUDY UNIT FOUR
STRATEGIC DECISIONS

(13 pages of outline)

The three subunits in this study unit use the methods of competitive analysis to discuss certain strategic decisions.

 The objectivity of an internal auditor is impaired if (s)he makes management decisions. However, as part of their role in improving governance processes, internal auditors must be able to assess strategic decisions made by management.

4.1 INTEGRATION STRATEGIES

1. **Vertical integration** combines within a firm production, distribution, selling, or other separate economic processes needed to deliver a product or service to a customer. All such processes could in principle be performed through market transactions with outside firms.

   a. However, vertical integration uses internal or administrative transactions for these purposes in the expectation they will increase efficiency or decrease costs and risks.

   b. The **decision to integrate** should consider direct economic issues (needed investment and effects on costs), broader strategic issues, and the potential difficulties of administering a vertically integrated firm. Thus, the extent of integration depends on the balance of economic and administrative benefits and costs.

      1) This balance varies with the industry, the firm's position, and whether the firm engages in

         a) Full integration,

         b) **Tapered (partial) integration**, or

         c) **Quasi-integration** (use of alliances, not ownership, to achieve the effects of integration).

Generic Strategic Benefits

2. The following are generic strategic benefits of vertical integration:

   a. **Upstream** (backward) integration is acquisition of a capability that otherwise would be performed by external parties that are suppliers of the firm.

      1) **Downstream** (forward) integration is acquisition of a capability performed by customers.

      2) Whether integration should occur depends on

         a) The firm's volume of transactions with the external parties **(throughput)** and

         b) The magnitude of the capability required to achieve necessary **economies of scale**.

      i)   If the integrating firm's need is for a capability **less than the efficient scale**, one option is to acquire a capability with a cost-inefficient scale.

      ii)   The other option is to acquire an efficient capability that provides **excess output** (in the upstream case) or creates **excess demand** (from, for example, a distribution capability in the downstream case).

        ● This option will require the integrated firm to sell or buy in the open market. Thus, the second option carries the risk of having to deal with competitors.

   b. **Economies of vertical integration** occur when throughput is great enough to achieve economies of scale. For example, economies of integration are available when the firm builds a supply facility that is large enough to be cost efficient, and the firm can use all of its output.

     1) **Economies of combined operations** may reduce production steps, handling and transportation, and slack time. For example, facilities for technologically different processes might be located near each other, or the same machines may be used for different steps.

     2) **Economies of control and coordination** result from

        a)   Better delivery scheduling,
        b)   Common oversight of functions,
        c)   Increased reliability of supply by a related entity,
        d)   Internal redesign or new product introductions, and
        e)   A leaner control structure.

     3) **Economies of information** are achieved by an integrated firm because

        a)   Some information may no longer be needed,
        b)   The fixed costs of competitive intelligence and forecasting are borne by additional subunits of the firm, and
        c)   Information may flow more rapidly between related than unrelated entities.

     4) Economies result from **avoiding some market transactions**. Transaction costs of dealing with outside parties are greater than those of dealing with inside parties.

     5) **Stable relationships** between internal sellers and buyers create economies because

        a)   They need not fear loss of the related buyers and sellers or undue economic pressure from each other.
        b)   They may more fully adapt to each other's needs than they would or could in dealings with outsiders.
        c)   The relationship is locked in, so more efficient procedures for their relationship (e.g., dedicated controls and records) may be implemented.

   c. A **tap into technology** of upstream or downstream firms is an integration benefit that is a vital economy of information. However, integration to obtain a better understanding of technology is usually tapered so as to manage risk.

   d. Providing **assurance of supply or demand** is an integration benefit because it reduces some of the uncertainty caused by market fluctuations. Thus, the firm has less risk of interruptions, changes in customers and suppliers, or payment of excessive prices in emergencies.

     1) However, demand in the absolute sense is not affected. For example, when a downstream subunit faces lower external demand, its internal supplier also faces lower demand.

2) To promote overall firm efficiency, **transfer prices** most likely should be market-based.

e. Integration benefits include **offsetting the bargaining power** of strong suppliers and customers.

1) If such parties have returns greater than the firm's opportunity cost of capital, the firm benefits even if no other advantages result from integration.

a) Thus, upstream integration eliminates **input cost distortion** caused by the supplier's power, and downstream integration eliminates the customer's power to obtain an unjustifiably low price.

i) Moreover, the special costs of dealing with powerful parties also are eliminated.

b) Upstream integration also has the advantage of disclosing the true cost of the input provided by the powerful supplier. This information helps the firm to adjust its input mix and prices.

f. An integrated firm may have a better **ability to differentiate** itself because it has greater opportunities to offer value to customers, such as by improved service through integrated distribution channels.

g. Integration that generates any of the benefits described above and on the previous pages also raises **entry and mobility barriers**. Integration may provide a competitive advantage not matched by a nonintegrated firm, especially if it requires large capital investment or economies of scale.

h. Integration may increase the firm's **overall** return on investment after considering any costs of overcoming barriers to integration.

i. Integration may be a **defense against foreclosure of access** to suppliers or customers. It is a response to integration by competitors who threaten to secure the low-cost or high-quality suppliers, favorable distribution channels, or largest customers.

1) Defensive integration also increases mobility when investment or economies of scale are large.

Generic Strategic Costs

3. The following are generic strategic costs of vertical integration:

a. Integration is a special case of entry into a new business. The firm must incur **costs to overcome mobility barriers** to enter the adjacent business, such as economies of scale, proprietary technology, capital investment, and sources of materials.

b. Integration **increases fixed costs and operating leverage**, which is in itself a cause of increased business risk.

1) Thus, an integrated firm is exposed to fluctuations affecting any of its components. For example, sales of an upstream component depend on sales of downstream components.

c. Integration **reduces the flexibility to change business partners** because it increases the costs of switching to different suppliers or customers.

1) For example, a supplier component may ultimately be providing an obsolete, overpriced, or poorly designed product. A customer component may lose market share.

d. Integration may increase any **exit barriers**.

e. Integration **requires investment capital**. The return must at least equal the firm's opportunity cost of capital (after considering all strategic analytical factors).

1) Furthermore, the integration decision is in part dependent on the **appetite for capital** of the adjacent business to be entered. The danger is that it may continually require capital that could be more profitably invested elsewhere in the firm.

   a) This loss of flexibility of capital allocation may prevent profitable diversification.

f. Integration may **foreclose access to supplier or customer technology**. The integrated firm may have to create its own technology rather than taking advantage of supplier/customer expertise.

g. Integration requires **maintaining a balance** among the operations of the firm's subunits. Excess output or demand of a subunit may require selling to, or buying from, competitors unless the needs can be satisfied by sales or purchases on the open market.

   1) Imbalance may result because of unequal changes in capacity caused by technological change or alterations in the product mix or quality.

h. Integration may **reduce incentives**. For example, a buyer may not bargain as aggressively with an in-house seller, and a seller may not compete as aggressively because it is ensured of a customer.

   1) Accordingly, internal projects may not be as carefully considered as external transactions. The response is for management to require that internal relationships be treated as if they are genuinely at arms' length.

   2) Furthermore, subunit managers must resist the natural temptation to assist a failing subunit, thereby damaging the successful subunits.

i. A significant cost and risk of integration is that subunits have **differing managerial requirements**. It is a mistake to apply the same methods used in the core business to other parts of the integrated firm.

Strategic Issues

4. **Forward Integration**

   a. **Enhanced product differentiation** may follow forward integration because of better control of production, marketing, retailing, or service that adds value.

   b. Forward integration may secure **access to distribution channels**.

   c. **Access to market information** is improved. A forward subunit (the **demand leading stage**) controls the amount and mix of demand to be satisfied upstream.

      1) At the very least, forward integration improves

         a) The timeliness of demand information,
         b) Production planning,
         c) Inventory control, and
         d) The costs of being under- or overstocked.

      2) It also may provide information about changing tastes, competitors' moves, and the ideal mix of products.

      3) Whether forward integration is indicated depends on the relative instability of demand and the effect on information reliability of the number of customers.

   d. Forward integration may permit **higher price realization**, for example, by moving into businesses in which the price elasticity of demand is relatively high and lower prices must be set.

      1) When demand is elastic, raising prices decreases revenue. Thus, the firm may benefit by acquiring customers with high elasticities while selling to customers with low elasticities.

5. **Backward Integration**

    a. Backward integration allows the firm to protect its **proprietary knowledge** from suppliers.

    b. Controlling inputs may permit the firm to **differentiate its product** more effectively, or at least to argue persuasively that it does so.

Contracts and Economies of Integration

6. Some of the economies of integration may be secured by contracts (long- or short-term) with independent parties, for example, through a long-term agreement with a supplier to provide all of the firm's needs for an input. However, such arrangements may be difficult to create because of the parties' dissimilar interests and the risks involved.

    a. **Tapered (partial) integration** implies that the firm can fully support an efficient subunit but has additional needs to be met in the market. If the in-house subunit will not be efficient, that inefficiency must be weighed against the benefits of tapering.

        1) Tapering results in **lower fixed costs** than full integration. Furthermore, the strategy may allow the firm's subunit(s) to maintain constant production rates while external parties bear the **risk of fluctuations**.

            a) Another use of tapering is to protect against operational **imbalances** (excesses of output or demand) among the subunits.

        2) Risks of tapering include greater coordination cost and selling to, or buying from, competitors.

        3) Advantages of tapering are

            a) Avoidance of locked-in relationships,

            b) Some access to external expertise,

            c) Increased managerial incentives,

            d) Offering a credible threat of full integration to suppliers or customers, and

            e) Obtaining knowledge of the adjacent business and an emergency supply source.

    b. **Quasi-integration** is something more than a long-term contract and less than full ownership. It may be achieved by a minority common stock interest, debt guarantees, cooperation in R&D, an exclusive dealing arrangement, etc.

        1) Buyer and seller may, as a result, have a common interest leading to lower costs, smoothing of supply/demand fluctuations, or mitigating against bargaining power.

        2) Quasi-integration may avoid commitment to an adjacent business with its investment and management requirements. But many benefits of full integration may not be achievable in this way.

7. **Common Illusions of Integration**

    a. Strength in one part of the chain necessarily carries over to the other parts.
    b. Doing something internally is less expensive.
    c. Integrating into a highly competitive business is often wise.
    d. Integration may save a strategically sick firm.
    e. Experience in one part of the chain always carries over to other parts.

Core Concepts

- The decision to integrate should consider direct economic issues (needed investment and effects on costs), broader strategic issues, and the potential difficulties of administering a vertically integrated firm.

- Upstream (backward) or downstream (forward) integration is the acquisition of a capability that otherwise would be performed by external parties that are suppliers or customers, respectively, of the firm.

- Whether integration should occur depends on the firm's volume of transactions with the external parties (throughput) and the magnitude of the capability required to achieve necessary economies of scale.

- Integration is a special case of entry into a new business. Thus, the firm must incur costs to overcome the mobility barriers when entering an adjacent business.

- The benefits of forward integration may include enhanced product differentiation, access to distribution channels, access to market information, and higher price realization.

- Backward integration allows the firm to protect its proprietary knowledge from suppliers as well as control inputs, which may permit the firm to differentiate its product more effectively.

- Instead of full integration, firms may choose to enter new businesses through tapered (partial) integration or quasi-integration.

  - Tapered, or partial, integration implies that the firm can fully support an efficient subunit but has additional needs to be met in the market.

  - Quasi-integration is something more than a long-term contract and less than full ownership. It involves the use of alliances, not ownership, to achieve the effects of integration.

- The following are common illusions of integration:

  - Strength in one part of the chain necessarily carries over to the other parts.
  - Doing something internally is less expensive.
  - Integrating into a highly competitive business is often wise.
  - Integration may save a strategically sick firm.
  - Experience in one part of the chain always carries over to other parts.

Stop and review! You have completed the outline for this subunit. Study multiple-choice questions 1 through 4 beginning on page 103.

4.2 CAPACITY EXPANSION

Overview

1. Whether to expand capacity is a major **strategic decision** because of (a) the capital required, (b) the difficulty of forecasting, (c) the long lead times, and (d) the commitment. The key forecasts are **long-term demand** and **behavior of competitors**. The key strategic issue is **avoidance of industry overcapacity**.

   a. Undercapacity in a profitable industry tends to be a short-term issue. Profits ordinarily attract more investors. Overcapacity tends to be a long-term problem because firms are more likely to compete intensely rather than reverse their expansion.

2. Formal **capital budgeting** involves predicting cash flows related to the expansion, discounting them at an appropriate interest rate, and determining whether the **net present value** is positive. This process permits comparison with other uses of the firm's resources.

   a. The apparent simplicity of this process is deceptive. It depends upon, among many other things, which expansion method is chosen, developments in technology, and profitability. Profitability in turn depends on such uncertainties as total long-term demand and the expansion plans of rival firms.

The Decision to Expand Capacity

3. Porter's **model of the decision process for capacity expansion** has the following interrelated steps:

    a. The firm must **identify the options** in relation to their size, type, degree of vertical integration (if any), and possible response by competitors.

    b. The second step is to **forecast demand, input costs, and technology developments**. The firm must be aware that its technology may become obsolete or that future design changes to allow expansion may or may not be possible.

        1) Moreover, the expansion itself may put upward pressure on input prices.

    c. The next step is **analysis of competitors** to determine when each will expand. The difficulty is that forecasting their behavior depends on knowing their expectations.

        1) Another difficulty is that each competitor's actions potentially affect all other competitors' actions, with the industry leader being most influential.

    d. Using the information from the first three steps, the firm predicts **total industry capacity and firms' market shares**. These estimates, together with the expected demand, permit the firm to predict **prices and cash flows**.

    e. The final step is **testing for inconsistencies**.

4. The **extent of uncertainty about future demand** is a crucial variable in industry expansion. For example, if uncertainty is great, firms willing to take greater risks because of their large cash resources or strategic stake in the industry will act first. Other firms will await events.

    a. When demand uncertainty is low, firms will tend to adopt a strategy of **preemption**, usually with strong market signals, to deter expansion by competitors.

        1) Excess preemption leads to excess industry capacity because firms

            a) Overestimate their competitive strengths,
            b) Misunderstand market signals, or
            c) Fail to accurately assess competitors' intentions.

Causes of Overexpansion

5. **Causes of overbuilding** extend beyond poorly played games of preemption.

    a. Overbuilding is most frequent in firms that produce **commodities**. One reason is that such firms are usually **cyclical** so that capacity is always excessive at low points in the cycle. Moreover, many tend to overestimate the strength of upturns.

        1) A second reason is that commodities tend to be **undifferentiated**. Thus, competition is based on price, cost efficiency is crucial, and sales depend on capacity.

    b. The following are **technological factors** that may lead to overbuilding:

        1) Capacity may need to be added in **large increments**.
        2) The presence of **economies of scale** or the **learning curve effect** encourages preemption (see page 99).
        3) **Long lead times** for adding capacity increase the risk of competitive inferiority if a firm does not act quickly to begin raising its capacity.
        4) When the **minimum efficient scale** increases, large plants are becoming more efficient. Unless demand is growing, the number of plants must decline to avoid overbuilding.
        5) **Changes in production technology** result in new construction while old plants remain in operation, particularly when exit barriers are high.

c. The following are **structural factors** that may lead to overbuilding:

1) **Exit barriers** are high. Thus, the period of overcapacity is extended.

2) **Suppliers** of capital, equipment, materials, etc., face their own competitive pressures. Thus, (a) lower supplier prices, (b) government subsidies, (c) favorable interest rates, and (d) similar incentives may promote expansion by customer industries.

3) **Credibility** of new products is promoted by capacity expansion that gives assurance to large buyers. Such customers need to know that capacity will exist to meet their long-term needs and that a few suppliers will not have excessive bargaining power.

4) When **competitors are integrated**, the pressure to build despite uncertain demand intensifies. Each firm wants to ensure that it can supply its downstream operations.

5) **Capacity leadership** is important in some industries as a means of increasing market share. Customers may be more likely to buy from the capacity leader.

    a) The **age and type of capacity** also may be competitive advantages.

d. The following are **competitive factors** that may lead to overbuilding:

1) **Many firms** with the ability to add capacity want to improve market share.

2) The **lack of a credible market leader(s)** makes for a less orderly expansion. A stronger leader can retaliate effectively against inappropriate expansion by others.

3) **New entrants**, possibly encouraged by low entry barriers and favorable economic conditions, may cause or intensify overcapacity.

4) **First mover advantages** may be significant. Thus, shorter lead times for ordering equipment, lower costs, and the ability to exploit an excess of demand over supply may encourage too many firms to expand.

e. The following are **information flow factors** that may lead to overbuilding:

1) **Future expectations** may be inflated because of industry buzz.

2) Firms' **assumptions or perceptions** about competitors' strengths, weaknesses, and plans may be inaccurate.

3) **Market signaling** may be ineffective because it is no longer regarded as credible. Firms' signals may no longer be trusted as indicators of planned moves, such as expansion, because of new entrants, a period of bitter rivalry, or other reasons.

4) **Changes in industry structure** may lead directly to new investment or create uncertainties leading to faulty decisions.

5) The **financial community** encourages overbuilding when analysts criticize firms that have not expanded. Also, management's optimistic comments to the financial community may be taken as aggressive signals by competitors.

f. The following are **managerial factors** that may lead to overbuilding:

1) Management that is **production-oriented** may be more likely to overbuild than marketing- or finance-oriented management.

2) A manager's career **risk is asymmetric** when the consequences of overcapacity appear to be less serious than those of undercapacity.

g. The following are **governmental factors** that may lead to overbuilding:

1) **Tax incentives** may promote excess capacity, for example, by permitting foreign subsidiaries to pay no tax on earnings retained in the business.

2) A nation may wish to create a **local industry**. When the minimum efficient scale is great in relation to worldwide demand, the excess production in the country may contribute to global overcapacity.

3) **Governmental employment pressures** may result in overbuilding to create jobs or avoid job loss.

h. The following are **limits on capacity expansion**:

1) Most firms have great **uncertainty** about future conditions.
2) The firm faces **financial limitations**.
3) The firm is **diversified**. As a result, the opportunity cost of capital is greater, and management's perspective is broader.
4) Senior managers have **finance backgrounds**.
5) **Expansion is costly**, e.g., because of environmental regulations.
6) The firm experienced distress during a **prior period of overbuilding**.
7) A firm's behavior sends **signals** to competitors that building is unwise. For example, it may announce an expansion project or indicate in some way that forecasts of demand are unfavorable or that current technology will soon be obsolete.

Preemptive Strategies

6. Preemption requires investments in plant facilities and the ability to accept short-term unfavorable results. The strategy is risky because it anticipates demand and often sets prices in the expectation of future cost efficiencies. Moreover, a failed preemption strategy may provoke intense, industry-damaging conflict. The following conditions must be met for the strategy to succeed:

a. The expansion must be **large relative to the market**, and competitors must believe that the move is preemptive. Hence, the firm should know competitors' expectations about the market or be able to influence them favorably. A move that is too small is by definition not preemptive.

b. **Economies of scale** should be large in relation to demand, or the **learning-curve effect** will give an initial large investor a permanent cost advantage.

1) For example, the preemptive firm may be able to secure too much of the market to allow a subsequent firm to invest at the efficient scale. That is, the residual demand available to be met by the later firm is less than the efficient scale of production. The later firm therefore must choose between intense competition at the efficient scale or a cost disadvantage.

c. The preempting firm must have **credibility** to support its statements and moves, such as resources, technology, and a history of credibility.

d. The firm must provide **credible signals before action by competitors**.

e. The **competitors** of the firm should be willing not to act. This condition may not be met if competitors have noneconomic objectives, the business is strategically vital to them, or they have greater ability or willingness to compete.

Core Concepts

- Whether to expand capacity is a major strategic decision because of (1) the capital required, (2) the difficulty of forecasting, (3) the long lead times, and (4) the commitment. The key forecasts are long-term demand and the behavior of competitors. The key strategic issue is avoidance of industry overcapacity.

- Porter's model of the decision process for capacity expansion has the following interrelated steps:

  - Identify the options
  - Forecast demand, input costs, and technology developments
  - Analyze the competition
  - Predict the total industry capacity and firms' market shares
  - Test for inconsistencies

- The extent of uncertainty about future demand is a crucial variable in industry expansion. When demand uncertainty is low, firms will tend to adopt a strategy of preemption, usually with strong market signals, to deter expansion by competitors.

- The factors that may lead to overbuilding are (1) technological, (2) structural, (3) competitive, (4) informational, (5) managerial, and (6) governmental.

- A preemptive strategy is risky because it anticipates demand and often sets prices in the expectation of future cost efficiencies. Moreover, a failed preemption strategy may provoke intense, industry-damaging conflict.

Stop and review! You have completed the outline for this subunit. Study multiple-choice questions 5 and 6 on page 105.

4.3 ENTRY INTO NEW BUSINESSES

Entry through Internal Development

1. Entry through internal development ordinarily involves creation of a new business entity. This **internal entrant** must cope with structural barriers and retaliation by existing firms.

   a. Thus, costs include

      1) Initial investments to overcome **entry barriers** (facilities, inventory, branding, technology, distribution channels, sources of materials, etc.),

      2) Operating losses in the start-up phase,

      3) The effects of **retaliation** (e.g., higher marketing costs, capacity expansion, or lower prices), and

      4) Price increases for factors of production that may result because of the new entry.

   b. Also, the **capacity** added to the industry by the entrant may affect the equilibrium level of supply and demand.

      1) The result may be additional competitive costs as firms with excess capacity cut prices.

   c. An internal entrant is most likely to cause industry disruption and **retaliation**, with a consequent negative effect on future results, in the following industries:

      1) In a **slow-growth** industry, existing firms cannot compensate for the loss in market share, and the added capacity will depress prices.

      2) If the product is a commodity or is commodity-like, brand identification and market segmentation do not exist to protect existing firms. Price cuts are probable.

      3) **High fixed costs** indicate that existing firms will retaliate if their capacity usage decreases materially.

      4) In a **highly concentrated industry**, the internal entrant is more likely to have a significant and noticeable effect on particular firms with the ability to retaliate.

         a) In a **fragmented industry**, many firms might be affected but not significantly. These firms also might have no ability to retaliate.

      5) Existing firms view the industry as **strategically important**, e.g., as a source of cash flow or growth or because of integration.

      6) **Management attitudes** of well-established firms, especially if engaged in a single business, may provide a psychological basis for retaliation. An internal entrant should consider the prior reactions of such firms to new entrants or to existing firms that attempted to move to a new strategic group.

d. The internal entrant should undertake a **structural analysis**, including consideration of profitability as a function of the **five competitive forces**, to **identify target industries**.

1) If the industry is **in equilibrium**, the internal entrant should expect normal (average) profits even if established firms earn above-average profits. The reason is that the internal entrant's costs exceed those of existing firms. It must pay the costs of overcoming entry barriers and coping with retaliation.

   a) If the entry costs did not negate above-average profits, other firms would previously have entered the industry and lowered the available profits.

   b) Consequently, unless the firm has special advantages, it should most likely not target an industry in equilibrium.

2) However, a firm may be able to achieve **above-average profits** by choosing appropriate targets.

   a) An industry may be in **disequilibrium**.

      i) In a **new industry**, (a) the structure is not established, (b) entry barriers are low, (c) retaliation is unlikely, (d) resource supplies are not yet controlled by existing firms, and (e) brands are not well developed.

         • However, initial firms may have greater costs than later entrants if entry barriers are low.

      ii) **Rising entry barriers** favor an early entrant whose subsequent competitors will incur higher costs. The early entrant also may have an advantage in product differentiation.

      iii) **Poor information** may perpetuate disequilibrium because firms that might enter the industry may not be aware of its potential.

      iv) An internal entrant must understand that the indicators of disequilibrium may be apparent to other firms.

         • Hence, the firm's decision to enter should be based on some advantage that will enable it to earn above-average profits.

   b) The balance of expected profits and entry costs may be favorable when existing firms do not or cannot **retaliate against the internal entrant swiftly and effectively**. Industries of this kind do not have the attributes discussed earlier (see 1.c.). The following are other relevant factors:

      i) The **costs to existing firms of retaliation** may exceed the benefits. The new firm also may be able to persuade existing firms that the costs are excessive.

      ii) The industry may have a **dominant firm or a long-time leadership group** that acts to protect the industry rather than maximize its own standing, e.g., by retaliating against a new entrant.

      iii) Existing firms' **costs of retaliation are high** in relation to the need to protect their business. For example, a response might alienate distributors, reduce sales of key products, or be inconsistent with the retaliating firm's image.

      iv) **Conventional wisdom** about industry operating practices may impair the ability of existing firms to retaliate. A new firm may perceive circumstances in which the conventional wisdom does not apply.

      c) **Lower industry entry costs** may be incurred by a firm with special advantages, such as a well-known brand, proprietary technology, or a strong distribution network.

          i) Moreover, the respect for such a powerful competitor may deter retaliation.

      d) A **distinctive ability to influence industry structure** is another basis for earning above-average profits. Thus, an ability to raise mobility barriers after the firm has entered the industry is a reason to target that industry. Furthermore, a firm may be able to recognize that entering a fragmented industry will start a process of consolidation and increased entry barriers.

      e) Internal entry having a **positive effect on the firm's existing businesses** is justified even if above-average profits cannot be earned in the new industry.

  e. The following **generic entry concepts** are methods of inexpensively overcoming entry barriers:

    1) **Product costs** may be reduced by use of new process technology, economies of scale, a modern plant, or sharing functions with existing businesses.

    2) A **low initial price** that sacrifices profits for market share may succeed if competitors do not retaliate.

    3) A **better product or service** overcomes the product differentiation barrier.

    4) Barriers can be overcome by finding an **unserved niche market**.

    5) A **marketing innovation** overcomes product differentiation and distribution barriers.

    6) Use of an **established distribution network** is another way to overcome entry barriers.

Entry by Acquisition

2. The analysis of entry by acquisition differs from that for entry by internal development. A key point is that prices are set in the **market for acquisitions**. In the industrialized countries, this market is active and well organized, indicating that it is also efficient and therefore tends to eliminate above-average profits.

  a. One factor contributing to **efficiency** (and the elimination of above-average profits for a buyer) is that a seller normally can choose to continue running the business.

    1) Accordingly, a bidder ordinarily must pay the seller a premium in excess of the expected present value to the seller of continuing operations. The price minus that **floor** value equals the premium.

  b. Acquisitions are most likely to earn **above-average profits** when

    1) The **floor is low**, e.g., because the seller perceives that it needs funds, has management weaknesses, or cannot grow or compete because of capital limits.

    2) The **market for acquisitions is imperfect**.

      a) The buyer may have better information.
      b) There are few bidders.
      c) The economy is weak.
      d) The seller is weak.
      e) The seller has reasons to sell other than profit maximization.

3) The **buyer may have a unique ability to operate the seller**.

    a) The buyer may be uniquely able to improve operations.

    b) The buyer purchases a firm in an industry that meets one of the conditions for an internal entrant to earn above-average profits.

    c) The purchase may improve the buyer's position in its current businesses.

4) A pitfall to avoid is competition from **irrational bidders**. An acquisition may be a genuine or perceived value to the irrational bidder, which exceeds the value to the firm.

c. **Sequential entry** may be the best entry strategy. It involves entering one **strategic group** in the industry with subsequent mobility to another group(s).

Core Concepts

- Entry through internal development ordinarily involves creation of a new business entity. This internal entrant must cope with structural barriers and retaliation by existing firms.

- The internal entrant should undertake a structural analysis, including consideration of profitability as a function of the five competitive forces, to identify target industries.

- Certain generic entry concepts provide methods of inexpensively overcoming entry barriers. They include (1) reduced product costs, (2) a low initial price, (3) a better product or service, (4) finding an unserved niche market, (5) introducing a marketing innovation, and (6) using an established distribution network.

- The analysis of entry by acquisition differs from that for entry by internal development. A key point is that prices are set in the market for acquisitions. In the industrialized countries, this market is active and well organized, indicating that it is also efficient and therefore tends to eliminate above-average profits.

- Sequential entry may be the best strategy for an entry by acquisition. It involves entering one strategic group in the industry with subsequent mobility to another group(s).

Stop and review! You have completed the outline for this subunit. Study multiple-choice questions 7 and 8 on page 106.

QUESTIONS

4.1 Integration Strategies

1. Backward integration strategy is **most** appropriate when the firm's current suppliers are

A. Highly reliable.

B. Not reliable.

C. Geographically dispersed.

D. Geographically concentrated.

Answer (B) is correct. *(CIA, adapted)*
    REQUIRED: The use of backward integration.
    DISCUSSION: Backward integration is appropriate when the firm's current suppliers are unreliable. Stable relationships between internal sellers and buyers create economies because they need not fear loss of the related buyers and sellers. They also need not fear undue economic pressure from each other. Furthermore, because the relationship is locked in, more efficient procedures for their relationship (e.g., dedicated controls and records) may be implemented. Another advantage is that internal sellers and buyers may more fully adapt to each other's needs than they would or could in dealings with outsiders.
    Answer (A) is incorrect. Backward integration is less likely if the firm's current suppliers are highly reliable. Answer (C) is incorrect. The reliability of suppliers is more important than whether they are geographically dispersed. Answer (D) is incorrect. The reliability of suppliers is more important than whether they are geographically concentrated.

2. The decision to engage in the vertical integration of a firm is in large part a function of an analysis of throughput and economies of scale. If throughput is less than the efficient scale, the firm

    A. Should acquire a capability equal to the firm's throughput.

    B. Must sell or buy in the open market if the firm vertically integrates at the efficient scale.

    C. Should engage in quasi-integration.

    D. Should not vertically integrate.

Answer (B) is correct. *(Publisher, adapted)*
    REQUIRED: The effect of the analysis of throughput and economies of scale in a vertical integration decision.
    DISCUSSION: Upstream (backward) or downstream (forward) integration is the acquisition of a capability that otherwise would be performed by external parties that are suppliers or customers, respectively, of the firm. Whether integration should occur depends on the firm's volume of transactions with the external parties (throughput) and the magnitude of the capability required to achieve necessary economies of scale. If the integrating firm's need is for a capability less than the efficient scale, one of its options is to acquire a capability with a cost inefficient scale. The other option is to acquire an efficient capability that provides excess output (in the upstream case) or creates excess demand (from, for example, a distribution capability in the downstream case). This option will require the integrated firm to sell or buy in the open market. Thus, the second option carries the risk of having to deal with competitors.
    Answer (A) is incorrect. A full analysis of strategic benefits and costs may indicate that acquiring a capability with a cost inefficient scale may be best. The cost disadvantage may be offset by many other factors. Answer (C) is incorrect. A full analysis of strategic benefits and costs may indicate that acquiring a capability with a cost inefficient scale may be best. The cost disadvantage may be offset by many other factors. Quasi-integration (use of alliances, not ownership) may not provide many of the benefits of full integration. Answer (D) is incorrect. The best strategic decision may be to integrate either at the efficient or inefficient scale.

3. Which of the following is an arrangement that involves partial integration and implies the ability to fully support an efficient subunit?

    A. Quasi-integration.

    B. Tapered integration.

    C. Upstream integration.

    D. Contract integration.

Answer (B) is correct. *(Publisher, adapted)*
    REQUIRED: The arrangement that involves partial integration and implies the ability to support fully an efficient subunit.
    DISCUSSION: Tapered (partial) integration implies that the firm can fully support an efficient subunit but has additional needs to be met in the market. If the in-house subunit will not be efficient, that inefficiency must be weighed against the benefits of tapering. Tapering results in lower fixed costs than full integration. Furthermore, the strategy may allow the firm's subunit(s) to maintain constant production rates while external parties bear the risk of fluctuations. Another use of tapering is to protect against operational imbalances among the subunits. A risk of tapering is selling to, or buying from, competitors. Another is greater coordination cost. Advantages of tapering are avoidance of locked-in relationships, some access to external expertise, increased managerial incentives, offering a credible threat of full integration to suppliers or customers, and obtaining knowledge of the adjacent business and an emergency supply source.
    Answer (A) is incorrect. Quasi-integration is something more than a long-term contract and less than full ownership. It may be achieved by a minority common stock interest, debt guarantees, cooperation in R&D, an exclusive dealing arrangement, etc. Answer (C) is incorrect. Upstream integration is backward integration by acquiring or building a supply capability. Answer (D) is incorrect. Some of the economies of integration may be secured by contracts (long- or short-term) with independent parties, for example, through a long-term agreement with a supplier to provide all of the firm's needs for an input. However, such arrangements may be difficult to create because of the parties' dissimilar interests and the risks involved.

4. A milk producer company acquires its own dairy farms to supply milk. The growth strategy adopted by the company is

A. Horizontal integration.

B. Vertical integration.

C. Concentric diversification.

D. Conglomerate diversification.

Answer (B) is correct. *(CIA, adapted)*
REQUIRED: The correct type of growth strategy.
DISCUSSION: Vertical integration occurs when a company becomes its own supplier or distributor. It combines within a firm production, distribution, selling, or other separate economic processes needed to deliver a product or service to a customer.
Answer (A) is incorrect. Horizontal integration is the acquisition of competitors. Answer (C) is incorrect. Concentric diversification results from developing or acquiring related businesses that do not have products, services, or customers in common with current businesses, but that offer internal synergies, e.g., through common use of brands, R&D, plant facilities, or marketing expertise. Answer (D) is incorrect. Conglomerate diversification is the acquisition of wholly unrelated businesses. The objectives of such an acquisition are financial, not operational, because of the absence of common products, customers, facilities, expertise, or other synergies.

4.2 Capacity Expansion

5. What is the key strategic issue when a firm is considering capacity expansion?

A. Forecasting long-term demand.

B. Analyzing the behavior of competitors.

C. Identifying options.

D. Avoiding industry overcapacity.

Answer (D) is correct. *(Publisher, adapted)*
REQUIRED: The key strategic issue when a firm is considering capacity expansion.
DISCUSSION: Whether to expand capacity is a major strategic decision because of the capital required, the difficulty of forming accurate expectations, and the long time frame of the lead times and the commitment. The key forecasting problems are long-term demand and behavior of competitors. The key strategic issue is avoidance of industry overcapacity. Undercapacity in a profitable industry tends to be a short-term issue. Profits ordinarily lure additional investors. Overcapacity tends to be a long-term problem because firms are more likely to compete intensely rather than reverse their expansion.
Answer (A) is incorrect. Forecasting long-term demand, input costs, and technology developments is a step preliminary to predicting total industry capacity and firms' market shares. Answer (B) is incorrect. Analyzing the behavior of competitors is a step preliminary to predicting total industry capacity and firms' market shares. Answer (C) is incorrect. Identifying options is a step preliminary to predicting total industry capacity and firms' market shares.

6. When demand uncertainty is low, firms tend to adopt a strategy of preemptive expansion. The conditions for successful preemption expansion include which of the following?

A. The firm should avoid market signals that alert competitors to the firm's plans.

B. The expansion should be small relative to the market to minimize risk.

C. Economies of scale should be large relative to demand.

D. The business should be strategically vital to competitors.

Answer (C) is correct. *(Publisher, adapted)*
REQUIRED: The condition for successful preemption.
DISCUSSION: Economies of scale should be large in relation to demand, or the learning-curve effect should give an initial large investor a permanent cost advantage. For example, the preemptive firm may be able to secure too much of the market to allow a subsequent firm to invest at the efficient scale. That is, the residual demand available to be met by the later firm is less than the efficient scale of production. The later firm therefore must choose between intense competition at the efficient scale or a cost disadvantage.
Answer (A) is incorrect. The firm must provide credible signals before action by competitors. Answer (B) is incorrect. The expansion must be large relative to the market, and competitors must believe that the move is preemptive. Hence, the firm should know competitors' expectations about the market or be able to influence them favorably. A move that is too small is by definition not preemptive. Answer (D) is incorrect. The competitors of the firm should be willing not to act. This condition may not be met if competitors have noneconomic objectives, the business is strategically vital to them, or they have greater ability or willingness to compete.

4.3 Entry into New Businesses

7. Entry into a new business may be made by internal development or acquisition. Entry through internal development usually involves creation of a full-fledged new business entity. The costs likely to be incurred by an internal entrant include

I. Investments to overcome entry barriers.

II. Change in the equilibrium level of supply and demand.

III. Lower prices charged by competitors.

IV. Higher marketing costs.

    A. I and II only.

    B. I and IV only.

    C. II, III, and IV only.

    D. I, II, III, and IV.

Answer (D) is correct. *(Publisher, adapted)*
    REQUIRED: The costs likely to be incurred by an internal entrant.
    DISCUSSION: An internal entrant must cope with structural barriers and retaliation by existing firms. Costs incurred by the internal entrant include initial investments to overcome entry barriers (facilities, inventory, branding, technology, distribution channels, sources of materials, etc.), operating losses in the start-up phase, and the effects of retaliation (e.g., higher marketing costs, capacity expansion, or lower prices). Other costs include the price increases for factors of production that may result because of the new entry. Also, the capacity added to the industry by the entrant may affect the equilibrium level of supply and demand. The result may be additional competitive costs as firms with excess capacity cut prices.

8. Entry into a new business may be made by acquisition. The analysis differs from that for entry by internal development. A key point is that prices are set in the market for acquisitions. Accordingly, a buyer should **most** likely expect to make above-average profits when the

    A. Market is active and well organized.

    B. Seller can choose to continue operating the business.

    C. Market for acquisitions is imperfect.

    D. Buyer adopts a sequential entry strategy.

Answer (C) is correct. *(Publisher, adapted)*
    REQUIRED: The circumstances in which entry through acquisition is most likely to result in above-average profits.
    DISCUSSION: Acquisitions are more likely to earn above-average profits when the expected present value to the seller of continuing operations is low, e.g., because the seller needs funds, has capital limits, or has management weaknesses. Above-average profits also are more likely when the market for acquisitions is imperfect. For example, (1) the buyer may have better information, (2) there are few bidders, (3) the economy is weak, (4) the seller is weak, or (5) the seller has reasons to sell other than profit maximization. Moreover, the buyer may have a unique ability to operate the seller.
    Answer (A) is incorrect. When the market is active and well organized, it is also efficient and therefore tends to eliminate above-average profits. Answer (B) is incorrect. One factor contributing to efficiency (and the elimination of above-average profits for a buyer) is that a seller normally can choose to continue running the business. Accordingly, a bidder ordinarily must pay the seller a premium in excess of the expected present value to the seller of continuing operations. The price minus that floor value equals the premium. Answer (D) is incorrect. Sequential entry may be the best entry strategy. It involves entering one strategic group in the industry with subsequent mobility to another group(s). However, sequential entry is less likely to result in above-average profits than the existence of market imperfections.

Use the additional questions in Gleim *CIA Test Prep* Software to create Test Sessions that emulate Pearson VUE!

STUDY UNIT FIVE
GLOBAL BUSINESS ISSUES

(13 pages of outline)

Globalization has progressed rapidly because of advances in communications, information technology, transportation, and trade liberalization. Accordingly, The IIA has added the global environment to the CIA exam syllabus.

5.1 ASPECTS OF GLOBAL BUSINESS DEVELOPMENT

In the 2000s, globalization of the world's economic system accelerated. Thus, besides such technical issues as exchange rates and tax differences, internal auditors also must be aware of the cultural aspects of global business. They affect marketing, human resource management, and many other aspects of commercial activity.

Overview

1. **Globalization** is driven by the **digital revolution** that facilitates international commerce by providing capabilities that did not exist relatively few years ago. It is also driven by such **political events** as the fall of the Soviet Union in the 1990s, the growth of China as an economic power, the emergence of other economic powers (e.g., India and Brazil), the expansion of the European Union, and the creation of other regional free trade zones.

   a. These technological and political factors are intertwined with **social changes**. They include (1) greater concern for the rights of women and minorities; (2) the advance of multilingualism; and (3) the convergence of tastes in fashion, music, and certain other cultural factors.

   b. Accordingly, these factors favor globalization by reducing trade barriers, reducing costs of coordination, increasing economies of scale, and encouraging standardization and global branding.

Methods of Expanding into International Markets

2. Methods of expanding into international markets include the following:

   a. **Licensing** gives firms in foreign countries the right to produce or market products or services within a geographical area for a fee.

      1) Licensing a process, patent, trade secret, etc., is a way to enter a foreign market with little immediate risk. However,

         a) The licensor may have insufficient control over the licensee's operations,
         b) The licensor loses profits if the arrangement succeeds, and
         c) The licensee ultimately may become a competitor.

   b. **Exporting** is the sale of goods manufactured in one country and then sold in other countries.

   c. In a **local storage and sale arrangement**, products manufactured in one country are then shipped to a marketing facility located in another country.

   d. **Local component assembly** involves shipping individual parts from one country to an assembly facility in a second country. They are then turned into a salable product and sold in the second country or exported to other countries.

e.   In **multiple or joint ventures**, several firms, even competitors, work together to create products that are sold under one or more brand names in different countries. They share responsibility, ownership, costs, and profits.

f.   An **indirect export strategy** operates through intermediaries, such as

1)   Home-country merchants who buy and resell the product,

2)   Home-country agents who negotiate transactions with foreign buyers for a commission,

3)   Cooperatives that represent groups of sellers, and

4)   Export-management firms that receive fees for administering the firm's export efforts.

g.   **Indirect export** requires lower investment than direct export and is less risky because of the intermediaries' expertise.

h.   **Direct investment** has many advantages and risks.

1)   The advantages include

a)   Cheaper materials or labor,

b)   Receipt of investment incentives from the host government,

c)   A strong relationship with interested parties in the host country,

d)   Control of the investment,

e)   A better image in the host country, and

f)   Market access when domestic content rules are in effect.

2)   Direct investment is risky because of

a)   Exposure to currency fluctuations,

b)   Expropriation,

c)   Potentially high exit barriers, and

d)   Restraints on sending profits out of the country.

i.   The **internationalization process** is of crucial interest to nations that wish to encourage local firms to grow and to operate globally. According to Swedish researchers, it involves the following steps:

1)   Lack of regular exports;

2)   Export via independent agents to a few markets, with later expansion to more countries;

3)   Creation of sales subsidiaries in larger markets; and

4)   Establishment of plants in foreign countries.

j.   **Attractiveness** of a foreign market is a function of such factors as geography, income, climate, population, the product, and the unmet needs of the market.

1)   Entry into a market abroad may be based on many factors, for example, **psychic proximity**. Thus, a first-time venture abroad might be in a market with a related culture, language, or laws.

Limited Entry

3.   According to Ayal and Zif, the following are factors indicating that few national markets should be entered:

a.   Entry costs are high;

b.   Market control costs are high;

c.   Product adaptation costs are high;

d.   Communication adaptation costs are high;

e.   The first countries selected have large populations, high income, and a high rate of growth; and

f.   A dominant firm can erect high entry barriers.

Organizational Progression of Marketing

4. International marketing has three broad stages:

   a. **Export division.** This is the first step for an organization when it begins selling products beyond its own borders. Generally, a firm's initial entry is in other markets that share a common language or similar cultural norms.

   b. **International division.** Large corporations make this step before becoming true global organizations. They generally focus their efforts in certain geographical regions that are led either from a central structure or are locally run and managed.

      1) Moreover, operating units report to the head of the division, not to a CEO or executive committee. Operating units may be geographical units, world product groups, or subsidiaries.

   c. **Global organization.** All elements of the organization are directed toward creating and selling products to a worldwide market. Thus, all elements of the firm can be made to be more efficient in the global arena.

      1) These elements include management, production facilities, and the procurement of raw materials and components.

      2) **Glocalization** of a global organization localizes some of its elements but standardizes other elements.

Comparative and Competitive Advantage

5. Porter's model describes the following elements:

   a. A country has a **comparative advantage** when it can achieve a lower cost of production due to a focus on, and a cooperative specialization in, a particular product.

   b. A firm has a **competitive advantage** when it can achieve a lower cost of production on particular items compared with firms in another country because of local factors. **Sources of competitive advantage** include

      1) A lower cost of production through natural resources or geography,
      2) Quality or market factor differences, and
      3) Supplementary supply patterns that enhance production advantages.

   c. For more on global competition, see Subunit 5.4.

Factors of National Advantage

6. The following are **Porter's four determinants** of why firms in some countries are more successful than others.

   a. The **diamond model** for determining factors of national advantage can be used by firms to identify their home-country advantages. It also can be used by governments to develop policies to create national advantages industries can exploit.

      1) **Factor conditions** are specific production factors that include skilled labor, infrastructure, etc. Firms in each country naturally select those industries that give them an advantage due to their unique factor conditions.

      2) **Home demand conditions** determine the inherent demand for goods or services that originate within the home country. Porter believes that home markets exert a much higher influence on a firm's ability to recognize consumer trends than those in a foreign market.

      3) **Related and supporting industries** determine whether industries within the home country provide support for a given industry. Firms in countries that have a close-knit group of industries that support each other have an advantage over firms in other nations that do not.

      4)   **Firm strategy, structure, and rivalry.** How much firms work together or compete with each other can determine the advantage firms in a particular nation may have over others. Also, organizational structure, how firms are established, and how they are managed contribute to effectiveness in the global business environment.

Strategies for Global Marketing Organization

    7.   Three strategy types are generally recognized:

      a.   A **multinational strategy** adopts a portfolio approach. Its emphasis is on national markets because the need for global integration is not strong, and the driving forces of localization (cultural, commercial, and technical) predominate.

          1)   The product is customized for each market and therefore incurs higher production costs.
          2)   Decision making is primarily local with a minimum of central control.
          3)   This strategy is most effective given large differences between countries.
          4)   Also, exchange rate risk is reduced when conducting business in this manner.

      b.   A **global strategy** regards the world as one market. Among its determinants are ambition, positioning, and organization.

          1)   The product is essentially the same in all countries.
          2)   Central control of the production process is relatively strong.
          3)   Faster product development and lower production costs are typical.

      c.   A **glocal strategy** seeks the benefits of localization (flexibility, proximity, and adaptability) and global integration.

          1)   Successful telecommunications firms are examples of balancing these elements of localization and global integration.
          2)   **Local responsiveness** is indicated when local product tastes and preferences, regulations, and barriers are significant.
          3)   **Global integration** is indicated when demand is homogeneous and economies of productive scale are large.

Global vs. Transnational Firms

    8.   Global and transnational firms can be distinguished as follows:

      a.   **Global firms** are primarily managed from one central country. Even though their products may be sold throughout the world, their headquarters and most of their policy decisions are set from a central base of operations.

          1)   According to Kotler, "Global firms plan, operate, and coordinate their activities on a worldwide basis." Thus, a global firm secures cost or product differentiation advantages not available to domestic firms.

      b.   **Transnational firms** lack a national identity, but they rely on a decentralized structure for management and decision-making.

          1)   They tend to be more aware of local customs and market forces because they take much more of their input from a local or regional management team.

International Trade Practices

    9.   Three important aspects of international trade are as follows:

      a.   **Regional Free Trade Zones**

          1)   The **European Union (EU)** is a group of 27 European nations that have lowered trade barriers among member states, 17 of which share a common currency and trade policy.

2) The nations bound by the **North American Free Trade Agreement (NAFTA)** are the U.S., Mexico, and Canada. NAFTA may be expanded into South American countries.

3) **Mercosul** is a free-trade agreement among South American nations. They include Argentina, Brazil, Uruguay, and Paraguay. Chile and Bolivia are associate members.

4) **APEC** (the Asian Pacific Economic Cooperation forum) is a collection of Pacific-rim nations, including the NAFTA countries, China, and Japan, dedicated to promoting increased trade with each other and the rest of the world.

b.   **Cartels.** A cartel is an organization of sellers (e.g., the oil cartel OPEC) who undertake joint action to maximize members' profits by controlling the supply, and therefore the price, of their product.

1) In many nations, such conduct is illegal. The reason is that the monopolistic and anticompetitive practices of cartels reduce supply, raise prices, and limit competition. Also, the relevant industry tends to be less efficient.

c.   **Dumping.** Dumping is an unfair trade practice that violates international agreements.

1) It occurs when a firm charges a price (a) lower than that in its home market or (b) less than the cost to make the product.

2) Dumping may be done to penetrate a market or as a result of export subsidies.

Core Concepts

- The methods of expanding into international markets include (1) licensing, (2) exporting, (3) local storage and sale arrangements, (4) local component assembly, (5) multiple or joint ventures, (6) indirect export, and (7) direct investment.

- The organizational progression of international marketing is from establishment of an export division to an international division to global organization. Glocalization of a global organization localizes some of its elements but standardizes others.

- A country has a comparative advantage when it can achieve a lower cost of production due to a focus on, and a cooperative specialization in, a particular product. A firm has a competitive advantage when it can achieve a lower cost of production on particular items compared with firms in another country because of local factors.

- Porter's diamond model for determining factors of national advantage can be used by firms to identify their home-country advantages and by governments to develop policies to create national advantages industries can exploit.

- A multinational global marketing strategy adopts a portfolio approach. Its emphasis is on national markets because the need for global integration is not strong. A global strategy regards the world as one market. A glocal strategy combines some elements of local responsiveness or adaptation with some elements of global integration.

- International trade practices have given rise to regional free trade zones. These include the European Union (EU), North American Free Trade Agreement (NAFTA), Mercosul in South America, and APEC (Asian Pacific Economic Cooperation forum).

- A cartel is an organization of sellers (e.g., the oil cartel OPEC) who undertake joint action to maximize members' profits by controlling the supply, and therefore the price, of their product.

Stop and review! You have completed the outline for this subunit. Study multiple-choice questions 1 through 10 beginning on page 120.

5.2 GLOBAL MARKETING ISSUES

International Marketing Programs

1. Firms that operate globally must choose a marketing program after considering the need for adaptation to local circumstances. The possibilities lie on a continuum from a purely **standardized marketing mix** to a purely **adapted marketing mix**.

    a. The first chooses to standardize products, promotion, and distribution. The second adapts the elements of the mix to each local market.

        1) Worldwide standardization of all elements should be the lowest cost marketing strategy. However, even well-established global brands ordinarily undergo some adaptation to local markets.

    b. Warren Keegan describes strategies for **product and promotion**.

        1) Using a **straight extension** strategy, a higher profit potential exists because virtually no changes are made in the product or its promotion.

            a) But the risk is that foreign consumers may not be familiar with this type of product or readily accept it.

        2) Using a **product adaptation** strategy, a firm makes changes in the product for each market but not in its promotion. This strategy may reduce potential profit but also may provide a marketing advantage by considering local wants and needs.

        3) Using a **product invention** strategy, a new product is created specifically for a certain country or regional market. A product may either include advancements for developed countries or have certain elements removed in places where a lower cost is important.

            a) **Backward invention** is the reintroduction of an earlier version of the product to meet local needs. This variation of the invention strategy reflects the possibility that different countries may be in different stages of the international product life cycle.

            b) **Forward invention** requires developing a new product for the unique needs of a foreign market.

        4) **Communication adaptation** is a strategy that does not change the product, but advertising and marketing campaigns are changed to reflect the local culture and beliefs.

        5) A **dual adaptation** strategy changes both the product and the promotion to provide the best chance of acceptance in a foreign market.

    c. **Price**

        1) The gray market is a problem for a firm that sells products at different prices in different countries.

            a) In a **gray market**, products imported from one country to another are sold in a third country or even in the original exporter's country. The purpose is to make a profit from differences in retail prices.

                i) These activities clearly lower the profits in some markets of the firm that was the initial seller.

            b) One response is to **monitor** the practices of distributors and retaliate if necessary.

            c) A second response is to charge **higher prices** to the low-cost distributors to reduce their incentives to participate in a gray market.

            d) A third response is to **differentiate products** sold in different countries, e.g., by adapting the product or offering distinct service features.

2) The **price escalation** problem requires setting different prices in different countries.

    a) Price escalation is caused by an accumulation of additional costs, for example,

        i) Changes in currency exchange rates;
        ii) Transportation expenses;
        iii) Profits earned by importers, wholesalers, and retailers; and
        iv) Import duties.

    b) Three strategies address this issue:

        i) A firm may set a **standard price** globally. However, this strategy may result in prices being unprofitable in some markets and too high in others.

        ii) A firm may set a **market-based price** in each market. The weakness of this strategy is that it ignores cost differences. It also may create a gray market between certain regions.

        iii) A firm may set a **cost-based price** in each market with a standard markup. In a region or country where costs are high, this strategy may result in prices that are too high to be competitive within the local market.

3) A **transfer price** is the price charged by one subunit of a firm to another. When the subsidiary-buyer is in a foreign country, the higher the transfer price, the higher the potential tariffs.

    a) However, the tax levied on a subsequent sale by the subsidiary will be lower because of its higher acquisition cost.

d. **Distribution channels** are a necessity to ensure goods are successfully transferred from the production facility to end users. These channels include three distinct links that must work well together.

1) The **international marketing headquarters** (export department or international division) is where decisions are made about the subsequent channels and other aspects of the marketing mix.

2) **Channels between nations** carry goods to foreign borders. They include air, land, sea, or rail transportation channels.

    a) At this stage, in addition to transportation methods, intermediaries are selected (e.g., agents or trading companies), and financing and risk management decisions are reached.

3) **Channels within nations** take the goods from the border or entry point to the ultimate users of the products.

    a) Among nations, the number of the levels of distribution, the types of channels, and the size of retailers vary substantially.

Steps to Brand Globally

2. The following steps should be taken to minimize the risks of expanding into foreign markets and to maximize growth potential:

a. A firm must understand how diverse markets connect to form a **global branding landscape**. Individual countries vary in their historical acceptance of products and services.

1) However, firms also may capitalize on similarities that are found in certain areas and regions.

    b.   Branding and brand-building must be a process. New markets must be developed where none previously existed.

        1)   Thus, global firms must build awareness of the product and then create sources of **brand equity**.

    c.   Establishing a **marketing infrastructure** is crucial. To create a successful marketing structure, the firm either must merge with the local marketing channels or create a completely new method of distribution.

    d.   **Integrated marketing communications** should be developed. Markets must be approached with a broad range of messages, and sole reliance on advertising should be avoided.

        1)   Other marketing communications include merchandising, promotions, and sponsorship.

    e.   The firm may create **branding partnerships**. Global firms often form alliances with local distribution channels to increase their profitability while decreasing their marketing costs.

    f.   The firm should determine the **ratio of standardization and customization**. Products that can be sold virtually unchanged throughout several markets provide a greater profit opportunity for a global firm.

        1)   However, cultural differences may require extensive customization to appeal to markets in different countries.

    g.   The firm should determine the **ratio of local to global control**. Local managers may understand the wants and needs of their market, but the global firm must still retain control of certain elements of the marketing process and strategy.

    h.   The firm should establish **local guidelines** so that local sales and profit goals are met.

    i.   The firm should create a **global brand equity tracking system**. This equity system is a set of research processes that provide the marketers with pertinent information.

        1)   The marketers can use this tracking system to create both long- and short-term strategies for expanding product sales and reach.

    j.   The firm should maximize **brand elements**. Large global firms can achieve much greater expansion rates when the brand elements are successfully employed at the launch of a product or service.

Core Concepts

- Product and promotion strategies in international marketing include (1) straight extension, (2) product adaptation, (3) product invention, (4) communication adaptation, and (5) dual adaptation.

- Firms engaged in global marketing may set (1) a standard price globally, (2) a market-based price in each market, or (3) a cost-based price in each market with a standard markup. The gray market and price escalation are issues.

- Distribution channels include distinct links that must work well together: (1) the international marketing headquarters where decisions are made about the subsequent channels and other aspects of the marketing mix, (2) channels between nations that carry goods to foreign borders, and (3) channels within nations that take goods from the border or entry point to ultimate users.

- Steps to brand globally include (1) forming a global branding landscape, (2) creating sources of brand equity, (3) establishing a marketing infrastructure, (4) developing integrated marketing communications, (5) creating branding partnerships, (6) determining the ratios of standardization-customization and local-to-global control, (7) establishing local sales and profit guidelines, (8) creating a global brand equity tracking system, and (9) maximizing brand elements.

Stop and review! You have completed the outline for this subunit. Study multiple-choice questions 11 through 20 beginning on page 123.

5.3 LEADERSHIP IN GLOBAL OPERATIONS

1. The most important characteristic of a successful leader has been determined to be the ability to develop additional leaders within his/her own team. The following are other **common characteristics of successful leaders in global organizations**:

    a. Extensive international travel during childhood prior to entering the working world.

    b. Influence and encouragement by family.

    c. A series of events that shaped their belief systems to include a foundation of honesty and trustworthiness.

    d. Key learning experiences that instilled the ability to be flexible and adaptable in a variety of situations.

    e. Strong role models who emphasized the importance of being fair, consistent, and true to inner principles and beliefs.

    f. Effective interpersonal skills and the ability to communicate successfully with a variety of individuals.

    g. Ability to speak one or more additional languages and extensive exposure to nonnative cultures.

    h. Effective problem-solving skills that draw from a multidisciplinary approach. The best candidates have varied backgrounds and can draw on a multitude of life experiences.

2. Research has been conducted on different **leadership styles** in various countries.

    a. These leadership styles are based on the **path-goal** approach.

        1) A **directive style** establishes specific expectations, guidelines, schedules, rules, and standards.

        2) A **supportive style** regards employees as equals and attempts to improve their circumstances.

        3) A **participative style** involves consultation with employees and serious attention to their ideas.

        4) An **achievement-oriented style** sets high goals, emphasizes continuous improvement, and maintains confidence that employees will perform.

    b. The participative style, although not always the best, is the most widely accepted internationally.

    c. The directive style is the least accepted internationally. It was not deemed appropriate in the U.S., the U.K., Canada, Australia, Germany, and Sweden.

    d. The achievement-oriented style was found unacceptable in such countries as Brazil, France, Italy, and Japan.

    e. The supportive style was not accepted in such countries as Brazil, France, India, and Sweden.

3. Howard Perlmutter stresses the importance of **managerial attitudes toward global operations**.

    a. An **ethnocentric attitude** assumes that the home country's people, practices, and ideas are superior to all others. Thus, the firm's identification is with the owner's nationality.

        1) Authority and decision making are centralized, so communication is likely to involve a high volume of information flow in the form of orders and advice to subsidiaries.

        2) Home-country standards are likely to be used for performance evaluation of entities and individuals.

3) The ethnocentric attitude is perpetuated by recruiting and developing home-country individuals for key posts throughout the firm.

4) The advantages of an ethnocentric attitude are simplicity and close control. The disadvantages are

    a) Social and political problems in foreign countries,
    b) Poor feedback,
    c) Ineffective planning,
    d) Lack of flexibility and innovative thinking, and
    e) High turnover of managers in foreign subsidiaries.

b. A **polycentric attitude** assumes that cultural differences require local managers to make most decisions because they are more knowledgeable about local conditions than are central administrators.

1) Thus, development of local managerial talent is crucial, and operating performance is primarily evaluated based on results.

    a) Consequently, methods, training, and incentives vary significantly among subsidiaries.

2) Furthermore,

    a) Control is predominantly local,
    b) The firm is identified with the nationality of the host nation, and
    c) Relatively little communication occurs with central administration or among subsidiaries.

3) One disadvantage is that local operations may have inefficiencies because of duplication of activities.

    a) Another disadvantage is that the goals of local entities may not be consistent with those of the firm as a whole.

4) Advantages are

    a) More capable and motivated local managers,
    b) Better results in local markets,
    c) Local development of new product ideas, and
    d) Stronger support by host governments.

c. A **geocentric attitude** is truly internationally oriented while absorbing the best that various cultures offer.

1) It is a completely balanced approach with the following qualities:

    a) Full collaboration between central administrators and subsidiaries,
    b) Control and evaluation methods that harmonize local and overall firm standards, and
    c) Frequent communication in all directions (i.e., between central administrators and subsidiaries and among subsidiaries).

2) Moreover, talent, not nationality, determines personnel decisions throughout the firm.

Core Concepts

- Varying leadership styles based on the path-goal approach have been researched. These include (1) a directive style that establishes specific expectations guidelines, schedules, rules, and standards; (2) a supportive style that regards employees as equals and attempts to improve their circumstances; (3) a participative style that involves consultation with employees and serious attention to their ideas; and (4) an achievement-oriented style that sets high goals, emphasizes continuous improvement, and maintains confidence that employees will perform.
- Managerial attitudes toward global operations differ. An ethnocentric attitude assumes that the home country's people, practices, and ideas are superior to all others. A polycentric attitude assumes that cultural differences require managers to make most decisions because they are more knowledgeable about local conditions than are central administrators. A geocentric attitude is truly internationally oriented while absorbing the best that various cultures offer.

Stop and review! You have completed the outline for this subunit. Study multiple-choice questions 21 through 26 beginning on page 126.

5.4 HUMAN RESOURCES ISSUES IN GLOBAL OPERATIONS

Overview

1. **Cross-cultural differences** are important for global firms. Edward T. Hall defined **culture** as "a population's taken-for-granted assumptions, values, beliefs, and symbols that foster patterned behavior" (see Kreitner, *Management*, 9th ed.).

    a. In international business, misunderstanding and conflict arise because people from different cultures have fundamentally different assumptions, values, etc.

2. Hall made a distinction between high-context and low-context cultures.

    a. In **high-context cultures** (e.g., Japanese, Chinese, Arabic, and Korean), much meaning is transmitted by nonverbal cues and situational circumstances.

        1) Thus, a person's status in a firm, rank in society, and reputation convey the primary message.

    b. In **low-context cultures** (e.g., Northern European and North American), primary messages are transmitted verbally.

        1) Accordingly, precise written contractual agreements are highly valued in a low-context culture.

            a) In contrast, social events are more valued in a high-context culture.

Other Causes of Cultural Diversity

3. Differences in cultures are apparent in multiple areas.

    a. **Individualistic cultures** are societies that place a higher value on the rights and accomplishments of individual persons within the society. Examples are the U.S., the U.K., Canada, and Australia.

        1) **Collectivist cultures** focus much more on the goals of family, friends, country, and the organization. Examples are China, India, Mexico, Japan, and Egypt.

    b. The perception of time as it relates to business and social life varies with the culture.

        1) **Polychronic time** is based on a perception that time is nonlinear, flexible, and multidimensional. This perception is typical of Mediterranean, Latin American, and Arabic cultures.

2)   **Monochronic time** is based on a perception that time is the same for everyone and is measurable in standard units. This perception is common in Northern Europe and the U.S.

   a)   These western cultures believe in punctuality and that time should not be wasted.

c.   **Interpersonal space** varies from only a few inches to several feet. Managers must be aware of these distances because they may be dramatically different from culture to culture.

   1)   For example, Northern Europeans and North Americans tend to prefer holding conversations at arm's length.

   2)   In Arabic and Asian cultures, however, the preferred conversational distance may be only 6 inches.

d.   Because of the **differences in language** even within the same country, special care must be taken not to make mistakes or offend others in a foreign land.

   1)   It is nearly impossible for someone who has studied a foreign language only briefly to understand its subtleties.

e.   Global firms must respect local **religious beliefs and customs** to be successful. For example, local religious holidays, days off from work, and food restrictions should be understood.

How American Management Theories Work in Other Countries

4.   Dutch researcher Geert Hofstede has compared and contrasted the management characteristics of American managers with prevailing styles in 40 other countries.

a.   The following are the four cultural dimensions Hofstede used to categorize his results:

   1)   **Power distance** is the degree of acceptance of unequal distribution of power in an organization.

   2)   **Uncertainty avoidance** concerns the extent of the threat posed by ambiguous circumstances, the significance of rules, and the pressure for conformity.

   3)   The **individualism-collectivism** dimension addresses whether the organization protects its members in return for their loyalty or the individual must meet his/her own security needs.

   4)   The **masculinity versus femininity** dimension is the balance of masculine traits (aggressiveness, acquisitions, and performance) compared with the traditionally female traits (concern for others and the quality of life).

b.   The U.S. received a low ranking on uncertainty avoidance, a less low ranking on power distance, a high ranking on masculinity, and the highest ranking on individualism.

   1)   The conclusion, given the wide variance of these results with those for many other countries, is that American management theories need to be altered when applied in other countries.

5.   Americans experience a high rate of failure when living and working abroad primarily as a result of not being adequately prepared to succeed within the new culture. Failure does not usually result from technical incompetence.

a.   American firms will probably enjoy greater success if they better prepare their executives for cultural differences.

Training for Work in a Foreign Culture

6. Any training program for those working internationally should contain the following:

   a. **Documentary programs** provide text-based or videotape preview of the history, culture, institutions, beliefs, and economy of the foreign country.

   b. **Cultural assimilation practice** is similar to role-play techniques that are frequently used to train salespeople. Problem scenarios are presented to managers and workers, and they are coached on how to respond to them.

   c. **Language instruction** is provided by various means to senior executives and mid-level managers who are now expected to learn the language of the country where they will be working.

      1) Some languages take years, not months, to master, but multilingual ability is a necessity.

   d. **Sensitivity training** is focused mainly on educating workers about the beliefs and mores of the foreign country. Special care is given to topics that might bring embarrassment to a manager or offend his/her hosts.

   e. **Experience in the field** involves actually traveling to the foreign country and interacting with its people. Usually, one or more guides are available to answer questions and provide feedback.

   f. A firm's **management training** for work in a foreign country should be part of a planned career path that includes selection, orientation and training, and repatriation (professional and cultural readjustment).

      1) The last step includes a commitment from the firm that the manager will not be at a professional disadvantage because of his/her work abroad.

         a) The process also should address the needs of families.

Core Concepts

- Cross-cultural differences are important for global firms. Edward T. Hall defined culture as "a population's taken-for-granted assumptions, values, beliefs, and symbols that foster patterned behavior." Hall made a distinction between high-context and low-context cultures. In high-context cultures (e.g., Japanese, Chinese, Arabic, and Korean), much meaning is transmitted by nonverbal cues and situational circumstances. In low-context cultures (e.g., Northern European and North American), primary messages are transmitted verbally.

- Dutch researcher Geert Hofstede used four cultural dimensions to categorize his results regarding how American management theories work in other countries: (1) power distance, (2) uncertainty avoidance, (3) the individualism-collectivism dimension, and (4) the masculinity versus femininity dimension.

Stop and review! You have completed the outline for this subunit. Study multiple-choice questions 27 through 30 on page 128.

QUESTIONS

5.1 Aspects of Global Business Development

1. Which of the following is the **most** significant reason that domestic governments and international organizations seek to eliminate cartels?

   A. The increased sales price reduces the amount of corporate tax revenues payable to the government.

   B. True competition keeps prices as low as possible, thus increasing efficiency in the marketplace.

   C. Small businesses cannot survive or grow without government protection.

   D. The economic stability of developing countries depends on a global free market.

Answer (B) is correct. *(CIA, adapted)*
REQUIRED: The best reason to eliminate cartels.
DISCUSSION: A cartel is an organization of sellers (e.g., the oil cartel OPEC) who undertake joint action to maximize members' profits by controlling the supply, and therefore the price, of their product. Under the laws of many nations, such conduct is illegal when engaged in by firms subject to those laws. The reason is that, as a result of the monopolistic and anticompetitive practices of cartels, supply is lower, prices are higher, competition is limited, and the relevant industry is less efficient. Accordingly, governmental and international organizations seek to protect consumers and the health of the domestic and global economy through anti-cartel efforts.
   Answer (A) is incorrect. An increased sales price would raise corporate profits. Thus, the tax revenue lost through eliminating cartel activity would serve as a disincentive to government anti-cartel efforts. Answer (C) is incorrect. Although the effect of cartel activities may be harmful to small businesses, the greatest impact is on the overall economy. Macroeconomic effects are the primary reasons for anti-cartel efforts by governments and international organizations. Answer (D) is incorrect. The contribution of a free market to the stability of developing countries' economies does not provide a compelling reason for domestic anti-cartel efforts in industrialized countries.

2. When a multinational firm decides to sell its products abroad, one of the risks the firm faces is that the government of the foreign market charges the firm with dumping. Dumping occurs when

   A. The same product sells at different prices in different countries.

   B. A firm charges less than the cost to make the product so as to enter or win a market.

   C. Lower quality versions of the product are sold abroad so as to be affordable.

   D. Transfer prices are set artificially high so as to minimize tax payments.

Answer (B) is correct. *(CIA, adapted)*
REQUIRED: The nature of dumping.
DISCUSSION: Dumping is an unfair trade practice that violates international agreements. It occurs when a firm charges a price (1) lower than that in its home market or (2) less than the cost to make the product. Dumping may be done to penetrate a market or as a result of export subsidies.
   Answer (A) is incorrect. In a gray market, the same product sells at different prices in different countries. The effect differs from that of dumping. A seller in a low-price market tries to sell the goods in a higher-price market. Unlike the dumping case, the objective is not to penetrate a market. Instead, a dealer seeks to resell at a favorable price. Answer (C) is incorrect. Selling a lower quality product at a fair price is a perfectly acceptable strategy. Answer (D) is incorrect. A transfer price is a price charged to a subunit of an enterprise. Setting a high price to avoid an unfavorable tax rate has the opposite effect of dumping, assuming the subunit passes the cost on to its customers.

3. A global firm

   A. Has achieved economies of scale in the firm's domestic market.

   B. Plans, operates, and coordinates business globally.

   C. Relies on indirect export.

   D. Tends to rely more on one product market.

Answer (B) is correct. *(Publisher, adapted)*
REQUIRED: The nature of a global firm.
DISCUSSION: According to Kotler, "Global firms plan, operate, and coordinate their activities on a worldwide basis." Thus, a global firm secures cost or product differentiation advantages not available to domestic firms.
   Answer (A) is incorrect. One reason to go abroad is that economies of scale are so great that they cannot be achieved in a domestic market. Answer (C) is incorrect. Global firms do not rely only on indirect export. They also rely on direct export, which is potentially more profitable. Answer (D) is incorrect. A global firm may be a small firm that sells one product or class of products, or it may be a large firm with a multiproduct line.

4. A firm wishing to become global must consider how many national markets to enter. A firm should enter fewer national markets when

   A. Communication adaptation costs are low.

   B. The product need not be adapted.

   C. Entry costs are low.

   D. The first countries chosen are heavily populated and have high incomes.

Answer (D) is correct. *(Publisher, adapted)*
   REQUIRED: The reason for a global firm to enter fewer national markets.
   DISCUSSION: According to Ayal and Zif, the following are factors indicating that few national markets should be entered: (1) entry costs are high; (2) market control costs are high; (3) product adaptation costs are high; (4) communication adaptation costs are high; (5) the first countries selected have large populations, high incomes, and high income growth; and (6) a dominant firm can erect high entry barriers.
   Answer (A) is incorrect. Low communication adaptation costs argue operations in many countries. Answer (B) is incorrect. Low product adaptation costs argue for operations in many countries. Answer (C) is incorrect. Low entry costs argue for operations in many countries.

5. The **least** risky method of entering a market in a foreign country is by

   A. Indirect exports.

   B. Licensing.

   C. Direct exports.

   D. Direct investments.

Answer (A) is correct. *(Publisher, adapted)*
   REQUIRED: The least risky method of entering a market in a foreign country.
   DISCUSSION: An indirect export strategy operates through intermediaries, such as home-country merchants who buy and resell the product, home-country agents who negotiate transactions with foreign buyers for a commission, cooperatives that represent groups of sellers, and export-management firms that receive fees for administering the firm's export efforts. Indirect export requires lower investment than direct export and is less risky because of the intermediaries' expertise.
   Answer (B) is incorrect. Licensing a process, patent, trade secret, etc., is a way to gain a foothold in a foreign market with little immediate risk. However, the licensor may have insufficient control over the licensee's operations, profits are lost if the arrangement succeeds, and the licensee ultimately may become a competitor. Answer (C) is incorrect. Direct export involves higher risk and investment but may yield higher returns. Answer (D) is incorrect. Direct investment has many advantages: (1) cheaper materials or labor, (2) receipt of investment incentives from the host government, (3) a strong relationship with interested parties in the host country, (4) control of the investment, (5) a better image in the host country, and (6) market access when domestic contest rules are in effect. However, direct investment is risky because of exposure to currency fluctuations, expropriation, potentially high exit barriers, and restraints on sending profits out of the country.

6. An advantage of a direct investment strategy when entering a foreign market is

   A. Reduction in the capital at risk.

   B. Shared control and responsibility.

   C. Assurance of access when the foreign country imposes domestic content rules.

   D. Avoidance of interaction with the local bureaucracy.

Answer (C) is correct. *(Publisher, adapted)*
   REQUIRED: The advantage of direct investment.
   DISCUSSION: Direct investment has many advantages: (1) cheaper materials or labor, (2) receipt of investment incentives from the host government, (3) a strong relationship with interested parties in the host country, (4) control of the investment, (5) a better image in the host country, and (6) market access when domestic contest rules are in effect. However, direct investment is risky because of exposure to currency fluctuations, expropriation, potentially high exit barriers, and restraints on sending profits out of the country.
   Answer (A) is incorrect. Direct investment maximizes capital at risk. Answer (B) is incorrect. Direct investment avoids shared control and responsibility. Answer (D) is incorrect. Direct investment means a closer relationship with governmental entities in the host country.

7. A firm that moves from not exporting on a regular basis to establishing plants in foreign countries has

A. Globalized.

B. Nationalized.

C. Glocalized.

D. Internationalized.

Answer (D) is correct. *(Publisher, adapted)*
REQUIRED: The process of moving from not exporting on a regular basis to establishing plants in foreign countries.
DISCUSSION: The internationalization process is of crucial interest to nations that wish to encourage local firms to grow and to operate globally. According to Swedish researchers, it involves the following steps: (1) Lack of regular exports; (2) export via independent agents with a few markets, with later expansion to more countries; (3) creation of sales subsidiaries in larger markets; and (4) establishment of plants in foreign countries.
Answer (A) is incorrect. All elements of a global organization are geared toward selling in a worldwide market. Answer (B) is incorrect. Nationalization is the takeover of an industry by a national government. Answer (C) is incorrect. Glocalization of a global organization localizes some of its elements but standardizes other elements.

8. The inherent attractiveness of a national market is **most** likely increased by which factor?

A. The firm's strategic position.

B. The market's exclusion from a regional free trade zone.

C. Unmet needs of a developing nation.

D. Product adaptation is costly.

Answer (C) is correct. *(Publisher, adapted)*
REQUIRED: The factor most likely increasing market attractiveness.
DISCUSSION: Attractiveness is a function of such factors as geography, income, climate, population, and the product. Another major factor is the unmet needs of a developing nation, for example, China or India.
Answer (A) is incorrect. The inherent attractiveness of a national market is primarily determined by its characteristics. Answer (B) is incorrect. Given the emergence of regional free trade blocs (e.g., the European Union, APEC, or Mercosul), a firm is more likely to enter a regional rather than a purely national market. Answer (D) is incorrect. Low adaptation costs are attractive.

9. A firm considering entry into a market abroad may make the selection based on many criteria. For example, a Portuguese firm applying a psychic proximity criterion will **most** likely choose to enter which market?

A. Afghanistan.

B. China.

C. India.

D. Brazil.

Answer (D) is correct. *(Publisher, adapted)*
REQUIRED: The market chosen on the basis of psychic proximity.
DISCUSSION: Psychic proximity means the nearness of the market's culture, language, and laws to those of the firm's home country. For example, Portuguese is spoken in Brazil.

10. The creation of regional free trade zones is a global phenomenon. Trade barriers are lowered in these areas, and other steps are taken to promote economic cooperation. For example, a common currency has been adopted by the nations of

A. NAFTA.

B. Mercosul.

C. APEC.

D. The European Union.

Answer (D) is correct. *(Publisher, adapted)*
REQUIRED: The nations that have adopted a common currency.
DISCUSSION: The European Union (EU) is a group of 27 European nations that have lowered trade barriers among member states, and most share a common currency and trade policy. The euro is the common currency of 17 members of the European Union.
Answer (A) is incorrect. The North American Free Trade Agreement (NAFTA) was created by the U.S., Mexico, and Canada. It will likely be expanded to South American countries. However, NAFTA does not provide for a common currency. Answer (B) is incorrect. Mercosul is a free-trade agreement of South American nations, which includes Argentina, Brazil, Uruguay, and Paraguay, with Chile and Bolivia as associate members. However, these nations have no common currency. Answer (C) is incorrect. APEC (the Asian Pacific Economic Cooperation forum) is a collection of Pacific-rim nations dedicated to promote increased trade with each other and the rest of the world. However, these nations have no common currency.

5.2 Global Marketing Issues

11. Firms that sell products worldwide are **most** likely to have the lowest costs with a marketing mix that is

- A. Adapted to each market.
- B. Standardized for all markets.
- C. A combination of new and adapted products in each market.
- D. A combination of standardized products and adapted promotions.

Answer (B) is correct. *(Publisher, adapted)*
REQUIRED: The marketing mix most likely to have the lowest costs.
DISCUSSION: Firms that operate globally must choose a marketing program after considering the need for adaptation to local circumstances. The possibilities lie on a continuum from a purely standardized marketing mix to a purely adapted marketing mix. The first chooses to standardize products, promotion, and distribution. The second adapts the elements of the mix to each local market. Worldwide standardization of all elements should be the lowest cost marketing strategy. However, even well-established global brands ordinarily undergo some adaptation to local markets.
Answer (A) is incorrect. Adaptation to each market incurs greater costs. Some economies of scale are lost. Answer (C) is incorrect. Pure standardization of products, promotion, and distribution is likely to be the lowest-cost, but not necessarily highest-revenue, strategy. Answer (D) is incorrect. Pure standardization of products, promotion, and distribution is likely to be the lowest-cost, but not necessarily highest-revenue, strategy.

12. A firm sells the same product in different countries and uses the same promotion methods. According to Keegan's model of adaptation strategies, this firm has adopted a strategy of

- A. Straight extension.
- B. Product adaptation.
- C. Product invention.
- D. Dual adaptation.

Answer (A) is correct. *(Publisher, adapted)*
REQUIRED: The adaptation strategy followed.
DISCUSSION: Using a straight extension strategy, a higher profit potential exists because virtually no changes are made in the products or its promotion. The risk is that foreign consumers may not be familiar with this type of product or readily accept it.
Answer (B) is incorrect. Using a product adaptation strategy, a firm makes changes to the product for each market but not its promotion. This can reduce profit potential but may also provide a marketing advantage by taking into account local wants and needs. Answer (C) is incorrect. Using a product invention strategy, a new product is created specifically for a certain country or regional market. A product may either include advancements for developed countries or have certain elements removed in places where a lower cost is a key selling point. Backward invention is the reintroduction of an earlier version of the product to meet local needs. This variant of the invention strategy reflects the possibility that different countries may be in different stages of the international product life cycle. Forward invention requires developing a new product for the unique needs of a foreign market. Answer (D) is incorrect. A dual adaptation strategy changes both the product and promotion to provide the best chance of acceptance in a foreign market.

13. A firm that manufactures refrigerators sold ice boxes in urban areas of less developed countries. Many residents lacked electricity to power refrigerators but could purchase blocks of ice from local vendors for use in ice boxes. According to Keegan's model of adaptation strategies, this firm adopted a strategy of

- A. Product adaptation.
- B. Dual adaptation.
- C. Backward invention.
- D. Forward invention.

Answer (C) is correct. *(Publisher, adapted)*
REQUIRED: The adaptation strategy followed.
DISCUSSION: Using a product invention strategy, a new product is created specifically for a certain country or regional market. A product may either include advancements for developed countries or have certain elements removed in places where a lower cost is important. Thus, an ice box, a precursor of the modern refrigerator, is a backward invention.
Answer (A) is incorrect. The refrigerator was not adapted. An older precursor product was reintroduced. Answer (B) is incorrect. Dual adaptation involves product adaptation, not invention. Answer (D) is incorrect. Forward invention is the development of a new product.

14. Gray market activity is in essence a form of arbitrage. To prevent this activity by their distributors, multinational firms

I.   Raise prices charged to lower-cost distributors.
II. Police the firms' distributors.
III. Change the product.

A. I only.

B. I and II only.

C. II and III only.

D. I, II, and III.

Answer (D) is correct.   *(Publisher, adapted)*
  REQUIRED: The reaction to gray market activities.
  DISCUSSION: In a gray market, products imported from one country to another are sold in a third country or even in the original exporter's country. The purpose is to make a profit from the difference in retail prices. These activities clearly lower the profits in some markets of the firm that was the initial seller. One response is to monitor the practices of distributors and retaliate if necessary. A second response is to charge higher prices to the low-cost distributors to reduce their incentives to participate in a gray market. A third response is to differentiate products sold in different countries, e.g., by adapting the product or offering distinct service features.

15. A firm buys new computer equipment from bankrupt companies and resells it in foreign markets at prices significantly below those charged by competitors. The firm is

A. Engaged in dumping.

B. Engaged in price discrimination.

C. Operating in a gray market.

D. Operating in a black market.

Answer (C) is correct.   *(Publisher, adapted)*
  REQUIRED: The term for sale in a higher-price market of goods acquired cheaply in another market.
  DISCUSSION: In a gray market, products imported from one country to another are sold in a third country or even in the original exporter's country. The purpose is to make a profit from the differences in retail prices. These activities clearly lower the profits in some markets of the firm that was the initial seller.
  Answer (A) is incorrect. Dumping is sale below cost or at less than the price charged in the home market. Answer (B) is incorrect. Price discrimination involves illegally selling the same products at different prices to different customers. Answer (D) is incorrect. Black market operations are illegal.

16. A firm ships its product to a foreign subsidiary and charges a price that may increase import duties but lower the income taxes paid by the subsidiary. The **most** likely reason for these effects is that the

A. Price is an arm's-length price.

B. Price is a cost-plus price.

C. Transfer price is too low.

D. Transfer price is too high.

Answer (D) is correct.   *(Publisher, adapted)*
  REQUIRED: The reason that sale to a subsidiary results in high import duties.
  DISCUSSION: A transfer price is the price charged by one subunit of a firm to another. When the subsidiary-buyer is in a foreign country, the higher the transfer, the higher the potential tariffs. However, the tax levied on a subsequent sale by the subsidiary will be lower because of its higher acquisition cost.
  Answer (A) is incorrect. An arm's-length price is what a competitor would charge in that market. Answer (B) is incorrect. A cost-plus price does not necessarily trigger higher import duties. Answer (C) is incorrect. If the transfer price is too low, import duties would be lower and taxes would be higher.

17. A global firm establishes a cost-based price for the firm's product in each country. The **most** likely negative outcome is that this pricing strategy will

A. Set too high a price in countries where the firm's costs are high.

B. Overprice the product in some markets and underprice the product in others.

C. Create a gray market.

D. Result in dumping.

Answer (A) is correct.   *(Publisher, adapted)*
  REQUIRED: The most likely negative result of a cost-based pricing strategy.
  DISCUSSION: A firm may set a cost-based price in each market with a standard markup. In a region or country where costs are high, this strategy may result in prices that are too high to be competitive within the local market.
  Answer (B) is incorrect. A uniform pricing policy may overprice the product in some markets and underprice it in others. Answer (C) is incorrect. Charging what consumers can afford in each country may create a gray market. Answer (D) is incorrect. Dumping often entails charging a below-cost price.

18. A firm sells its product in a foreign market for a much higher price than in the firm's home market. The reason is **most** likely

A. Price elasticity of demand.

B. Dumping.

C. Gray market activity.

D. Price escalation.

Answer (D) is correct. *(Publisher, adapted)*
   REQUIRED: The most likely reason for disparate prices in different national markets.
   DISCUSSION: Price escalation is caused by an accumulation of additional costs, for example, (1) changes in currency exchange rates; (2) transportation expenses; (3) profits earned by importers, wholesalers, and retailers; and (4) import duties.
   Answer (A) is incorrect. Price elasticity of demand is the relationship of total revenue to a change in price. If demand is price elastic, a price increase results in lower revenue. Answer (B) is incorrect. Dumping is sale at a price below cost or below the price in the home country. Answer (C) is incorrect. In a gray market, products imported from one country to another are sold by persons trying to make a profit from the difference in retail prices between the two countries.

19. A firm that sells in foreign markets should consider all aspects of how products move from the firm to ultimate users. Where in the whole channel are marketing mix decisions **most** likely made?

A. Export department of the seller firm.

B. Import department of the buyer firm.

C. Channels within nations.

D. Channels between nations.

Answer (A) is correct. *(Publisher, adapted)*
   REQUIRED: The place in an international marketing channel where marketing mix decisions are most likely made.
   DISCUSSION: Distribution channels are a necessity to ensure that goods are successfully transferred from the production facility to end users. These channels include three distinct links that must work well together.

1) The international marketing headquarters (export department of international division) is where decisions are made with regard to the subsequent channels and other aspects of the marketing mix.

2) Channels between nations carry goods to foreign borders. They include air, land, sea, or rail transportation channels. At this stage, in addition to transportation methods, intermediaries are selected (e.g., agents or trading companies) and financing and risk management decisions are reached.

3) Channels within nations take the goods from the border or entry point to the ultimate users of the products. Among nations, the number of levels of distribution, the types of channels, and the size of retailers vary substantially.

   Answer (B) is incorrect. The seller makes marketing-mix decisions. Answer (C) is incorrect. The seller's export department makes marketing-mix decisions. Answer (D) is incorrect. The seller's export department makes marketing-mix decisions.

20. Developing brand equity in a foreign market may be desirable but is subject to considerable risk. A global firm launching a new product in a new market **most** likely should

A. Initially place most of the firm's emphasis on advertising geared to the local culture.

B. Fully decentralize control of the marketing process.

C. Avoid creating partnerships with local distribution channels to avoid dilution of the brand.

D. Balance standardization and customization of the product.

Answer (D) is correct. *(Publisher, adapted)*
   REQUIRED: The most likely step taken by a global firm launching a new product in a new market.
   DISCUSSION: The firm should determine the ratio of standardization and customization. Products that can be sold virtually unchanged throughout several markets provide a greater profit opportunity for a global firm. However, cultural differences may require extensive customization to appeal to markets in different countries.
   Answer (A) is incorrect. Integrated marketing communications should be developed. Markets must be approached with a broad range of messages. Sole reliance on advertising should be avoided. Other marketing communications include merchandising, promotions, and sponsorship. Answer (B) is incorrect. The firm should determine the ratio of local to global control. Local managers may understand the wants and needs of their market, but the global firm must still retain control of certain elements of the marketing process and strategy. Answer (C) is incorrect. The firm may create branding partnerships. Global firms often form alliances with local distribution channels to increase their profitability while decreasing their marketing costs.

5.3 Leadership in Global Operations

21. Managerial attitudes toward global operations are viewed by researcher Howard Perlmutter as a key to understanding multinational firms. An ethnocentric attitude is indicated by

    A. An identification with the nationality of the host country.

    B. Collaboration between the firm's subsidiaries and the firm's central administration.

    C. A high volume of information flow in the form of orders and advice to subsidiaries.

    D. A staffing emphasis on finding and developing the best people in the world for key positions anywhere in the firm.

Answer (C) is correct. *(Publisher, adapted)*
    REQUIRED: The indicator of an ethnocentric attitude.
    DISCUSSION: An ethnocentric attitude assumes that the home country's people, practices, and ideas are superior to all others. Thus, the firm's identification is with the owner's nationality. Authority and decision making are centralized, so communication is likely to involve a high volume of information flow in the form of orders and advice to subsidiaries. Moreover, home-country standards are apt to be used for performance evaluation of entities and individuals. Also, this ethnocentric attitude is perpetuated by recruiting and developing home-country individuals for key posts throughout the firm. The advantages of an ethnocentric attitude are simplicity and close control. The disadvantages are social and political problems in foreign countries, poor feedback, ineffective planning, lack of flexibility and innovative thinking, and higher turnover of managers in foreign subsidiaries.
    Answer (A) is incorrect. A polycentric attitude is indicated by an identification with the nationality of the host country. An ethnocentric attitude is indicated by an identification with the nationality of the owner. Answer (B) is incorrect. A geocentric attitude is indicated by collaboration between the firm's subsidiaries and its central administration. Answer (D) is incorrect. A geocentric attitude is indicated by a staffing emphasis on finding and developing the best people in the world for key positions anywhere in the firm.

22. Managerial attitudes toward global operations are viewed by researcher Howard Perlmutter as a key to understanding multinational firms. A polycentric attitude is indicated by

    A. An identification with the nationality of the owner.

    B. Evaluation and control standards that are both local and global.

    C. High information flow in multiple directions.

    D. Relatively little decision making by the central administrative authority.

Answer (D) is correct. *(Publisher, adapted)*
    REQUIRED: The indicator of a polycentric attitude.
    DISCUSSION: A polycentric attitude assumes that cultural differences require local managers to make most decisions because they are more knowledgeable about local conditions than are central administrators. Thus, development of local managerial talent is crucial, and operating performance is primarily evaluated based on results. As a consequence, methods, training, and incentives vary significantly among subsidiaries. Furthermore, control is predominantly local, the firm is identified with the nationality of the host nation, and relatively little communication occurs with central administration or among subsidiaries. One disadvantage is that local operations may have inefficiencies because of duplication of activities. Another disadvantage is loss of goal congruence between local entities and the firm as a whole. Advantages are more capable and motivated local managers, better results in local markets, local development of new product ideas, and stronger support by host governments.
    Answer (A) is incorrect. An identification with the nationality of the owner is an indicator of an ethnocentric attitude.
Answer (B) is incorrect. Evaluation and control standards that are both local and global is an indicator of a geocentric attitude.
Answer (C) is incorrect. High information flow in multiple directions is an indicator of a geocentric attitude.

23. According to research on the international contingency model of leadership, which path-goal leadership style is **most** likely to be accepted around the world as culturally appropriate?

    A. Directive.

    B. Participative.

    C. Supportive.

    D. Achievement-oriented.

Answer (B) is correct. *(Publisher, adapted)*
    REQUIRED: The path-goal leadership style most likely to be accepted around the world.
    DISCUSSION: A participative style entails consultation with employees and serious attention to their ideas. The participative style, although not always the best, is the most widely accepted internationally. Every country surveyed found it to be culturally acceptable.
    Answer (A) is incorrect. The directive style is the least accepted internationally. It was not deemed appropriate in the U.S., U.K., Canada, Australia, Germany, and Sweden.
Answer (C) is incorrect. The supportive style was not accepted in such countries as Brazil, France, India, and Sweden.
Answer (D) is incorrect. The achievement-oriented style was found unacceptable in such countries as Brazil, France, Italy, and Japan.

24. Managerial attitudes toward global operations are viewed by researcher Howard Perlmutter as a key to understanding multinational firms. A geocentric attitude is indicated by

A. An identification with national perspectives even though the firm is genuinely international.

B. Control and evaluation methods that are locally determined.

C. Decision making concentrated in the central administrative authority.

D. Little communication among subsidiaries.

Answer (A) is correct. *(Publisher, adapted)*
REQUIRED: The indicator of a geocentric attitude.
DISCUSSION: A geocentric attitude is truly internationally oriented while absorbing the best that various cultures offer. It is a completely balanced approach with full collaboration between central administrators and subsidiaries, control and evaluation methods that harmonize local and overall firm standards, and frequent communication in all directions (i.e., between central administrators and subsidiaries and among subsidiaries). Moreover, talent, not nationality, determines personnel decisions throughout the firm.
Answer (B) is incorrect. Control and evaluation methods that are locally determined is an indicator of a polycentric attitude. Answer (C) is incorrect. Decision making concentrated in the central administrative authority is an indicator of an ethnocentric attitude. Answer (D) is incorrect. Little communication among subsidiaries is an indicator of an ethnocentric attitude.

25. Research on the common characteristics of leaders of global firms found that

A. Ambition and relentless drive were more significant than honesty and trustworthiness.

B. The leaders tended to have multidisciplinary problem solving ability.

C. Being multilingual was unimportant.

D. Having traveled extensively before entering the working world was relatively uncommon.

Answer (B) is correct. *(Publisher, adapted)*
REQUIRED: The common characteristic of leaders of global firms.
DISCUSSION: A common characteristic of successful leaders of global firms is that they have effective problem-solving skills that draw from a multidisciplinary approach. The best candidates have varied backgrounds and can draw on a multitude of life experiences. They also tend to be flexible and adaptable, have good interpersonal skills, and communicate successfully.
Answer (A) is incorrect. These leaders were found to have been exposed to a series of events that shaped their belief systems to include a foundation of honesty and trustworthiness. They also had strong role models who emphasized the importance of being fair, consistent, and true to inner principles and beliefs. Answer (C) is incorrect. These leaders had the ability to speak one or more additional languages. In addition, they had extensive exposure to cultures that were nonnative. Answer (D) is incorrect. These leaders had engaged in extensive international travel during childhood prior to entering the working world.

26. For a multinational firm, which of the following is a disadvantage of an ethnocentric staffing policy in which all key management positions are filled by parent-company nationals?

A. An ethnocentric staffing policy significantly raises compensation, training, and staffing costs.

B. An ethnocentric staffing policy produces resentment among the firm's employees in host countries.

C. An ethnocentric staffing policy limits career mobility for parent-country nationals.

D. An ethnocentric staffing policy isolates headquarters from foreign subsidiaries.

Answer (B) is correct. *(CIA, adapted)*
REQUIRED: The disadvantage of ethnocentric staffing of key positions.
DISCUSSION: An ethnocentric staffing policy assumes that the home country's people, practices, and ideas are superior to all others. Thus, the firm's identification with the owner's nationality. Authority and decision making are centralized, so communication is likely to involve a high volume of information flow in the form of orders and advice to subsidiaries. Home-country standards are likely to be used for performance evaluation of entities and individuals.
Answer (A) is incorrect. The key disadvantages of a geocentric staffing policy are that it significantly raises compensation, training, and staffing costs. Although an ethnocentric strategy involves relocation costs and higher compensation for expatriate managers, it allows the overall compensation structure to follow national levels in each country. Answer (C) is incorrect. This strategy limits career mobility of host country employees, not parent company employees. Answer (D) is incorrect. A polycentric staffing policy isolates headquarters from foreign subsidiaries.

5.4   Human Resources Issues in Global Operations

27. Cultures have been described as low-context or high-context. Which culture is high-context?

A. Germany.

B. Saudi Arabia.

C. Great Britain.

D. Switzerland.

Answer (B) is correct.   *(Publisher, adapted)*
REQUIRED: The high-context culture.
DISCUSSION: Edward T. Hall drew a distinction between high-context and low-context cultures. In high-context cultures (e.g., Japanese, Chinese, Arabic, and Korean), much meaning is transmitted by nonverbal cues and situational circumstances. Thus, a person's status in a firm, rank in society, and reputation convey the primary message. In low-context cultures (e.g., Northern Europe and North America), primary messages are transmitted verbally. Hence, precise written contractual agreements are highly valued. In contrast, social events are more highly valued in a high-context culture.

28. Which country is **best** described as having an individualistic culture?

A. India.

B. Japan.

C. Canada.

D. China.

Answer (C) is correct.   *(Publisher, adapted)*
REQUIRED: The individualistic culture.
DISCUSSION: Individualistic cultures are societies that place a higher value on the rights and accomplishments of individual persons within the society. Examples are the U.S., the U.K., Canada, and Australia. Collectivist cultures focus much more on the goals of family, friends, country, and the organization. Examples are China, India, Mexico, Japan, and Egypt.
   Answer (A) is incorrect. India is an example of a collectivist culture. Answer (B) is incorrect. Japan is an example of a collectivist culture. Answer (D) is incorrect. China is an example of a collectivist culture.

29. According to Edward T. Hall, the perception of time is monochronic or polychronic. Which cultures perceive time as monochronic?

A. Northern European.

B. Latin American.

C. Arabic.

D. Mediterranean.

Answer (A) is correct.   *(Publisher, adapted)*
REQUIRED: The cultures that perceive time as monochronic.
DISCUSSION: The perception of time as it relates to business and social life varies with the culture. Polychronic time is based on a perception that time is nonlinear, flexible, and multidimensional. This perception is typical of Mediterranean, Latin American, and Arabic cultures. Monochronic time is based on a perception that time is the same for everyone and is measurable in standard units. This perception is common in Northern Europe and the U.S. These western cultures believe in punctuality and that time is money and should not be wasted.
   Answer (B) is incorrect. In a Latin American culture, time tends to be perceived as polychronic. Answer (C) is incorrect. In an Arabic culture, time tends to be perceived as polychronic. Answer (D) is incorrect. In a Mediterranean culture, time tends to be perceived as polychronic.

30. Dutch researcher Geert Hofstede has examined the cultural dimensions of organizational behavior in 40 countries. The United States ranked the highest in which dimension?

A. Power distance.

B. Uncertainty avoidance.

C. Individualism.

D. Masculinity.

Answer (C) is correct.   *(Publisher, adapted)*
REQUIRED: The cultural dimension in which the United States ranked the highest.
DISCUSSION: The individualism-collectivism dimension addresses whether the organization or individual must meet his/her own security needs.
   Answer (A) is incorrect. The U.S. had a moderately low ranking on power distance. Answer (B) is incorrect. The U.S. had a low ranking on uncertainty avoidance. Answer (D) is incorrect. The U.S. had a high, but not the highest, ranking on masculinity.

STUDY UNIT SIX
MOTIVATION AND COMMUNICATIONS

(20 pages of outline)

This study unit begins with a discussion of the individual needs that are the basis for motivation. It continues with a review of various theories about the motivation of employees in an organization. The remaining subunits address the closely related subject of communication, including its nature and forms and the obstacles it encounters.

6.1 INDIVIDUAL DYNAMICS

1. Individual dynamics is fundamental to an understanding of motivation. It is a psychological model of a single personality. In contrast, group dynamics attempts to explain the behavior of people in groups.

Maslow

2. According to **Abraham Maslow**, human needs are a hierarchy, from lowest to highest. Lower-level needs must be satisfied before higher-level needs can influence (motivate) the individual.

   a. Maslow's **hierarchy of needs** is listed below, from lowest to highest:

      1) **Physiological needs** are the basic requirements for sustaining human life, such as water, food, shelter, and sleep. Until these needs are satisfied to the degree needed to maintain life, higher-level needs will not be motivators.

      2) **Security or safety needs** include freedom from physical or emotional harm, the loss of a job, and other threats.

      3) **Affiliation or acceptance needs** are the needs of people as social beings for love, affection, friendship, and belonging.

      4) **Esteem** is the need to be valued by both one's self and others. These needs are satisfied by power, prestige, status, and self-confidence.

      5) **Self-actualization** is the highest need in the hierarchy. It is the need to realize one's own potential for growth and continued development.

         a) Thus, the job itself is an **intrinsic** motivation; no **extrinsic** motivation (such as rewards or reinforcements) is needed.

            i) Intrinsic motivation provides the worker with psychological utility.

   b. Research does not support the concept of a strict hierarchy, except for the requirement that biological needs be satisfied before other needs become motivators.

      1) Physiological and safety needs tend to decrease in importance for fully employed people. Needs for acceptance, esteem, and self-actualization tend to increase.

      2) Higher-level needs, esteem and self-actualization, are variable in their motivational effects, depending upon the individual.

    c.   Maslow's hierarchy does not apply equally to all situations. It is dependent on the social, cultural, and psychological backgrounds of the people involved.

        1)   People of different cultures respond differently.

        2)   Professional workers, skilled workers, and unskilled workers react differently.

        3)   Other social, ethnic, and cultural factors make people react differently.

        4)   The hierarchy is not a smooth, step-by-step path. It is a complicated and interdependent set of relationships.

            a)   However, the tendency to move upward as lower needs are satisfied does exist.

Other Theories

3.   According to **David McClelland**, motivation is based on the **needs** for achievement, power, and affiliation.

    a.   The need for **achievement** is the drive to succeed in relation to a set of standards. Thus, high achievers wish to do something better than it has been done before. They thrive when the job provides personal responsibility, feedback, and moderate risks. They avoid very easy or very difficult tasks, and they do not like to succeed by chance.

    b.   The need for **power** is a desire to compel others to behave in certain ways, to influence or control others. Individuals with a high need for power are concerned with prestige and status and prefer to be in charge.

    c.   The need for **affiliation** is the need for close interpersonal relationships. Individuals with a high need for affiliation seek friendship, cooperative rather than competitive situations, and mutual understanding.

4.   The **ERG theory** developed by Clayton Alderfer states that the core needs are existence (physiological and security needs), relatedness (affiliation and external esteem needs), and growth (self-actualization and internal esteem needs).

    a.   According to ERG theory, multiple needs may serve as motivators at the same time.

    b.   Frustration of a higher need may lead to regression to a lower need. For example, frustration of growth needs through inability to find more fulfilling work may result in a heightened need to make money.

5.   **Individual Values**

    a.   Values are specific to each individual and involve moral and personal issues.

    b.   Values are learned from family, friends, school, and life experience.

    c.   Values can be modified throughout life but ordinarily tend to stay the same.

    d.   It is important to reward good values in a corporation to prevent fraud, theft, and deception and to improve worker morale.

        1)   The value structure is an important part of the corporate culture.

    e.   Personal beliefs, such as those on religious and political matters, cannot be the basis of personnel actions. Discrimination on the basis of personal beliefs could expose the organization to legal action.

6.   **Human Defense Mechanisms**

    a.   A defense mechanism is an often unconscious mental process that permits the individual to reach compromise solutions to personal problems. Some of the most common are listed below and on the next page.

        1)   **Rationalization** is giving more acceptable reasons for behavior than the actual ones.

        2)   **Regression** is reversion to child-like behavior.

        3)   **Repression** eliminates stressful items from working memory.

4) **Projection** is the attribution of one's own ideas, feelings, or attitudes to others, especially the externalization of blame, guilt, or responsibility as a defense against anxiety.

5) **Compensation** attempts to offset bad qualities with good qualities.

6) **Withdrawal** is simply avoidance.

7) **Aggression** involves a direct attack on the perceived causes of the problem.

8) **Sublimation** diverts the expression of a basic impulse or instinct to a more acceptable form, such as physical exercise instead of arguing with a coworker.

Core Concepts

- Individual dynamics is fundamental to an understanding of motivation. It is a psychological model of a single personality. In contrast, group dynamics attempts to explain the behavior of people in groups.

- Abraham Maslow's hierarchy of needs (in ascending order) consists of (1) physiological needs, (2) security or safety needs, (3) affiliation or acceptance needs, (4) esteem, and (5) self-actualization.

- According to David McClelland, motivation is based on the needs for achievement, power, and affiliation.

- The ERG theory developed by Clayton Alderfer states that the core needs are existence (physiological and security needs), relatedness (affiliation and external esteem needs), and growth (self-actualization and internal esteem needs).

- Values are specific to each individual and involve moral and personal issues.

- Defense mechanisms include (1) rationalization, (2) regression, (3) repression, (4) projection, (5) compensation, (6) withdrawal, (7) aggression, and (8) sublimation.

Stop and review! You have completed the outline for this subunit. Study multiple-choice questions 1 through 3 beginning on page 148.

6.2 MOTIVATION

Overview

1. Motivation describes an entire class of drives, desires, needs, fears, and similar forces that cause behavior.

   a. The ideal management action motivates subordinates by structuring situations and requiring behaviors that will simultaneously satisfy the needs of subordinates and the organization.

   b. The organization's needs and those of the individual **need not conflict**.

   c. The **level of motivation** is determined by individuals' opportunity to satisfy their needs within the organizational setting. The greater the ability to satisfy these needs, the greater the motivational level.

      1) The inducements that an organization offers an individual should be matched with the contributions expected from that individual. Thus, each side should be willing to give up something to receive a desired benefit.

      2) The task of a **leader** is to make available the kinds and amounts of rewards an individual requires in exchange for the kinds and amounts of contributions the organization requires.

Classical Views

2. Classical views stress fear and economics as motivators.

   a. The following are examples:

      1) Economic incentive programs and bonuses are economic rewards.
      2) Loss of employment and demotion are feared by employees.

   b. According to **Frederick Taylor's** scientific school of management, motivation in the business organization was simple. It consisted of monetary incentives.

      1) Because money was the common ground between workers and management, prosperity for the company must be accompanied by prosperity for the worker and vice versa.

Behaviorism

3. Behaviorists believe that economic motivation is effective only for the short run or for people who do not have job alternatives. This approach focuses on participation and personal involvement in the work situation as motivational factors.

   a. For a **participative management** approach to succeed,

      1) The parties must have sufficient time,
      2) The issues must be relevant to employees' interests,
      3) Employees must have the abilities (training and communication skills) to participate, and
      4) The organizational culture should support participation.

   b. Accordingly, a limitation of the participative approach is that it is unlikely that all employees are willing and able to be involved in decision making.

4. **Chris Argyris** proposed a theory of motivation that integrates the needs of the individual with those of the organization.

   a. Conflict arises when a mature, independent adult who seeks self-actualization joins a highly structured, demanding, and limiting organization.

      1) For example, a highly competent engineer who takes a job with a governmental unit may be frustrated in the pursuit of technical excellence by the procedures that are characteristic of a bureaucracy.
      2) **Self-actualization** is the process of accomplishing goals to the limit of one's ability because of the personal need to excel.
      3) Challenging new job assignments are a means of satisfying an employee's self-actualization needs.

Theory X and Theory Y

5. **Douglas McGregor's** Theory X and Theory Y are simplified models that define the extremes of managers' opinions on employee conduct. They permit a manager to evaluate his/her own tendencies.

   a. **Theory X** is the perspective of the autocratic manager.

      1) "Average human beings have an inherent dislike of work and will avoid it if possible."
      2) "Because of this dislike for work, most people must be coerced, controlled, directed, and threatened with punishment to get them to put forth adequate effort toward the achievement of organizational objectives."
      3) "Average human beings prefer to be directed, have relatively little ambition, and want security above all."

    b.   **Theory Y** is the extreme opposite of Theory X. The permissive manager assumes the following:

        1)   "The expenditure of physical and mental effort in work is as natural as play or rest -- to average human beings."

        2)   "External control and the threat of punishment are not the only means for bringing about individual effort toward organizational objectives. Employees will exercise self-direction and self-control in their efforts to accomplish goals thought to be worthwhile."

        3)   "Commitment to objectives is proportional to the rewards associated with their achievement."

        4)   "Average human beings learn, under proper conditions, not only to accept responsibility, but to seek it."

        5)   "The capacity to exercise a relatively high degree of imagination, ingenuity, and creativity in the solution of organizational problems is widely, not narrowly, distributed in the population."

        6)   "Under the conditions of modern industrial life, the intellectual potential of the average human being are only partially realized."

    c.   McGregor did not suggest that Theory Y was the only correct managerial behavior. He suggested these theories as starting points from which a manager can examine his/her own views about human nature.

Theory Z

6.   **William Ouchi** analyzed the characteristics of **Japanese companies** that produce high employee commitment, motivation, and productivity.

    a.   At many of these companies, employees are guaranteed a position for life, increasing their loyalty to the organization.

        1)   Careful evaluation occurs over a long period, and the responsibility for success or failure is shared among employees and management.

        2)   Most employees do not specialize in one skill area. Their career paths are **cross-functional**. That is, they work at several different tasks, learning more about the company as they develop.

        3)   The Japanese companies are often concerned about all aspects of their employees' lives, on and off the job.

    b.   Ouchi also identified American companies that are **hybrid or Theory Z organizations**. They tended to have stable employment, high productivity, and high employee satisfaction. The following are traits of Theory Z organizations:

        1)   The **goal** is to achieve a long-range orientation among workers.

        2)   The promise of long-term employment creates intense **job loyalty**.

        3)   **Teamwork** is a key requirement. Collective decision making occurs in all activities.

            a)   This bottom-up process is slower than a top-down approach.

        4)   **Promotion and performance evaluation** occur more slowly than is typical in American companies.

            a)   The emphasis is more on long-range orientation than short-term success.
            b)   However, performance must be recognized in other ways.

        5)   Despite the focus on group decision making, Theory Z still emphasizes **individual responsibility**. Because sole reliance on a group decision is hard for Western businesses to accept, Theory Z recommends that an individual be assigned responsibility for carrying out the group's decision.

6) Theory Z requires **trust** among employees and between employees and management.

    a) The concept of egalitarianism stresses that each person can work autonomously and without supervision because (s)he is to be trusted.

7) A **holistic orientation** includes employees and their families in all decisions. Work and social life are integrated.

8) The concept of **self-control** is balanced with external control.

Two-Factor Theory of Motivation

7. **Frederick Herzberg's** two-factor theory is based on satisfaction. The following two classes of motivational factors exist in the job situation:

    a. **Dissatisfiers (maintenance or hygiene factors)** are found in the **job context**.

        1) Their presence will not especially motivate people, but their absence will lead to diminished performance. They include

            a) Organizational policy and administration,
            b) Supervision,
            c) Working conditions,
            d) Interpersonal relations,
            e) Salary and status, and
            f) Job security.

    b. **Satisfiers (motivational factors)** relate to **job content**.

        1) Their absence will not diminish performance, but their addition or availability will motivate employees. They include

            a) Achievement,
             b) Recognition,
             c) Challenging work,
             d) Advancement,
             e) Growth in the job, and
            f) Responsibility.

8. Satisfaction and dissatisfaction are on a continuum. In the middle is the point at which an employee experiences neither job satisfaction nor dissatisfaction.

    a. At this point, (s)he is not dissatisfied with the job context but also is not positively motivated.

    b. If Herzberg is correct, considerable attention should be given to upgrading job content through the use of job enrichment strategies.

    c. Based on Herzberg's analysis, some jobs obviously do not contain many motivators, but others have more than are being fully used by management. For example,

        1) Routine, low-status work such as mail sorting has few motivators.

        2) A company that may be paying above the industry average (maintenance factor) could also increase satisfaction by openly acknowledging sales or other efforts by initiating a salesperson of the week recognition program.

Job Design

9. **Job design** links tasks to particular jobs in a way consistent with the organization's strategies, structure, and resources (including technology).

   a. One approach is to **adapt people to the jobs**. The following are techniques for avoiding job dissatisfaction when this approach is used:

      1) A **realistic job preview** is a full explanation of what the job involves, including its negative aspects. The purpose is to reduce or eliminate false expectations. Written previews should be provided before hiring, and verbal previews should be provided after hiring.

      2) **Job rotation** may introduce a welcome element of change in boring, highly specialized jobs. It also may have such benefits as cross-functional training and avoidance of repetitive stress injuries.

      3) **Contingent time off** is an award earned by early completion of a fair performance quota for a day's work without loss of pay.

   b. Another approach to job design is to **adapt the job to the people** performing them. The following are common methods:

      1) **Job enlargement** is primarily intended to reduce boredom in repetitive or fast-paced jobs through the assignment of a variety of simple tasks as part of one job. Such jobs are **horizontally loaded**.

      2) **Job enrichment** attempts to structure the job so that each worker participates in planning and controlling. The purpose is to maximize the satisfaction of both social and ego needs and to avoid the disadvantages of routine, highly specialized work.

         a) Job enrichment should improve motivation by **vertically loading** the job, that is, increasing its complexity and challenge.

         b) According to the **core job characteristics** described by Hackman and Oldham, jobs are enriched by improving their basic aspects:

            i) **Skill variety**, or the diversity of talents required

            ii) **Task identity**, or the performance of a job from start to finish of an identifiable, entire work product

            iii) **Task significance**, or the effect on other people within or outside the firm

            iv) **Autonomy**, or greater discretion over methods, sequence, and pace of work

            v) **Feedback**, or receipt of information about performance

         c) Enrichment should produce three **critical psychological states**:

            i) **Meaningfulness** is determined by the first three core job characteristics.

            ii) **Responsibility for work outcomes** results from autonomy.

            iii) **Knowledge of actual work outcomes** is provided by feedback.

         d) The critical psychological states should produce high motivation, performance, and satisfaction; low turnover; and low absenteeism.

            i) However, studies have shown that worker satisfaction does not necessarily lead to improved productivity (performance). In fact, studies indicate that it is more likely that a productive worker is a happy worker.

Expectancy Theory

10. **Victor Vroom's** expectancy theory is based on the commonsense idea that people have (a) subjective expectations of rewards, (b) beliefs as to what is valuable, and (c) expectations of receiving these rewards if they exert effort.

    a. Thus, expectancy theory addresses individualized (1) motivations and (2) perceptions of the probability of success.

    b. High effort expended, ability, and accurate role assessment will lead to a high performance level. That is, putting appropriate effort into the right task and having the right amount of ability to do it will lead to high performance.

        1) Insufficient ability will impede performance despite effort.
        2) Executing a task that is not desired or is improperly performed according to role definition will impede performance despite effort or ability.

    c. Expectancy theory is based on **individual perception** of

        1) The value of rewards,
        2) The probability the required effort will result in the required performance, and
        3) The probability that the required performance will result in receipt of the desired rewards.

    d. **Expectancy** results from past experiences and measures the strength of belief (the probability assessments) that a particular act will be followed by a specific outcome.

        1) **Management** is more able to control the expectancy factor than the individual perception of the value of rewards because expectations are based on past experiences.

            a) A consistent management policy will reinforce employee expectations.

    e. **Performance** leads to rewards.

        1) Individuals evaluate rewards on the basis of the fairness of their treatment compared with others in similar jobs.
        2) If unfairness exists, individuals react, usually negatively.

    f. Perception of the equity of rewards leads to **satisfaction**.

        1) The level of satisfaction or dissatisfaction feeds back into the next cycle's estimates of reward values, individual abilities, and role perceptions.

Goal-Setting Theory

11. According to Edwin Locke's goal-setting theory, specific, difficult goals to which the employee is committed provide the best motivation tool.

    a. Performance improves when goals are **specific** rather than general, **difficult** rather than easy, and **participative** (self-set) rather than imposed by others.

    b. Furthermore, **specific feedback**, especially self-generated feedback, also improves performance compared with lack of feedback.

    c. Goals serve as motivators because they

        1) Focus **attention** on specific objectives,
        2) Require **effort** to achieve,
        3) Necessitate continued actions (**persistence**), and
        4) Create an incentive for developing **strategies and action plans**.

Other Theories

12. **Equity theory** states that employee motivation is affected significantly by relative as well as absolute rewards. An employee compares the **ratio** of what (s)he receives from a job (outcomes such as pay or recognition) to what (s)he gives to the job (inputs such as effort, experience, ability, or education) with the ratios of relevant others.

    a. If the ratios are equal, equity exists, but if they are unequal, equity tension exists, and the employee will be motivated to eliminate the tension.

    b. The **referent** chosen (the employee's experience inside or outside the organization or the experiences of others inside or outside the organization) tends to be affected by the employee's job tenure, education, and salary level.

        1) For example, better-educated employees are more likely to make comparisons with outsiders, and longer-tenured employees may rely on coworkers.

    c. **Equity tension** leads to changes in inputs or outcomes, distorted perceptions of one's effort or of the referent, choice of a different referent, or abandonment of the job.

13. **Cognitive evaluation theory** states that **intrinsic rewards** (such as competence, responsibility, and achievement) tend to be reduced when **extrinsic rewards** (such as higher pay, promotion, and better working conditions) are provided for superior performance.

    a. The reason may be that the individual perceives a loss of control over his/her behavior. However, research suggests that the negative effects of extrinsic rewards on motivation do not apply when a job provides either a very high or a very low level of intrinsic rewards.

        1) In the second case, extrinsic rewards may actually increase intrinsic motivation.

Rewards

14. Rewards are the benefits, psychological and otherwise, of work to employees. Proper management of reward systems should improve job satisfaction and performance.

    a. **Extrinsic rewards** are received from others. They range from pay to praise.

        1) **Social rewards** normally include acknowledgment of employee achievement through actions, such as solicitation of advice.

        2) **Token rewards** are normally nonrecurring. They show appreciation for the role of the employee. Examples are gift coupons, stock options, early time off with pay, dinner and theater tickets, or a paid vacation trip.

        3) Examples of **visual or auditory awards** include a private office, book-club discussions, or redecoration of the work environment.

        4) Examples of manipulatables are gifts, such as desk accessories, watches, trophies, clothing, or jewelry.

    b. **Intrinsic rewards** are the internal psychological payoffs that an employee gives to him/herself. The higher levels of Maslow's hierarchy consist of such rewards.

    c. **Employee compensation** accounts for a high proportion of the organization's total costs. It also involves many complex legal and taxation questions.

        1) **Nonincentive plans** include payment of hourly wages or annual salaries. These plans are easy to manage but provide no performance incentives.

        2) **Incentive plans** include **piece rate** (a fixed amount for each unit of physical output) and **sales commission** compensation. **Merit pay** provides bonuses for excellent performance. **Sharing** of profits, productivity gains, or cost savings gives employees a vested interest in the organization's success. However, performance may be affected by factors that employees cannot control. **Stock-based employee compensation** has advantages and disadvantages similar to those of profit sharing. **Knowledge-based** plans pay employees for skills learned or completion of degree requirements.

3) A **cafeteria-plan** (life-cycle benefits plan) provides for employee choices that suit their personal circumstances. For example, age or marital status may determine whether an employee desires health insurance, pension benefits, or family leave.

4) A compensation plan should be perceived by employees as fair. It meets the **personal equity** test if rewards are proportional to effort. (But overpaid employees also may perceive inequity.) It meets the **social equity** test if an employee believes that his/her effort-to-reward ratio is proportionate to that of others in similar circumstances.

5) In accordance with **expectancy theory**, an effective plan should be administered so that employees believe that their efforts will be rewarded.

6) A plan also should provide additional rewards for excellent **performance**. Hourly and annual compensation plans may not be effective in this respect.

7) Other types of employee compensation include

a) **Flextime** (flexible working hours). Granting reasonable scheduling flexibility tends to improve manager-employee relations, promote better performance, and minimize absenteeism. Disadvantages are higher administrative costs and ensuring that job duties are performed.

b) **Job-sharing**, a practice favored by many parents.

c) Permanent part-time work.

d) Compressed work weeks (e.g., 40 hours over 4 days).

e) **Wellness programs**, such as those promoting physical fitness, smoking cessation, weight loss, or stress reduction.

f) **Family support**, such as paid or unpaid parental leave, family sickness leave, on-site daycare, emergency childcare, and eldercare.

8) Family support may be required by law.

15. For outlines of subjects closely related to this subunit, see Study Unit 9, "Influence and Leadership."

Core Concepts

- Classical views of motivation stress fear and economics as motivators.

- According to Frederick Taylor's scientific school of management, motivation in the business organization was simple. His concept of motivation began and ended with monetary incentives.

- Chris Argyris proposed a theory of motivation that involves integrating the needs of the individual with those of the organization. Conflict arises when a mature, independent adult who seeks self-actualization joins a highly structured, demanding, and limiting organization.

- Douglas McGregor's Theory X and Theory Y are simplified models that define the extremes of managers' views on employee conduct. They permit a manager to evaluate his/her own tendencies. Theory X is the viewpoint of the autocratic manager. Theory Y (the permissive manager) is the extreme opposite of Theory X.

- William Ouchi's Theory Z resulted from studies of Japanese management styles. Theory Z emphasizes motivating employees through developing loyalty to the company and emphasizing teamwork.

- Frederick Herzberg's two-factor theory of motivation is based on satisfaction. Two classes of motivational factors exist in the job situation: dissatisfiers (maintenance or hygiene factors) and satisfiers (motivational factors).

- Job design links tasks to particular jobs in a way consistent with the organization's strategies, structure, and resources (including technology). Two approaches are to adapt people to jobs or adapt jobs to people. Job enlargement and job enrichment are subtopics.
- Expectancy theory is based on the commonsense idea that people have (1) subjective expectations of rewards, (2) beliefs as to what is valuable, and (3) expectations of receiving these rewards if they exert effort.
- Goal-setting theory, equity theory, and cognitive evaluation theory are other attempts to explain motivation.
- Rewards are the benefits, psychological and otherwise, of work to employees. Proper management of reward systems should improve job satisfaction and performance.

Stop and review! You have completed the outline for this subunit. Study multiple-choice questions 4 through 11 beginning on page 149.

The word "communicate" appears several times in The IIA's exam content outline. The ability to communicate effectively with upper management and the board, as well as with other internal auditors and client personnel, is a critical skill for an internal auditor.

6.3 NATURE OF COMMUNICATION

Overview

1. **Communication** is the process of conveying and understanding information between one person and another. It affects all organizational activities and moves in many directions.

2. The **communication process** has five elements (the mnemonic is SSMRF):

   a. **Sender**, the person who originates the message
   b. **Symbols**, in which the message is **encoded**
   c. **Medium**, the channel through which the message flows
   d. **Receiver**, the person who decodes the message and interprets the sender's meaning
   e. **Feedback**, acknowledging to the sender that the message was correctly understood

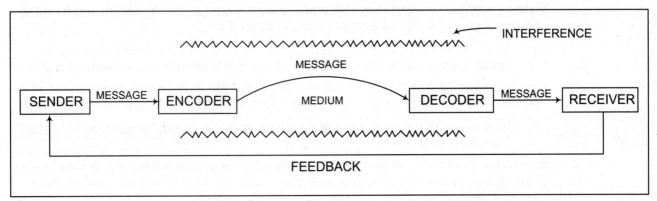

Figure 6-1

Types of Communication

3. Because all managerial functions require communication, it is **the secret to the success of any manager**. A manager's ability to understand other people and their ability to understand the manager are crucial to accomplishing organizational objectives. Communication is the link that ties an organization together and transforms a diverse group of people into a cohesive whole.

a.   An organization's internal communications network should (1) facilitate decision making among managers, (2) promote goal congruence among employees, (3) integrate the efforts of all employees, and (4) build high morale and mutual trust.

   1)   Managers must spend most of their time communicating with subordinates, peers, and superiors. They communicate

      a)   Organizational goals and plans downward,

      b)   Lower-level results and problems upward, and

      c)   Coordinating information horizontally (among peers or across organizational channels).

b.   **Formal communication** is conducted through the formal structure of the organization, e.g., budgets, bonus programs, memoranda, or technical manuals.

c.   Informal communication (the **grapevine**) operates outside of formal structural media.

   1)   The grapevine exists wherever there are people.

   2)   Grapevines can exist in several **patterns**. For example,

      a)   One person may tell one other person who tells one other person, etc. (a **single strand** pattern);

      b)   One person may tell all people in a group **(gossip)**;

      c)   Individuals may tell selected others (a **cluster** pattern, the most common); or

      d)   Individuals may tell others at random (a **probability** pattern).

   3)   The grapevine is usually accurate, but it can carry gossip and rumor, and it serves as an emotional outlet for employees. It also satisfies employees' innate desire to know what is actually happening.

      a)   The emergence of electronic media in the workplace has made the grapevine even more pervasive and important.

   4)   Managers can minimize the damage that a grapevine can cause by transmitting accurate and timely information and maintaining open media of communication. The effective manager stays tuned in to the grapevine and uses it constructively.

d.   **Written communication** provides a permanent record of the message and tends to be accurate, but it can be time consuming to prepare.

   1)   An inherent weakness of written communication is that it inhibits feedback because the sender and the receiver are not in simultaneous communication.

e.   **Oral communication** is less formal and less accurate than written communication but permits immediate feedback. It also permits messages to be transmitted rapidly.

   1)   Most managers spend more of their time in oral communication than in written communication.

f.   **Electronic communication.** Modern technology (e.g., voice mail, fax, texting, social networking, and email) blurs the distinction between written and oral communications. The benefits of electronic communication include

   1)   Better control of information,
   2)   More timely information,
   3)   Elimination of tedious tasks,
   4)   Improvement of competitiveness due to improved technology,
   5)   Standardization of procedures by computer programs,
   6)   Assistance for strategic planning, and
   7)   Optimization of organizational resources to improve productivity.

Aspects of Communication

4. **Directions of Communication**

   a. **Downward communication** (from superior to subordinate) is vertical communication consisting of orders, instructions, notices, memos, bulletins, newsletters, handbooks, loudspeakers, and the chain of command.

   b. **Upward communication** (from subordinate to superior) is vertical communication consisting of morale surveys, traditional grievance procedures, peer review of grievances, suggestion systems, informal meetings, Internet chat, exit interviews, and conferences.

      1) Upward communication must overcome more barriers and is slower than downward communication.

   c. **Horizontal (lateral) communication** is from one peer to another.

5. Lengel and Daft have proposed a **contingency model for media selection**. Its fundamental concept is **media richness**, which is the ability "to convey information and promote learning."

   a. Media richness may be high, e.g., in a face-to-face meeting or in another interactive framework. A rich medium is characterized by many cues (content, tone of voice, body language, its personal emphasis, and immediate feedback).

   b. Media richness may be lean (low), e.g., company memos or general email that may be viewed as impersonal static. A lean medium is essentially the opposite of a rich medium.

   c. The **management problem** is to choose the appropriate medium with the degree of richness appropriate to the circumstances. For example, rich (lean) media should be used for nonroutine (routine) problems.

Interaction with Receiver

6. The **effectiveness of communication** can be determined only when the sender seeks feedback and observes the effect of the communication on the receiver.

   a. The sender is obligated to solicit feedback to ensure the communication process is complete.

   b. The receiver is obligated to give feedback to the sender.

   c. The importance of feedback to verify the effectiveness of the communication process indicates the limitations of one-way communications (e.g., memos).

   d. The best indicator of the effectiveness of a communication is the change in the receiver's behavior in the direction requested or required by the communication. The sender has the responsibility to solicit feedback (or observe results) to determine the communication's effectiveness.

      1) A receiver who understands a message may change attitude but may not necessarily change behavior.

7. Managers must consider the **nature of the message receiver**. Receivers vary in their **perception** of messages because of language, education, culture, attitudes toward the sender and job, etc. This variance may result in communication distortion.

   a. The following are some examples of this phenomenon:

      1) In some cultures, to move toward a person while speaking is expected. In others, it is considered an act of aggression.

      2) In some cultures, consistently being late to appointments means laxness, lack of concern, discourtesy, and disinterest. In others, it is normal, expected, and carries no particular meaning.

3) A speaker analyzes the audience to gather the right information. Understanding the other participants' opinions and needs enables the speaker to express his/her ideas in the way best calculated to be persuasive.

b. **Perception** is the process through which someone gives meaning to the surrounding environment. Perception consists of three subprocesses.

1) **Selectivity** screens out certain stimuli to focus on details. Without selectivity, one would be overwhelmed by sensory overload.

2) **Organization** groups disorganized stimuli to give meaning to otherwise meaningless information.

3) **Interpretation** gives meaning to a set of stimuli based on the individual's experience.

8. **Nonverbal Communication**

a. **Nonverbal signals** occur in clusters, whether or not accompanied by verbal communication. The following are examples:

1) Vocal characteristics and tone of voice
2) Facial expressions and eye contact
3) Hand and body gestures and other movements
4) Breathing, sighs, and other noises that are not words
5) Physical distance between the sender and the receiver
6) Posture and other aspects of physical appearance
7) Touch
8) Mode of attire
9) Decoration and layout of rooms

b. Nonverbal communication is easily misunderstood because

1) Different cultures and languages employ different nonverbal signals, and
2) Clarifying the ambiguities inherent in nonverbal communication is difficult.

c. **Interpreting nonverbal communication** requires the establishment of the norms in a particular person's nonverbal repertoire.

1) For example, folded arms may signify resistance or inflexibility or may simply be a habit.

2) People should not be judged solely on established or learned norms of nonverbal communication but instead on an individual basis.

d. For any communication to be effective, both verbal and nonverbal messages should complement each other.

Organizational Aspects

9. **Organizational structure** is a determinant of how communication is transmitted.

a. **Traditional or classical management** stresses the sending of one-way communications from top management down to the subordinates. This military model of organization (command and control) is autocratic or mechanistic and ignores the need for feedback.

b. **Participative management** stresses multidirectional communication. All parts of the organization are allowed and expected to communicate with each other, not merely along lines of authority.

c. **Systems theory** stresses the importance of feedback in determining the effectiveness of communications. Without a channel from the receiver back to the sender, the sender has no idea how the information has affected the performance or actions of the receiver, if at all.

10. **Organizational communication strategy continuum.** Clampitt, DeKoch, and Cashman have devised a model with two dimensions. **Communication effectiveness** (the vertical dimension) is the degree to which meaning is fully and precisely transmitted. The **amount of information** (the horizontal dimension) may be large or small.

   a. The **spray-and-pray strategy** ineffectively conveys too great an amount of information using one-way, impersonal methods, such as corporate email, that require receivers to determine the central issues.

   b. The **tell-and-sell strategy** conveys less information and indicates what is important. It is often used by senior managers attempting to gain support for major corporate changes. The result is greater effectiveness. A weakness is that refining the presentation may be done at the expense of not addressing the needs of the receiver.

   c. The **underscore-and-explore strategy** is interactive. It states priorities and reasons for action and allows employees to give feedback in a disciplined way. Its success depends on communicating the appropriate amount of information, effective listening, resolution of misunderstandings, and striving for consensus.

   d. The **identify-and-reply strategy** is reactive, and the emphasis is on listening. Employees are presumed to understand the central issues. Moreover, they effectively set the agenda. Managers may use this strategy to reply to leaks or rumors.

   e. The **withhold-and-uphold strategy** is characterized by stringent control of information and a Theory X view of management. Managers view secrecy as promoting (upholding) their power. Communication effectiveness is low because too little information is shared and both rumors and resentment abound.

   f. The optimal·strategy is underscore and explore. Tell-and-sell and identify-and-reply strategies should be used infrequently. The other, low-effectiveness strategies should not be used.

   g. Within cost limits, managers should adopt the **richest medium** to implement a communications strategy.

Core Concepts

- Communication is the process of conveying and understanding information between one person and another. It affects all organizational activities and moves in many directions. The communication process has five elements: sender, symbols, medium, receiver, and feedback.

- Because all managerial functions require communication, it is the secret to the success of any manager.

- Formal communication is conducted through the formal structure of the organization, e.g., budgets, bonus programs, memoranda, or technical manuals. Informal communication (the grapevine) operates outside of formal structural media. The grapevine exists wherever there are people.

- Communication may be written, oral, or electronic. Its directions are downward, upward, or horizontal (lateral).

- Lengel and Daft have proposed a contingency model for media selection. Its fundamental concept is media richness, which is the ability "to convey information and promote learning."

- The effectiveness of communication can be determined only when the sender seeks feedback and observes the effect of the communication on the receiver.

- Managers must consider the nature of the message receiver. Receivers vary in their perception of messages because of language, education, culture, attitudes toward the sender and job, etc.

- Organizational structure is a determinant of how communication is transmitted.

- Nonverbal signals occur in clusters, whether or not accompanied by verbal communication. They include vocal characteristics (e.g., tone of voice), facial expressions, gestures, and eye contact.

- The organizational communication strategy continuum is a model for communication that consists of two dimensions: effectiveness (vertical) and amount of information (horizontal). Possible strategies include (1) spray and pray, (2) tell-and-sell, (3) underscore-and-explore (optimal), (4) identify-and-reply, and (5) withhold-and-uphold.

Stop and review! You have completed the outline for this subunit. Study multiple-choice questions 12 through 18 beginning on page 152.

6.4 PROBLEMS IN COMMUNICATION

1. **Encoding** is the way that meaning is transmitted in communication. **Decoding** is the way a recipient of a message applies meaning to what is received. **Poorly encoded messages** result from the following:

   a. Inappropriate choice of words or phrases

      1) An example is using technical language (jargon) in speaking with a lay person. The skill levels of both the sender and the recipient are pertinent to the manner in which a message should be encoded.

   b. Careless omissions of key ideas

   c. Lack of coherence in forming the message

   d. Inconsistency between verbal and nonverbal messages

   e. Incomplete ideas or ideas out of the receiver's context

   f. **Projection**, which is the tendency of the sender to attribute his/her traits, values, and emotions to the receiver and vice versa

   g. **Filtering** the message so that it reflects more favorably on the sender, a typical problem in upward communication

2. The following are examples of **faulty medium selection**:

   a. Trying to speak while a loud airplane flies overhead

   b. Gesturing to someone who cannot see the gesture

   c. Using a medium that creates no permanent record to send a purchase order with detailed specifications

3. **Noise in the communications medium** is an outside disruption that impedes the flow of a message, for example,

   a. Asking for a raise during discussion of an operational problem,

   b. Random events that cause a breakdown in communication (lost mail, phone service disruption, etc.), or

   c. Use of technical language by the sender that is unlikely to be understood by the receiver.

4. **Perceptual problems** may arise from the following:

   a. The sender's dislike of the receiver or vice versa

   b. Distortion created by personal enthusiasm for embellishing good news and downplaying the bad or vice versa

   c. Status differences among people that impede free and open communication

      1) Few people are secure enough to tell a superior that what was just said was not understood.

    d.   **Selective perception** caused by the receiver's needs, motives, projections, experiences, and expectations

        1)   People tend to interpret what they see and hear in the light of their own needs, etc., and to regard that interpretation as reality.

        2)   Moreover, people necessarily must narrow their perception to avoid sensory overload. Such screening is required to organize and interpret experience.

    e.   **Stereotyping** or attributing to another person traits that are commonly associated with a category or group to which that person belongs

5.   Perceptual problems can be minimized by

    a.   Feedback from the receiver concerning his/her perceptions and interpretations of the message,

    b.   Understanding of the sender's perspective by the receiver,

    c.   The sender's sensitivity to the receiver's problems, and

    d.   Implementation of an organization-wide training program to improve communication skills.

6.   **Use of Communication Media for Enhancement of Personal Status**

    a.   Some lower-level employees who have access to management become influential among their peers. These individuals are, in effect, **gatekeepers** because they can determine which messages will be communicated.

        1)   For example, an editor of a newspaper is a gatekeeper. (S)he can control what is communicated through the newspaper.

    b.   **Opinion leaders** can be used to enhance the reception that a message obtains. Celebrities may or may not be good opinion leaders.

        1)   For example, the opinion of a local mechanic about a new car might carry greater weight than would a celebrity endorsement of the same car.

    c.   A **media liaison** is an individual in an organization who has been formally charged with the job of facilitating communication. An example is a public relations director.

7.   **Loss in Transmission and Poor Retention**

    a.   As much as 30% of the information in oral communication is lost in each transmission. Even written communications are subject to some loss. After passing through a chain of command, little of the message may have been retained.

    b.   Poor retention. One study found that as little as 50% of communicated information was retained by employees.

8.   **Nonreception.** The following are common reasons for a receiver not to receive any communication.

    a.   Inattention or disinterest in the message. Messages are sometimes screened, and those in which the recipient has no interest are ignored.

    b.   Information overload. The receiver is already receiving so many messages that (s)he cannot process what (s)he is hearing.

    c.   Confusing messages. The sender is not sending enough information to fully communicate thoughts, and the receiver must allocate too much time to interpreting what the sender is saying.

9.   **Formal Breakdowns of Communications Media**

    a.   An example is omission from a mailing list.

10. **Solutions to Communications Problems**

   a. The message should be in the context of the receiver's perceptions.

      1) Explaining an accounting concept to a nonaccountant will require terms different from those used with someone who has an accounting background.

   b. The sender must monitor media to ensure they are free from distortion or breakdown.

   c. The sender must actively solicit feedback to ensure reception and understanding.

   d. The organizational climate should encourage the elimination of interpersonal barriers to communication.

   e. The sender should look for nonverbal cues or feedback (such as body language).

   f. The sender must remember that it is his/her responsibility to deliver the communication with appropriate symbols through appropriate media and never to make assumptions about the receiver's reaction.

   g. Two-way (interactive) communication should be used whenever possible to permit ease of feedback.

   h. Communication can be improved through redundancy, that is, by repeating the message in several different formats and in several media.

Core Concepts

- Problems in communication include (1) poorly encoded messages, (2) faulty media selection, (3) noise, (4) perceptual problems, (5) loss in transmission, (6) poor retention, (7) nonreception, and (8) media breakdown.

Stop and review! You have completed the outline for this subunit. Study multiple-choice questions 19 through 27 beginning on page 154.

6.5 LISTENING AND ELECTRONIC COMMUNICATION

1. **Listening** is the responsibility of both the speaker (sender) and the listener (receiver). Listening is one of the problems in communication that can be improved by the manager. The art of listening must be exercised effectively to

   a. Gain more information about the work situation and

   b. Have a positive effect on both superiors and subordinates through showing concern for their views.

Problems in Listening

2. People can listen several times **faster** than words can be spoken, which may result in inattention and mind-wandering.

3. **Evaluating**, or prejudgment of the message, before or during the communication process may reduce the ability to listen objectively. In other words, the recipient could be biased and may fail to give the message adequate consideration.

4. A decoding problem occurs when concentration is focused on the **words used** to the exclusion of the ideas.

Guides to More Effective Listening

5. **Empathy** is the process of mentally putting oneself in another person's position to better understand his/her feelings, attitudes, and thoughts. Empathy

   a. Enables the sender and the receiver to consider each other's backgrounds, biases, beliefs, and values;

   b. Aids in anticipating others' reactions to messages; and

    c.   Aids in effective communication by guiding the choice of

        1)   Words used and their meanings,

        2)   Word inflection and emphasis, and

        3)   Tone of voice and gestures.

6.   **Sensitivity training** gives managers a greater awareness of, or sensitivity to, their own attitudes, feelings, and beliefs. This understanding helps them perceive how their behavior affects the people with whom they communicate.

    a.   Such training is designed to result in better listening skills, tolerance for individual differences, and an awareness of the effect of one's personality on other people.

    b.   The disadvantage is that some managers may spend a disproportionate amount of time focusing on relationships rather than on the day-to-day problems of the job.

7.   **Interpersonal communications training** helps supervisors and their subordinates learn how to give and receive both written and oral communications. The advantage is that everyone has the same training and can practice working together using specific problems.

8.   Effective listening tools include

    a.   Paraphrasing what has been heard,

    b.   Being attentive physically and mentally,

    c.   Asking relevant questions,

    d.   Avoiding premature judgments, and

    e.   Summarizing after the speaker has finished.

Electronic Communication

9.   **Telecommuting.** In recent years, many people have begun working from outside the office. They correspond with their offices by means of telecommunication.

    a.   Advantages are (1) savings of travel time and expenses, (2) reduced cost of office space, (3) access to larger pool of employees, (4) avoidance of office distractions, and (5) potentially greater productivity.

    b.   Problems associated with these employees include (1) a tendency to fall behind in their fields of specialization, (2) a lack of strong working relationships with other employees, (3) a loss of career opportunities, and (4) inadequate organizational socialization.

    c.   The primary strength of these individuals, however, has been their communication skills.

    d.   Many corporations have taken advantage of fax machines, email, file transfer protocol (ftp), high-speed modems, the Internet, and various network configurations to make telecommuting more practical and useful.

10.   **Email** is part of a global communications revolution. To avoid its excessive, inefficient, or offensive use, an organization should adopt an email **policy**.

    a.   Employees should understand that the organization has the legal right to monitor their use of the email system.

    b.   The policy should stress that the system is not for private use.

    c.   Filters should be installed to protect against spam. If it eludes the filters, it should be promptly deleted.

    d.   The principles of good writing apply to email messages, especially the need for concision.

    e.   The policy should provide guidelines for transmission, receipt, and retention of email.

11. **Cell phones** provide mobile communications at reasonable cost. Because they provide a means of performing work outside a traditional work place, business communications may be more timely, flexible, and convenient.

   a. The disadvantage of cell phones is the increased **risk of security**. Thus, critical information might be revealed to eavesdroppers.

   b. Cell phone use should be consistent with the principles of good manners, including consideration for people nearby.

12. **Videoconferencing** permits people at distant locations to meet without the cost and expenditure of time required for travel.

   a. Videoconferencing via live television or the **Internet** may enhance productivity. Its expense has decreased, and its availability (e.g., through rental of a video-conferencing facility) has increased.

Core Concepts

- Listening is the responsibility of both the speaker (sender) and the listener (receiver). Listening is one of the problems in communication that can be improved by the manager.
- Effective listening tools include (1) paraphrasing what has been heard, (2) being attentive physically and mentally, (3) asking relevant questions, (4) avoiding premature judgments, and (5) summarizing after the speaker has finished.
- Electronic communication may be by telecommuting, email, cell phone, or video-conferencing.

Stop and review! You have completed the outline for this subunit. Study multiple-choice questions 28 through 30 on page 157.

QUESTIONS

6.1 Individual Dynamics

1. A company, the largest provider of mental health services in its area, was encountering personnel problems. The company's facilities housed many clients, but funding never seemed adequate to hire quality, live-in staff. A new administrator is determined to facilitate long-term employment of the best possible care-giving staff. Besides paying better wages, the administrator believes that the staff should be strongly motivated by the work itself. According to Maslow's hierarchy of needs, the best employees would have a need for

A. Esteem.

B. Belonging.

C. Self-actualization.

D. Safety and security.

Answer (C) is correct. *(CMA, adapted)*
   REQUIRED: The aspect of Maslow's hierarchy of needs that refers to the motivation by the work itself.
   DISCUSSION: Self-actualization is the highest level need in Maslow's hierarchy. Self-actualization refers to the desire to become what one is capable of becoming, to realize one's potential and accomplish to the limit of one's ability. It becomes important only after the lower level needs have been met. The work itself becomes the motivator after all lower level needs are satisfied.
   Answer (A) is incorrect. Esteem is the need to be valued, which is satisfied by power, prestige, status, and self-confidence. Answer (B) is incorrect. Belonging is the need to be accepted by others, which would not be applicable when the desire is to have people motivated by the work itself. Answer (D) is incorrect. Safety and security are met by higher wages. The question asks about something above and beyond higher wages.

2. A manager has a small team of employees, but each individual is self-motivated and could be termed a "high achiever." The manager has been given a particularly difficult assignment. Even for a high achiever, the probability that this job can be completed by one individual by the required deadline is low. Select the **best** course for the audit manager.

- A. Assign one individual since high achievers thrive on high risks.
- B. Assign two employees to moderate the risk of failure.
- C. Assign all employees to ensure the risk of failure is low.
- D. Ask company management to cancel the job.

Answer (B) is correct. *(CIA, adapted)*
REQUIRED: The best course of action for a manager whose team consists of high achievers.
DISCUSSION: High achievers wish to do something better than it has been done before. According to McClelland's theory of needs, high achievers thrive when the job provides for personal responsibility, feedback, and moderate risks. They avoid very easy or very difficult tasks, and they do not like to succeed by chance. Accordingly, one high achiever should not be assigned a job when the probability of its successful completion is very low.

3. Which of the following statements is true with respect to a change in values?

- A. Values are neither stable nor enduring.
- B. The process of questioning values will result in a change.
- C. Values are not fixed, and when they change, they change quickly.
- D. Values are established in early years and are unlikely to change.

Answer (D) is correct. *(CIA, adapted)*
REQUIRED: The true statement about values.
DISCUSSION: Values are specific to each individual and involve moral and personal issues. They tend to be learned in childhood from parents, friends, and others. Values can be modified throughout life but ordinarily tend to stay the same.
Answer (A) is incorrect. Values are stable and enduring. Answer (B) is incorrect. Questioning values may result in their reinforcement. Answer (C) is incorrect. Values are relatively fixed and change only slowly.

6.2 Motivation

4. Frederick Herzberg postulated a two-factor theory of human behavior that included satisfiers and dissatisfiers. Which of the following is a dissatisfier?

- A. Promotion to another position.
- B. Salary.
- C. Challenging work.
- D. Responsibility.

Answer (B) is correct. *(CIA, adapted)*
REQUIRED: The item that is a dissatisfier.
DISCUSSION: Frederick Herzberg's two-factor theory of human behavior postulates that there are two classes of factors in the job situation. Maintenance of hygiene factors (dissatisfiers) are those the presence of which will not especially motivate people but the absence of which will diminish performance. These factors are extrinsic to the work itself. They include supervision, working conditions, interpersonal relations, salary, and status. Motivational factors (satisfiers) are those the absence of which will not diminish performance but the addition or availability of which will motivate employees. Intrinsic to the work itself, these include achievement, recognition, challenging work, advancement, growth in the job, and responsibility.
Answer (A) is incorrect. Recognition and status are satisfiers. Answer (C) is incorrect. Challenging work is a satisfier. Answer (D) is incorrect. Responsibility is a satisfier.

5. Alternative work schedules for employees are said to increase the efficiency of business operations. Alternative work schedules are consistent with the underlying concepts of which theory?

    A. Motivation-hygiene theory.

    B. Theory X.

    C. Equity theory.

    D. Cognitive evaluation theory.

Answer (A) is correct. *(CIA, adapted)*
    REQUIRED: The theory that supports alternative work schedules.
    DISCUSSION: Herzberg's two-factor theory of human behavior postulates two classes of factors: motivational and hygiene. Hygiene factors (dissatisfiers) include those factors whose presence will not especially motivate people but whose absence will lead to diminished motivation. These factors are extrinsic to the work itself. They include status, interpersonal relations, and alternative work schedules. Hygiene factors such as work schedules need to be adequate so that workers will have little dissatisfaction. The absence of motivational factors (satisfiers) will not diminish performance, but their addition or availability will motivate employees. Intrinsic to the work itself, they include achievement, advancement, and recognition.
    Answer (B) is incorrect. Theory X assumes that workers have to be coerced, controlled, or threatened to achieve goals. Answer (C) is incorrect. According to equity theory, individuals compare their inputs and outputs with those of others. Answer (D) is incorrect. According to cognitive evaluation theory, allocating extrinsic rewards for behavior that had been previously intrinsically rewarded tends to decrease the overall level of motivation.

6. An employee's self-actualization need would be met by

    A. Attractive pension provisions.

    B. Challenging new job assignments.

    C. Good working conditions.

    D. Regular positive feedback.

Answer (B) is correct. *(CIA, adapted)*
    REQUIRED: The item that meets an employee's self-actualization need.
    DISCUSSION: Self-actualization is the highest level need in Maslow's hierarchy. It is the desire to become what one is capable of becoming, to realize one's potential and accomplish to the limit of one's ability. In other words, the job itself is an intrinsic motivation; no extrinsic motivation (such as rewards or reinforcements) is needed. Intrinsic motivation provides the worker with psychological income. Thus, challenging new job assignments meet an employee's self-actualization needs.
    Answer (A) is incorrect. Attractive pension provisions meet an employee's physiological needs. Answer (C) is incorrect. Good working conditions meet an employee's physiological needs. Answer (D) is incorrect. Regular positive feedback meets an employee's esteem needs.

7. Both Maslow and Herzberg have developed popular motivational theories. Which statement **best** distinguishes Herzberg's theory?

    A. Job performance improves as job satisfaction increases.

    B. Job performance improves as physiological needs are met.

    C. Job esteem improves as physiological needs are met.

    D. Job esteem improves as job satisfaction increases.

Answer (A) is correct. *(CIA, adapted)*
    REQUIRED: The statement that best distinguishes Herzberg's theory.
    DISCUSSION: Frederick Herzberg's two-factor theory of human behavior postulates that there are two classes of factors in the job situation. Maintenance or hygiene factors are those whose presence will not especially motivate people but whose absence will diminish performance. These factors are extrinsic to the work itself. They include supervision, working conditions, interpersonal relations, salary, and status. Motivational factors are those the absence of which will not diminish performance but the addition or availability of which will motivate employees. Intrinsic to the work itself, these include achievement, recognition, challenging work, advancement, growth in the job, and responsibility.
    Answer (B) is incorrect. Physiological needs are at the base of Maslow's hierarchy of needs. Answer (C) is incorrect. Maslow's theory is that higher needs emerge as lower needs are met. Answer (D) is incorrect. Esteem and satisfaction are almost synonymous.

8. Some behavioral models stress employee participation as a key to motivation. A limitation of the participative approach is

A. Workers are intrinsically lazy and must be driven.

B. A number of dissatisfiers must be present in order for the approach to work.

C. It is difficult to elicit the participation of all employees.

D. Unresolvable conflicts arise when a mature, capable, creative person joins a structured, demanding, and limiting organization.

Answer (C) is correct. *(CIA, adapted)*
REQUIRED: The limitation of the participative approach.
DISCUSSION: For a participative management approach to succeed, the parties must have sufficient time, the issues must be relevant to employees' interests, employees must have the abilities (training and communication skills) to participate, and the organizational culture should support participation. Accordingly, a limitation of the participative approach is that it is unlikely that all employees are willing to participate in decision making.
Answer (A) is incorrect. The participative approach assumes that workers are positively motivated. Answer (B) is incorrect. The presence of dissatisfiers is not consistent with the participative approach. Answer (D) is incorrect. Such conflicts arise when the needs of individuals are not integrated with the needs of the organization.

9. In many jobs, excessive specialization can eventually lead to poor motivation, boredom, and alienation. In order to cope with the potential problems in such a situation, managers should

A. Focus on the employees' higher-level needs in order to help them achieve self-actualization.

B. Remove dissatisfiers such as low salary, bad supervision, lack of job security, and poor working conditions.

C. Implement an optimal organizational rewards system and provide all needed training to keep employees up to date on technology.

D. Change the jobs to fit the employees' needs or rotate employees to jobs that satisfy the employees' needs.

Answer (D) is correct. *(CIA, adapted)*
REQUIRED: The approach to cope with employee boredom, poor motivation, and alienation.
DISCUSSION: Job design theories of motivation specifically address the issue of overspecialization. These theories focus on the match between the person and the job as the key to motivation. The recommendation for dealing with the potential problems of overspecialization and boredom is either to enrich the job or to move the employee to a job that provides the appropriate level of challenge.
Answer (A) is incorrect. Focusing on employees' higher-level needs in order to help them achieve self-actualization is a recommendation based on Maslow's hierarchy of needs that does not address the job itself as a source of motivation. Answer (B) is incorrect. Removing dissatisfiers does not address the issue of overspecialization, although it may remove some of the obstacles to motivation. Answer (C) is incorrect. Implementing an optimal organizational rewards systems and providing extensive training to keep employees up to date do not address the job and the issue of overspecialization.

10. Two managers were discussing the merits of goal setting to improve employee performance. One manager felt that specific goals should not be established and that, to provide for flexibility, only generalized goals should be used. The other manager felt that specific, difficult goals produce the best results. As the discussion continued, other methods of goal setting were identified. Select the **best** method for setting goals.

A. The manager should provide generalized goals.

B. The manager should select specific, difficult goals.

C. The employee should develop generalized goals and obtain management concurrence.

D. The employee should develop specific, difficult goals and obtain management concurrence.

Answer (D) is correct. *(CIA, adapted)*
REQUIRED: The best method for setting goals.
DISCUSSION: According to Edwin Locke's goal-setting theory, specific, difficult goals to which the employee is committed provide the best motivation tool. Performance improves when goals are specific rather than general, difficult rather than easy, and participative (self-set) rather than imposed by others. Feedback, especially self-generated feedback, also improves performance compared with lack of feedback. Commitment to goals, that is, a determination not to reduce or abandon them, and self-efficacy, that is, a belief in one's ability to accomplish the task, are additional qualities that result in better performance.
Answer (A) is incorrect. Specific, difficult goals provide more motivation than generalized goals. Answer (B) is incorrect. Employee involvement in goal setting provides better assurance that employees will be committed to the goals. Answer (C) is incorrect. Specific, difficult goals provide more motivation than generalized goals.

11. The human resource department of an organization observed that accounting staff turnover was unusually high. Exit interviews indicated that the accounting department work schedule was highly restrictive for accountants who had young children. To improve the retention of skilled employees in the accounting department, the **best** solution would be to

A. Implement a program of job rotation within the accounting department.

B. Promote job enlargement for the positions experiencing the greatest turnover.

C. Provide job sharing and flextime opportunities for accounting department employees.

D. Enrich the jobs of accounting department employees.

Answer (C) is correct. *(CIA, adapted)*
REQUIRED: The best way to improve employee retention.
DISCUSSION: Job sharing and flextime allow employees to adjust their work schedules and hours to better achieve personal objectives. These programs can increase worker loyalty and motivation.
Answer (A) is incorrect. Job rotation would not adequately address the scheduling issue. Answer (B) is incorrect. Job enlargement would not adequately address the scheduling issue. Answer (D) is incorrect. Job enrichment would not adequately address the scheduling issue.

6.3 Nature of Communication

12. Communication plays an important role in the successful operation of all organizations. Which of the following statements concerning organizational communications is **false**?

A. Communication involves at least two people: a sender and a receiver.

B. Communication is what the sender says, not what the receiver understands.

C. Every act of communication influences the organization in some way.

D. Management spends the majority of its time communicating with other members of the organization.

Answer (B) is correct. *(CIA, adapted)*
REQUIRED: The false statement concerning organizational communications.
DISCUSSION: The communication process has five elements: the sender, the symbols in which the message is encoded, the medium through which the message flows, the receiver, and feedback. Because the effectiveness of communication can be known only by its impact on the receiver and the perceived change in the receiver's behavior, the received message must govern the definition. The sent message may be garbled in encoding, in transmission, or in the receiver's decoding.
Answer (A) is incorrect. Communication involves at least a sender and a receiver. Answer (C) is incorrect. An organization is, by definition, two or more people gathered together for a common purpose. These people agree on organizational goals via communicating their objectives, and management spends the majority of its time influencing the achievement of goals by communicating with other members of the organization. Answer (D) is incorrect. An organization is, by definition, two or more people gathered together for a common purpose. These people agree on organizational goals via communicating their objectives, and management spends the majority of its time influencing the achievement of goals by communicating with other members of the organization.

13. Which of the following is **least** appropriate with regard to management's approach to informal group or grapevine communication? Management should

A. Use informal group information to supplement communication channels of the formal organization.

B. Try to suppress informal group information as a possible source of conflicting information.

C. Take advantage of informal group information as a device to correct misinformation.

D. Make use of informal group information as a means of transmitting information not appropriate for formal communication channels.

Answer (B) is correct. *(CIA, adapted)*
REQUIRED: The least appropriate management actions regarding the grapevine.
DISCUSSION: The effective manager stays tuned into the grapevine and uses it constructively.
Answer (A) is incorrect. Management can use a grapevine or informal communication network to supplement the formal communication process. Answer (C) is incorrect. Management can use a grapevine or informal communication network to correct misinformation. Answer (D) is incorrect. Management can use a grapevine or informal communication network to transmit information not appropriate for formal communication channels.

14. Which of the following is the **best** indicator of the effectiveness of a communication on a receiver?

A. Understanding of message received.

B. Clarity of message.

C. Change in receiver's attitude.

D. Change in receiver's behavior.

Answer (D) is correct. *(CIA, adapted)*
REQUIRED: The best indicator of a communication's effectiveness.
DISCUSSION: The best indicator of the effectiveness of a communication on the receiver is the change in the receiver's behavior in the direction requested or required by the communication. The sender has the responsibility to solicit feedback (or observe results) to determine the communication's effectiveness.
Answer (A) is incorrect. A receiver who understands a message may change attitude but may not necessarily change behavior. Answer (B) is incorrect. Although the clarity of the message is a receiver perception necessary to understanding (believing) the message, the receiver must respond appropriately before the message is effective. Answer (C) is incorrect. A receiver who understands a message may change attitude but may not necessarily change behavior.

15. A company is rumored to be considering downsizing. Because a manager stops the use of all temporary employees, the staff concludes that some jobs will be lost. Which of the following is true about the manager's communication about job losses?

A. The staff decoded the formal communication sent by the manager correctly.

B. The manager properly encoded the idea in a message.

C. The lack of a formal message had a negative impact on staff.

D. The channel through which the message was sent was appropriate.

Answer (C) is correct. *(CIA, adapted)*
REQUIRED: The true statement about the manager's communication regarding job losses.
DISCUSSION: Management's lack of formal communication regarding possible downsizing caused the employees to draw their own negative conclusions based on a manager's actions. Management should formally communicate the reasons for eliminating the use of temporary employees or refute the rumor about downsizing.

16. When evaluating communication, the accountant should be aware that nonverbal communication

A. Is independent of a person's cultural background.

B. Is often imprecise.

C. Always conveys a more truthful response.

D. Always conveys less information than verbal communication.

Answer (B) is correct. *(CIA, adapted)*
REQUIRED: The true statement about nonverbal communication.
DISCUSSION: Nonverbal communication (body language) consists of facial expressions, vocal intonations, posture, gestures, and appearance, and physical distance. Thus, by its nature, nonverbal communication is much less precise than verbal communication.
Answer (A) is incorrect. Nonverbal communication is heavily influenced by culture. For example, a nod of the head may have opposite meanings in different cultures. Answer (C) is incorrect. Nonverbal communication is not necessarily more truthful. Answer (D) is incorrect. Nonverbal communication can sometimes convey more information.

17. Which of the following is an example of upward communication?

A. Management's notices on bulletin boards.

B. Grievance actions.

C. Informational inserts in pay envelopes.

D. Personnel policy manuals.

Answer (B) is correct. *(CIA, adapted)*
REQUIRED: The item that is an example of upward communication.
DISCUSSION: Grievance actions are a formal means of bringing employee dissatisfaction to the attention of management, i.e., from the bottom upward.
Answer (A) is incorrect. This is an example of downward communication. Official changes in procedures or benefits can be announced by notices on bulletin boards. Answer (C) is incorrect. This is an example of downward communication. Official changes in procedures or benefits can be announced by notices on bulletin boards. Answer (D) is incorrect. This is an example of downward communication. Official changes in procedures or benefits can be announced by notices on bulletin boards.

18. Effective communication is **most** likely to take place when the

   A. Sender and receiver share similar frames of reference.

   B. Message is stated in general rather than specific terms.

   C. Message is delivered as quickly as possible.

   D. Sender ignores any underlying assumptions.

Answer (A) is correct. *(CIA, adapted)*
  REQUIRED: The situation most likely to encourage effective communication.
  DISCUSSION: Effective communication is likely to have the least amount of distortion when the sender and the receiver share similar frames of reference. If both sender and receiver understand the symbols used to communicate and the underlying assumptions concerning the problem, the message will be easier to write, to send, and to understand.
  Answer (B) is incorrect. Stating a message in general terms will not create effective communication if the message concerns a specific problem. Answer (C) is incorrect. Haste can make waste. A message cannot be effective if it is coded too quickly or if some is lost in transit. Answer (D) is incorrect. The sender should not assume that the receiver will recall all underlying assumptions. If both ends of the message share a frame of reference, underlying assumptions need not be spelled out, but they should not be ignored.

6.4 Problems in Communication

19. In some organizations, first-line supervisors withhold or alter unfavorable information that the supervisors do not want higher management to know. This selective withholding of information is widely known as

   A. Selective reception.

   B. Filtering.

   C. Regulating information flow.

   D. Perceptual defense.

Answer (B) is correct. *(CIA, adapted)*
  REQUIRED: The true term for withholding information from higher management.
  DISCUSSION: Communication within an organization must be clear, appropriate, and properly transmitted. Distortion can be unintentional (e.g., a phone line going dead), or it may follow from deliberate filtering either by the sender or an intermediary. The auditor should watch for indications that first-line or lower-level management is "filtering" out bad news or covering up irregularities.
  Answer (A) is incorrect. Selective reception (perceptual defense), the tendency for people to hear what they want or expect to hear, is filtering by the recipient. Answer (C) is incorrect. Regulating information flow deals more with volume than content. Answer (D) is incorrect. Selective reception (perceptual defense), the tendency for people to hear what they want or expect to hear, is filtering by the recipient.

20. In a report, an internal auditor stated that communication in the auditee area was poor with employees deciding in advance which information should be given to management so as to present themselves in the best possible light. This is an example of

   A. Filtering.

   B. Selective perception.

   C. Emotion.

   D. Language.

Answer (A) is correct. *(CIA, adapted)*
  REQUIRED: The definition of filtering.
  DISCUSSION: Filtering of a message is the sender's manipulation of information so that it will be viewed more favorably by the receiver. Filtering is a typical problem in upward communication, e.g., from employee to manager.
  Answer (B) is incorrect. Selective perception involves the receiver selectively interpreting what they see or hear based on their interest, background, experience, and attitudes. Answer (C) is incorrect. Emotions affect the interpretation of the message, not the contents. Answer (D) is incorrect. Choice of language involves the personal selection of words to communicate the same message without distorting it.

21. A purchasing agent placed a rush telephone order with a supplier. The clerk in the supplier's office repeated the order specifications back to the purchasing agent. No written confirmations were exchanged. The shipment arrived late and was of the wrong quantity. However, the purchasing agent was unable to prove that the shipment was unsatisfactory. What link of the communication chain has failed in this scenario?

    A. Encoding.

    B. Decoding.

    C. Medium.

    D. Feedback.

Answer (C) is correct. *(CIA, adapted)*
    REQUIRED: The link of the communication chain that failed.
    DISCUSSION: In the communication process, the medium is the channel through which the communication flows. The failure in this case was caused by the choice of a medium that did not create a permanent record of the facts of the communication.
    Answer (A) is incorrect. The order information was repeated back correctly to the sender, so it was encoded properly.
    Answer (B) is incorrect. The order information was repeated back correctly to the sender, so it was decoded properly.
    Answer (D) is incorrect. The supplier's clerk gave accurate verbal feedback on the essentials of the order.

Questions 22 and 23 are based on the following information. A multinational firm was attempting to buy a controlling interest in a medium size (US $10 million annual sales) foreign metal-working firm. The multinational firm's negotiator in the foreign country sent the following email: "The foreign firm won't deal unless 51% ownership." The executive committee of the multinational firm, not wanting a minority interest, then canceled the deal. Upon returning to the multinational firm, the negotiator pointed out that the foreign firm wanted to sell no more than 51% ownership in order to retain at least 49%. Thus, the deal could have been made.

22. The email received by the executive committee was faulty. In terms of the links in the communications process, the error occurred because of

    A. Noise in the communication chain.

    B. The sender's perception.

    C. Message encoding.

    D. The choice of transmission medium.

Answer (C) is correct. *(CIA, adapted)*
    REQUIRED: The reason for the communications error.
    DISCUSSION: Encoding is the sender's packaging of an idea for better understanding. It involves translating the message into symbols that can be transmitted through the chosen medium of communication and then decoded by the recipient. In this example, the sender's wording of the message was misleading.
    Answer (A) is incorrect. The message was received exactly as transmitted. Answer (B) is incorrect. The sender had the correct perception of the message as it was actually encoded. Answer (D) is incorrect. No transmission errors occurred.

23. The faulty email led to a communications error by the executive committee of the multinational firm. The error was in

    A. Decoding of the message.

    B. Choice of transmission medium.

    C. Understanding of the message.

    D. Response to the message.

Answer (C) is correct. *(CIA, adapted)*
    REQUIRED: The nature of the communications error.
    DISCUSSION: Because of faulty encoding, the message was open to two different interpretations. The committee chose the wrong one.
    Answer (A) is incorrect. The committee applied a reasonable meaning to the message. Answer (B) is incorrect. The medium was capable of completing the exchange. Answer (D) is incorrect. The action taken was appropriate given how the email was decoded by the committee.

24. Studies of managerial communications have indicated that

A. Most managers are excellent communicators.

B. Managers spend most of their time communicating.

C. Written communication takes more of a manager's time than oral communication.

D. Most effective communicators will be good managers.

Answer (B) is correct.   *(CIA, adapted)*
REQUIRED: The true statement concerning managerial communications.
DISCUSSION: Because communication is the process of conveying meaning or understanding from one person to another, managers must spend most of their time communicating with subordinates, peers, and superiors. They communicate organizational goals and plans downward, lower-level results and problems upward, and coordinating information horizontally (among peers or across organizational channels).
Answer (A) is incorrect. One of the problems within management is the inability of many managers to clearly and concisely communicate ideas, concepts, directives, policies, results, etc. Answer (C) is incorrect. Managers spend more time in oral than in written communication. Answer (D) is incorrect. Good management requires more than just effective communication. If a manager cannot motivate subordinates, even clearly communicated information will be ineffective to achieve organizational objectives.

25. Which of the following is unlikely to cause changes in attitudes?

A. Make sure that the message is credible.

B. Present many different issues in as short a time as possible.

C. Shape the argument to the listener.

D. Focus the presentation on the ultimate objective.

Answer (B) is correct.   *(CIA, adapted)*
REQUIRED: The communication technique unlikely to cause changes in attitudes.
DISCUSSION: Presenting many different issues in as short a time as possible will confuse the listener and cause the message to be lost or disregarded. To convey a persuasive message effectively, the communicator should make a clear presentation that focuses on the ultimate objective. The argument should be stated one idea at a time, and unrelated subjects and jumping from issue to issue should be avoided. The presentation should guide the recipient of the communication directly to the desired conclusion.
Answer (A) is incorrect. Trust, competence, objectivity, and high ethical standards are important in changing attitudes. Answer (C) is incorrect. Effective persuasion demands flexibility so that the arguments presented have a better chance of changing the person's attitudes. Answer (D) is incorrect. To convey a persuasive message effectively, the communicator should make a clear presentation that focuses on the ultimate objective.

26. "But I mailed the order 4 weeks ago, giving the supplier plenty of time," said the parts manager when asked why a critical part was not available. The **most** likely reason for this failed communication between the parts manager and the supplier was

A. Lack of feedback.

B. Confusing language.

C. Inappropriate medium.

D. Perceptual selectivity.

Answer (A) is correct.   *(CIA, adapted)*
REQUIRED: The most likely reason for failed communication between the parts manager and the supplier.
DISCUSSION: The effectiveness of communication can be determined only by the sender seeking feedback and observing the impact of the communication on the receiver. The sender is obligated to solicit feedback to ensure that the communication process is complete. The receiver should give feedback to the sender. The importance of feedback to check the effectiveness of the communication process indicates the limitations of one-way communications (e.g., memos). Effectiveness can only be measured when the sender perceives a change in the receiver's behavior. Thus, the parts manager (the sender) should have sought and the supplier (the receiver) should have provided, feedback.
Answer (B) is incorrect. The facts do not suggest that the language used was confusing. Answer (C) is incorrect. The mail is an acceptable medium of transmission. Answer (D) is incorrect. The supplier had no reason to ignore (selectively screen out) an order. A supplier's perceptual selection obviously includes rather than excludes customer orders.

27. A manager found that instructions given to a subordinate were not followed. A review of the cause of the failure revealed that the manager was interrupted by several telephone calls while issuing the instructions. In terms of problems in the communications chain, the interruptions are

A. Noise.

B. Nonverbal feedback.

C. Semantics.

D. Closure.

Answer (A) is correct. *(CIA, adapted)*
   REQUIRED: The interruptions encountered in the communications process.
   DISCUSSION: Noise in the communication channel refers to any disruption that impedes the encoding, sending, or receipt of a message, such as being interrupted by several telephone calls while issuing instructions.
   Answer (B) is incorrect. Nonverbal feedback, or body language, encompasses the facial expressions, gestures, and posture that send various messages. Answer (C) is incorrect. Semantics is the study of meanings, especially connotative nuances. Answer (D) is incorrect. Closure is the process of filling in the blanks of an incomplete message.

6.5 Listening and Electronic Communication

28. Which of the following is a potential disadvantage of listening by a manager?

A. Demonstrates concern for subordinates by the manager.

B. Concentration may be focused on the words spoken to the exclusion of the ideas.

C. Gain more information about the workplace.

D. May result in higher employee morale.

Answer (B) is correct. *(Publisher, adapted)*
   REQUIRED: The advantages of effective listening.
   DISCUSSION: If a manager is focused on the words spoken by someone else and not the intended ideas, a decoding problem exists. Effective listening requires understanding the message the communicating party is trying to convey.
   Answer (A) is incorrect. Effective listening has a positive effect on both superiors and subordinates through showing concern for each others views. Answer (C) is incorrect. Effective listening by managers often gives the manager a better idea of what employees are thinking and potential problems. Answer (D) is incorrect. Effective listening by a manager shows subordinates that their input is valued and often raises employee morale.

29. Which of the following is **false** with regard to email policies?

A. Employees may use informal writing because email is often informal in nature.

B. Employees should understand that the organization has a legal right to monitor the employees' use of the email system.

C. Filters should be used to protect against spam.

D. Emails should be concisely written.

Answer (A) is correct. *(Publisher, adapted)*
   REQUIRED: The policies associated with email use in an organization.
   DISCUSSION: The principles of good writing still apply to emails. Thus, emails should be written with the same care as formal communications within the organization.
   Answer (B) is incorrect. Employers are legally permitted to keep track of employee activities while employees are at work, including monitoring emails. Answer (C) is incorrect. Filters should be used to prevent incoming spam. If spam eludes the filters, it should be deleted. Answer (D) is incorrect. Emails are still supposed to be written with good writing skills.

30. Telecommuting, working away from the office and communicating via electronic media, has become more widespread as advances in communication devices have made telecommuting more practical. All of the following are problems that are beginning to be associated with employees using telecommuting **except** that the telecommuting employees

A. Fall behind in their fields of specialization.

B. Lack strong working relationships.

C. Experience a loss of career opportunities.

D. Lack sufficient communication skills.

Answer (D) is correct. *(CMA, adapted)*
   REQUIRED: The item that is not a problem associated with employees who telecommute from their homes.
   DISCUSSION: People who are computer literate have in recent years begun working from their homes via telecommunication devices. Problems include lack of reliable telephone lines, a potential increase in management's work load, the loss of in-office contributions, a tendency to fall behind in fields of specialization, a lack of strong working relationships with other employees, a loss of career opportunities, and inadequate socialization. The primary strength of these individuals, however, has been their communication skills.
   Answer (A) is incorrect. Telecommuters have tended to fall behind in their fields of specialization. Answer (B) is incorrect. Telecommuters may be unable to form normal manager-employee and employee-employee relationships. Interaction with telecommuters poses obvious problems. Answer (C) is incorrect. Telecommuters sometimes experience a loss of career opportunities as a result of not being in the office on a day-to-day basis.

Use the additional questions in Gleim *CIA Test Prep* Software to create Test Sessions that emulate Pearson VUE!

STUDY UNIT SEVEN
ORGANIZATIONAL STRUCTURE AND EFFECTIVENESS

(20 pages of outline)

This study unit addresses the organizing function of management. It outlines the major theories of organizational design and describes the elements of organizational effectiveness. Particular emphasis is placed on the contingency approach to design developed from systems thinking. Other subunits concern some of the principal formats for integrating and coordinating an organization's activities.

The design of an organization's structure is a crucial part of its governance process. An internal auditor is ideally placed to make recommendations about improvements in lines of reporting.

7.1 THE ORGANIZING PROCESS

Overview

1. **Edgar Schein** describes the following elements of organizations:

    a. **Coordination of effort** in a cooperative social arrangement
    b. A **common goal or purpose**
    c. **Division of labor** (efficient specialization)
    d. A **hierarchy of authority**

        1) Authority is the right to direct, and to expect performance from, other people. Those people are **accountable** to their superiors in the hierarchy.

2. **Robert Kreitner** classifies organizations as follows:

    a. **Businesses** are engaged in economic activities with the intent to make a profit.
    b. **Nonprofit service organizations**, such as charities and universities, serve particular groups of clients. Money may come from donations, appropriations, or grants.
    c. **Mutual benefit organizations** are groups that exist to serve their members, e.g., labor unions, political parties, or credit unions.
    d. **Commonweal organizations** provide a standard service to all members of a population. Examples are local police departments and public school systems.

3. **Organizational charts** represent the formal organizational structure in two dimensions: vertical hierarchy and horizontal specialization. They often resemble a pyramid, with the chief executive on top and the operating workforce on bottom.

    a. Recent trends in management, including increased span of control and decreased hierarchy, have resulted in flatter organizational charts.

    b.   The typical organizational chart can be designed to do the following:

        1)   Reflect classical, formal vertical authority channels **(chain of command)**

        2)   Show reporting relationships and task groupings **(departmentation)**

        3)   Describe communication channels

        4)   Identify location of sources of organizational expertise

        5)   Show promotional or career tracks

        6)   Depict the span of control and number of organizational levels

        7)   Show major **functions** and their respective relationships **(horizontal specialization)**

    c.   The following are weaknesses of organizational charts:

        1)   Limited presentation of information, which may be overcome by supplementing the chart with a detailed manual

        2)   Tendency to become obsolete due to rapid change

        3)   Failure to show informal communication, influence, power, or friendships

        4)   Tendency to ignore informal job trade-offs among titles on the chart

        5)   Possibility of misleading management by giving an appearance of structure and order that might not exist

        6)   Possibility that position titles do not reflect actual functions

Theories of Organizing

    4.   Theories of organizing may be divided into two categories: traditional, closed-system theories and modern, open-system theories.

    5.   The **closed-system perspective** treats the organization as focused on economic efficiency in a reasonably predictable environment. Planning and control processes can substantially eliminate uncertainty.

        a.   The **scientific school of management** focused on the production process and ways to make it more efficient. It is based on the work of **Frederick W. Taylor**, who advocated a systematic quantitative approach oriented towards individual job design. Taylor's **principles of scientific management** are the following:

            1)   Scientific analysis of work

            2)   Scientific selection, training, and development of workers

            3)   Cooperation among work planners and operators

            4)   Equal sharing of responsibility by labor and management, who perform the tasks for which they are best suited

        b.   **Henri Fayol**, sometimes called the father of administration, advocated the separation of administration from technical, commercial, financial, and accounting operations. Fayol's **functions of management** listed below form the foundation for the modern functional or process approach to classifying a manager's activities.

            1)   Planning

            2)   Organizing

            3)   Commanding

            4)   Coordinating

            5)   Controlling

        c.   Taylor, Fayol, and other traditionalists advocated the creation of authoritarian organizations with narrow spans of control, close supervision, and the top-down flow of authority.

            1)   The **hierarchy of authority** should be precisely determined to foster pursuit of common objectives **(unity of objective)**.

2)   The **principle of unity of command** should be followed. Each subordinate should have only one superior (though a superior may have as many subordinates as allowed by the superior's span of control).

    a)   Violation of this principle leads to confusion and frustration for the subordinate.

3)   **Authority should be** proportionate to **responsibility**. Thus, a person should not be held accountable for performance unless (s)he has the power to perform.

4)   Authority but not responsibility may be **delegated**.

d.   According to **Max Weber**, a **bureaucracy** is a traditionalist organization founded on efficient military principles, including "impartiality," or the making of personnel decisions based on merit.

    1)   It is characterized by

        a)   Division of labor,
        b)   A hierarchy of authority,
        c)   A framework of rules, and
        d)   Impersonality.

    2)   Despite its bad reputation, bureaucracy is a feature of every large organization. Because bureaucracy is necessary, managers should be aware of the symptoms of an inefficient and otherwise **dysfunctional bureaucracy**. These include the following:

        a)   A high degree of bureaucratization
        b)   Too many boring jobs
        c)   Obedience to authority at all costs
        d)   Development of rules that are pointless or that obscure accountability
        e)   Impersonality in the sense of ignoring the human needs of customers and employees

    3)   As an organization increases in **size**, its structure tends to become more **formal and mechanistic** (bureaucratic). More **policies and procedures** are necessary to coordinate the increased number of employees, and more managers must be hired.

        a)   However, the relationship between size and changes in structure is linear only within a certain range. For example, adding 100 employees to an organization with 100 employees is likely to cause significant structural change, but adding the same number to a workforce of 10,000 is likely to have little effect.

        b)   When an organization reaches a certain size (1,500 to 2,000 or more), it usually has most of the qualities of a mechanistic structure.

6.   The **open-system perspective** treats the organization as focused on survival in an uncertain environment. The organization itself and the environment contain variables that may not be controllable.

a.   **Chester Barnard** described an organization as a **cooperative system** with a bottom-up flow of authority. According to his **acceptance theory of authority**, a manager's leadership depends on employees' acceptance.

    1)   Thus, compliance with a message from a superior is dependent on employees'

        a)   Understanding of the message
        b)   Belief that it serves an organizational objective
        c)   Belief that it serves their objectives
        d)   Ability to comply

b.   A successful organization must **adapt** rapidly to changes in such factors as

   1)   Technology progress,
   2)   Product evolution,
   3)   Market conditions,
   4)   Competitive challenges, and
   5)   Globalization.

c.   An **organizational system** is a group of subsystems that are interrelated and form parts of a larger whole. According to the open-systems perspective, an organization cannot succeed without considering the larger system of which it is a part.

   1)   It also considers both human relations and structural issues.

   2)   **Closed systems** are closed to the external environment. Few systems are truly closed, but boundaries may be artificially drawn to facilitate analysis by treating a system as if it were closed.

      a)   Early writers on management treated it as a closed system and ignored most things external to the organization.

         i)   Such policy is limited and dangerous in that effective management of a social system is not deterministic or mechanistic.

   3)   **Open systems** are not self-sufficient. They must interact with an **external environment**. The **system boundaries** are drawn to reflect external inputs and system outputs.

      a)   A closed system suffers **entropy**, or progressive degradation and disorganization. An open system seeks replenishment through its boundaries with the larger system (environment).

         i)   Accordingly, an open system is in **dynamic equilibrium**. For example, a business may obtain external financing to modernize its plant.

   4)   An open system is **synergistic**. Its parts interact so that the total effect exceeds the sum of the effects of the separate parts.

   5)   Another attribute of open systems is **equifinality**, or the ability to achieve desired results by using different methods.

      a)   For example, a manufacturer may vary such inputs into the production process as labor and materials.

   6)   A business or other open system obtains **inputs** (information, capital, labor, materials, etc.) and produces **outputs** (goods, services, earnings, nonrecycled scrap, etc.).

   7)   An open system consists of the following:

      a)   The **technical subsystem** (the production function)

      b)   The **boundary-spanning subsystem**, which interacts with the environment (sales, purchasing, public relations, planning, etc.)

      c)   The **management subsystem**, which coordinates the other subsystems

   8)   An open-systems organization also should be a **learning organization**. According to David Garvin, it should effectively create, acquire, and transfer knowledge. Moreover, it must change its behavior in response.

      a)   Organizational learning proceeds by **cognition** (acquiring new knowledge), **behavior** (acquiring new skills), and **performance**.

       b)   The following are **skills** required for an organization to prosper as it copes with inevitable change:

          i)   Problem solving

          ii)   Learning by systematic experimentation

          iii)   Learning from its experience

          iv)   Learning from customers, competitors, and others

          v)   Transferring and implementing what has been learned, e.g., through training and communication

Organizational Effectiveness

7.   In the narrowest sense, effectiveness is achievement of objectives. It is contrasted with **efficiency**, which is the ratio of output to input. In the broadest sense, an organization must achieve its objectives efficiently to be considered effective.

    a.   Economists define **productivity** as the ratio of real output to a unit of input. Increased productivity is the goal of every organization because its effect is to improve the ultimate measures of performance, such as the profits of a business.

        1)   For example, in a retail store, a critical output of interest is revenue per square foot. The floor space in the store is a limited resource whose productivity should be analyzed.

8.   Continued profitability and growth are the obvious effectiveness criteria for businesses. However, **society's expectations** expressed through laws and regulations (antitrust, securities regulation, labor law, worker safety, environmental protection, pension security, antidiscrimination, consumer protection, etc.) provide many other criteria.

    a.   The weighting of these concerns raises difficult issues for all businesses.

9.   **Time** is a component of organizational effectiveness. Consequently, an organization should be effective and efficient, grow, be profitable, satisfy society's and its stakeholders' expectations, learn, adapt, develop, and survive over a period of years.

    a.   The organization needs to be effective and efficient and meet expectations of society, owners, employees, customers, and creditors in the **near term** (about 1 year).

    b.   It must **adapt** to change and **develop** its capacities in the **intermediate term** (about 2-4 years).

    c.   It must **survive** in an uncertain environment full of threats and opportunities in the **long term** (about 5 years or more).

10.   **Organizational decline** (inflexibility and loss of effectiveness and efficiency) may lead to downsizing, merger, reorganization, or liquidation. It results from decreased demand, resource limitations, or mismanagement.

    a.   The following are **characteristics** of organizations that are stable or in decline:

        1)   Centralization

        2)   Lack of long-term planning because of a short-term crisis mentality

        3)   Lack of innovation

        4)   A tendency to place blame on leaders

        5)   Rejection of change when most needed

        6)   High turnover of the best leaders

        7)   Poor morale

        8)   Not setting priorities for cutbacks

        9)   Conflict over control and resources when teamwork is most needed

b. **Management complacency** is the most important cause of organizational decline. The following are its characteristics:

1) A lack of innovation
2) Faulty perception of markets and competition
3) Failure to observe or properly appraise the initial warnings of decline
4) Not focusing on daily objectives

c. An **adaptive organization**

1) Monitors problems and watches for the symptoms of decline.
2) Restates and clarifies its objectives on a timely basis.
3) Identifies the best markets and customers and the most threatening competitors.
4) Promotes experimentation, communication, and participation.
5) Recognizes that it may be the most vulnerable when it is the most successful. Overconfidence tends to be greatest then.

d. **Downsizing** results from organizational decline, changes in the business cycle, or business combinations. The objectives are cost reduction, improved efficiency, and higher profits.

1) These purposes often are not achieved. Many organizations follow cycles of hiring, firing, and rehiring that do not yield the expected benefits to offset the harm to terminated employees, the loss of morale of the survivors, and the damage to communities.
2) Downsizing also tends to have a disproportionate effect on women and members of minorities, who tend to be the last hired and first fired.
3) The more enlightened view is that employees are not readily disposable commodities but valuable resources who should be terminated only as a last resort. This view seeks alternatives to involuntary termination.

   a) Redeployment involves retraining or transferring employees or lending them to other companies.
   b) Voluntary retirement programs offer accelerated retirement benefits, severance allowances, or other compensation.
   c) Employees may share jobs or be shifted to lower-level positions.
   d) All employees may be asked to accept reduced hours or pay.
   e) Outplacement assists laid-off employees in finding new jobs.
   f) The law may require notice of facilities' closings or layoffs.
   g) A job bank provides downsized employees with work that is usually outsourced.
   h) Counseling and training may be offered to counter the stress felt by employees who are retained.

Core Concepts

- Organizational charts represent the formal organizational structure in two dimensions: vertical hierarchy and horizontal specialization. They often resemble a pyramid, with the chief executive on top and the operating workforce on bottom. However, they present limited information and fail to show informal communication, influence, power, or friendships.

- The closed-system perspective treats the organization as focused on economic efficiency in a reasonably predictable environment. Planning and control processes can substantially eliminate uncertainty. This perspective is identified with the work of Frederick W. Taylor (the scientific school of management), Henri Fayol (functions of management), and Max Weber (bureaucracy).

■ The open-system perspective treats the organization as focused on survival in an uncertain environment. The organization itself and the environment contain variables that may not be controllable. This perspective reflects the reality that a successful organization must adapt rapidly to changes in such factors as (1) technology progress, (2) product evolution, (3) market conditions, (4) competitive challenges, and (5) globalization. It is identified with the work of Chester Barnard (acceptance theory of authority) and David Garvin (the learning organization).

■ In the narrowest sense, effectiveness is achievement of objectives. It is contrasted with efficiency, which is the ratio of output to input. In the broadest sense, an organization must achieve its objectives efficiently to be considered effective.

■ Organizational decline (inflexibility and loss of effectiveness and efficiency) may lead to downsizing, merger, reorganization, or liquidation. It results from decreased demand, resource limitations, or mismanagement. Management complacency is the most important cause of organizational decline.

Stop and review! You have completed the outline for this subunit. Study multiple-choice questions 1 through 4 beginning on page 178.

7.2 THE CONTINGENCY APPROACH

1. According to the contingency approach (derived from **open systems** concepts), answers to organizational design problems depend on contingencies that can be discovered and studied. No one design format fits all organizations.

    a. Because solutions are situationally determined, the key is finding the relevant factors in the organization's **environment**.

    b. Moreover, the greater the environmental uncertainty, the more **adaptive** the organization must be.

2. Contingency design determines the **structure** that suits the **environmental (state) uncertainty** faced by the organization. Environmental uncertainty is a function of, among other things,

    a. Stability of demand for the organization's goods or services,
    b. Reliability of supply,
    c. Rate of technological change, and
    d. Socioeconomic and political pressures.

Mechanistic vs. Organic Organizations

3. Burns and Stalker distinguished between mechanistic and organic organizations.

    a. A **mechanistic organization** (an inflexible bureaucracy), is most likely to succeed in **stable and certain environments**. In such an entity,

        1) Tasks are specifically defined and have little flexibility.
        2) Knowledge tends to be task-specific.
        3) Hierarchical authority is strong, with an emphasis on employee obedience.
        4) Communication is mostly top-down.
        5) Rights and obligations are clearly defined, but how individual efforts relate to achieving organizational objectives is not.

b.   An **organic organization** is most likely to succeed in **unstable and uncertain environments** because it is adaptive. In such an entity,

1)   Tasks are broadly and flexibly defined.
2)   The relationship of individual effort and organizational objectives is clear.
3)   Knowledge tends to be professional.
4)   Work methods, rights, and obligations are purposely left unclear.
5)   Self-control is preferred to hierarchical control.
6)   Superiors have an informational and advisory role.
7)   Communication is participative and horizontal.

Differentiation vs. Integration

4.   Lawrence and Lorsch addressed the relationship between environmental complexity and the organization's balance between differentiation and integration.

a.   **Differentiation** is caused by the division of labor and technical specialization. Thus, specialists in, for example, marketing and IT may have substantial differences in skills, attitudes, and behavior.

1)   Differentiation leads to **organizational fragmentation** because specialists tend to have a narrow focus.

b.   **Integration** is the coordination of effort required for achievement of mutual objectives. Typical structural arrangements for achieving integration include

1)   A hierarchy of authority,
2)   A framework of rules,
3)   Departmentation,
4)   Formation of cross-functional groups,
5)   Computer systems,
6)   Liaison bodies, and
7)   Human relations training.

c.   In successful organizations (and in their subunits), a **dynamic equilibrium** exists between the tendencies of differentiation and coordination. Furthermore,

1)   Differentiation and integration are directly correlated with **environmental complexity**.
2)   The higher the differentiation, the greater the obstacles to integration.
3)   An unsuccessful organization in a complex environment is likely to be highly differentiated but poorly integrated.

Organizational Components

5.   According to Henry Mintzberg, an organization has five components. Depending on which is in control, one of five different structures will evolve. The following are the organizational components:

a.   **Operating core** -- workers who perform the basic tasks related to production
b.   **Strategic apex** -- top managers
c.   **Middle line** -- managers who connect the core to the apex
d.   **Technostructure** -- analysts who achieve a certain standardization in the organization
e.   **Support staff** -- indirect support services

6.   Mintzberg's five organizational structures include the following:

a.   A **simple structure**, such as that of a small retailer, has a low complexity and formality, and authority is centralized. Its small size and simplicity usually precludes significant inefficiency in the use of resources.

1)   The strategic apex is the dominant component.

b. A **machine bureaucracy** is a complex, formal, and centralized organization.

    1) A machine bureaucracy

        a) Performs highly routine tasks.
        b) Groups activities into functional departments.
        c) Has a strict chain of command.
        d) Distinguishes between line and staff relationships.

    2) The technostructure dominates.

c. A **professional bureaucracy** (e.g., a university or library) is a complex and formal but decentralized organization in which highly trained specialists have great autonomy. Duplication of functions is minimized. For example, a university would have only one history department.

    1) The operating core is in control.

d. A **divisional structure** is essentially a self-contained organization. Hence, it must perform all or most of the functions of the overall organization of which it is a part. It has substantial duplication of functions compared with more centralized structures.

    1) The middle line dominates.

e. An **adhocracy** (an organic structure) has low complexity, formality, and centralization. Vertical differentiation is low, and horizontal differentiation is high. The emphasis is on flexibility and response.

    1) The support staff dominates.

Core Concepts

- According to the contingency approach, (derived from open systems concepts), answers to organizational design problems depend on contingencies that can be discovered and studied. No one design format fits all organizations. Contingency design determines the structure that suits the environmental (state) uncertainty faced by the organization.

- Burns and Stalker distinguished between mechanistic and organic organizations. In a mechanistic organization (an inflexible bureaucracy), tasks are specifically defined and have little flexibility. Moreover, knowledge tends to be task-specific. An organic organization is adaptive. Tasks are broadly and flexibly defined, and the relationship of individual effort and organizational objectives is clear. In addition, knowledge tends to be professional.

- Lawrence and Lorsch addressed the relationship between environmental complexity and the organization's balance between differentiation and integration. Differentiation is caused by the division of labor and technical specialization. Thus, specialists in, for example, marketing and IT may have substantial differences in skills, attitudes, and behavior. Differentiation leads to organizational fragmentation because specialists tend to have a narrow focus. Integration is the coordination of effort required for achievement of mutual objectives.

- According to Henry Mintzberg, an organization has five components. Depending on which is in control, one of five different structures will evolve. The five organizational components are the (1) operating core, (2) strategic apex, (3) middle line, (4) technostructure, and (5) support staff. Mintzberg's five organizational structures are (1) simple structure, (2) machine bureaucracy, (3) professional bureaucracy, (4) divisional structure, and (5) adhocracy.

Stop and review! You have completed the outline for this subunit. Study multiple-choice questions 5 through 7 beginning on page 179.

7.3 DEPARTMENTATION

1. **Division of labor** divides complex processes into their simpler components. This makes task specialization by employees possible. However, dividing labor creates a need for efficient coordination of those performing the separate tasks.

    a. One response to the problem is departmentation, a structural format for organizational integration that is intended to promote coordination. It is the grouping of related activities into significant organizational subsystems (groups, divisions, units, departments, etc.).

Types of Departmentation

2. **Departmentation by function** is found in almost every organization at some level, whether for-profit or nonprofit. The most common departments in for-profit organizations are marketing, production, and finance (though other terms may be used). These often extend upward in the organizational chart to the level below the chief executive.

    a. **Advantages** include occupational specialization, simplified training, and representation of primary functions at the top level of the organization.

    b. **Disadvantages** include lack of coordination among primary functions and absence of profit centers within the organization.

3. **Departmentation by territory** (geographic location) is favored by national or multinational firms and government agencies with scattered resources, offices, or plants.

    a. **Advantages** include

        1) Quicker reaction to local market changes,
        2) Greater familiarity with local problems or unique geographic concerns, and
        3) Logistical savings in freight costs and travel time.

    b. Advances in telecommunications counteract some of the **disadvantages**, which include

        1) More delegation of authority to regional managers,
        2) Problems of control for headquarters, and
        3) Duplication of facilities and service functions (personnel, purchases, etc.).

4. **Departmentation by product or service** is typical in multiline, large-scale enterprises. It often results from functional departmentation.

    a. Thus, product or service subunits may be treated as separate businesses with a high degree of autonomy. Managers must therefore have a broad perspective, not a merely functional orientation.

    b. **Advantages** include

        1) Better use of specialized capital and skills,
        2) Ease of coordination,
        3) Simpler assignment of profit responsibility,
        4) Compatibility with a decentralization strategy, and
        5) A basis for allocating capital efficiently to products or services likely to achieve the best returns.

    c. **Disadvantages** include

        1) The requirement for a greater number of persons with managerial ability,
        2) Duplication of facilities and service functions, and
        3) Difficulty integrating operations.

5.   **Departmentation by customer** allows for service to a particular customer to be provided under the management of a subunit.

   a.   This form of departmentation seldom appears at the top level of an organizational structure, but it is common at middle levels (e.g., the loan officer of a large bank who handles one account exclusively).

       1)   Customer departmentation is typical in the sales department of a firm organized by function.

   b.   **Advantages** include

       1)   Improved customer service as a result of greater expertise in a particular business and

       2)   Ease in identifying contributions to profit by different types and locations of customers.

   c.   **Disadvantages** include

       1)   Difficulties in coordination with other units in the organization,
       2)   Pressure to give preferential treatment to a given manager's customers, and
       3)   Duplication of facilities and service functions.

6.   **Project departmentation** is appropriate for experimental or one-time activities, e.g., the construction of a ship or large building, or a major design project (such as the development of a new generation of large-scale passenger aircraft).

   a.   **Advantages** include specialization and ease of communication and coordination of efforts required within a particular project.

   b.   **Disadvantages** include need for reorganization at the end of the project, problems of recruitment at the start of the project, and difficulty of maintaining control at the central office.

7.   **Departmentation by work flow process** is used in reengineered organizations.

   a.   Reengineering involves starting anew to redesign an organization's core processes rather than attempting to improve the current system. Reengineering is not merely downsizing or continuous improvement, but a complete change in ways of doing business.

       1)   In the modern, highly competitive business environment, an organization needs to adapt quickly and radically to change. Thus, reengineering is usually a cross-functional process of innovation requiring substantial investment in information technology and retraining.

           a)   Successful reengineering may bring dramatic improvements in customer service and the speed with which new products are introduced.

   b.   Organizations that use **work flow process** design are **horizontal organizations**. Their objective is an outward focus on customer satisfaction.

       1)   For this purpose, the horizontal work flow between **identification of customer needs** and satisfaction of those needs is to be managed quickly and efficiently.

Matrix Design

8.   Matrix design may combine any of the previously mentioned approaches. For example, a manager for each product may be appointed to supervise personnel who simultaneously report to a manager for each function. This form is used in R&D and in **project management**.

   a.   The emphasis of the arrangement is on the result or the product.

   b.   The functional organization remains, but parts of it are temporarily assigned to a given project.

c. The project may be to make a product indefinitely or to accomplish a limited but lengthy task, such as construction of a football stadium.

d. Matrix design provides the security and accountability of the functional form. However, it also provides expert personnel to the project only when needed and only to the extent required.

  1) It allows personnel as well as functions to be most effectively and efficiently used.

e. The technical ability of employees is better appraised by the functional managers than by the project manager.

f. Practical applications skills can be appraised by the project manager on site.

g. Unnecessarily large swings in levels of personnel and equipment are minimized.

  1) The major disadvantage is that the **unity-of-command** principle is violated. Hence, the authority, responsibility, and accountability of the parties involved must be clearly defined to avoid confusion and employee dissatisfaction.

  2) A second disadvantage is the possible inefficient use of employees. Individuals may be idle while waiting for project assignments that require their specific talents.

h. It is difficult for large organizations to use matrix design because they typically have many levels (both vertical and horizontal), thus slowing communications.

Core Concepts

■ Division of labor divides complex processes into their simpler components. This makes task specialization by employees possible. However, dividing labor creates a need for efficient coordination of those performing the separate tasks. One response to the problem is departmentation. Departmentation may be by function, territory, product or service, customer project, or work flow process.

■ Matrix design may be a combination of any of the approaches to departmentation. For example, a manager for each product may be appointed to supervise personnel who simultaneously report to a manager for each function. This form is used in R&D and in project management.

Stop and review! You have completed the outline for this subunit. Study multiple-choice questions 8 through 12 beginning on page 180.

7.4 LINE AND STAFF DESIGN

Major Approaches

1. The **classical** approach views **line** activities as those directly responsible for the primary function, product, or service of the organization. Staff members provide supporting technical expertise.

a. In **mechanistic organizations**, a line-and-staff design helps to preserve unity of command.

b. Production is a line activity, but more current writers include sales (marketing) and sometimes finance, depending on the objectives of the organization.

c. **Staff** activities are advisory. They are necessary to the organization but secondary to the line functions.

  1) A distinction should be made between **personal staff** and **specialized staff**. The first are individuals assigned to a given manager, and the second are functions that serve the whole organization.

2. **Behavioral theorists'** concerns with **acceptance of authority** define their approach to line and staff relationships. They see exercise of **informal authority** as a very important constraint on formal chains of command.

   a. Advice offered by senior staff members is similar to a command. They have access to senior management and can exercise more informal authority than a junior line manager.

   b. Even the classical school acknowledged the dilemma of how to ensure adoption of specialized staff advice without subverting line authority.

      1) If line management refuses to accept staff's advice, what can senior management do?

   c. A staff group with **advisory authority** can offer only suggestions, prepare plans for consideration by line managers, and evaluate organizational performance.

      1) A staff member often has an area of technical expertise, such as law, industrial labor relations, operations research, or personnel.

      2) The staff member's goal is the approval (or rejection) of a complete recommended solution, but a line manager may want a quick fix to a problem rather than a complete solution.

      3) Consultation with line personnel is essential.

   d. A staff group may have **concurrent** authority. Line management must persuade experts in specified areas to agree to an action or decision.

      1) For example, a line production manager may be required to obtain a second signature on a lease agreement from the legal department.

   e. A staff group may be given complete authority in a specialized area, and its specialized activities are separated from line management.

      1) Unlike advisory activities, the line manager must use the services of the staff organization.

      2) Examples include information systems, purchasing, and personnel.

   f. A staff group may occasionally be given **control** authority. Thus, line authority may be superseded by that of the specialist staff designated by higher levels of management to make certain decisions in the area of staff expertise.

      1) Control staff authority appears to violate classical principles of unity of command. However, no violation occurs when members of the control staff act as agents for the higher-level line manager, who has delegated authority.

         a) For example, quality-control inspectors have the authority to reject marginal products, but because this authority is exercised on behalf of the manufacturing manager, the chain of command actually remains intact.

   g. If the organization adopts **total quality management** concepts with an emphasis on internal as well as external service, line managers and staff personnel may be viewed as having a **customer-service provider** relationship.

3. A hybrid of the control authority relationship of line and staff is **functional authority**. This kind of design is common in **organic organizations**.

   a. An individual is given functional authority outside the chain of command for certain specified activities. The individual may be either a line or a staff manager who is a specialist in a particular field.

      1) For example, the vice president in charge of sales may be given functional authority over manufacturing executives in scheduling customer orders, packaging, or making service parts available.

b.   Functional authority may be created for numerous reasons when a line manager is not the person best suited to oversee a given activity.

   1)   For example, the vice president for industrial labor relations may have functional authority over the production manager for the purpose of negotiating a new labor contract, though no line relationship exists at other times.

c.   Functional specialists have the authority to determine the appropriate standards in their own field of specialization and to enforce those standards.

   1)   For example, the chief engineer of an airline may have the authority to remove airplanes from service, overriding the wishes of the vice president for operations.

Line and Staff Conflicts

4.   Line and staff conflicts are almost inevitable given the considerable difference in their backgrounds and activities. These individuals tend to have different training and education, perspectives on the organization, career and other objectives, and temperaments.

a.   Line and staff conflicts are classic results of the **differentiation and fragmentation** process discussed in Subunit 7.2.

b.   Operating executives with line authority often see a high potential for harm in staff activity. A staff member with vaguely defined authority from a chief executive may effectively undermine line managers.

c.   Staff members are not responsible for the success of a line department, but only for generating suggestions. If an implemented suggestion fails, line managers will blame the suggestion, and staff will blame the poor implementation of the suggestions.

   1)   Thus, conflict may arise because line managers may have no authority to influence staff behavior when it is inconsistent with the achievement of objectives.

d.   Setting staff members apart from line responsibilities gives them the time and environment in which to think. However, this separation also can lead to thinking in a vacuum and suggestions by staff that are inappropriate or not feasible.

e.   Excessive staff activity may violate the principle of **unity of command**. Subordinates may become confused and wonder whether they are primarily responsible to the staff member or to their line manager.

5.   Line-staff conflicts may be **minimized** by

a.   Clearly defining areas of activity and authority.

b.   Sharply defining the nature and place of line and staff. For example, line managers may have authority and responsibility, and staff members may be required to sell their ideas to line managers.

c.   Stressing the systems approach to all employees, whether line or staff, to encourage them to work together toward organizational goals.

d.   Reducing areas of possible conflict, e.g., keeping functional authority to a minimum and providing feedback to staff of line's reaction to proposals.

e.   Using the concept of **completed staff work** when possible. Thus, recommendations should be complete enough to make possible yes-or-no responses from line managers. Advice should be clear and complete.

6.   The modern approach to line and staff activities is based on **systems theory**.

a.   Every position and task must contribute to achievement of organizational objectives.

b.   Distinctions between producers and helpers are irrelevant.

    c.   The changing nature of work environments from predominantly production firms to predominantly service providers makes it harder to pinpoint who exactly is responsible for producing.

        1)   For example, at a motor inn with the objective of customer satisfaction, who is line and who is staff?

Core Concepts

- The classical approach to organization theory views line activities as those directly responsible for the primary function, product, or service of the organization. Staff members provide supporting technical expertise. In mechanistic organizations, a line-and-staff design helps to preserve unity of command. Staff activities are advisory. They are necessary to the organization but secondary to the line functions.

- Behavioral theorists' concerns with acceptance of authority define their approach to line and staff relationships. They see exercise of informal authority as a very important constraint on formal chains of command.

- A hybrid of the control authority relationship of line and staff is functional authority. This kind of design is common in organic organizations.

- Line and staff conflicts are almost inevitable given the considerable difference in their backgrounds and activities. These individuals tend to have different training and education, perspectives on the organization, career and other objectives, and temperaments. Line and staff conflicts are classic examples of differentiation and fragmentation.

Stop and review! You have completed the outline for this subunit. Study multiple-choice questions 13 through 15 beginning on page 182.

7.5 SPAN OF CONTROL

1.   **Span of control** (span of management or span of authority) is an upper limit to the number of people who can be effectively and efficiently supervised by one person.

2.   The **classical view** is that the universal span of control is five or six people.

3.   **Behaviorists** advocate expanding the span of control if possible. The following are advantages:

    a.   **Increasing autonomy and morale** of individual workers by reducing the time available to a manager to direct them (the more people per manager, the less time available per person)

    b.   **Decreasing communication problems** by reducing organizational levels (given a fixed number of employees, the narrower the span of control, the taller the organization, and the greater the number of levels)

4.   The **modern or contingency approach** suggests that the appropriate span of control varies widely. The following are the situational variables that determine the span of control:

    a.   The supervisor's training, interests, abilities, personality, time available, etc.

    b.   Workers' interests, drives, commitment to the job, training, attitudes, aptitudes, etc.

    c.   The work situation, including the technological process used (job shop, mass production, continuous process), frequency of change in job method, complexity of the task, dependence on the work of others, and supervision required

    d.   The organizational culture and established policies and procedures

    e.   The organization's environment, including how rapidly it is compelled to change by technological innovation or market pressure and the amount of **uncertainty** in the environment

5.   Spans of control tend to move from wider to narrower as

    a.   The work done becomes **less similar**.
    b.   Workers being supervised become more **dispersed** geographically.
    c.   The work done becomes more **complex**.
    d.   The frequency and intensity of **required supervision** increase.
    e.   The time needed for **coordination** with other supervisors increases.
    f.   The time needed for **planning** increases.

6.   The number of levels in an organization will be greatly influenced by the span of control.

    a.   **Flat organizational structures** have relatively few levels from top to bottom. They have wide spans of control.

        1)   Flat structures provide fast information flow from top to bottom of the organization and increased employee satisfaction.

        2)   Disadvantages of reduced supervision are poorer employee training, lack of coordination, and behavioral problems.

    b.   **Tall organizational structures** have many levels between top and bottom. They have relatively narrow spans of control.

        1)   Tall structures are faster and more effective at problem resolution than flat structures. They increase frequency of interaction between superior and employee and impose greater order.

        2)   Disadvantages are slow decision making, excessive supervision, greater administrative costs, and lack of initiative resulting from too little delegation of authority.

    c.   Studies do not indicate great advantages for either flat or tall structures.

Core Concepts

-    Span of control is an upper limit to the number of people who can be effectively and efficiently supervised by one person.

-    The behavioral school advocates expanding the span of control if possible. The modern or contingency approach suggests that the appropriate span of control varies widely. It identifies the situational variables that determine the span of control. The number of levels in an organization will be greatly influenced by the span of control.

-    Flat organizational structures have relatively few levels from top to bottom. They have wide spans of control. Flat structures provide fast information flow from the top to the bottom of the organization and increased employee satisfaction. Disadvantages of reduced supervision are poorer employee training, lack of coordination, and behavioral problems.

-    Tall organizational structures have many levels between top and bottom. They have relatively narrow spans of control.

Stop and review! You have completed the outline for this subunit. Study multiple-choice questions 16 through 23 beginning on page 183.

7.6 CENTRALIZATION AND DECENTRALIZATION

Overview

1.   Major design issues are the concentration of authority in an organization, its degree, and the levels at which it occurs.

    a.   Centralization and decentralization are relative terms. Absolute centralization or decentralization is impossible.

    b.   **Classicists** view decentralization with distrust because they seek to avoid any dilution of control by senior managers.

    c.   **Behaviorists** view decentralization in the same way as delegation, that is, as a good way to improve motivation and morale of lower-level employees.

2. The **modern or contingency view** is that neither centralization nor decentralization is good or bad in itself. The degree to which either is stressed depends upon a given situation.

    a. Decisions cannot be decentralized to those who do not have necessary **information**, e.g., knowledge of job objectives or measures for evaluation of performance.

    b. Decisions cannot be decentralized to people who do not have the training, experience, knowledge, or **ability** to make them.

    c. Decisions requiring a **quick response** should be decentralized to those near the action.

    d. Decentralization should not occur below the organizational level at which **coordination** must be maintained (e.g., each supervisor on an assembly line cannot be allowed to decide the reporting time for employees).

    e. Decisions that are **important** to the survival of the organization should not be decentralized.

    f. Decentralization has a positive influence on **morale**.

3. Decentralization is a philosophy of organizing and managing. Careful selection of which decisions to push down the hierarchy and which to make at the top is required. The **degree of decentralization** will be greater if

    a. More decisions are made lower in the hierarchy.
    b. More of the important decisions are made lower in the hierarchy.
    c. More functions are affected by decisions made at lower levels.
    d. Fewer decisions made lower in the hierarchy are monitored by senior management.

4. Organizational design should achieve a **balance** between centralization and decentralization. The main benefits of centralization are more **effective control and reduced costs** through resource sharing. The main benefits of decentralization are **flexibility and adaptability** that permit a rapid response to changes in circumstances.

    a. The more centralized organization tends to thrive in a relatively stable and certain environment.

    b. The more decentralized organization tends to be more successful in a relatively unstable and uncertain environment.

5. Establishment of **strategic business units (SBUs)** is a means of decentralization used by large corporations seeking to enjoy the entrepreneurial advantages of smaller entities.

    a. An SBU in principle is permitted by its parent to function as an **independent business**, including development of its own strategic plans. A true SBU

        1) Is not merely a supplier of the parent, but serves its own markets
        2) Encounters competition
        3) Is a **profit center**
        4) Makes all important decisions about its business although it may share resources with the parent

Delegation

6. Delegation is the formal process of assigning authority downward. Delegation is similar to decentralization in philosophy, process, and requirements.

    a. The **classical approach** is to avoid delegation because the superior is deemed to be both responsible and knowledgeable. Under that view, delegation avoids responsibility.

    b. The **behavioral view** sees delegation as useful in every organization because no one has time to make every decision, and employees like to make decisions affecting their work.

   c.   The **modern or contingency approach** is to view delegation as dependent on the situation and the people involved. Delegation requires

      1)   Skill, self-confidence, and knowledge of organizational objectives
      2)   A feedback system to allow objective assessment of performance
      3)   Faith in employees' abilities
      4)   Clear recognition of the basic need to delegate
      5)   Willingness to accept risk
      6)   Desire to develop and train employees

   d.   The **delegation process** involves

      1)   Determination of results expected
      2)   Assignment of tasks and responsibilities
      3)   Delegation of authority for accomplishing these tasks
      4)   Recruitment of responsible people for the accomplishment of tasks
      5)   Clear communication of what is expected in objective terms
      6)   Follow-up, because the delegator still has **ultimate responsibility**

   e.   The **benefits of delegation** are time savings for the delegator, training and development of lower-level managers, and improved morale.

   f.   The following are **obstacles to delegation**:

      1)   The delegator is a perfectionist, has low self-esteem, fears criticism or competition, lacks confidence in lower-level managers, or has low risk tolerance.
      2)   Jobs are poorly defined.
      3)   Controls are ineffective.
      4)   Superiors are not role models for delegation.

   g.   The following is the **continuum of delegation** in ascending order of the authority assigned to the subordinate from low to high:

      1)   Investigation and reporting back to the superior
      2)   Investigation and recommendations of actions to the superior
      3)   Investigation and advising the superior about plans
      4)   Investigation and undertaking action, with reporting to the superior on what was done
      5)   Investigation and undertaking action

New Types of Organizations

   7.   New types of organizations tend to have **flatter structures** (fewer layers), make more use of **teams**, and avoid the disadvantages of the complex large entity by creating **entrepreneurial units**.

   a.   An **hourglass organization** has three layers:

      1)   The **strategic layer** determines the mission of the organization and ensures that it is successful.

      2)   A few **middle managers** coordinate a variety of lower-level cross-functional activities. These managers are generalists, not specialists, and they are not simply conduits for operating information.

         a)   Computer systems can instantly transfer such information directly to the top layer.

      3)   On the lowest level are **empowered technical specialists** who are most often self-supervised. They lack promotion possibilities but are motivated by lateral transfers, challenging work, training in new skills, and pay-for-performance plans.

    b.   A **cluster organization** is in essence a group of teams. Workers are multiskilled and shift among teams as needed. Communication and group skills are vital, requiring special training and team-building exercises. Pay is for knowledge.

    c.   **Network organizations.** The relative independence of the various firms in a network differentiates it from a vertically integrated organization.

        1)   A network is not based on the price mechanism or on a hierarchical relationship but on coordination through adaptation.

        2)   It is a long-term, strategic relationship based on implicit contracts without specific legal ties.

        3)   A network allows member firms to gain a competitive advantage against competitors outside the network.

        4)   A network may be viewed as a group of **activities involving suppliers and customers that add value**. Each activity may be performed internally at an **internal cost** or subcontracted at an **external cost**.

           a)   When an activity is subcontracted, a **transaction cost** will be incurred.

           b)   A technological restriction on the existence of a network is that **external costs must be less than internal costs**.

              i)   The firms in the network must be able to reduce the transaction costs so that the combination of external and transaction costs is less than internal costs.

           c)   The difference between a network and a normal market is that transaction costs in the market are low enough for any player.

              i)   In a network, the participating firms reduce initially high transaction costs through cooperative efforts.

        5)   A network is an ultimate expression of **outsourcing**, which involves obtaining goods or services from outside sources that could be acquired internally.

           a)   For example, a firm may choose to outsource its computer processing or legal work, and a manufacturer may buy rather than make components.

    d.   **Virtual organizations** are "flexible networks of value-adding subcontractors, linked by the Internet, email, fax machines, and telephones" (Kreitner, 9th ed., pages 343-344).

        1)   The emphasis is on speed and constant, if not too rapid, change.
        2)   Constant learning is essential.
        3)   Cross-functional teams are emphasized.
        4)   Stress is high.

Core Concepts

- Major design issues are the concentration of authority in an organization, its degree, and the levels at which it occurs. Centralization and decentralization are relative terms. Absolute centralization or decentralization is impossible.

- Classicists view decentralization with distrust because they seek to avoid any dilution of control by senior managers. Behaviorists view decentralization in the same way as delegation, that is, as a good way to improve the motivation and morale of lower-level employees. The modern or contingency view is that neither centralization nor decentralization is good or bad in itself. The degree to which either is stressed depends upon a given situation.

- Decentralization is a philosophy of organizing and managing. Careful selection of which decisions to push down the hierarchy and which to make at the top is required.

- Establishment of strategic business units (SBUs) is a means of decentralization used by large corporations seeking to enjoy the entrepreneurial advantages of smaller entities. An SBU in principle is permitted by its parent to function as an independent business, including development of its own strategic plans.

- Delegation is the formal process of assigning authority downward. Delegation is similar to decentralization in philosophy, process, and requirements. The contingency approach views delegation as dependent on the situation and people involved.

- New types of organizations tend to have flatter structures (fewer layers), make more use of teams, and avoid the disadvantages of the complex large entity by creating entrepreneurial units. Examples include the hourglass organization, the cluster organization, and the network organization. Kreitner identifies virtual organizations as being "flexible networks of value-adding subcontractors, linked by the Internet, email, fax machines, and telephones."

Stop and review! You have completed the outline for this subunit. Study multiple-choice questions 24 through 30 beginning on page 185.

QUESTIONS

7.1 The Organizing Process

1. The organizational chart

A. Is used only in centralized organizations.

B. Is applicable only to profit-oriented companies.

C. Depicts only line functions.

D. Depicts the lines of authority linking various positions.

Answer (D) is correct. *(CMA, adapted)*
REQUIRED: The true statement about an organizational chart.
DISCUSSION: An organizational chart is used to represent the organizational structure of an entity in two dimensions, vertical hierarchy and horizontal specialization. It often resembles a pyramid, with the chief executive on top and the operating work force on the bottom. Lines show reporting relationships, lines of authority, and task groupings. An organizational chart depicts promotional or career tracks and illustrates the span of control and the number of organizational levels.
Answer (A) is incorrect. An organizational chart can be used in decentralized as well as centralized organizations. Answer (B) is incorrect. Not-for-profit agencies use organizational charts for the same reasons as profit-oriented companies. Answer (C) is incorrect. Both staff and line functions are depicted on organizational charts.

2. Which of the following concepts is **not** consistent with a successful authoritarian organization?

A. Each subordinate should only have one superior.

B. Superiors may have as many subordinates as possible within the superior's span of control.

C. Responsibility may be delegated.

D. The hierarchy of authority should be precisely defined.

Answer (C) is correct. *(Publisher, adapted)*
REQUIRED: The characteristics of a successful authoritarian organization.
DISCUSSION: Taylor, Fayol, and other traditionalists advocated the creation of authoritarian organizations. One of the criteria for success was the ability to delegate authority but not responsibility. Responsibility should always remain with the person who made the decision.
Answer (A) is incorrect. The unity of command principle states that each subordinate should only have one superior in order to prevent confusion and frustration. Answer (B) is incorrect. The unity of command principle states that a superior can have as many subordinates as he or she can reasonably manage. Answer (D) is incorrect. The unity of objective principle requires that the hierarchy of authority be precisely defined to pursue common objectives.

3. Although bureaucracy is often perceived negatively by the public, bureaucracy is a feature of nearly every large company. Which of the following is a sign that a bureaucracy is dysfunctional?

    A. A diversity of jobs.

    B. Rules that obscure responsibility.

    C. A large number of rules necessary for day to day operations.

    D. Obedience to authority.

Answer (B) is correct. *(Publisher, adapted)*
    REQUIRED: The symptoms of a dysfunctional bureaucracy.
    DISCUSSION: A sign that a bureaucracy is dysfunctional is the development of rules that are meaningless or that obscure accountability. A lack of accountability shows that the bureaucracy is ineffective at identifying the source problems and creating solutions to solve the problems.
    Answer (A) is incorrect. A diversity of jobs prevents employees from becoming bored with routine and unchallenging tasks. Answer (C) is incorrect. Many bureaucracies have rules to guide day-to-day operations. As long as the rules have a purpose and are not meaningless, the rules do not create a dysfunctional environment. Answer (D) is incorrect. Obedience to authority is required for a corporation's operations to run smoothly. However, obedience at all costs is a sign that the bureaucracy is dysfunctional.

4. Faced with 3 years of steadily decreasing profits despite increased sales and a growing economy, which of the following is the healthiest course of action for a chief executive officer to take?

    A. Set a turnaround goal of significantly increasing profits within 2 months.

    B. Reduce staff by 10% in every unit.

    C. Reduce staff in the nonvalue-adding functions by 20%.

    D. Encourage innovation at all levels and use an early retirement program to reduce staff size.

Answer (D) is correct. *(CIA, adapted)*
    REQUIRED: The healthiest course of action given decreasing profits despite increasing sales.
    DISCUSSION: Organizational decline (loss of effectiveness and efficiency coupled with inflexibility) may lead to downsizing, merger, reorganization, or liquidation. It results from decreased demand, resource limitations, or mismanagement. One characteristic of a declining organization is lack of innovation. Moreover, the most important cause of organizational decline is management complacency. In turn, a characteristic of management complacency is lack of innovation. Consequently, the CEO should encourage innovation at all levels. Also, downsizing has many negative effects. The enlightened view is that employees are not readily disposable commodities, but rather valuable resources who should be terminated only as a last resort. This view seeks alternatives to involuntary termination. One such alternative is a voluntary retirement program that offers accelerated retirement benefits, severance allowances, or other compensation.
    Answer (A) is incorrect. This response illustrates two of the characteristics of organizational decline: increased centralization of decision making and lack of long-term planning. The exclusive emphasis on short-term results is likely to be counterproductive. Answer (B) is incorrect. Another characteristic of organizational decline is nonprioritized downsizing. By itself, downsizing rarely turns a company around. Answer (C) is incorrect. Reducing staff disproportionately in control functions could have disastrous consequences.

7.2 The Contingency Approach

5. Which of the following is true with regard to the contingency approach to solving problems within an organization?

    A. The organization's environment plays the largest role in finding situationally determined answers.

    B. The organization may be less adaptive when the environment is more uncertain.

    C. The organization should search for a design format that can be used in all cases.

    D. The contingency approach focuses on a closed systems thinking.

Answer (A) is correct. *(Publisher, adapted)*
    REQUIRED: The true statement regarding the contingency approach to solving problems within an organization.
    DISCUSSION: The contingency approach argues for situationally determined answers, the key is finding the relevant factors in the organization's environment.
    Answer (B) is incorrect. The organization should be more adaptive when the environment is uncertain. Answer (C) is incorrect. No single design format fits all organizations and situations. Answer (D) is incorrect. The contingency approach focuses on an open systems thinking.

6. In a dynamic equilibrium, successful organizations have a balance between fragmentation and coordination. Which of the following may cause an organization to risk the loss of this equilibrium?

A. A framework of rules.

B. A hierarchy of authority.

C. Formation of cross-functional groups.

D. Division of labor and technical specialization.

Answer (D) is correct. *(Publisher, adapted)*
REQUIRED: The problems encountered with integration.
DISCUSSION: The division of labor and technical specialization often lead to differentiation within an organization. Differentiation leads to fragmentation because specialists often have a narrow focus and make integration more difficult.
Answer (A) is incorrect. A framework of rules is necessary for an organization to coordinate to achieve mutual objectives. Answer (B) is incorrect. A hierarchy of authority prevents fragmentation of the organization by having a central authority direct when necessary. Answer (C) is incorrect. The formation of cross-functional groups helps employees integrate into the organization and prevents the fragmentation of specialization.

7. Which of the following is a characteristic of a mechanistic organization?

A. Knowledge by employees tends to be task-specific.

B. Self-control is preferred to hierarchical control.

C. Superiors usually have an informational and advisory role.

D. Communication is horizontal.

Answer (A) is correct. *(Publisher, adapted)*
REQUIRED: The characteristics of a mechanistic organization.
DISCUSSION: A mechanistic organization designs tasks that are specifically designed and have little flexibility. Therefore, the mechanistic organization focuses on task-specific knowledge by its employees.
Answer (B) is incorrect. An organic organization prefers self-control instead of hierarchical control. Answer (C) is incorrect. In most organic organizations, management often plays an informal role and allows employees to make many decisions providing input as needed. Answer (D) is incorrect. Organic organizations focus on communication that is participative and horizontal.

7.3 Departmentation

8. Departmentalization is a common form of business integration. Grouping together all related jobs, activities, and processes for a given business objective into a major organizational subunit is an example of

A. Product-service departmentalization.

B. Functional departmentalization.

C. Geographic location departmentalization.

D. Customer classification departmentalization.

Answer (A) is correct. *(CIA, adapted)*
REQUIRED: The type of departmentation defined.
DISCUSSION: Departmentation by product or service is growing in importance for multiline, large-scale enterprises and is an outgrowth of functional departmentation. The result is that product-service subunits may be treated as separate businesses with a high degree of autonomy. Managers must therefore have a broad perspective, not a merely functional orientation.
Answer (B) is incorrect. Functional departmentation categorizes jobs according to the activity performed. Answer (C) is incorrect. Geographic location departmentation categorizes based upon the area in which a part of the business is located. Answer (D) is incorrect. Customer classification departmentation categorizes based upon the differing needs of discrete groups of customers.

9. Departmentalization may be performed by

I.   Function
II. Product
III. Geography

A. I only.

B. II only.

C. I and II only.

D. I, II and III.

Answer (D) is correct. *(CIA, adapted)*
REQUIRED: The way departmentation may be performed.
DISCUSSION: Departmentation may be performed by function, product, and geography. Departmentation by function is found in almost every organization at some level, whether for-profit or nonprofit. The most common departments in for-profit organizations are marketing, production, and finance (though other terms may be used). These often extend upward in the organizational chart to the level below the chief executive. Departmentation by product or service is growing in importance for multiline, large-scale enterprises. It is often an outgrowth of functional departmentation. The result is that product-service subunits may be treated as separate businesses with a high degree of autonomy. Managers must therefore have a broad perspective, not a merely functional orientation. Departmentation by territory (geographic location) is favored by national or multinational firms and government agencies with scattered resources, offices, or plants.
Answer (A) is incorrect. Departmentation may be performed by product and geography. Answer (B) is incorrect. Departmentation may be performed by function. Answer (C) is incorrect. Departmentation may be performed by geography.

10. Which particular type of organization structure will likely have unity-of-command problems unless there is frequent and comprehensive communication between the various functional and project managers?

    A. Line and staff.

    B. Strategic business unit.

    C. Centralized.

    D. Matrix.

Answer (D) is correct. *(CIA, adapted)*
    REQUIRED: The organization structure with unity-of-command problems absent frequent communication among managers.
    DISCUSSION: A matrix structure allows authority to flow both vertically and horizontally. A manager is appointed for each project and draws on personnel who are organized by function and report to a manager for each function. This violates the principle of unity of command, which states that each subordinate should have only one superior.
    Answer (A) is incorrect. A line and staff structure is designed to maximize unity of command by giving only line managers the authority to make decisions affecting those in their chain of command. Answer (B) is incorrect. A strategic business unit is a subunit that is treated as an independent business. Thus, unity of command is not an issue for a strategic business unit. Answer (C) is incorrect. A centralized structure need not have unity-of-command problems if management is organized in a line and staff fashion.

11. Of the following entities, a matrix organization would be **most** appropriate for

    A. A company operating a set of geographically dispersed telephone call centers that provide technical support.

    B. A company which starts several complex, multidisciplinary engineering and construction projects each year.

    C. A retail company, which sells to customers through multiple stores, located in shopping malls, as well as through a website and mailed catalogs.

    D. A company that provides temporary staffing help to a wide variety of commercial and governmental agencies.

Answer (B) is correct. *(CIA, adapted)*
    REQUIRED: The entity most appropriate for a matrix organization.
    DISCUSSION: A matrix organization consists of a project team of people from various functional areas within the organization. These specialists report simultaneously to the project manager and the managers of their functional departments. At the end of the project, the team is disbanded. Accordingly, a matrix organization that assigns specialists as needed to various projects is appropriate for such a company.
    Answer (A) is incorrect. Individuals assigned to work in a call center have only one supervisor. Moreover, they are not employees from different functions. Answer (C) is incorrect. Although multichannel sales require coordination, staff are not necessarily moved from one sales channel to another for project work, and they are not likely to report to different supervisors. Answer (D) is incorrect. Temporary staff do not report to any manager within a temporary agency. They simply work for a wide variety of employers who have full authority. They are not necessarily "specialized staff." If not needed, they are simply not paid.

12. In what form of organization does an employee report to multiple managers?

    A. Bureaucracy.

    B. Matrix.

    C. Departmental.

    D. Mechanistic.

Answer (B) is correct. *(CIA, adapted)*
    REQUIRED: The organization in which an employee reports to multiple managers.
    DISCUSSION: A matrix organization (project management) is characterized by vertical and horizontal lines of authority. The project manager borrows specialists from line functions as needed. This manager's authority is limited to the project, and the specialists will otherwise report to the line managers.
    Answer (A) is incorrect. In a bureaucracy, each subordinate reports to a single manager. Answer (C) is incorrect. Departmental organization structures represent the typical organization with unified and clear single lines of authority. Answer (D) is incorrect. Mechanistic organization structure is another term for a bureaucracy.

7.4 Line and Staff Design

Questions 13 and 14 are based on the following information.

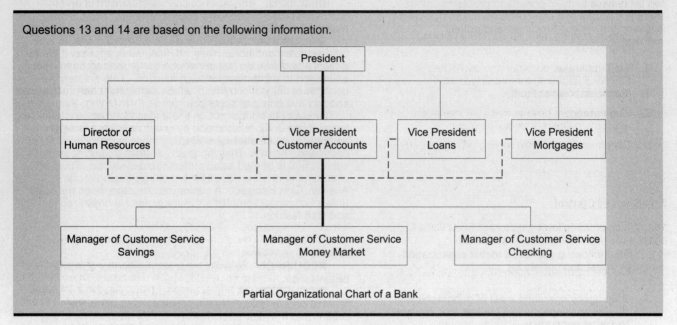

Partial Organizational Chart of a Bank

13. Which of the following is a staff position in the bank?

   A. The manager of customer service-checking, the department that handles checking account inquiries and transactions.

   B. The director of personnel, the department that handles the hiring, firing, promotion, etc., of all employees.

   C. The chief loan officer, who is in charge of final approval of all loans.

   D. The vice president in charge of the mortgage department, which handles mortgages on business and residential property.

Answer (B) is correct. *(Publisher, adapted)*
   REQUIRED: The example of a staff position in a bank.
   DISCUSSION: Staff positions in any organization advise and support the line positions. They indirectly help to achieve the organization's basic objective. Each staff position's authority is, at most, functional. Such authority is exercised only over activities related to the staff's function or specialty.
   Answer (A) is incorrect. The manager of customer service checking is an example of a line position that is directly involved in the achievement of the organization's objectives and directly related to the service(s) and/or product(s) offered by the firm. Answer (C) is incorrect. The chief loan officer is an example of a line position that is directly involved in the achievement of the organization's objectives and directly related to the service(s) and/or product(s) offered by the firm. Answer (D) is incorrect. The vice president in charge of the mortgage department is an example of a line position that is directly involved in the achievement of the organization's objectives and directly related to the service(s) and/or product(s) offered by the firm.

14. The manager of customer service checking at the bank is **most** likely to encounter conflict(s) because of

   A. The department's reliance on the savings manager and the money market manager.

   B. The manager of customer service checking providing services for customers who do not have checking accounts.

   C. The requirement that the manager of customer service checking must report directly to both the president and the vice president for customer accounts.

   D. A potential disagreement with the director of personnel about a subordinate's performance appraisal.

Answer (D) is correct. *(Publisher, adapted)*
   REQUIRED: The conflict most likely to be encountered by a line manager.
   DISCUSSION: The director of personnel (DP) must coordinate all employee evaluations. Although the manager of checking services is in a line position that is not under the DP, (s)he works with the DP when hiring, dismissing, transferring, or evaluating employees.
   Answer (A) is incorrect. The manager of checking is a line position that does not rely on the other customer service managers. Answer (B) is incorrect. The department only provides services for the customers with checking accounts. Answer (C) is incorrect. The manager of checking reports to the president indirectly through a vice president.

15. Line and staff positions are **most** likely to be in conflict because

A. Line managers have no authority over staff employees.

B. Staff managers consider line managers' functional authority threatening to staff managers' own authority.

C. Line managers believe that staff managers are resistant to line managers' advice.

D. Staff managers dislike relying on line expertise.

Answer (A) is correct. *(Publisher, adapted)*
REQUIRED: The cause of conflict between line and staff positions.
DISCUSSION: Line managers are directly responsible for achieving the organization's objectives, but staff managers are not directly accountable. However, line managers may have no authority to influence staff behavior when it is inconsistent with the achievement of objectives.
Answer (B) is incorrect. Staff managers may have functional authority that line managers perceive as threatening. Answer (C) is incorrect. Staff managers give line managers advice, not vice versa. Answer (D) is incorrect. Line managers are likely to become reliant on staff expertise.

7.5 Span of Control

16. Which of the following factors is **least** likely to affect a manager's direct span of control?

A. Frequency of supervisor-subordinate contact.

B. The manager's willingness to delegate authority.

C. The manager's training and communication skills.

D. Number of people in the corporation.

Answer (D) is correct. *(CIA, adapted)*
REQUIRED: The factor least likely to affect a manager's direct span of control.
DISCUSSION: The optimal span of control is the number of subordinates that a given manager can effectively supervise. It is a function of many situational factors. However, the total number of people in an organization has no bearing on the optimal span of control of a particular manager.
Answer (A) is incorrect. Managers who can contact subordinates frequently are able to control more people than those who have relatively infrequent contact with subordinates. Answer (B) is incorrect. Managers who delegate authority have more time to control the subordinates who report to them. These individuals can therefore supervise more people than managers who prefer not to delegate authority. Answer (C) is incorrect. Managers who have received effective training and are skillful communicators are equipped to control more individuals than managers who are untrained and/or have deficient communication skills.

17. Which of the following is generally true regarding a manager's span of control?

A. Narrow spans of control are typically found in flat organizations, those with few hierarchical levels.

B. An organization with narrow spans of control needs more managers than those with wide spans.

C. Wider spans of control mean higher administrative expense and less self-management.

D. Wider spans of control help ensure good internal controls and policy compliance throughout an organization.

Answer (B) is correct. *(CIA, adapted)*
REQUIRED: The true statement regarding a manager's span of control.
DISCUSSION: Span of control (span of management or span of authority) is an upper limit to the number of people who can be effectively and efficiently supervised by one person. Narrow spans of control mean that the ratio of those supervised (subordinates) to those doing the supervision (managers) is lower. Hence, more managers are required.
Answer (A) is incorrect. Narrow spans of control mean a tall organization with many more levels. Answer (C) is incorrect. Narrow spans of control result in higher administrative expense (coordination) and less self-management. Answer (D) is incorrect. Wider spans of control give subordinates more discretion.

18. The difference between a tall organization structure and a flat organization structure is that, in the former,

A. The communication process takes longer and is of poorer quality.

B. Maintenance of the organization is less costly.

C. The morale of lower-level employees is generally higher.

D. A higher degree of coordination and cooperation is created.

Answer (A) is correct. *(CIA, adapted)*
REQUIRED: The difference between tall and flat organization structures.
DISCUSSION: Flat organizational structures have relatively few levels from top to bottom. Tall organizational structures have many levels between top and bottom. Flat structures have the advantages of fast information flow from top to bottom of the organization and increased employee satisfaction. Tall structures are faster and more effective at problem resolution because of the increased frequency of interaction between superior and subordinate and the greater order imposed by the hierarchy. Studies do not indicate great advantages for either flat or tall structures.

19. The most likely span of control to apply over 14 data-entry clerks who do essentially the same job and work in the same office would be

- A. Close.
- B. Narrow.
- C. Moderate.
- D. Wide.

Answer (D) is correct. *(CIA, adapted)*
    REQUIRED: The span-of-control category that would be most applicable.
    DISCUSSION: Underlying variables influence the number of subordinates a manager can supervise. In general, if jobs are similar, procedures are standardized, and physical dispersion is minimized, a wide span of control is most effective.
    Answer (A) is incorrect. Close is not a span-of-control category. Answer (B) is incorrect. A narrow span of control is useful where jobs are dissimilar, procedures are not standardized, and subordinates are more dispersed. Answer (C) is incorrect. A moderate span of control is useful in situations that have some characteristics of both extremes: wide and narrow.

20. In which of the following situations would a narrower span of control be more appropriate?

- A. Managers do not spend a great deal of time on planning or strategic management.
- B. Managers must spend a great deal of time coordinating with other managers.
- C. Subordinates work in the same area rather than being geographically dispersed.
- D. Work performed by subordinates is substantially identical.

Answer (B) is correct. *(CIA, adapted)*
    REQUIRED: The situation in which a narrower span of control is appropriate.
    DISCUSSION: If substantial coordination is required, a manager benefits from reduced supervision requirements. In addition, increased coordination implies that the work done by subordinates is not standardized. As spans of control move from wider to narrower, the work done becomes less similar and more complex.
    Answer (A) is incorrect. If substantial planning is required, a manager benefits from the reduced supervision requirements characteristic of a wider span of controls. Also, increased planning implies a changing environment in which work of subordinates will be changing over time, requiring significant managerial work for training. Answer (C) is incorrect. Geographical dispersion of subordinates justifies a narrow span of control. Answer (D) is incorrect. When subordinates perform very similar work, they can train one another, provide backup if one subordinate is not present, and verify one another's work. In addition, work procedures are relatively easy to document, and a manager can be knowledgeable about the work of everyone. Thus, a wider span of control is appropriate.

21. The optimal span of control of a manager is contingent upon several situational variables. For instance, a manager supervising workers within the same work area who are performing identical tasks that are simple and repetitive would **best** be able to supervise

- A. An unlimited number of employees.
- B. Only a few workers (a narrow span of control).
- C. A relatively large number of employees (a wide span of control).
- D. Fewer workers than if the workers were geographically dispersed.

Answer (C) is correct. *(CIA, adapted)*
    REQUIRED: The optimal span of control of a manager supervising workers within the same work area who are performing identical tasks that are simple and repetitive.
    DISCUSSION: Underlying variables influence the number of subordinates a manager can supervise. In general, if jobs are similar, procedures are standardized, and physical dispersion is minimized, a wide span of control is most effective.
    Answer (A) is incorrect. Although a manager under these conditions would be able to supervise a large number of employees, an upper limit must exist. Answer (B) is incorrect. The conditions described support a wide rather than a narrow span. Answer (D) is incorrect. Geographical dispersion would decrease rather than increase the span of control.

22. Which of the following is a likely effect of a narrow span of control?

- A. The manager closely supervises employees.
- B. Each employee is given more responsibility.
- C. The organizational structure is flexible.
- D. The manager's control over employees is limited.

Answer (A) is correct. *(Publisher, adapted)*
    REQUIRED: The effect most likely to result from a narrow span of control.
    DISCUSSION: The span of control is the number of subordinates for which a manager or supervisor is responsible. When the span of control is narrow, a few subordinates are tightly controlled. A narrow span of control is typical of tall organizational structures.
    Answer (B) is incorrect. Each employee receiving more responsibility is a likely effect of a wide span of control, which is likely to be found in flat organizational structures. Answer (C) is incorrect. A flexible organizational structure is a likely effect of a wide span of control, which is likely to be found in flat organizational structures. Answer (D) is incorrect. Limited manager control over employees is a likely effect of a wide span of control, which is likely to be found in flat organizational structures.

23. A flat organization structure is one with relatively few levels of hierarchy and is characterized by wide spans of management control. A tall organization has many levels of hierarchy and narrow spans of control. Which of the following situations is consistent with a flat organization structure?

    A. Tasks require little direction and control of subordinates.

    B. Work areas are geographically dispersed.

    C. Tasks are highly complex and varied.

    D. Subordinates perform distinctly different tasks.

Answer (A) is correct. *(CIA, adapted)*
    REQUIRED: The situation consistent with a flat organization structure.
    DISCUSSION: Flat structures have the advantages of fast information flow from the top to the bottom of the organization and increased employee satisfaction. Tall structures are faster and more effective at problem resolution because of the increased frequency of interaction between superior and subordinate and the greater order imposed by the hierarchy. For a flat structure to be successful, employees must be able to work without supervision much of the time because a manager with many employees has little time for each one.
    Answer (B) is incorrect. Geographically dispersed work areas are very difficult for a manager with many subordinates to control. Answer (C) is incorrect. Tasks that are highly complex and varied are more appropriate for a narrow span of control. Answer (D) is incorrect. A narrow span of control (a tall structure) is more appropriate when subordinates perform distinctly different tasks.

7.6 Centralization and Decentralization

24. Centralization and decentralization are defined according to the relative delegation of decision-making authority by top management. Many managers believe that decentralized organizations have significant advantages over centralized organizations. A major advantage of a decentralized organization is that

    A. Decentralized organizations are easier to control.

    B. Decentralized structures streamline organizations and eliminate duplication of resources.

    C. Decentralized organizations have fewer managers than centralized organizations.

    D. Decentralized organizations encourage increased initiative among employees.

Answer (D) is correct. *(CIA, adapted)*
    REQUIRED: The major advantage of a decentralized organization.
    DISCUSSION: A decentralized organization allows lower level employees to participate in decision making. This increased involvement encourages initiative and creative thinking and is especially appropriate in complex and rapidly changing environments.
    Answer (A) is incorrect. Decentralized organizations are more difficult to control. Answer (B) is incorrect. Centralized structures streamline organizations and eliminate duplication of resources. Answer (C) is incorrect. The number of managers is not related to the degree of centralization or decentralization but is a function of the span of control.

25. A claimed advantage of decentralizing is

    A. Concentration of authority.

    B. Manager development.

    C. Elimination of duplication of effort.

    D. Departmentalization.

Answer (B) is correct. *(CIA, adapted)*
    REQUIRED: The advantage of decentralizing an organization.
    DISCUSSION: When an organization changes from a centralized to a decentralized structure, top management is delegating more authority to middle and lower levels. Thus, managers at these lower levels are usually hired and developed more rigorously than under the centralized structure.
    Answer (A) is incorrect. Authority is more concentrated in centralized management structures. Answer (C) is incorrect. Some effort will inevitably be duplicated under decentralization, of which departmentalization is a moderate form. Answer (D) is incorrect. Departments are formed when one manager can no longer supervise the entire organization; departmentalization is therefore a characteristic of centralized as well as decentralized organizations.

26. Which of the following is a reason for delegating?

    A. The manager wants to make more decisions.

    B. Subordinates lack initiative.

    C. The manager wants to remain the sole expert in the manager's field.

    D. Subordinates have too many responsibilities.

Answer (B) is correct. *(Publisher, adapted)*
    REQUIRED: The reason for delegating authority within a firm.
    DISCUSSION: Delegation is the assignment of a manager's authority and/or workload to the manager's subordinates. By increasing subordinates' responsibilities, the manager gives them more opportunity to exercise judgment and become more confident.
    Answer (A) is incorrect. Delegation passes some decision-making power to subordinates. Answer (C) is incorrect. Delegation gives subordinates the opportunity to increase their expertise. Answer (D) is incorrect. Delegation gives subordinates more responsibilities.

27. Advantages of decentralization include all of the following **except**

    A. Decisions are more easily made.

    B. Managers' motivation increases.

    C. Greater uniformity in decisions.

    D. Problems can be dealt with on the spot.

Answer (C) is correct. *(CIA, adapted)*
    REQUIRED: The statement that is not an advantage of decentralization.
    DISCUSSION: Organizational design should achieve a balance between centralization and decentralization. The main benefits of centralization are more effective control and reduced costs through resource sharing. The main benefits of decentralization are flexibility and adaptability that permit a rapid response to changes in circumstances. Accordingly, increased uniformity in decision making is an advantage of centralization. It reflects the benefit of more effective control.
    Answer (A) is incorrect. Ease of decision making is an advantage of decentralization. Answer (B) is incorrect. An increase in managers' motivation is an advantage of decentralization. Answer (D) is incorrect. Immediacy of problem resolution is an advantage of decentralization.

28. Which of the following is **most** likely to be a disadvantage of decentralization?

    A. Lower-level employees will develop less rapidly than in a centralized organization.

    B. Top management will have less time available to devote to unique problems.

    C. Lower-level managers may make conflicting decisions.

    D. Lower-level managers may lose motivation.

Answer (C) is correct. *(CIA, adapted)*
    REQUIRED: The item most likely to be a disadvantage of decentralization.
    DISCUSSION: The disadvantages of decentralization include a tendency to focus on short-run results to the detriment of the long-term health of the entity, an increased risk of loss of control by top management, the increased difficulty of coordinating interdependent units, and less cooperation and communication among competing decentralized unit managers.
    Answer (A) is incorrect. Decentralization encourages development of lower-level managers. They will have greater responsibilities and authority. Answer (B) is incorrect. Top managers will be freed from operating problems. Answer (D) is incorrect. Decision-making power should motivate lower-level managers.

29. The CEO of a rapidly growing high-technology firm has exercised centralized authority over all corporate functions. Because the company now operates in four geographically dispersed locations, the CEO is considering the advisability of decentralizing operational control over production and sales. Which of the following conditions probably will result from and be a valid reason for decentralizing?

    A. Greater local control over compliance with governmental regulations.

    B. More efficient use of headquarters staff officials and specialists.

    C. Less overall operating costs.

    D. Quicker and better operating decisions.

Answer (D) is correct. *(CIA, adapted)*
    REQUIRED: The condition that would be a valid reason for decentralizing.
    DISCUSSION: Decentralization results in greater speed in making operating decisions because they are made by lower-level managers instead of being referred to top management. The quality of operating decisions should also be enhanced, assuming proper training of managers, because those closest to the problems should be the most knowledgeable about them.
    Answer (A) is incorrect. Compliance with governmental regulations is probably more easily achieved by centralization. A disadvantage of decentralization is the difficulty of ensuring uniform action by units of the entity that have substantial autonomy. Answer (B) is incorrect. Decentralization may result in duplication of efforts, resulting in less efficient use of headquarters staff officials and specialists. Answer (C) is incorrect. Decentralization may result in duplication of efforts, thereby increasing overall costs.

30. Which type of organization is based upon strategic long-term relationships based upon implicit contracts and coordination through adaptation?

- A. Hourglass organization.
- B. Cluster organization.
- C. Network organization.
- D. Virtual organization.

Answer (C) is correct. *(Publisher, adapted)*

REQUIRED: The organization based upon strategic long-term relationships based upon implicit contracts and coordination through adaption.

DISCUSSION: A network organization is a network based upon coordination through adaptation. It also is based upon long-term relationships without specific legal ties.

Answer (A) is incorrect. An hourglass organization has three layers consisting of a strategic layer, a group of middle managers, and lower level technical specialists. There are also specific legal contracts in the form of employer-employee contracts. Answer (B) is incorrect. A cluster organization is essentially a group of teams. The teams are still part of an organization with explicit contracts such as employer-employee contracts. Answer (D) is incorrect. A virtual organization is a network of value-adding subcontractors who are linked by electronic mediums.

Use the additional questions in Gleim *CIA Test Prep* Software to create Test Sessions that emulate Pearson VUE!

STUDY UNIT EIGHT
MANAGING GROUPS

(13 pages of outline)

8.1	Group Dynamics	189
8.2	Stages of Group Development	194
8.3	Organizational Politics	195
8.4	Team Building	197

This study unit addresses the nature and types of groups, their characteristics and behavior, how they evolve, and how they should be managed.

> **GLEIM SUCCESS TIPS**
>
> Internal auditors encounter many situations in which group dynamics affect control procedures. Group dynamics also affect the internal audit activity. An understanding of this subdiscipline can help internal auditors fulfill their responsibilities.

8.1 GROUP DYNAMICS

1. Management should improve the **social capital** of the organization by enhancing the relationships of the groups within its structure. A **group** consists of at least two individuals who

   a. Interact freely,
   b. Recognize themselves as group members **(common identity)**, and
   c. Agree on the reason for the group **(common purpose)**.

Formal and Informal Groups

2. **Formal groups** are work groups (designated as committees, teams, etc.) within the organization assembled to perform a productive activity.

   a. Individuals are assigned to formal groups based on the organization's purposes and their qualifications for serving those purposes.
   b. Formal groups have explicitly designated **leaders** with authority and responsibility for directing the members.
   c. **Membership** in formal groups is relatively more permanent than in informal groups.

      1) Membership in informal groups may not be the same as in formal groups.

   d. Formal groups are more **structured** than informal groups.

3. People naturally seek association and group acceptance and tend to form informal as well as formal groups as a result. Thus, effective managers recognize, accept, and take advantage of the **informal organization**.

   a. Informal groups are created within organizations because of the following:

      1) Authority relationships not definable on an organizational chart
      2) Unwritten rules of conduct
      3) Group preferences

   b. **Characteristics of informal groups** include

      1) Development of informal groups primarily to satisfy esteem needs (friendship).
      2) Membership of almost all employees, including managers, in some informal group(s).

3) Reaction of members to group pressures. These pressures are difficult to resist, and most members conform.

4) The tendency of informal groups to be small and often very complex. They develop their own leaders, exist to fill the needs of the members, and usually result from the frequent interaction among individuals in the course of their work.

c. **Favorable effects of informal groups** include the following:

1) Reducing tension and encouraging production

2) Improving coordination and reducing supervision required

3) Assistance in problem-solving

4) Providing another (often faster) channel of communication

a) The **grapevine** is the informal, unofficial communication system found in every kind of organization. The emergence of computer networks in the workplace has strengthened the grapevine.

5) Providing social satisfactions that supplement job satisfaction

d. Informal groups have **potentially unfavorable effects**. The following are examples:

1) Circumventing managerial actions

2) Reducing production (slowdowns caused by counterproductive social interactions)

3) Causing dissension in the formal organization

4) Spreading rumors and distorting information

5) Adding to the cost of doing business

6) Forming subgroups that hinder group cohesiveness

7) Pressuring members to adopt group norms that may be contrary to the objectives of the organization

8) Developing dominant members

Group Commitment

4. Commitment to a group depends on its attractiveness and cohesiveness.

a. **Attractiveness** is a favorable view from the outside.

b. **Cohesiveness** is the tendency of members to adhere to the group and unite against outside pressures.

c. Group attractiveness and cohesiveness are increased by

1) Its prestige and status,

2) Cooperation among the members,

3) Substantial member interaction,

4) Small size of the group,

5) Similarity of members,

6) Good public image, and

7) Common external threat.

d. Group attractiveness and cohesiveness are decreased by

1) Its unpleasant demands on members,

2) Disagreements about activities and procedures,

3) Bad experiences with the group,

4) Conflict between the group's demands and those of other activities,

5) Its bad public image, and

6) The possibility of joining other groups.

Roles and Norms

5.   **Role playing** is an important concept that emerged from group dynamics theory. A **role** is the behavior expected of a person who occupies a particular position. Everyone is expected to play or assume different roles in different situations.

   a.   The term also refers to actual behavior.

   b.   Different people in the same position should behave similarly.

   c.   **Role conflict** emerges when two or more roles, making conflicting demands, are simultaneously expected of, or imposed on, a person.

   1)   **Role models** may be crucial in helping individuals resolve role conflicts.

   d.   Roles may be formally defined, for example, in job descriptions and procedures manuals.

6.   **Norms** are general standards of conduct and have a broader effect than roles. Groups are guided by self-set norms of performance and behavior.

   a.   Norms vary from culture to culture and most often are unwritten.

   b.   The following are the **functions of norms**:

   1)   Protect the group (survival)
   2)   Better define role behavior and expectations
   3)   Safeguard members from embarrassment (self-image)
   4)   Reinforce the group's values and common identity

   c.   **Enforcement of norms** in the positive sense follows from attention, recognition, and acceptance (social reinforcement).

   1)   Enforcement of norms in the negative sense may be by ridicule, condescension, or criticism. The ultimate punishment is **ostracism**, or rejection by the group.

Conformity

7.   An important element of group dynamics is **conformity**, which is compliance with roles and norms.

   a.   The **benefit** of conformity is predictability of behavior, e.g., performance of assigned tasks. The **cost** of conformity may, in the extreme, be tolerance of illegal, unethical, or incompetent conduct.

   b.   According to Irving Janis, one of the dangers of **cohesive groups** is **groupthink**. It is the tendency of individuals deeply committed to the group to conform and ignore relevant input that varies from the perceived group opinion.

   1)   The following are **symptoms** of groupthink:

   a)   Over-optimism
   b)   Assumed morality of the preferred action
   c)   Intolerance of dissent
   d)   An urgent search for unanimity

   2)   The following are ways of **avoiding groupthink**:

   a)   Being aware of its dangers
   b)   Encouraging members to think critically
   c)   Seeking outside opinions
   d)   Expressly assigning a member of the group to advocate contrary positions
   e)   Expressly considering the consequences of different actions
   f)   Not using a group to approve without discussion or dissent a decision already made by senior management

3)   Groupthink may have been a major factor in well-known **corporate governance scandals**. Directors often failed to perform their duty to protect shareholders by critically evaluating the actions of senior management.

4)   **Cooperative (constructive) conflict** is a means not only of managing change but also of avoiding groupthink.

Group-Aided Decision Making

8.   Group-aided decision making and problem solving have the following advantages:

  a.   The group has greater knowledge and experience than an individual.

  b.   **Lateral thinking** allows the group to be **creative** by exploring multiple perspectives and a wider diversity of views than in individual decision making.

  c.   Members participating in a group process tend to have a better understanding of the reasons for different actions.

  d.   Those actively participating in the group process tend to accept the result.

  e.   Group involvement provides training for the less experienced members.

9.   The following are the disadvantages of group-aided decision making:

  a.   The social pressure to conform may inhibit creativity.

  b.   The group may be dominated by a few aggressive members.

  c.   The decision or solution may be a product of political dealing.

  d.   The goal of reaching a good decision or solution may be replaced by a secondary concern, e.g., competing with a rival.

  e.   The process may suffer from groupthink (preference for unanimity over the quality of the decision or solution).

  f.   Groups tend to take longer than individuals.

10.   **Group decision making** differs from group-aided decision making.

  a.   Groups tend to submerge individual identity and responsibility and conceal the link between individual effort and outcome. Thus, one result of decision making by a group may be a greater acceptance of risk because of the dispersal of accountability.

  1)   **Groupshift** is the difference between the decisions that members of a group would make singly and the group's decision. Sometimes the group's decision is more conservative, but more often it is riskier.

  a)   What apparently occurs is that the group discussion emphasizes the initial tendency of the group. The most likely reason for the more frequent shift toward the riskier course is diffusion of responsibility among members of the group. Thus, no one will be wholly to blame for failure.

11.   The following are methods that may be applied to improve creativity:

  a.   **Attribute listing** is applied primarily to improve a tangible object. It lists the parts and essential features of the object and systematically analyzes modifications intended as improvements.

  b.   **Brainstorming** is an unstructured group approach that relies on spontaneous contribution of ideas. This technique breaks down broadly based problems into their essentials. A nonjudgmental environment is necessary.

  c.   **Creative leap** is a process that formulates an ideal solution and then works back to a feasible one.

  d.   The **Delphi technique** is an approach in which the manager solicits opinions on a problem from experts in the field, summarizes the opinions, and feeds the summaries back to the experts (without revealing any of the participants to each other).

  1)   The process is reiterated until the opinions converge on an optimal solution. This method attempts to avoid **groupthink**.

e. The **Edisonian approach** is a trial-and-error experimental method. It should usually not be applied unless other approaches have been unsuccessful.

f. **Forced relationship** is a structured adaptation of free association. The elements of a problem are analyzed, and the associations among them are identified so as to detect patterns that may suggest new ideas.

g. **Free association** is a method of idea generation that reports the first thought to come to mind in response to a given stimulus, for example, a symbol or analogy pertaining to a product for which an advertising slogan is sought. The objective is to express the content of consciousness without censorship or control.

h. **Morphological matrix analysis** is a structured technique that plots decision variables along the axes of a matrix. The relationships of these variables are found in the squares within the chart.

i. **Synectics** is a highly structured group approach to problem statement and solution based on creative thinking. It involves free use of analogies and metaphors in informal exchange within a carefully selected small group of individuals of diverse personality and areas of specialization.

Core Concepts

- Management should improve the social capital of the organization by enhancing the relationships of the groups within its structure. A group consists of at least two individuals. They interact freely, they recognize themselves as group members (common identity), and they agree on the reason for the group (common purpose).

- Formal groups are work groups (designated as committees, teams, etc.) within the organization assembled to perform a productive activity. Individuals are assigned to formal groups based on the organization's purposes and their qualifications for serving those purposes.

- People naturally seek association and group acceptance and tend to form informal as well as formal groups as a result. Thus, effective managers recognize, accept, and take advantage of the informal organization.

- Commitment to a group depends on its attractiveness and cohesiveness. Attractiveness is a favorable view from the outside. Cohesiveness is the tendency of members to adhere to the group and unite against outside pressures.

- A role is the behavior expected of a person who occupies a particular position. Everyone is expected to play or assume different roles in different situations.

- Norms are general standards of conduct and have a more general effect than roles. Groups are guided by self-set norms of performance and behavior. Norms vary from culture to culture and most often are unwritten.

- Conformity is compliance with roles and norms. The benefit of conformity is predictability of behavior, e.g., performance of assigned tasks. The cost of conformity may, in the extreme, be tolerance of illegal, unethical, or incompetent conduct. A danger of conformity in cohesive groups is groupthink.

- Group decision making is subject to certain disadvantages, such as inhibition of creativity and domination by a few aggressive members. To overcome these obstacles and improve the creativity of groups, certain methods may be applied, such as attribute listing, brainstorming, creative leap, and the Delphi technique.

Stop and review! You have completed the outline for this subunit. Study multiple-choice questions 1 through 13 beginning on page 201.

8.2 STAGES OF GROUP DEVELOPMENT

1. The process of group development proceeds through a succession of stages in which conflicts over power, authority, and interpersonal relationships must be overcome.

    a. Mutual understanding, trust, and commitment to the group tend to be absent in the beginning.

    b. Group objectives, members' roles, and leadership are initially uncertain.

2. A **mature group**, that is, the end stage of group development, tends to be effective and productive compared with groups in earlier stages of development. A mature group has the following traits according to L.N. Jewell and H.J. Reitz:

    a. Member awareness of individuals' strengths and weaknesses in relation to the group's function

    b. Acceptance of individuals' differences

    c. Acceptance of group authority and interpersonal relationships

    d. Rational discussion of decisions with tolerance of dissent and no attempt to force unanimity

    e. Limitation of conflict to substantive rather than emotional issues, e.g., group objectives and the means of reaching them

    f. Members' awareness of their roles in group processes

3. Jewell and Reitz also have defined the **stages of group development**. The principal issue in the early stages is uncertainty about power and authority relationships. The principal issue in the later stages is uncertainty about interpersonal relationships.

    a. In its **orientation stage**, the group is the least mature, effective, and efficient. Uncertainties are high and temporary leaders emerge.

    b. During the **conflict and challenge stage**, emerging leaders are opposed by people or subgroups with differing agendas. Redistribution of power and authority may occur during what may be a lengthy stage.

        1) It also may be the final stage if conflicts cannot be resolved.

    c. The consolidation of the power shifts begun during the conflict and challenge stage occurs during the **cohesion stage**. The members reach agreement about authority, structure, and procedures. They also begin to identify with the group.

        1) If progress is to continue, the stage should be brief.

    d. The **delusion stage** is a period during which the members must overcome a false sense that all emotional issues have been resolved. Hence, harmony is emphasized at the expense of properly addressing problems.

    e. When the group reaches the **disillusion stage**, cohesiveness diminishes as the members realize that their expectations are not being met. Absenteeism increases. Some members take the risk of urging the group to do better.

    f. Groups that evolve into the **acceptance stage** of group development tend to be both effective and efficient. Trust produces cohesiveness and a free exchange of information among group members. This stage is characterized by

        1) Personal and mutual understanding,
        2) Tolerance of individual differences,
        3) Constructive conflict about substantive matters,
        4) Realistic expectations about group performance, and
        5) Acceptance of the authority structure.

Core Concepts

- Group development proceeds through stages in which conflicts over power, authority, and interpersonal relationships must be overcome. Mutual understanding, trust, and commitment to the group tend to be absent in the beginning. Group objectives, members' roles, and leadership are initially uncertain. However, a mature group tends to be effective and productive compared with groups in earlier stages of development.

- Jewell and Reitz have defined the stages of group development: (1) orientation, (2) conflict and challenge, (3) cohesion, (4) delusion, (5) disillusion, and (6) acceptance.

Stop and review! You have completed the outline for this subunit. Study multiple-choice questions 14 through 16 beginning on page 205.

8.3 ORGANIZATIONAL POLITICS

1. Organizational politics, or **impression management**, is defined by Andrew DuBrin as "the pursuit of self-interest at work in the face of real or imagined opposition."

2. Managers must understand organizational politics as a matter of self-interest. Moreover, they also must understand its negative effects on morale, the effectiveness of needed change, and ethical behavior.

3. Self-interested behaviors are those not based solely on competence and diligence or resulting from good fortune.

    a. **Positive political behaviors** include coalition building, networking, and seeking mentors.

    b. **Negative political behaviors** include whistleblowing, sabotage, threats, taking credit for others' work or ideas, and building revolutionary coalitions.

        1) Negative political behavior is considered by some managers to include **whistleblowing**. It is the reporting to internal or external parties (e.g., internal auditors, a compliance officer, government bodies, the media, or private watchdog groups) of entity conduct asserted to be wrongful.

            a) Some managers believe whistleblowing to be an act of revenge that is disloyal to the organization. Moreover, some whistleblowers may have personal financial motives.

            b) However, the prevailing view is that whistleblowing is a net social good. Revealing unethical behavior may be the only way to end misconduct that has substantial negative effects on the public interest.

            c) Thus, many governments have enacted **whistleblower protection statutes**. These laws prohibit retaliation against insiders who appropriately disclose wrongdoing.

            d) Some statutes even provide financial incentives. For example, a statute may allow employees of the government or of contractors to receive a percentage of any recovery of fraudulent payments made under defense contracts, provision of healthcare, etc.

4. The **organizational culture** may encourage politics by creating unreasonable obstacles to group and individual advancement.

5.   The following **perceptions about organizational politics** are widely held:

    a.   Political behavior increases as managers rise in the hierarchy.

    b.   The frequency of political behavior increases as the organization grows.

    c.   Line managers are less political than staff managers.

    d.   Marketing managers are the most political, and production managers are the least.

    e.   Reorganization results in more political behavior than other changes.

    f.   Political behavior helps career advancement.

    g.   Political behavior may be beneficial to the organization by promoting ideas, building teams, enhancing communication, and improving morale.

    h.   Political behavior may have a negative effect on the organization by distracting managers from focusing on entity objectives.

6.   The following are common **political tactics**:

    a.   **Posturing** is an attempt to make a good impression, for example, by taking credit for others' work or seeking to stay ahead of a rival (one-upmanship).

    b.   **Empire building** is an attempt to control greater resources. Thus, a manager with a larger budget may believe that (s)he is in a safer position and is more influential.

    c.   **Making the supervisor look good** is an effort to impress the person who controls one's career path.

    d.   **Collecting and using social IOUs** is a tactic employed by someone who views favors as the currency of advancement, not as unselfish acts. Such a manager may help another to look good or not to look bad, for example, by concealing a mistake.

    e.   **Creating power and loyalty cliques** is a tactic based on the premise that a cohesive group has more power than an individual.

    f.   **Engaging in destructive competition** includes such behaviors as gossip, lying, and sabotage.

7.   **Limiting organizational politics** is desirable because such behavior may hinder the achievement of organizational objectives. To avoid this result, DuBrin suggests

    a.   Creating an open, trusting environment;

    b.   Focusing on performance;

    c.   Not modeling political behavior for lower-level managers;

    d.   Using work and career planning to make individual objectives consistent with organizational objectives; and

    e.   Job rotation to develop a broader perspective and understanding of the problems of others.

Core Concepts

- Organizational politics, or impression management, is defined by Andrew DuBrin as "the pursuit of self-interest at work in the face of real or imagined opposition." Managers must understand organizational politics as a matter of self-interest. Moreover, they also must understand its negative effects on morale, the effectiveness of needed change, and ethical behavior.

- Positive political behaviors include coalition building, networking, and seeking mentors. Negative political behaviors include (1) whistleblowing (in some cases), (2) sabotage, (3) threats, (4) taking credit for others' work or ideas, and (5) building revolutionary coalitions.

- The organizational culture may encourage politics by creating unreasonable obstacles to group and individual advancement. The following are common political tactics: (1) posturing, (2) empire building, (3) making the supervisor look good, (4) collecting and using social IOUs, (5) creating power and loyalty cliques, and (6) engaging in destructive competition.

- Limiting organizational politics is desirable because such behavior may hinder the achievement of organizational objectives.

Stop and review! You have completed the outline for this subunit. Study multiple-choice questions 17 through 19 on page 206.

8.4 TEAM BUILDING

Participative Management

1. Participative management is a Theory Y approach (see Subunit 6.2). It gives employees greater control of the workplace when they can establish objectives, be involved in decision making, solve problems, or effect organizational change.

    a. Employees are more highly motivated and productive and turnover is lower when effective participative management programs are in place.

2. Quality control circles, self-managed teams, and open-book management reflect the participative principle.

    a. **Quality circles (QCs)** are groups, usually of five to ten employees (management or subordinates), doing similar work who volunteer to meet at a specified time (e.g., once a week for an hour) to discuss and solve problems associated with their work areas.

        1) The objectives of QCs are to use employee capabilities more fully, build a more congenial workplace, and contribute to the improvement and development of both the organization and individual employees.

        2) Introduction of QCs is evolutionary through training, support, and team building. They are not imposed by management directive.

        3) The mechanics of a QC include the following problem-solving steps:

            a) Circle members bring problems before the group.

            b) The problems or projects are analyzed.

            c) Solutions are developed and presented to management.

            d) Management follows up on the suggestions by either approving or disapproving the ideas, with feedback to circle members.

            e) Members help to implement and evaluate the solutions.

        4) The following are advantages of quality circles:

            a) Easy implementation without major organizational change
            b) More efficient and effective operation of the organization
            c) Better-quality products
            d) Improved employee morale and better cohesion among coworkers

        5) The following are disadvantages of quality circles:

            a) Objections from unions

            b) Reduced morale if suggestions are not accepted by management and management fails to explain nonacceptance adequately

            c) Potential loss of management control

    b. **Self-managed teams** are a facet of total quality management (TQM). They are autonomous groups that go beyond quality circles because they represent a major organizational change.

        1) Team members are not volunteers but have been assigned to the teams.

        2) Teams are assembled to produce a complete product or service. Accordingly, they are empowered to perform traditional management tasks, such as scheduling, ordering materials, and even hiring.

3) Members' jobs are enriched or **vertically loaded** not only by performing some management functions but also by cross-training and job rotation.

4) The benefits of teams flow from the principle that employee self-management (and self-organization) is best.

    a) Motivation is improved because decision making is decentralized. The increased authority of autonomous work groups is intended to create a sense of ownership in the work product.

        i) Better decision making, productivity, quality, and goal congruence should be the results.

    b) An advantage of cross-functional teams is improved communication because all members have a better understanding of all team activities.

    c) If teams are staffed appropriately and have the necessary resources and support from management, they should be able to improve the processes of production. The individuals who perform the work have the power to make decisions about the way it is done.

5) **Managerial resistance** is the primary obstacle to adoption of self-managed teams. Fundamental organizational change is difficult. Thus, tradition-oriented managers tend to regard self-managed teams as endangering their status.

c. **Open-book management (OBM)** involves sharing important financial information with trained and empowered employees. This approach is founded on trusting employees, commitment to their training, and waiting patiently for results (usually at least 2 years).

1) Kaj Aggarwal and Betty Simkins developed the **STEP** (share, teach, empower, pay) model for OBM described below.

    a) Step one is to **share** important financial information (sales, expenses, profits, stock prices). It should be displayed prominently, e.g., on an internal website or in hallways.

    b) Step two is to **teach** employees how to understand this information and the organization's operations. Simulations and board games are possible methods.

    c) Step three is to **empower** employees to make needed changes.

    d) Step four is to **pay** employees fairly as recognition of their accomplishments. Profit-sharing, stock options, and bonuses are among the methods of compensation.

d. The success of participative management rests upon **employee support**. According to David Levine, this support is most likely when four conditions are present:

1) Profit-sharing
2) Job security (a long-term relationship)
3) Strong efforts to sustain group cohesiveness
4) Protection of employee rights

Teams

3. A **team** is a group whose members work intensively with each other to achieve a specific common goal. A **group** consists of two or more people who interact to accomplish a goal. All teams are groups, but not all groups are teams.

a. Teams can improve organizational performance, but they are often difficult to form because it takes time for members to learn to work together. Normally, the smaller the team, the better. A maximum of nine members is recommended.

b. A team differs from a group because team leadership often rotates, and team members are accountable to each other.

c. Members of a team are empowered when they are properly trained and equipped, have the relevant information they need, are fully involved in decision making, and receive fair compensation for their work.

1) Teams can be empowered by monitoring their progress and offering timely feedback on performance.

2) Performance feedback also counteracts **social loafing**, the situation in which a team member puts forth less effort in a group than (s)he would individually. Thus, individual efforts should be identifiable and subject to evaluation.

d. A **cross-functional** team includes members who have different areas of expertise. A **research-and-development team** is an example of a team that is typically cross-functional in that many skills are needed to identify and create a new product.

1) A cross-functional team need not be **self-managed**, but a self-managed team ordinarily is cross-functional.

2) Unlike the members of a quality circle, cross-functional team members are assigned.

3) The major difficulty is to integrate the work of individuals from diverse specialties (and possibly cultures).

e. A **virtual team** uses computer and telecommunications technology (email, voice mail, fax, Internet-based project software, videoconferencing, etc.) so that geographically distant members can work together on projects and reach common goals.

1) Such a team may be able to work faster than a traditional team. Nevertheless, experience indicates that occasional in-person interaction and trust- and team-building procedures are still vital.

2) Roles, expectations, performance standards, objectives, and deadlines must be clearly communicated.

3) Deborah Duarte and Nancy Snyder recommend the following procedure for **building a virtual team**:

a) Specify the individuals (sponsors and other stakeholders) who connect the team to the organization's power centers.

b) Draft a charter stating the team's purposes and objectives.

c) Choose the members. Core members are regular participants, extended members provide support, and ancillary members approve the work.

d) Introduce the members. At this first meeting, leaders make certain determinations about members. For example,

i) Members should know why they were chosen,
ii) Their computers should be compatible,
iii) They should have a way of finding answers to questions, and
iv) They should not be working on too many other projects.

e) Conduct an in-person team orientation that includes an overview of the charter and guidance regarding the development of team norms. Examples of these team norms are

i) The choice of, and the etiquette for, various communications media;
ii) How work is to be reviewed;
iii) The scheduling of meetings; and
iv) Which meetings will be in person.

f) The team process should address such matters as

i) Management of the work,
ii) Information storage and sharing,
iii) Designation of the reviewers of documents, and
iv) Frequency of review.

f.   **Team effectiveness** is reflected in achievement of objectives, innovation, adaptability, commitment, and favorable evaluations by senior management.

1)   According to Hans Thamhain, team effectiveness is determined by three sets of interdependent factors. Team effectiveness requires that all factors need to be addressed continually. A high performance team is committed to the personal growth of its team members.

a)   **People** - Job satisfaction, trust and team spirit, effective communication, successful conflict resolution, and job security

b)   **Organization** - Stability, job security, supportive management, a fair compensation system, and stable objectives and priorities

c)   **Tasks** - Clear objectives, direction, and planning; capable technical management; leadership; stimulating work; employee independence; experienced employees; team involvement; and visibility of the task

g.   **Trust** is a key factor in any participative management approach. According to Douglas Houston, it is "a belief in the integrity, character, or ability of others." Thus, management should take action to build trust from the time that teams or other work groups are formed.

1)   The following is Dale Zand's **model for building trust**:

a)   A commitment to **trust** means that managers strive to improve personal interaction by being open, honest, and willing to change.

b)   Managers' commitment to trust includes disclosure of **information**, emotions, and opinions.

c)   The commitment to trust also extends to receptiveness to **influence** by others.

d)   When mutual trust is achieved, **control** will be self-imposed. Direct supervision will not be necessary when all persons involved know that others will perform.

2)   Fernando Bartolomé states that managers build trust through the following:

a)   Timely and accurate **communication**
b)   **Supportive behavior**
c)   Showing **respect**, e.g., by delegation and effective listening
d)   **Fairness** of evaluations
e)   **Predictability** of behavior and promise-keeping
f)   **Competence** exemplified by sound judgment and technical proficiency

3)   Trust inspires trust. Hence, **being trusted** tends to lead to **trust in others**.

h.   **Roles** of team members include the following:

1)   A **contributor** is a task-oriented team member who provides the team with good technical information and pushes the team to set high-performance goals.

2)   A **collaborator** binds the whole team and is open to new ideas. (S)he is willing to work outside the defined role and to share the recognition and credit with other team members.

3)   A **communicator** is a people-oriented member. (S)he is process-driven and an effective listener. Thus, a communicator plays the role of a facilitator and a consensus builder who focuses on the overall perspective and reminds others of the vision, mission, or goal of the team.

4)   A **challenger** is candid and open, questions the team goals, is willing to disagree with the team leader, and encourages well-conceived risk taking.

Core Concepts

- Participative management gives employees greater control of the workplace when they can establish objectives, be involved in decision making, solve problems, or effect organizational change. Employees are more highly motivated and productive and turnover is lower when effective participative management programs are in place.

- Quality circles (QCs) are groups, usually of five to ten employees (management or subordinates), doing similar work who volunteer to meet at a specified time to discuss and solve problems associated with their work areas. The objectives of QCs are to use employee capabilities more fully, build a more congenial workplace, and contribute to the improvement and development of both the organization and individual employees.

- Self-managed teams are assembled to produce a complete product or service. Accordingly, they are empowered to perform traditional management tasks such as scheduling, ordering materials, and even hiring.

- Open-book management (OBM) involves sharing important financial information with trained and empowered employees. This approach is founded on trusting employees, commitment to their training, and waiting patiently for results (usually at least 2 years).

- A team is a group whose members work intensively with each other to achieve a specific common goal. A group consists of two or more people who interact to accomplish a goal. A cross-functional team includes members who have different areas of expertise.

- A virtual team uses computer and telecommunications technology (email, voice mail, fax, Internet-based project software, videoconferencing, etc.) so that geographically distant members can work together on projects and reach common goals.

- Team effectiveness is reflected in achievement of objectives, innovation, adaptability, commitment, and favorable evaluations by senior management. Trust and employee support are key factors in any participative management approach.

Stop and review! You have completed the outline for this subunit. Study multiple-choice questions 20 through 30 beginning on page 207.

QUESTIONS

8.1 Group Dynamics

1. Which of the following can be a limiting factor associated with group decision making?

    A. Groups generally do not analyze problems in enough depth.

    B. It is very difficult to get individuals to accept decisions made by groups.

    C. Groups have a difficult time identifying the important components of decision making.

    D. Accountability is dispersed when groups make decisions.

Answer (D) is correct. *(CIA, adapted)*
    REQUIRED: The limiting factor associated with group decision making.
    DISCUSSION: The difficulty associated with group decision making (as opposed to group-aided decision making) is accountability for the decision. If a decision is made by a group, no one person is responsible. The best method is for the group to recommend a decision but for a manager to assume responsibility for making the final decision.
    Answer (A) is incorrect. Groups may analyze problems in greater depth. Answer (B) is incorrect. Individuals who participate in the decision may accept it more readily. Answer (C) is incorrect. Greater experience and expertise of a group may render it more effective than a single manager in identifying key components of decision making.

2. Which of the following is **not** an advantage of group decision making as compared to individual decision making?

    A. Groups obtain an increased degree of acceptance of a solution so that it may be more easily implemented.

    B. Group decision making is consistent with democratic methods.

    C. Group members bring more complete information and knowledge into the decision process.

    D. Group members avoid expressing opinions that deviate from what appears to be the group consensus.

Answer (D) is correct. *(CIA, adapted)*
    REQUIRED: The item that is not an advantage of group decision making.
    DISCUSSION: The groupthink phenomenon is undesirable, whether a group makes the decision or aids the decision maker. Groupthink occurs when group members accept what appears to be the group consensus rather than giving their honest input. The result may be decisions with which some members of the group are not happy.
    Answer (A) is incorrect. If members of the group are responsible for the decision making, their participation in the implementation process will increase the ease with which the decisions are carried out. Answer (B) is incorrect. Group decision making adds legitimacy to the solution by following democratic methods. Answer (C) is incorrect. A group possesses greater resources than an individual.

3. Which of the following is **not** an advantage of group effort compared with work performed by individuals?

    A. Groups provide support to members.

    B. Groups make decisions that are more easily accepted.

    C. Groups provide a clear link between effort and outcome.

    D. Groups control and discipline members.

Answer (C) is correct. *(CIA, adapted)*
    REQUIRED: The item not an advantage of group effort.
    DISCUSSION: In a culture that strongly emphasizes individual identity and competition, the preference tends to be for a clear link between effort and outcome. However, groups tend to submerge individual identity and responsibility and therefore to blur the link between individual effort and its results.
    Answer (A) is incorrect. Providing support and meeting other needs of members is an advantage. Answer (B) is incorrect. Members who participate in a group decision-making process tend to understand and accept the result. Answer (D) is incorrect. Groups develop and enforce behavioral norms that (1) protect the group, (2) define roles and expectations, (3) safeguard members from loss of face, and (4) reinforce group values and identity.

4. Which of the following statements about group decision making is **most** likely false?

    A. There is a lack of responsibility for group decisions.

    B. Group decision making is almost always less efficient than individual decision making.

    C. The desire by individual members to be accepted by the group often restrains open disagreement.

    D. Group decision making tends to be less creative than individual decision making.

Answer (D) is correct. *(CIA, adapted)*
    REQUIRED: The false statement about group decision making.
    DISCUSSION: Groups tend to be more creative than individuals because diversity of member views generally results in the consideration of more alternatives for solving a problem (but the social pressure to conform also may inhibit creativity).
    Answer (A) is incorrect. Individuals do not accept responsibility for group decisions. Answer (B) is incorrect. Group decision making almost always takes more time than individual decision making, except when the need for diverse views is so great that an individual decision maker needs to consult many people or perform research. Answer (C) is incorrect. Group members generally have diverse views, but their common need to be accepted and respected by the group often restrains the full, open expression of their views when they fear strong disagreement.

5. An audit manager allowed a work group to make a decision about whether to adopt a new work procedure. In allowing the group to make the decision, the manager should be aware that groups tend to make

- A. Very conservative decisions and do not want to assume risk.
- B. Faster decisions than do individuals because groups have more expertise than does any one person.
- C. Decisions that are less accurate than those made by individuals.
- D. Riskier decisions than do individuals, and individual responsibility for the group's decision is lessened.

Answer (D) is correct. *(CIA, adapted)*
   REQUIRED: The decisions made by work groups.
   DISCUSSION: Groupshift is the difference between the decisions that members of a group would make singly and the group's decision. Sometimes the group's decision is more conservative, but more often it is riskier. What apparently occurs is that the group discussion accentuates the initial tendency of the group. The most likely reason for the more frequent shift toward the riskier course is diffusion of responsibility among members of the group. Thus, no one will be wholly to blame for failure.
   Answer (A) is incorrect. Groups tend to make riskier decisions than individuals (part of the group shift phenomenon). Answer (B) is incorrect. Group decisions take longer than individual decisions. Answer (C) is incorrect. Group decisions tend to be more accurate than individual decisions.

6. Under "groupthink,"

- A. There is a tendency to conform to the majority's will and to ignore relevant individual input that is at variance with group opinion.
- B. The group is not required to reach consensus.
- C. The extent of groupthink is proportional to the size of the group.
- D. There are too many alternatives to facilitate decision making.

Answer (A) is correct. *(CIA, adapted)*
   REQUIRED: The true statement regarding "groupthink."
   DISCUSSION: Groupthink is the tendency to conform to the majority's will when individual input is at variance with the group opinion. Groupthink is a cause of faulty decision making in a group. Groups may not consider all alternatives because they desire unanimity at the expense of quality decisions. Groupthink occurs when groups are highly cohesive and under considerable pressure to make a decision.
   Answer (B) is incorrect. Consensus is desirable even when groupthink is avoided. Answer (C) is incorrect. Groupthink is not limited to groups of only certain sizes. Answer (D) is incorrect. Few alternatives may be addressed by a group afflicted with groupthink.

7. Which of the following is **not** a characteristic of informal groups?

- A. Informal groups are developed to establish friendships.
- B. Informal groups tend to be small and very complex.
- C. Membership in informal groups lasts longer than membership in formal groups.
- D. Informal groups develop their own leaders.

Answer (C) is correct. *(Publisher, adapted)*
   REQUIRED: The statement that does not characterize informal groups.
   DISCUSSION: Membership in formal groups tends to last longer than membership in informal groups. Membership in both groups is usually different as well.
   Answer (A) is incorrect. Informal groups are often developed to satisfy esteem needs such as the desire to form friendships. Answer (B) is incorrect. Informal groups are often small and complex because they evolve from interaction in the course of work. There are no predetermined leaders and therefore the structure of the group is complex. Answer (D) is incorrect. Informal groups often develop their own leaders from interaction during the course of work.

8. Groupthink is defined as

- A. The tendency to conform and ignore relevant individual input that is at variance with the majority opinion.
- B. The guidance of groups based upon self-set standards of performance and behavior.
- C. The members of a group developing a solution to a problem after all the relevant information has been considered.
- D. A way of brainstorming ideas to address an issue presented to a group by management.

Answer (A) is correct. *(Publisher, adapted)*
   REQUIRED: The definition of groupthink.
   DISCUSSION: Research into cohesive groups has revealed the prevalence of groupthink. Groupthink is conformity to a group's opinion despite information that it may be incorrect.
   Answer (B) is incorrect. Norms are defined as the guidance of groups based upon self-set standards of performance and behavior. Answer (C) is incorrect. Considering all relevant information avoids the problem of groupthink. The group addresses issues that may change its opinion. Answer (D) is incorrect. Groupthink is not a way of developing ideas to address an issue. Groupthink is using the ideas of the group to address an issue, regardless of outside information.

9. When compared to individuals, groups have advantages and disadvantages for decision making. Which of the following is true regarding group-aided decisions?

	Advantage	Disadvantage
A.	Increased personal accountability	Disagreements do not surface because of pressures to conform
B.	Increased acceptance of a decision by participants	Takes more time to arrive at a decision
C.	Takes less time to arrive at a decision	Lack of personal accountability
D.	Increased diversity of expertise	Reduced acceptance of decision by participants

Answer (B) is correct. *(CIA, adapted)*
REQUIRED: The advantages and disadvantages of group-aided decision making.
DISCUSSION: Group-aided decision making and problem solving has the following advantages: (1) The group has greater knowledge and experience than an individual; (2) the group provides multiple perspectives; (3) members participating in a group process tend to have a better understanding of the reasons for different actions; (4) those actively participating in the group process tend to accept, and have ownership of, the result; and (5) group involvement provides training for the less experienced members. The following are the disadvantages: (1) The social pressure to conform may inhibit creativity; (2) the group may be dominated by a few aggressive members; (3) the decision or solution may be a product of political dealing; (4) the goal of reaching a good decision or solution may be displaced by a secondary concern, e.g., competing with a rival; and (5) the process may suffer from groupthink, or preference for unanimity over the quality of the decision or solution.
Answer (A) is incorrect. Group decisions lead to lack of personal accountability. Answer (C) is incorrect. An individual makes decisions more quickly than a group. Answer (D) is incorrect. Those who participated in a group process are more likely to accept and support the group's decisions.

10. There has been an increased emphasis on group decision making in organizations. Which of the following statements has been found to hold true in studies of individual decision making as compared to group decision making? Individual decision making tends to

A. Be more conservative.
B. Evaluate more complete information.
C. Generate more alternatives.
D. Increase the perceived legitimacy of the decision.

Answer (A) is correct. *(CIA, adapted)*
REQUIRED: The true comparison of group and individual decision making.
DISCUSSION: Group decision making is often characterized by greater acceptance of risk because of the dispersal of accountability. Individual decision making tends to be more conservative because accountability can be specifically assigned.
Answer (B) is incorrect. A group has greater resources of knowledge and experience than an individual. Answer (C) is incorrect. A group has a wider diversity of views and should be able to offer a wider range of solutions. Answer (D) is incorrect. Group decisions are more likely to be accepted by those affected.

11. Which of the following characteristics do both informal and formal groups share?

A. Both groups are structured similarly.
B. Commitment to both groups depends on the group's attractiveness and cohesiveness.
C. Membership in both groups is usually the same.
D. Both groups exist within the community to perform a productive activity.

Answer (B) is correct. *(Publisher, adapted)*
REQUIRED: The characteristics that informal and formal groups share.
DISCUSSION: The commitment to a group depends on the group's attractiveness and cohesiveness. Employees are more likely to join a group that has a favorable view from the outside and whose group members adhere to the group and resist outside pressure.
Answer (A) is incorrect. Formal groups are often more structured than informal groups. Answer (C) is incorrect. Membership in formal groups may not be the same as in informal groups. Answer (D) is incorrect. Informal groups form to fill the needs of the members, not to perform a productive activity.

12. Groups have often evolved by self-set standards of performance and behavior, usually based on the personal and social backgrounds of the individuals on the job. This establishment of a group culture is referred to as developing

A. Role models.
B. Cohesiveness.
C. Conformity.
D. Norms.

Answer (D) is correct. *(Publisher, adapted)*
REQUIRED: The definition of norms.
DISCUSSION: Norms are the standards of behavior adopted by a group when it is in its early stages. The norms of the group are often a composite of the personal and social backgrounds of the individuals who comprise the group.
Answer (A) is incorrect. Role models set an example for other employees to follow, but role models are not usually responsible for establishing the culture of a group. Answer (B) is incorrect. Cohesiveness is the tendency of members to adhere to the group and unite against outside pressures. Answer (C) is incorrect. Conformity involves complying with the prevailing role expectations and norms of a group.

13. A new production team has been formed by taking experienced high achievers from existing teams within the factory. The members of the new team have not been required to learn any new skills, and the machines used are identical to those used in their former teams. The team's production supervisor is a longtime employee of the organization but has not previously worked with any members of the new team. Despite the abilities and previous individual achievements of the individual team members, management is surprised by the mediocre performance of the new team. The **best** approach for the production supervisor to improve performance would be to

A. Increase pressure on the team through higher goals and reprimands.

B. Replace the individuals on the team.

C. Provide opportunities for the team members to socialize with each other.

D. Do nothing now because it is too soon to draw any conclusions.

Answer (C) is correct. *(CIA, adapted)*
REQUIRED: The best approach for improving team performance.
DISCUSSION: As the team members work and socialize, cohesiveness will be enhanced because of the opportunity to discover commonalities and share experiences. However, performance may or may not improve as cohesiveness increases. Improvement is also contingent on the group's performance norms. A cohesive group enforces norms. Thus, if norms are high, greater cohesiveness should result in better performance.
Answer (A) is incorrect. External pressure sometimes increases group cohesiveness and improves performance. However, these team members do not know each other well, and they may perceive that the team will not respond adequately to adversity. Answer (B) is incorrect. Group cohesiveness has not had sufficient opportunity to develop. Starting over will be counterproductive. Answer (D) is incorrect. Cohesiveness will probably improve over time, but the supervisor can speed the process by encouraging social interaction.

8.2 Stages of Group Development

14. Which of the following characteristics is common with a mature group?

A. Harmony is emphasized at the expense of addressing the problems.

B. No attempt to force unanimity.

C. Members begin to identify with the group.

D. Redistributions of power and authority may occur.

Answer (B) is correct. *(Publisher, adapted)*
REQUIRED: The characteristics of a mature group.
DISCUSSION: A mature group is in the end stage of group development and tends to be more effective and productive compared to groups in earlier stages. A mature group engages in rational discussion of decisions with tolerance of dissent and no attempt to force unanimity.
Answer (A) is incorrect. Harmony is emphasized at the expense of addressing problems during the delusion stage when members have the false sense that all emotional issues have been resolved. Answer (C) is incorrect. Members begin to identify with the group during the cohesion stage. In a mature group, members already identify with the group. Answer (D) is incorrect. Redistributions of power and authority occur during the conflict and challenge stage when leaders are opposed by members of the group with differing agendas.

15. A mature group lacks which of the following characteristics?

A. Acceptance of individuals' differences.

B. Members' awareness of individual roles in group processes.

C. Attempts to compel unanimity.

D. Acceptance of group authority and interpersonal relationships.

Answer (C) is correct. *(Publisher, adapted)*
REQUIRED: The characteristic not found in a mature group.
DISCUSSION: A mature group has rational discussion of decisions with tolerance of dissent and no attempt to force unanimity. Groups that are in their early stages attempt to force unanimity.
Answer (A) is incorrect. A mature group acknowledges that each member is unique and that the objectives can be accomplished without each group member being the same. Answer (B) is incorrect. Members of a group are often aware of the role they play in a mature group. Answer (D) is incorrect. A mature group already has structured itself so that each member understands the hierarchy of authority and the interpersonal relationships.

16. During which stages do the primary issues among group members involve uncertainty about power and authority relationships?

	Early Stages	Later Stages
A.	Yes	Yes
B.	Yes	No
C.	No	Yes
D.	No	No

Answer (B) is correct. *(Publisher, adapted)*
REQUIRED: The identification of the principal issues encountered in the early and later stages in groups.
DISCUSSION: According to Jewell and Reitz, the principal issue in the early stages is uncertainty about power and authority relationships. The principal issue in the later stages is uncertainty about interpersonal relationships.
Answer (A) is incorrect. Groups in later stages of development already have defined power and authority relationships, and there is little uncertainty. Answer (C) is incorrect. Groups in early stages of development have problems defining power and authority relationships, while groups in later stages of development do not. Answer (D) is incorrect. Groups in early stages of development have problems defining power and authority relationships.

8.3 Organizational Politics

17. Which of the following tactics may employees use when feeling that employees' individual power is insignificant?

A. Employees may engage in posturing by taking credit for the work of a coworker.

B. Employees may engage in destructive competition by spreading false rumors.

C. Employees may engage in creating power and loyalty cliques with other coworkers.

D. Employees may attempt to conceal errors made by a supervisor in order to aid the employees' own future advancement within the corporation.

Answer (C) is correct. *(Publisher, adapted)*
REQUIRED: The tactics employees engage in when they feel a cohesive group has more power than an individual.
DISCUSSION: Employees will often form groups when they feel their collective bargaining power is greater than the power of an individual.
Answer (A) is incorrect. Posturing is the attempt to make a good impression and is often used when an individual feels his/her power is adequate. Answer (B) is incorrect. Engaging in destructive competition does not reveal that an individual feels his/her power is insignificant. Answer (D) is incorrect. Concealing errors by an employee demonstrates that (s)he feels his/her power is great enough to hide errors and not get caught.

18. In which of the following situations will organizational politics **most** likely have a significant impact?

A. When space allocations are made according to objective criteria.

B. When the budget allows for generous salary increases for all employees.

C. When promotions are based on an employee's attitude.

D. When performance outcomes are clearly stated and objective.

Answer (C) is correct. *(CIA, adapted)*
REQUIRED: The situation most likely significantly affected by organizational politics.
DISCUSSION: Organizational politics, or impression management, is defined by Andrew DuBrin as "the pursuit of self-interest at work in the face of real or imagined opposition." Also, employees tend to believe that pursuit of self-interest at work in the form of career advancement is aided by playing politics. Hence, employees will try to, among other things, manage the impression of their attitudes held by superiors.
Answer (A) is incorrect. Objective space allocations are not affected by politics. Answer (B) is incorrect. If each employee receives a salary increase, politics will be less relevant. Answer (D) is incorrect. If an employee meets objectives, politics should not significantly affect his/her performance evaluations.

19. The organizational culture may encourage politics by creating unreasonable obstacles to group and individual advancement. Which type of political tactic involves taking credit for another person's work?

A. Loyalty cliques.

B. Destructive competition.

C. Empire building.

D. Posturing.

Answer (D) is correct. *(Publisher, adapted)*
REQUIRED: The type of political tactic involving taking credit for another person's work.
DISCUSSION: Posturing is an attempt to make a good impression, for example, by taking credit for others' work or seeking to stay one jump ahead of a rival.
Answer (A) is incorrect. Creating power and loyalty cliques is a tactic based on the premise that a cohesive group has more power than an individual. Answer (B) is incorrect. Engaging in destructive competition includes activities such as gossip, lying, and sabotage. Answer (C) is incorrect. Empire building is an attempt to control greater resources. A manager who supervises many employees may feel more secure and influential.

8.4 Team Building

20. Which of the following is **not** one of the advantages of self-managed teams?

   A. Motivation is improved because decision making is decentralized.

   B. Improved processes of production if the teams are supported properly.

   C. Managerial acceptance by tradition-oriented managers.

   D. Improved communication because all members understand the team's activities better.

Answer (C) is correct. *(Publisher, adapted)*
   REQUIRED: The characteristic that is not an advantage of self-managed teams.
   DISCUSSION: Managerial resistance is often the primary obstacle of self-managed teams. Organizational change is difficult and tradition-oriented managers tend to regard self-managed teams as a threat to their status.
   Answer (A) is incorrect. The increased authority of autonomous work groups creates a sense of ownership of the final product. Answer (B) is incorrect. Teams are often able to improve production processes if the team is properly supported by management. Answer (D) is incorrect. Cross-functional teams result in improved communication because all the members have a better understanding of the team activities.

21. Which of the following is key to any plan to empower teams?

   A. Give structure to team members.

   B. Monitor progress and offer timely feedback on performance.

   C. Reduce authority of the team when mistakes are made.

   D. Avoid tension and conflict within the team.

Answer (B) is correct. *(CIA, adapted)*
   REQUIRED: The key item to any plan to empower teams.
   DISCUSSION: Members of a team are empowered when they are properly trained and equipped, have the relevant information they need, are fully involved in decision making, and receive fair compensation for their work. Monitoring and feedback are keys to maintaining empowerment because they are necessary to team effectiveness. Team effectiveness is reflected in achievement of objectives, innovation, adaptability, commitment, and favorable evaluations by senior management.
   Answer (A) is incorrect. Empowered team members may determine their own structure. Answer (C) is incorrect. A tolerance for problems and mistakes is part of empowerment. Answer (D) is incorrect. Tension and conflict are a normal part of team development.

22. The sharing of important financial information with employees based upon a foundation of trust and commitment to training is known as

   A. Self-managed teams.

   B. Open-book management.

   C. Quality circles.

   D. Impression management.

Answer (B) is correct. *(Publisher, adapted)*
   REQUIRED: The definition of open-book management.
   DISCUSSION: Open-book management involves sharing important financial information with trained and empowered employees. This approach is founded on trusting employees, commitment to their training, and waiting patiently for results.
   Answer (A) is incorrect. Self-managed teams involve teams that are empowered to perform traditional management tasks. Self-managed teams may be able to view financial information, but not in all cases. Answer (C) is incorrect. Quality groups usually meet to discuss and solve problems associated with their work areas. Quality circles are usually not able to view important financial information without management approval. Answer (D) is incorrect. Impression management is the pursuit of self-interest in the fear of a real or perceived risk.

23. Which of the following actions can management take to build trust with groups?

   A. Disclose information, emotions, and opinions.

   B. Engaging in timely and accurate communication.

   C. Showing respect to the group.

   D. All of the answers are correct.

Answer (D) is correct. *(Publisher, adapted)*
   REQUIRED: The actions management can take to build trust with groups.
   DISCUSSION: All three of the described actions show that management desires to build a trusting relationship between the group and management.
   Answer (A) is incorrect. Engaging in timely and accurate communication and showing respect to the group will also help build mutual trust. Answer (B) is incorrect. Disclosing information, emotions, and opinions also help build mutual trust. Showing respect to the group also demonstrates that management desires a trusting relationship. Answer (C) is incorrect. Disclosure of information, emotions, and opinions and engaging in timely and accurate communication also demonstrates that management desires to build trust with the group.

24. Which of the following factors is critical for the success of participative management?

    A. Trust.

    B. Control.

    C. Information.

    D. Influence.

Answer (A) is correct. *(Publisher, adapted)*
    REQUIRED: The factor critical to the success of participative management.
    DISCUSSION: Trust is the key factor in any participative management approach. Management should take action to build trust as soon as groups are formed. If there is a lack of trust, then success is unlikely because both the team and management will act in their own self-interest and not the interest of the organization.
    Answer (B) is incorrect. Control comes after there is mutual trust. Direct supervision will be unnecessary if both management and the teams trust that each will act in the organization's best interest. Answer (C) is incorrect. Managers will not disclose information if they do not trust the team first. Answer (D) is incorrect. Neither party will be able to influence the other if there is not mutual trust for each party's position.

25. Which of the following is **not** an appropriate approach to team building?

    A. Ensuring a balance of complementary team roles.

    B. Choosing members who need to improve skills.

    C. Developing clear and shared values.

    D. Selecting team members based on how the members are likely to relate to each other.

Answer (B) is correct. *(CIA, adapted)*
    REQUIRED: The inappropriate approach to team building.
    DISCUSSION: A team is most likely to be effective when it is fully empowered. Empowerment follows from properly training and equipping team members, and providing them with all necessary information. A team will not be effective if its members lack the needed skills.
    Answer (A) is incorrect. Role definition is a recognized approach to team building. Answer (C) is incorrect. Value development is a recognized approach to team building. Answer (D) is incorrect. Interpersonal relations is a recognized approach to team building.

26. Which of the following statements regarding virtual teams is false?

    A. Virtual teams may be able to work faster than a traditional team.

    B. In-person interaction and team-building exercises are unnecessary.

    C. Roles and objectives must be clearly communicated.

    D. Team leaders should meet members in person before the members are chosen for participation in the group.

Answer (B) is correct. *(Publisher, adapted)*
    REQUIRED: The false statement regarding a virtual team.
    DISCUSSION: In-person and team-building exercises are often necessary to create the cohesion and trust for a group to operate effectively. If there are no team-building exercises, the team may fracture and become ineffective at achieving its objective.
    Answer (A) is incorrect. Virtual teams have an advantage of being able to meet anywhere at anytime and therefore may be able to complete tasks faster than traditional teams. Answer (C) is incorrect. In any group, roles and objectives should be clearly communicated to ensure that the team is working together productively towards a common goal. Answer (D) is incorrect. It is recommended that team leaders meet with prospective team members to ensure that the members are compatible with the group and are not working on too many other projects.

27. The STEP model is consistent with which organizational philosophy?

    A. Self-managed teams.

    B. Open-book management.

    C. Impression management.

    D. Group development.

Answer (B) is correct. *(Publisher, adapted)*
    REQUIRED: The organizational philosophy that is consistent with the STEP model.
    DISCUSSION: Open-book management involves sharing important financial information with trained and empowered employees. The first step is to share (S) the financial information with the employees. Next, management must teach (T) the employees how to understand the information and use it to the benefit of the organization. Then, management empowers (E) the employees to act on the information given. Finally, the employees are paid (P) for their accomplishments.
    Answer (A) is incorrect. Self-managed teams are not part of the STEP model. The STEP model involves providing employees with important financial information and teaching the employees how to use it. Answer (C) is incorrect. Impression management involves acting in self-interest in the face of a real or perceived threat. Answer (D) is incorrect. Group development is the stage of bringing a group together that extends from development to maturity.

28. A team is a group whose members work together to achieve a specific common goal. Which of the following is true with respect to teams?

A. All groups are teams, but not all teams are groups.

B. Teams improve organizational performance because teams are easy to form.

C. A team is similar to a group because team leadership often rotates and members are accountable to each other.

D. Smaller teams are recommended.

Answer (D) is correct. *(Publisher, adapted)*
REQUIRED: The characteristics of teams.
DISCUSSION: Normally, smaller teams are recommended. Two to nine members is recommended because working in teams requires accepting a diversity of ideas and opinions. Larger groups require more time for each of the members to develop trust in one another and to work together productively.
Answer (A) is incorrect. All teams are groups, but not all groups are teams. Each team, by definition, is a group of people. Answer (B) is incorrect. Teams often improve organizational performance but teams are not easy to form because it takes time for group members to learn to work together. Answer (C) is incorrect. A team differs from a group because team leadership often rotates and team members are accountable to each other.

29. Which of the following indicates a high-performance team?

A. Pride in the team leader.

B. Quick agreement on the first proposed solution for problems facing the team.

C. Care in risk-taking.

D. Commitment to personal growth of team members.

Answer (D) is correct. *(CIA, adapted)*
REQUIRED: The characteristic that indicates a high-performance team.
DISCUSSION: Team effectiveness is reflected in achievement of objectives, innovation, adaptability, commitment, and favorable evaluations by senior management. According to Hans Thamhain, team effectiveness is determined by three sets of interdependent factors. Team effectiveness requires that all factors need to be addressed continually. A high-performance team is committed to the personal growth of its team members.
Answer (A) is incorrect. High performance teams recognize the value of all members. Answer (B) is incorrect. Quick agreement reflects a lack of diversity characteristic of "groupthink." Answer (C) is incorrect. Individuals tend to be more risk averse than teams.

30. Which one of the following statements about quality circles is false?

A. A quality circle is typically comprised of a group of 8 to 10 subordinates and supervisors.

B. Part of the quality circle concept includes teaching participants communication skills, quality strategies, and problem analysis techniques.

C. Quality circles meet on the company premises and on company time.

D. The quality circle has the final control over implementation of recommended solutions.

Answer (D) is correct. *(CIA, adapted)*
REQUIRED: The false statement about quality circles.
DISCUSSION: Use of quality circles is a form of participative management. A quality circle is a group of up to 10 individuals (managers and subordinates) who do similar work and who volunteer to meet weekly to discuss and solve work-related problems. However, management retains the right to make the final decisions.
Answer (A) is incorrect. A quality circle is a small group of subordinates and supervisors, usually 8 to 10 people. Answer (B) is incorrect. Each member is responsible for the success of the circle, and success depends on the ability of members to analyze and solve problems. Answer (C) is incorrect. Quality circles are used by companies to accomplish objectives. Participation is part of each worker's job.

Use the additional questions in Gleim *CIA Test Prep* Software to create Test Sessions that emulate Pearson VUE!

STUDY UNIT NINE
INFLUENCE AND LEADERSHIP

(11 pages of outline)

This study unit describes the research on influence processes used by managers in organizations. Such processes range from influence tactics, the application of various sources of power, employee empowerment, and behavior modification to the many theories of leadership and its development.

 Influence tactics, the exercise of power, and leadership are, like group dynamics, intangible qualities that substantially if not decisively affect organizational success. An internal auditor therefore must be alert to their effects on governance, risk management, and control processes.

9.1 INFLUENCE AND POWER

Influence

1. **Robert Kreitner** defines **influence** in the work environment as "any attempt by a person to change the behavior of superiors, peers, or lower-level employees."

    a. Influence may be exerted in many ways, including the use of power and the exercise of leadership.

2. Management literature (Kipnin, Schmidt, Wilkinson, and others) describes **generic influence tactics**.

    a. They may be directed upward to influence superiors, laterally to influence peers, and downward to influence lower-level employees.

    b. The following are the generic influence tactics noted by researchers:

        1) **Consultation** permits the other person(s) to participate in the decision or change.

        2) **Rational persuasion** tries to convince others by reliance on a detailed plan, supporting evidence, and reason.

        3) **Inspirational appeals** are based on emotions, values, or ideals.

        4) **Ingratiating tactics** attempt to raise the other person's self-esteem prior to a request.

        5) **Coalition tactics** seek the aid of others to persuade someone to agree.

        6) **Pressure tactics** involve intimidation, threats, and demands.

        7) **Upward appeals** are based on the formal or informal support of higher management.

        8) **Exchange tactics** may involve an exchange of favors, a reminder of a past favor, or an offer of a personal sacrifice.

    c. The most commonly used influence tactics are consultation, rational persuasion, and inspirational appeals. The least commonly used are pressure tactics, upward appeals, and exchange tactics.

        1) Research suggests that male and female managers do not differ significantly in their use of influence tactics.

2)   Upward influence methods used by employees of **authoritarian managers** are most likely to consist of ingratiating tactics and upward appeals.

3)   Rational persuasion is the method used most often by employees of **participative managers**.

Power

3.   Power is the ability to influence employees to do what they would not ordinarily do. It also has been defined as the ability to use people, information, and material resources to accomplish something (Morgan McCall, Jr.).

a.   Power and influence may be used formally or informally.

b.   The following are **power sources**:

1)   **Legitimate or position power** (closely associated with formal authority)

a)   Employees tend not to completely obey someone who relies solely on legitimate authority. Moreover, managers may not have the right to direct (exert formal authority over) some people whom they need to influence.

2)   **Expertise**

a)   The most notable example is the power exerted by IT professionals.

3)   **Referent power** (derived from the leader's charisma or employees' identification with the leader)

a)   The negative aspect of referent power is that the individuals who have it often abuse it.

4)   **Coercive power**

a)   This power is based on the fear or threat of punishment.

5)   **Control of rewards**

a)   Performance may determine pay raises and promotions.

c.   The greater the sources of power possessed by a manager, the more likely an employee will accept his/her authority.

1)   Thus, a manager who has formal and informal sources of power will be more influential than one with a single source.

d.   **Authority** is the **right** to manage others. It differs from power, which is the **ability** to accomplish something.

1)   A manager may have one without the other.

e.   The **dimensions of power** include the ability to control others, act freely, or resist control by others.

f.   The exercise of power affects the **decisions**, for example, as the result of advice offered by someone with expert power.

1)   It also affects **behavior**, for example, as the result of a warning from someone with coercive power.

2)   Moreover, the exercise of power affects **situations**, for example, a change in the nature or type of resources used in operations effected by someone with any base of power.

g.   Modern management theory emphasizes **employee empowerment**. The question is not whether employees should be empowered but the circumstances in which it should occur.

1)   Individuals need to be honest, trustworthy, unselfish, and skilled.

2)   Empowerment is not the same as lack of control. Appropriate oversight is necessary.

3) Employees should have adequate training, relevant information, and other necessary tools.

4) Employees should participate fully in making important decisions.

5) Employees should be fairly compensated.

6) Managers who appropriately surrender power by empowering employees actually gain power. They have an increased ability to achieve desired results.

Behavior Modification

4. Behavior modification is the management of environmental factors to encourage desirable behavior and to discourage undesirable behavior. Environmental factors include antecedents and consequences of behavior.

  a. **Antecedents** are cues that encourage but do not cause a given behavior. Managing antecedents involves eliminating barriers to good performance and replacing them with helpful aids.

    1) **Barriers** include unattainable objectives, poor training, confusing rules, and conflicting directions from management.

    2) **Aids** include challenging but attainable objectives, clear instructions, realistic plans, constructive suggestions, and acceptable work rules.

  b. **Consequences** include the following:

    1) **Positive reinforcement** provides rewards for certain responses. It emphasizes desirable rather than undesirable behavior.

      a) Theorists regard positive reinforcement as the most effective approach.

      b) Examples are merit-based salary bonuses and payment based on the level of output.

      c) **Continuous reinforcement** rewards every occurrence of a desirable new behavior.

      d) **Intermittent reinforcement** provides occasional rewards for an established behavior.

        i) **Variable-interval schedules** of intermittent reinforcement lead to better performance. Employees are more alert because of the uncertainty involved, and performance and reward are connected.

        ii) **Fixed-interval schedules** of reinforcement do not clearly link performance and reward.

    2) **Negative reinforcement** is the withdrawal of an existing unpleasant condition (such as a threat) when the desired behavior occurs.

    3) **Extinction** discourages a behavior by ignoring it (not reinforcing it).

    4) **Punishment** discourages a behavior by following it with a negative consequence.

      a) Punishment is most effective when it immediately follows an undesirable behavior.

Core Concepts

- Influence may be exerted in many ways, including the use of power and the exercise of leadership.
- Generic influence tactics may be used in any direction (upward to influence superiors, laterally to influence peers, and downward to influence lower-level employees). They include (1) consultation, (2) rational persuasion, (3) inspirational appeals, (4) ingratiating tactics, (5) coalition tactics, (6) pressure tactics, (7) upward appeals, and (8) exchange tactics.

- Power is the ability to influence employees to do what they would not ordinarily do. It also has been defined as the ability to use people, information, and material resources to accomplish something.

- Power sources include (1) legitimate or position power, (2) expertise, (3) referent power, (4) coercive power, and (5) control of rewards.

- Authority is the right to manage others. It differs from power, the ability to accomplish something. A manager may have one without the other.

- The exercise of power affects (1) decisions (e.g., the result of advice offered by someone with expert power), (2) behavior (e.g., the result of a warning from someone with coercive power), or (3) situations (e.g., a change in the nature or type of resources used in operations effected by someone with any base of power).

- Modern management theory emphasizes employee empowerment. The question is not whether employees should be empowered but the circumstances in which it should occur.

- Behavior modification is the management of environmental factors to encourage desirable behavior and to discourage undesirable behavior. Environmental factors include antecedents and consequences. Antecedents are cues that encourage but do not cause a given behavior. Consequences include reinforcement (positive, continuous, intermittent, and negative), extinction, and punishment.

Stop and review! You have completed the outline for this subunit. Study multiple-choice questions 1 through 11 beginning on page 221.

9.2 LEADERSHIP

Overview

1. **Leadership** is the act or process of influencing, inspiring, and guiding people so they will strive willingly toward the achievement of group objectives through common effort.

    a. **Formal leadership** pursues the organization's objectives, but **informal leadership** may pursue objectives different from the organization's.

        1) Formal (not informal) leaders ordinarily have **formal authority** and **legitimate power**. However, both kinds of leaders may have any other type of power.

        2) Informal leaders whose **objectives** are the same as (different from) those of the organization are assets (liabilities).

    b. According to the **classical position**, authority, decision making, and responsibility all may be decentralized to some extent.

        1) But leadership is a characteristic of the individual's personality and cannot be subdivided.

    c. The **traitist approach** has produced such a long list of leadership traits that, in effect, it identifies nothing. Nevertheless, a few traits have a significant correlation with a leader's effectiveness:

        1) Intelligence
        2) Scholarship
        3) Dependability
        4) Social participation and interest
        5) Socioeconomic status (in comparison with nonleaders)

    d. A more recent traitist approach is based on the **emotional intelligence** of leaders, that is, their social skills and judgment, maturity, and emotional control.

        1) These abilities can be learned, especially when a person understands that immaturity, erratic behavior, and uncontrolled negative emotions have a bad effect on the workplace.

2) According to Daniel Goleman, a leader can acquire social capital through exhibiting the following **leadership traits**:

    a) **Self-awareness** is knowing oneself.

    b) **Self-management** is the ability to prevent changes in one's mood from interfering with positive relationships.

    c) **Social awareness** is understanding the actions and emotions of others. This ability helps a person to adapt in a productive way.

    d) **Relationship management** is an ability possessed by a person who communicates and resolves conflict effectively. Humor and a benign approach are characteristics of people who develop good relationships.

e. Some writers assert that men and women have different leadership traits.

    1) However, the research indicates male and female managers do not match the stereotypes (task orientation versus relationship orientation, respectively).

Leader Behavior

2. Behavior-oriented researchers have examined **leader behavior** to determine whether leaders conduct themselves in certain ways.

3. **Styles of leadership** are emphasized in behavioral approaches. The following are the classic styles:

    a. **Authoritarian**

        1) The manager does not share authority and responsibility. (S)he dictates all decisions to employees, so communication is downward with little employee input.

        2) Tasks are clearly defined.

        3) Authoritarian leaders rely on threats and punishment and do not trust employees.

        4) Such leadership can sometimes be the most effective, such as when the time to make a decision is limited or when employees do not respond to any other leadership style.

    b. **Democratic**

        1) The leader delegates substantial authority.

        2) Employees participate in defining and assigning tasks, and communication is actively upward as well as downward. Thus, employees are more committed.

    c. **Laissez faire**

        1) Employees in a group are given the authority and responsibility to make their own decisions.

        2) Communication is mostly horizontal.

        3) This style works best when employees show personal initiative, but the group also may be ineffective without the leader's guidance.

4. According to a **model developed at Ohio State University**, two behavior patterns that are consistently found in the study of leadership are the initiation of structure and consideration by the leader. The first is production-centered and the second is employee-centered.

    a. **Initiating structure** is directed towards accomplishing tasks. Structure includes the following:

        1) Defining duties
        2) Establishing procedures
        3) Planning and organizing work

    b.   **Consideration** is the establishment of a personal relationship between the leader and the subordinate. High consideration by the leader includes the following:

        1)   Warmth toward the employee as a person
        2)   Psychological support for the employee
        3)   Helpfulness with work-related problems

    c.   Both structure initiation and consideration are present in **all job situations**. The relative amounts of each must be appropriate to the situation. For example,

        1)   A highly structured situation (e.g., assembly-line work) may respond negatively to further structure initiated by the manager but positively to increased consideration.

        2)   A manager of R&D may find the initiation of structure much more productive than increased consideration. Creative personnel working on a disorganized project may find a better-defined project plan much more satisfying than a demonstration of concern by the manager.

    d.   The following are the four leadership styles in the Ohio State model:

        1)   **Low structure and low consideration** indicates a passive leader.
        2)   **Low structure and high consideration** results from an emphasis on satisfying employee needs.
        3)   **High structure and low consideration** results from a primary focus on task accomplishment.
        4)   **High structure and high consideration** reflects a strong emphasis on both task accomplishment and satisfying employee needs.

  5.   The **leadership grid** developed by Robert Blake and Jane Mouton is a trademarked classification scheme. **Concern for production** is on the horizontal (x) axis, and **concern for people** is on the vertical (y) axis.

    a.   Concern for production emphasizes output, cost control, and profit.

    b.   Concern for people emphasizes friendship, aiding employees in accomplishing tasks, and addressing employee issues (e.g., compensation).

    c.   Each axis has a scale of 1 to 9. Thus, the primary styles are the following:
        <u>X,Y</u>

        1)   **1,1:** Little concern for production or people (impoverished management)
        2)   **1,9:** Primary concern for people, little concern for production (country club management)
        3)   **9,1:** Primary concern for production, little concern for people (authority-compliance management)
        4)   **5,5:** Moderate concern for production and people to maintain status quo (middle-of-the-road management)
        5)   **9,9:** Great concern for production and people, trust, teamwork, and commitment (team management)

           a)   Blake and his associates assert that the 9,9 style is best because it produces the best operating results, health outcomes, and conflict resolutions.

Situational Theories

  6.   The assumption of situational theories of leadership is that the appropriate leadership style depends on the situation. The emphasis is on flexibility because no one style is best in every situation.

  7.   According to Fred E. Fiedler's **contingency theory**, people become leaders because of personality attributes, various situational factors, and the interaction between the leaders and the situation.

a.   Thus, the **right person at the right time** may rise to a position of leadership if his/her personality and the needs of the situation complement each other.

    1)   The same person might not become a leader in different circumstances because of failure to interact successfully with that situation.

b.   The contingency theory model has **three dimensions**:

    1)   **Position power** is based on the formal authority structure. It is the degree to which the position held enables a leader to evaluate, reward, punish, or promote group members.

        a)   It is independent of other sources of power, such as personality or expertise.

    2)   **Task structure** is how clearly and carefully members' responsibilities for various tasks are defined.

        a)   Quality of performance is more easily controlled when tasks are clearly defined.

    3)   **Leader-member relations** reflect the extent to which group members like and trust and are willing to follow a leader.

c.   Leaders tend to be task motivated or relationship motivated.

    1)   The **task-motivated style** is most effective when the situation is very favorable or very unfavorable.

        a)   The situation is **very favorable** when the leader's position of power is high, tasks are well defined, and leader-member relations are good. The situation is **very unfavorable** when the reverse is true.

        b)   In the favorable situation, a leader has little need to address relationship issues and should therefore concentrate on the work. In the unfavorable situation, the leader must emphasize close supervision.

    2)   The **relationship-motivated style** is most effective in the middle, less extreme situations when favorable and unfavorable factors are mixed.

d.   The most effective leadership style depends upon the degree to which the three dimensions are present in a situation.

e.   Leadership is therefore as much a responsibility of the organization's placement of leaders as it is of the leaders themselves.

    1)   Thus, an organization should identify leadership situations and its managers' leadership styles and design the job to suit the manager if necessary.

8.   According to Hersey and Blanchard's **situational leadership theory**, the appropriate leadership style depends on the followers' maturity, which is their degree of willingness to be responsible for directing their behavior.

a.   The dimensions of the four styles of leadership described in the model are task and relationship behaviors.

    1)   **Selling.** A selling leadership style explains decisions and provides opportunity for clarification (high task and high relationship).

    2)   **Telling.** A telling leadership style provides specific instructions and closely supervises performance (high task and low relationship).

    3)   **Participating.** A participating leadership style encourages the sharing of ideas and facilitates decision making (low task and high relationship).

    4)   **Delegating.** A delegating leadership style turns over responsibility for decisions and implementation (low task and low relationship).

9.   **Path-goal theory** emphasizes **motivation**. It combines the research on initiating structure and consideration with expectancy theory.

   a.   Leaders should motivate employees by clarifying employees' understanding of

      1)   Work goals,

      2)   The relationship of achievement of those goals with rewards that matter to employees, and

      3)   How the goals may be achieved.

   b.   Leaders should increase payoffs, define the path to success, remove obstacles, and increase the chances of individual satisfaction while the path is being traveled.

   c.   Two groups of contingency factors affect the relationship between leadership behavior and the outcomes of employee performance and satisfaction.

      1)   **Environmental contingency factors** are those beyond employees' control (task structure, the formal authority system, and the work group).

      2)   **Subordinate contingency factors** are the personal characteristics of employees (locus of control, experience, and perceived ability).

   d.   A leadership style should be chosen that complements but does not duplicate the factors in the environment and is consistent with employees' characteristics.

      1)   The **directive** leader lets employees know what is expected of them, schedules work to be done, and gives specific guidance on how to accomplish tasks.

         a)   A directive style is most effective when the employees are externally controlled, tasks are ambiguous or stressful, and substantial conflict exists in the work group.

            i)   Thus, a directive style is appropriate when employees do not have high perceived ability or experience.

      2)   The **supportive** leader is friendly and shows concern for the needs of the employees.

         a)   The supportive style is best when tasks are highly structured and the authority relationships are clear and bureaucratic.

         b)   This approach depends on people who want to work, grow, and achieve.

         c)   The supportive style may be best when tasks are unsatisfying.

      3)   The **participative** leader consults with employees and considers their suggestions before making a decision.

         a)   The participative style is most useful when employees believe they control their own destinies, that is, when they have an internal locus of control.

            i)   Such individuals may be resentful if they are not consulted.

      4)   The **achievement-oriented** leader is a facilitator who sets challenging goals and expects employees to perform at their highest level.

         a)   Achievement-oriented leadership is appropriate when tasks are nonrepetitive and ambiguous and employee competence is high.

   e.   In contrast with Fiedler's approach, path-goal theorists believe that managers are able to adapt their styles to the situation.

Other Leadership Theories

10. A **transformational leader** is an agent of change who combines initiating structure and consideration with such other behaviors as charisma. The transformational leader is able to inspire the members of the organization to aspire to, and to achieve, more than they thought was possible.

a. Transformational leadership emphasizes

1) Vision,
2) Development of the individual,
3) Empowerment of the worker, and
4) The challenging of traditional assumptions.

b. Transformational leaders

1) Articulate a vision,
2) Use nontraditional thinking,
3) Encourage individual development,
4) Provide workers with regular feedback,
5) Use participative decision making, and
6) Promote a cooperative and trusting work environment.

c. The transformational leader normally has charisma, is inspirational, provides intellectual stimulation to workers, and gives individualized consideration.

d. A **transactional leader** emphasizes monitoring of employees so that they adhere to standards.

1) Thus, the transactional leader ensures that expectations are met, but the transformational leader motivates employees to go beyond expectations.

11. Robert Greenleaf's philosophy of **servant leaders** is founded on the following principles:

a. They have an instinctive desire to serve others and must therefore consciously decide to become leaders.

b. They clearly define a vision (goals).

c. They are trusted by their followers.

d. They listen first.

e. They accept people, if not their performance.

f. They have intuitive foresight that allows them to make sound judgments.

g. They believe that every problem begins inside themselves. Thus, personal development is their focus.

Mentoring

12. Mentoring is systematic development of leadership by providing career counseling and social nurturing.

a. According to Abraham Zaleznik, it requires intensive tutoring, coaching, and guidance.

b. Some organizations have formal mentoring programs that assign mentors to junior employees. However, some research indicates that a mentoring arrangement that occurs informally and voluntarily may have better results.

c. According to Kathy Kram, mentoring serves career and psychosocial functions.

1) **Career functions** include sponsorship, visibility, coaching, protection, and assigning challenges.

a) For example, a technically proficient auditor who works well with clients might be challenged to develop leadership skills by being assigned to lead a small team. The project should involve specific objectives and a well-trained staff. The experience should prepare the auditor for larger projects.

2) **Psychosocial functions** include role modeling, acceptance, confirmation, counseling, and friendship.

d. Mentors also may benefit from intrinsic pleasure in helping others to succeed or from gaining power by transferring values and skills to the people they mentor.

Core Concepts

- Leadership is the act or process of influencing, inspiring, and guiding people so they will strive willingly toward the achievement of group objectives through common effort.

- Formal leadership pursues the organization's objectives, but informal leadership may pursue objectives at variance with the organization's.

- Traits significantly correlated with a leader's effectiveness include (1) intelligence, (2) scholarship, (3) dependability, (4) social participation and interest, and (5) socioeconomic status (in comparison with nonleaders).

- Traits based on the emotional intelligence of leaders (social skills and judgment, maturity, and emotional control) include (1) self-awareness, (2) self-management, (3) social awareness, and (4) relationship management.

- Styles of leadership emphasized in behavioral approaches include (1) authoritarian (e.g., the manager dictates all decisions to the employees), (2) democratic (e.g., the leader delegates substantial authority), and (3) laissez faire (e.g., employees in a group are given the authority and responsibility to make their own decisions).

- According to the Ohio State model, two behavior patterns that are consistently found in the study of leadership are the initiation of structure and consideration by the leader. The first is production-centered, and the second is employee-centered. Both are present in all job situations.

- The four leadership styles are (1) low structure and low consideration (a passive leader), (2) low structure and high consideration (emphasis on satisfying employee needs), (3) high structure and low consideration (primary focus on task accomplishment), and (4) high structure and high consideration (strong emphasis on both task accomplishment and satisfying employee needs).

- The leadership grid developed by Robert Blake and Jane Mouton is a trademarked classification scheme. Concern for production is on the horizontal axis, and concern for people is on the vertical axis. Each axis has a scale of 1 to 9.

- According to Fred E. Fiedler's contingency theory, people become leaders because of personality attributes, various situational factors, and the interaction between the leaders and the situation. The contingency model has three dimensions: (1) position power, (2) task structure, and (3) leader-member relations. Fiedler's research showed that leaders tend to be either task motivated or relationship motivated.

- Hersey and Blanchard describe four styles of leadership. They are (1) selling (explains decisions and provides opportunity for clarification), (2) telling (provides specific instructions and closely supervises performance), (3) participating (encourages the sharing of ideas and facilitates decision making), and (4) delegating (turns over the responsibility for decisions and implementation).

- According to path-goal theory, a directive leader lets employees know what is expected of them, schedules work to be done, and gives specific guidance on how to accomplish tasks. A supportive leader is friendly and shows concern for the needs of the employees. A participative leader consults with employees and considers their suggestions before making a decision. An achievement-oriented leader is a facilitator who sets challenging goals and expects employees to perform at their highest level.

- The transformational leader is able to inspire the members of the organization to aspire to, and to achieve, more than they thought was possible. A transactional leader emphasizes monitoring of employees so that they adhere to standards.

- Robert Greenleaf's philosophy of servant leaders is founded on the following principles: (1) an instinctive desire to serve others; (2) clearly defined visions or goals; (3) ability to win the trust of their followers; (4) listening first; (5) accepting people, if not their performance; (6) intuitive foresight; and (7) belief that every problem begins inside themselves.

- Mentoring is the systematic development of leadership by providing career counseling and social nurturing. It requires intensive tutoring, coaching, and guidance, and serves career and psychosocial functions.

Stop and review! You have completed the outline for this subunit. Study multiple-choice questions 12 through 28 beginning on page 224.

QUESTIONS

9.1 Influence and Power

1. A manager can use power and authority to accomplish objectives. The relationship between these two important concepts is **best** explained as follows:

A. Power is the right to do things, while authority is the ability to do things.

B. Authority is the right to do things, while power is the ability to do things.

C. Power and authority are both required to accomplish a task.

D. Power and authority are simply two words that describe the same concept -- how to get things done in organizations.

Answer (B) is correct. *(CIA, adapted)*
   REQUIRED: The relationship between power and authority.
   DISCUSSION: Authority is the officially sanctioned privilege to direct others. A clear hierarchy of authority enhances coordination and accountability. Power is the ability to marshal organizational resources to obtain results. A manager may have both authority and power, or one without the other.
   Answer (A) is incorrect. Authority is the right to do things, and power is the ability to do things. Answer (C) is incorrect. A manager may accomplish a task without having formal authority. Answer (D) is incorrect. Authority is the right to do things, and power is the ability to do things.

2. A company's decisions are made solely by one person, who is the CEO and major shareholder. Which of the following powers is this person **least** likely to have?

A. Coercive power.

B. Legitimate power.

C. Referent power.

D. Reward power.

Answer (C) is correct. *(Publisher, adapted)*
   REQUIRED: The power that the sole decision maker is least likely to have.
   DISCUSSION: A person who is the head of a company may exert influence through five types of power. Referent power is the capacity of the individual's personality and style to cause others to identify with or like him or her. Thus, it is the one type of power not necessarily held by a CEO and major shareholder. This person has the ability to reward others and apply pressure. (S)he also has the right to expect cooperation.
   Answer (A) is incorrect. Coercive power is the ability of the individual to make others cooperate by applying pressure. Answer (B) is incorrect. Legitimate power is the leader's right to expect cooperation from others. Answer (D) is incorrect. Reward power is the individual's ability to influence others through their expectation that good behavior will be rewarded.

3. Which of the following is true concerning generic influence tactics?

A. Consultation involves appealing to emotions, values, or ordeals.

B. Ingratiating tactics attempt to raise the other person's self-esteem prior to a request.

C. Coalition tactics try to convince others by reliance on a detailed plan, supporting evidence, and reason.

D. Pressure tactics are based on the formal or informal support of higher management.

Answer (B) is correct. *(Publisher, adapted)*
   REQUIRED: The true statement concerning generic influence tactics.
   DISCUSSION: Management literature describes generic influence tactics that may be upward, lateral, or downward. As noted by researchers, ingratiating tactics attempt to raise the other person's self-esteem prior to a request.
   Answer (A) is incorrect. Consultation permits the other person to participate in the decision or change. Answer (C) is incorrect. Coalition tactics seek the aid of others to persuade someone to agree. Answer (D) is incorrect. Pressure tactics involve intimidation, threats, and demands.

4. Which of the following is **not** an example of positive reinforcement of behavior?

A. Paying a bonus to employees who had no absences for any 4-week period.

B. Giving written warnings to employees after only every other absence.

C. Assigning a mentor to each employee who exhibits a desire to develop leadership skills.

D. Having a lottery every month where 10% of the employees with no absences receive a US $200 bonus.

Answer (B) is correct.   *(CIA, adapted)*
REQUIRED: The action not an example of positive reinforcement.
DISCUSSION: Positive reinforcement encourages a desired behavior by following it with the presentation of a reward. Punishment, on the other hand, discourages an undesired behavior by following it with a negative consequence. While punishment ideally should follow every occurrence of an undesirable behavior, this is not always possible. Thus, even though written warnings are given to employees only after every other absence, the action is considered punishment, not positive reinforcement.
Answer (A) is incorrect. Paying a bonus is a positive reinforcement. Answer (C) is incorrect. Assigning a mentor is a positive reinforcement. Answer (D) is incorrect. Holding a lottery is an intermittent positive reinforcement.

5. The director of internal auditing for a large company has established an excellent reputation because of her strong professional credentials and tactful but firm handling of auditor-auditee relationships. With regard to auditees, she must rely upon what sources of power?

A. Expert and coercive.

B. Referent and reward.

C. Referent and expert.

D. Legitimate and coercive.

Answer (C) is correct.   *(Publisher, adapted)*
REQUIRED: The sources of power relied on by a particular manager.
DISCUSSION: The internal audit director has neither formal (legitimate or position) power over auditees nor the power to coerce (punish) or reward them. Rather, her ability to exert power (influence others) must derive from her specialized ability and knowledge and the force of her personal qualities.
Answer (A) is incorrect. She does not have the power to coerce others. Answer (B) is incorrect. She has no power to reward others. Answer (D) is incorrect. She does not have the power to coerce others.

6. The punishing of employees is made less effective by

A. Stating the offending behavior specifically.

B. Postponing the start of disciplinary procedures.

C. Permitting employees to challenge individual culpability.

D. Focusing the discussion on the offending behavior instead of the offender.

Answer (B) is correct.   *(CIA, adapted)*
REQUIRED: The action that renders the discipline process less effective.
DISCUSSION: The most effective discipline requires immediate corrective action to eliminate the negative effects of the undesirable employee conduct and to establish and reinforce appropriate behavior. Delay merely invites more serious consequences. Moreover, the punishment should be commensurate with the offense, and the employee should clearly perceive the relationship between the punishment and the behavior.
Answer (A) is incorrect. Stating the undesirable behavior clarifies for the employee the link between conduct and consequences. Answer (C) is incorrect. In U.S. legal culture, the accused has the right to be heard in his/her defense. Answer (D) is incorrect. Focusing on the offense rather than the offender is less likely to engender fear and resentment on the part of the employee.

7. Power is synonymous with leadership. Simply, it is the ability to influence other people. The sources of power are various. For example, the kind of power arising from the strength of the leader's personality is known as

A. Coercive power.

B. Legitimate power.

C. Expert power.

D. Referent power.

Answer (D) is correct.   *(Publisher, adapted)*
REQUIRED: The kind of power arising from the strength of the leader's personality.
DISCUSSION: Power may be classified as reward power (the leader controls resources), coercive power (the leader may punish the subordinate), legitimate power (the leader has the right to lead), referent power (the leader has fame, charisma, etc.), and expert power (the leader has specialized ability or knowledge).

8. A leader who is able to gain compliance from a group based solely on personal attraction is said to have

- A. Reward power.
- B. Coercive power.
- C. Referent power.
- D. Legitimate power.

Answer (C) is correct. *(CIA, adapted)*
REQUIRED: The type of power held by a leader who uses personal attraction to gain compliance from a group.
DISCUSSION: Referent power is based on identification of subordinates with a superior. Thus, personal magnetism (charisma) may be a basis for influencing others to comply with a manager's directives.
Answer (A) is incorrect. Reward power is based on a person's ability to grant benefits. Answer (B) is incorrect. Coercive power is rooted in the fear or threat of punishment. Answer (D) is incorrect. Legitimate power is based on a person's superior position.

9. A manager believes that positive reinforcement is the most appropriate way to deal with employees. Which of the following actions demonstrates the principle of positive reinforcement?

- A. Employees are given 2-day suspension without pay if errors exceed a predefined level.
- B. Employees are praised when the detected error rate in their work stays below a predefined level.
- C. Time budgets, which have forced employees to rush and consequently make errors, are eliminated.
- D. Employees are not required to work overtime if errors stay below a predefined level.

Answer (B) is correct. *(CIA, adapted)*
REQUIRED: The action that demonstrates positive reinforcement.
DISCUSSION: Positive reinforcement is a behavior modification technique that provides rewards for certain responses. It focuses on desirable rather than undesirable behavior. The practice of praising employees when the detected error rate in their work stays below a predefined level demonstrates positive reinforcement.
Answer (A) is incorrect. Suspending employees is punishment. Answer (C) is incorrect. Eliminating time budgets is extinction, which is the elimination of reinforcement that is maintaining a behavior. Answer (D) is incorrect. Not requiring employees to work overtime is negative reinforcement, which is the elimination of something unpleasant when a desired behavior occurs.

10. When supervising employees, the behavior **most** likely to attain long-term positive results for a manager would be to

- A. Discipline employees immediately using oral reprimands, written warnings, and temporary suspensions.
- B. Hold weekly meetings during which employees are reminded of work procedures and are praised for the week's accomplishments.
- C. Praise employees on a random schedule and link rewards to performance.
- D. Tell employees that working overtime now will result in a better performance review in 6 months.

Answer (C) is correct. *(CIA, adapted)*
REQUIRED: The supervisory behavior most likely to have long-term positive results.
DISCUSSION: Variable-interval schedules of reinforcement lead to higher performance. Employees are more alert because of the uncertainty involved, and performance and reward are connected.
Answer (A) is incorrect. Punishment only leads to short-term suppression of the behavior and may cause the staff member to avoid the manager, who is seen as punishing rather than helpful. Answer (B) is incorrect. Fixed-interval reinforcement schedules do not clearly link performance and rewards. Answer (D) is incorrect. Six months is too long an interval for linking performance and reward.

11. A production worker in a plant often speaks for the entire work force when problems arise between labor and management. Although this individual has the same level of authority and expertise as the individual's co-workers, the worker seems to possess a degree of power that others do not have. What type of power does this individual apparently have?

- A. Coercive.
- B. Referent.
- C. Legitimate.
- D. Reward.

Answer (B) is correct. *(CIA, adapted)*
REQUIRED: The type of power held by a worker who leads fellow workers despite having no advantage in expertise or authority.
DISCUSSION: Referent power is based on identification of subordinates with a superior. Thus, personal magnetism (charisma) may be a basis for influencing others to comply with a manager's directives.
Answer (A) is incorrect. Coercive power is rooted in fear or threat of punishment. Answer (C) is incorrect. Legitimate power is based on formal authority or the organizational position held by a leader. Answer (D) is incorrect. Reward power is based on a person's ability to grant benefits.

9.2 Leadership

12. According to the contingency theory of leadership, a manager will be **most** effective when the manager

- A. Consistently initiates structure.
- B. Adapts style to specific circumstances.
- C. Is task oriented.
- D. Is relationship oriented.

Answer (B) is correct. *(Publisher, adapted)*
REQUIRED: The most effective management approach according to contingency theory.
DISCUSSION: Fred E. Fiedler's contingency theory of management holds that no single style of directing is best for all occasions. A successful director (leader) must, for each situation, balance his/her formal authority, the task structure, and the leader's relationships with the pertinent group members.
Answer (A) is incorrect. A relationship- (employee-) oriented approach may be preferable when tasks are highly structured. Answer (C) is incorrect. A relationship- (employee-) oriented approach may be preferable when tasks are highly structured. Answer (D) is incorrect. When tasks are ill-defined, the more effective manager may be one who concentrates on defining and organizing the jobs to be done rather than on motivating employees.

13. Which of the following leadership types is **best** known as an agent of change?

- A. Participative leader.
- B. Traitist leader.
- C. Transformational leader.
- D. Free-rein leader.

Answer (C) is correct. *(Publisher, adapted)*
REQUIRED: The leadership style that is best used when an agent of change is needed.
DISCUSSION: A transformational leader is an agent of change who attempts to inspire the members of the organization to aspire to, and to achieve, more than they thought was possible. Transformational leadership emphasizes vision, development of the individual, empowerment of the worker, and the challenging of traditional assumptions. The transformational leader normally has charisma, is motivational, provides intellectual stimulation to workers, and gives individualized consideration.
Answer (A) is incorrect. A participative leader is simply one who allows employees to have input into the decision-making process. Answer (B) is incorrect. Traitist leader is essentially a nonsense term as used here. Answer (D) is incorrect. A free-rein leader is one who allows employees to make their own decisions.

14. Which of the following is true regarding the approach to leadership based on emotional intelligence?

- A. It attempts to identify traits possessed by leaders.
- B. It has produced such a long list of leadership traits that, in effect, the approach identifies nothing.
- C. It is based on scholarship, dependability, and social participation.
- D. It is based on social skills, judgment, maturity, and emotional control.

Answer (D) is correct. *(Publisher, adapted)*
REQUIRED: The true statement about the traitist approach based on emotional intelligence.
DISCUSSION: One traitist approach is based on the emotional intelligence of leaders, that is, their social skills and judgment, maturity, and emotional control. These abilities can be learned, especially when a manager or employee understands that immaturity, erratic behavior, and uncontrolled negative emotions have a bad effect on the workplace.
Answer (A) is incorrect. All traitist approaches attempt to identify leadership traits. Answer (B) is incorrect. Other approaches have produced such a long list of leadership traits that, in effect, each approach identifies nothing. Answer (C) is incorrect. The leader with emotional intelligence is self aware and socially aware and can manage him/herself and relationships.

15. Leadership situations vary with regard to the degree to which the leader can determine what subordinates will do, how the subordinates will do it, and what the results will be. According to Fiedler's contingency theory, a leader with a relationship-oriented management style will be **most** effective when exerting

- A. Great control.
- B. Moderate control.
- C. Little control.
- D. Great or little control.

Answer (B) is correct. *(Publisher, adapted)*
REQUIRED: The situation in which a relationship-oriented management style will be most effective.
DISCUSSION: A relationship-oriented manager is employee centered. His/her self-esteem is strongly affected by personal interactions with subordinates. Fiedler indicated that such a manager is most effective when not faced with the extremes of high or low control situations. High control follows from strong position power, a structured task, and good leader-member relations. A low-control situation has just the opposite characteristics. In a high-control environment, a concern for personal relations may be unimportant. In a low-control situation, the relationship-oriented leader may be unable to provide the needed task structuring. Thus, the moderate-control situation is best. An example is an assembly-line situation (a structured task) in which leader-member relations are poor.

16. If a supervisor uses a supportive management approach, evidenced by positive feelings and concern for subordinates, a problem might result because

   A. An approach based on pure power makes it difficult to motivate staff.

   B. This approach depends on material rewards for the worker.

   C. This approach depends on people who want to work, grow, and achieve.

   D. The manager must believe in the teamwork approach.

Answer (C) is correct. *(CIA, adapted)*
   REQUIRED: The problem that could result from using a supportive management approach.
   DISCUSSION: Supportive management techniques orient workers toward performance rather than obedience or happiness. The leader should have positive feelings for his/her employees and should attempt to encourage participation and involvement. This approach is effective when used with employees who are motivated to work, improve themselves and their abilities, and accomplish goals.
   Answer (A) is incorrect. An approach based on pure power is an autocratic style of leadership, not a supportive approach. Answer (B) is incorrect. The custodial model depends on material rewards for the worker. This model is predicated on the belief that a happy worker is a productive worker. Answer (D) is incorrect. The manager's beliefs are not sufficient. The workers also must believe in the system.

17. Which of the following statements is true regarding leadership styles?

   A. The manager dictates all decisions to the employees, so communication is downward and tasks are clearly defined in authoritarian leadership.

   B. Employees in a group are given the authority and responsibility to make individual decisions in democratic leadership.

   C. The leader delegates substantial authority and employees participate in defining and assigning tasks in laissez-faire leadership.

   D. None of the answers are correct.

Answer (A) is correct. *(Publisher, adapted)*
   REQUIRED: The true statement regarding leadership styles.
   DISCUSSION: When a manager uses an authoritarian leadership style, (s)he dictates all decisions to the employees, so communication is downward. Moreover, tasks are clearly defined. This is considered the classical approach to leadership. Employees are not allowed to give input.
   Answer (B) is incorrect. The leader delegates substantial authority in democratic leadership. In addition, employees participate in defining and assigning tasks. Therefore, communication is actively upward as well as downward. Answer (C) is incorrect. Employees in a group are given the authority and responsibility to make their own decisions in laissez-faire leadership. Answer (D) is incorrect. One of the answer choices is correct.

18. A leader who explains decisions and provides opportunity for clarification is described as having which leadership style?

   A. Selling.

   B. Telling.

   C. Participating.

   D. Delegating.

Answer (A) is correct. *(CIA, adapted)*
   REQUIRED: The leadership style that includes explaining decisions and providing an opportunity for clarification.
   DISCUSSION: According to Hersey and Blanchard, a selling style of leadership provides a high degree of task orientation and a high degree of relationship orientation. This type of leader explains decisions and provides opportunities for clarification. Thus, upward and downward, two-way communication is active. This approach is more democratic than authoritarian.
   Answer (B) is incorrect. A telling leadership style (high task and low relationship) provides specific instructions and closely supervises performance. Answer (C) is incorrect. A participating leadership style (low task and high relationship) encourages the sharing of ideas and facilitates decision making. Answer (D) is incorrect. A delegating leadership style (low task and low relationship) turns over responsibility for decisions and implementation.

19. Which of the following constitute initiating structure behavior?

I. Defining duties
II. Planning and organizing work
III. Helping with work-related problems

   A. I and II only.

   B. I and III only.

   C. II and III only.

   D. I, II, and III.

Answer (A) is correct. *(Publisher, adapted)*
   REQUIRED: The definition of initiating structure behavior.
   DISCUSSION: Initiating structure behavior is directed towards accomplishing tasks. Structure includes defining duties, establishing procedures, planning and organizing work. Consideration, on the other hand, is the establishment of a personal relationship between the leader and the subordinate. High consideration by the leader includes warmth toward the employee as a person, psychological support for the employee, and helpfulness with work-related problems.
   Answer (B) is incorrect. Helping with work-related problems is consideration behavior. Answer (C) is incorrect. Helping with work-related problems is consideration behavior. Answer (D) is incorrect. Helping with work-related problems is consideration behavior.

20. A manager implementing the directive leader approach should

    A. Closely supervise each employee.

    B. Display confidence in each employee's ability.

    C. Work with the employee when developing goals.

    D. Clearly signal that the employee is expected to be successful.

Answer (A) is correct. *(Publisher, adapted)*
    REQUIRED: The action that should be taken by a manager using the directive leader approach.
    DISCUSSION: The situational approach to leadership (called path-goal theory) allows a manager to choose one of four approaches for implementing his/her leadership style. Using the directive leader approach, a manager provides close guidance to the employee through the use of specific rules, policies, and procedures.

Questions 21 through 24 are based on the following information.

The following question presents a scenario in which a manager needs to decide what leadership style to use to obtain employee satisfaction and effective employee performance. For the purposes of this question, the manager has a choice of four styles.

- The **directive** leader lets subordinates know what is expected of subordinates, schedules work to be done, and gives specific guidance on how to accomplish tasks.
- The **supportive** leader is friendly and shows concern for the needs of the subordinates.
- The **participative** leader consults with employees and considers their suggestions before making a decision.
- The **achievement-oriented** leader sets challenging goals and expects subordinates to perform at their highest level.

---

21. The manager of a team of actuaries has been asked to develop the basic pricing structure for a new health insurance product. The team has successfully designed other pricing structures in recent years. The manager was assigned to the team 6 months ago. What is the **best** leadership style for the manager of this team?

    A. Directive.

    B. Supportive.

    C. Participative.

    D. Achievement-oriented.

Answer (C) is correct. *(CIA, adapted)*
    REQUIRED: The best leadership style for a new manager of a team that has successfully completed similar projects.
    DISCUSSION: Participative style is most useful when subordinates believe they control their own destinies, that is, when they have an internal locus of control. Such individuals may be resentful if they are not consulted.
    Answer (A) is incorrect. Directive leadership provides the highest subordinate satisfaction when a team encounters substantive internal conflict, when tasks are ambiguous, and when subordinates' loci of control are external. Answer (B) is incorrect. Supportive style is best when tasks are highly structured and the authority relationships are clear and bureaucratic. Answer (D) is incorrect. Achievement-oriented style will increase subordinates' expectations that high performance will result from their best efforts.

22. The workers in a factory have been told that the current machines are obsolete and will be replaced by new, computer-assisted machines. The workers must be retrained and are eager to learn everything about the new machines. The manager was recently hired from a company where the new machines were extensively used and is very familiar with them. In this case, what is the **best** leadership style for the manager?

    A. Directive.

    B. Supportive.

    C. Participative.

    D. Achievement-oriented.

Answer (A) is correct. *(CIA, adapted)*
    REQUIRED: The best leadership style for the manager when workers must be retrained and are eager to learn.
    DISCUSSION: According to path-goal theory, two groups of contingency factors affect the relationship between leadership behavior and outcomes (performance and satisfaction): environmental factors beyond subordinates' control (task structure, the formal authority system, and the work group) and subordinate factors. The latter include the subordinate's locus of control, experience, and perceived ability. A leadership style should be chosen that complements but does not duplicate the factors in the environment and is consistent with subordinates' characteristics. A directive style is most effective when the subordinate's locus of control is external, tasks are ambiguous or stressful, and substantial conflict exists in the work group. Thus, a directive style is appropriate when subordinates do not have high perceived ability or experience.
    Answer (B) is incorrect. Subordinates who are neither competent nor confident are best led using the directive style. Answer (C) is incorrect. Subordinates with an internal locus of control need a leader with a participative style. Answer (D) is incorrect. Achievement-oriented leadership is appropriate when tasks are nonrepetitive and ambiguous and employee competence is high.

23. A production team has been together for several years and has worked well together. However, severe arguments have recently occurred between two members of the group, and other members have begun to take sides. This problem has had a negative effect on production performance. The **best** leadership style for the manager in this situation is

A. Directive.

B. Supportive.

C. Participative.

D. Achievement-oriented.

Answer (A) is correct. *(CIA, adapted)*
REQUIRED: The best leadership style for the manager, given substantive internal conflict.
DISCUSSION: Directive leadership provides highest subordinate satisfaction when a team encounters substantive internal conflict. Thus, directive leadership is the appropriate complement to the environmental factors. The leader should intervene to compensate for the stress and strife in the workplace.
Answer (B) is incorrect. Supportive style is best when tasks and authority relationships are highly structured. Answer (C) is incorrect. Participative style is most useful when subordinates believe they control their own destinies. Answer (D) is incorrect. Achievement-oriented leadership is appropriate when tasks are nonrepetitive and ambiguous and employee competence is high.

24. A manager in a government agency supervises a section of clerical employees who review license applications for approval or denial. The clerical jobs are well defined procedurally and are covered by government regulations. In this case, what is the **best** leadership style for the manager?

A. Directive.

B. Supportive.

C. Participative.

D. Achievement-oriented.

Answer (B) is correct. *(CIA, adapted)*
REQUIRED: The best leadership style for the manager of clerical workers.
DISCUSSION: A supportive style is best when tasks are highly structured and the authority relationships are clear and bureaucratic. This approach depends on people who want to work, grow, and achieve. The supportive style may be best when tasks are unsatisfying.
Answer (A) is incorrect. A directive style is most effective when the employees' loci of control are external, tasks are ambiguous or stressful, and substantial conflict exists in the work group. Thus, a directive style is appropriate when employees do not have high perceived ability or experience. Answer (C) is incorrect. A participative style is most useful when subordinates believe they control their own destinies. Answer (D) is incorrect. Achievement-oriented leadership is appropriate when tasks are nonrepetitive and ambiguous and employee competence is high.

25. Which of the following is true regarding Fiedler's studies of contingency theory?

A. The three dimensions of contingency theory are position power, task structure, and relationship structure.

B. The two types of leaders that emerged from Fiedler's studies include task-oriented style and leader-member style.

C. Placement of leaders in the organization is not as important as the leaders' leadership skills.

D. People become leaders not only because of personality attributes, but also because of various situational factors and the interaction between the leaders and the situation.

Answer (D) is correct. *(Publisher, adapted)*
REQUIRED: The true statement concerning Fiedler's studies of contingency theory.
DISCUSSION: According to Fred E. Fiedler's contingency theory, people become leaders not only because of personality attributes, but also because of various situational factors and the interaction between the leaders and the situation. Thus, the right person at the right time may rise to a position of leadership if his/her personality and the needs of the situation complement each other.
Answer (A) is incorrect. The three dimensions of contingency theory are position power, task structure, and leader-member relations. Answer (B) is incorrect. The two types of leaders that emerged from Fiedler's studies are task-oriented style and relationship-oriented style. Answer (C) is incorrect. Leadership is as much a responsibility of the organization's placement of leaders as it is of the leaders themselves.

26. Which of the following is a benefit of implementing the achievement-oriented leader approach rather than the directive leader approach?

A. Employee development is enhanced.

B. The structured environment allows employees to better achieve the organization's goals.

C. Closer supervision is provided for employees who perform better in a structured work atmosphere.

D. Employees have more opportunities to develop creativity and meet challenges.

Answer (D) is correct. *(Publisher, adapted)*
REQUIRED: The benefit of using the achievement-oriented leader approach.
DISCUSSION: The benefits to the company of the achievement-oriented leader approach include (1) greater employee confidence and commitment, (2) more employee decision making, (3) increased employee creativity, (4) more challenging objectives, and (5) reduced supervision for employees who work best independently.
Answer (A) is incorrect. Employee development also is enhanced under the directive leader approach. Answer (B) is incorrect. A structured environment results from the directive leader approach. It is not a characteristic of the achievement-oriented leader approach. Answer (C) is incorrect. Close supervision results from the directive leader approach. It is not a characteristic of the achievement-oriented leader approach.

27. The leadership grid developed by Robert Blake and Jane Mouton has axes with a scale of 1 to 9. A primary style of 9,9 indicates

- A. Little concern for production or people (impoverished management).
- B. Moderate concern for production and people to maintain status quo (middle-of-the-road management).
- C. Great concern for production and people, trust, teamwork, and commitment (team management).
- D. Primary concern for production, little concern for people (authority-compliance management).

Answer (C) is correct. *(Publisher, adapted)*
REQUIRED: The true statement concerning the leadership grid.
DISCUSSION: A primary style of 9,9 is a maximum on both axes. Thus, this style indicates great concern for production and great concern for people. This leadership style emphasizes output, cost control, and profit in addition to friendship, aiding employees, and addressing employee issues.
Answer (A) is incorrect. Little concern for production or people is equivalent to 1,1 on the leadership grid. Answer (B) is incorrect. Moderate concern for production and people to maintain status quo is equivalent to a 5,5 on the leadership grid. Answer (D) is incorrect. Primary concern for production with little concern for people is equivalent to a 9,1 on the leadership grid.

28. Which of the following is false regarding transformational leadership?

- A. Transformational leadership emphasizes vision, development of the individual, empowerment of the worker, and the challenging of traditional assumptions.
- B. Transformational leaders use traditional thinking to monitor employees so that the employees adhere to standards.
- C. Transformational leaders have charisma and provide intellectual stimulation to the workers.
- D. Transformational leaders expect employees to achieve more than the employees thought was possible.

Answer (B) is correct. *(Publisher, adapted)*
REQUIRED: The false statement regarding transformational leadership.
DISCUSSION: Transformational leaders have charisma and provide intellectual stimulation to the workers. In addition, they emphasize (1) vision, (2) development of the individual, (3) empowerment of the worker, and (4) the challenging of traditional assumptions. A transactional leader, on the other hand, would monitor employees to ensure that they adhered to standards.

Use the additional questions in Gleim *CIA Test Prep* Software to create Test Sessions that emulate Pearson VUE!

STUDY UNIT TEN
TIME MANAGEMENT, CONFLICT, AND NEGOTIATION

(9 pages of outline)

This study unit begins with a discussion of how an individual manager may improve his/her mastery of daily workflow by applying time management skills. It also addresses the related subjects of conflict management and negotiation. The nature and causes (triggers) of conflict and the means of resolving it are discussed. After negotiation is defined, the elements of effective negotiation are described.

An internal auditor is a highly visible component of the organization's governance process. Accordingly, internal auditors must be efficient time managers. Also, the ability to deal with the inevitable conflicts that arise in the course of their work is a critical skill for individual internal auditors.

10.1 TIME MANAGEMENT SKILLS

1. To function effectively, managers must learn to manage time properly. The **key principle** is to focus on results rather than on staying busy.

   a. This idea is reflected in **Pareto analysis** (named for an Italian economist). It states the **80:20 rule**, based on the observation that typically 80% of unfocused effort generates only 20% of results.

      1) Thus, a manager needs to concentrate time and energy on the tasks with the highest payoffs or the most benefit.

   b. Time management is actually self management. The skills needed to manage others are the same: the ability to plan, delegate, organize, direct, and control.

   c. Time management does require self-discipline and control until it becomes an everyday habit. Plans and schedules for managing time are useless if one does not follow them.

2. The following are **common techniques for effective time management**:

   a. **Finding out how much time is worth.** A manager should calculate his/her annual cost to the organization, including salary, office space, equipment, facilities, and taxes. The excess of the annual expected profit to be generated by the manager over the total cost should be divided by the annual hours expected to be worked. The result is the manager's **hourly worth** to the organization.

      1) If the net benefit of the manager's performing a task is less than this amount, it should be delegated to an assistant whose time is less costly.

      2) A manager can free up considerable time by appropriate delegation.

b. **Prioritizing work.** One technique is for the manager to concentrate on the things that (s)he enjoys. The result should be better quality work.

 1) A second method is for the manager to concentrate on tasks most closely related to his/her strengths.

 2) A third method is for the manager to determine how (s)he is being evaluated and to prioritize tasks accordingly. This approach requires the manager to pose certain questions, for example,

  a) What is the purpose of this job?
  b) What are the measures of success?
  c) What are the deadlines?
  d) What are the resources available?

c. **Keeping an activity log for a week.** The log should be an accurate record of how long is spent doing different tasks. Most people are surprised at how much time they waste on unproductive activities such as talking to colleagues or making coffee.

 1) The log raises awareness and promotes avoidance of time-wasting behavior.

 2) The log also helps a manager determine when during the day (s)he is the most or least productive.

  a) Identifying the pattern of productivity permits managers to schedule the most important tasks when they are at their best.

d. **Developing an action plan.** This tool requires listing all the tasks that need to be performed to achieve a goal.

 1) It is not a to-do list, which focuses on different tasks that need to be done during the day. An action plan focuses on a single goal.

  a) During any given day, a manager may follow several action plans to achieve multiple short-term goals.

e. **Creating a prioritized to-do list.** This tool is best used when a manager has many different, unrelated tasks to perform during the day. It consists of all the tasks completed during a day ranked according to their importance.

 1) A manager should start with the most important task and finish with the least important.

f. **Learning to say "NO."** This tool is often overlooked but can save a lot of time. People may make offers that are not part of the daily plan and will not help the manager to complete any necessary tasks. In these circumstances, the manager must learn to politely say no.

Core Concepts

- The key principle for managers to function effectively is to focus on results rather than on staying busy. Thus, a manager needs to concentrate time and energy on the tasks with the highest payoffs for the most benefit. This idea is reflected in Pareto analysis (named for an Italian economist), which states the 80:20 rule. It is based on the observation that typically 80% of unfocused effort generates only 20% of results.

- The following are common techniques for effective time management: (1) finding out how much time is worth, (2) prioritizing work, (3) keeping an activity log for a week, (4) developing an action plan, (5) creating a prioritized to-do list, and (6) learning to say "NO."

Stop and review! You have completed the outline for this subunit. Study multiple-choice questions 1 through 4 beginning on page 237.

10.2 CONFLICT

Nature of Conflict

1. Effective interpersonal relationships and organizational change are closely tied to conflict management.

    a. According to Dean Tjosvold, **conflict** involves "incompatible behaviors; one person interfering, disrupting, or in some other way making actions less effective."

        1) However, conflict may be cooperative as well as competitive.

    b. **Cooperative conflict** is constructive. The existence of cooperative (shared) goals is the basis for treating the conflict as a mutual problem.

        1) In this context, the parties may be able to trust each other's motives and believe what the other says.

        2) Discussions are productive, the attitude (and the result) is win-win, and the parties move ahead together.

    c. **Competitive conflict** is destructive. Opposite goals are pursued, and neither side trusts or believes the other.

        1) The parties avoid genuine dialogue, and the attitude is win-lose.
        2) Ultimately, the parties take separate paths.

Conflict Triggers

2. Conflict triggers raise the probability of conflict between groups or individuals.

    a. They should be allowed to exist if they cause cooperative conflict. Otherwise, they should be eliminated.

    b. Conflict may be triggered by the following:

        1) **Badly defined job descriptions** (jurisdictional boundaries)

            a) Reorganization may be the solution.

        2) **Scarcity** of people, funds, or other resources

            a) Increasing resources may be the solution.

        3) **Failure of communication**

            a) Removing obstacles that hinder effective two-way communication is essential, but the problem is perennial.

        4) **Deadlines**

            a) Time pressure may induce better performance (constructive) or anger and frustration (destructive).

        5) Policies, procedures, rules, or other standards viewed by employees as **unfair**

            a) If very unpopular, they should be changed to avoid competitive conflict.

        6) Individual **personality differences**

            a) Reassignment or termination of employees may be the solution.

        7) **Differences in status**, an issue in any hierarchical entity

            a) The remedy is respect for the ideas, values, and concerns of lower-level employees.

        8) **Not meeting expectations**

            a) The problem can be avoided through clarifying in advance the expectations employees have about their jobs.

9) **Role incompatibility**

a) Better coordination is the solution.

b) For example, a sales manager may make delivery promises to customers that are incompatible with the low inventory levels maintained by the production managers.

i) The sales manager's role is to maximize sales, but one of the production manager's roles is to achieve production efficiencies, such as by maintaining low inventories.

ii) Thus, individual and intergroup conflict has occurred because functional responsibilities of these parties are independent in an interfunctional organization.

Addressing Conflicts

3. Managers may address competitive conflicts in a variety of ways.

a. **Problem solving** is a means of resolving the conflict by confronting it and removing its causes. The emphasis is on facts and solutions, not personalities and assignment of blame.

1) The disadvantage is that problem solving is time consuming.

b. **Smoothing (diffusion)** is a short-term avoidance approach. The parties in conflict are asked by management to submerge their differences temporarily, e.g., until a project is completed. It does not resolve the conflict.

c. **Forcing** occurs when a superior uses his/her formal authority to order a particular outcome. It does not resolve the conflict. Indeed, forcing may intensify it.

d. **Superordinate goals** are the overriding goals of the entity to which subunit and personal goals are subordinate. An appeal to these goals is another short-term solution that does not resolve the conflict.

e. **Compromise** requires negotiation by the parties in conflict. The conflict is resolved through a process by which each side makes concessions. Thus, both parties gain and lose.

1) However, if the negotiators on both sides are not skillful (see the earlier description of cooperative conflict), the conflict is suppressed, not resolved.

2) The disadvantage of fully negotiating a compromise is that the process is time consuming.

f. **Expanding resources** resolves conflicts that result from scarcity.

g. **Avoidance (withdrawing)** is nonaction. It withdraws from and suppresses the conflict but does not solve the underlying problem.

h. **Accommodation** is the willingness of one party to the conflict to place another's needs and concerns above his/her own.

4. Cooperative conflict drives the change processes that all organizations need to survive and prosper.

a. Cooperative conflict may result in

1) Better decision making,
2) A reduction in complacency,
3) More self-criticism,
4) Greater creativity, and
5) Solutions to problems.

    b.   Thus, **intentional stimulation of conflict** may be desirable. For example, management may intentionally trigger conflict by

        1)   Making changes in the organizational structure;

        2)   Hiring new employees with different values, managerial styles, attitudes, and backgrounds; or

        3)   Designating individuals to oppose the majority views of the group.

Core Concepts

- Effective personal relationships and organizational change are closely tied to conflict management. Cooperative conflict is constructive. The existence of cooperative or shared goals is the basis for treating the conflict as a mutual problem. Indeed, the intentional stimulation of conflict may be desirable. Competitive conflict is destructive. Opposite goals are pursued, and neither side trusts or believes the other.

- Conflict triggers raise the probability of conflict between groups or individuals. They should be allowed to exist if they cause cooperative conflict. Otherwise, they should be eliminated.

- Managers may address competitive conflicts by (1) problem solving, (2) smoothing, (3) forcing, (4) superordinate goals, (5) compromise, (6) expanding resources, (7) avoidance, and (8) accommodation.

Stop and review! You have completed the outline for this subunit. Study multiple-choice questions 5 through 12 beginning on page 238.

10.3 NEGOTIATION

Overview

1.   Robert Kreitner cites Northwestern University scholars who define **negotiation** as "a decision-making process among interdependent parties who do not share identical preferences." The parties must decide through bargaining what values will be exchanged (given and taken) by each side.

    a.   This definition is broad enough to encompass negotiating processes of all kinds from private interpersonal relations to commercial activities to agreements among nations.

    b.   Two-party and three-party negotiations are common.

        1)   For example, a **two-party negotiation** occurs when a person sells his/her car to a used car dealer.

        2)   An example of a **three-party negotiation** is a person's sale of stock through a broker.

Effective Negotiation

2.   Effective negotiation allows the parties to meet their needs and to establish the **trust** necessary for future bargaining. It emphasizes a **win-win attitude**.

    a.   In some cultures, the dominant approach is **competitive**. Rewards are given for winning and punishment is given for losing.

        1)   This **win-lose attitude** views negotiation using a sports metaphor, that is, as a zero-sum game.

        2)   The win-win attitude is to treat negotiation as a positive-sum game.

    b.   The win-win attitude is **cooperative**, seeking mutual benefit and satisfaction.

        1)   It is founded on the principle that resources are sufficient for all and that the **third alternative** (not one side's way or the other side's way) is preferable.

        2)   An advantage of win-win negotiation is that it promotes support of, and commitment to, the agreement.

3)   For example, the benefits of effective negotiation of employee-supervisor differences include

    a)   Communicating both sides of an issue without litigation,

    b)   Recognizing employee concerns to indicate that management values each subordinate's needs and rights, and

    c)   Impartially managing tensions in the work environment while finding compromise solutions.

c.   For a successful negotiation, the negotiator should understand the implications for both sides if the negotiation fails.

    1)   **Precedents** (previous demands, concessions, and settlements) help to determine what can be achieved. The history of past practices and interactions tends to define current standards of fairness in negotiations.

d.   The negotiator should present facts and precedents in an organized manner when negotiating with an analytical personality.

3.   Effective negotiators understand their **best alternative to a negotiated agreement (BATNA)**, an idea developed by Harvard University researchers.

a.   The BATNA is the acceptable minimum outcome if a negotiator cannot obtain the desired result.

b.   Understanding the BATNA helps a negotiator to avoid the following two mistakes:

    1)   Accepting an unfavorable agreement
    2)   Rejecting a favorable agreement

c.   A reasonable BATNA protects against bad decisions caused by the following:

    1)   **Framing error** is a perceptual problem. The presentation or context of information may bias its interpretation and the resulting decision.

        a)   Accordingly, favorably (unfavorably) presented information may be viewed more (less) favorably than is justified.

            i)   For example, a job seeker may hope that the attractive appearance of a resumé will sway the judgment of a potential employer.

            ii)   Purely semantic effects also may result in framing error. For example, a glass still holds 50% of its capacity whether it is described as half full or half empty. However, the first (second) characterization may lead to a more (less) favorable opinion.

    2)   **Escalation of commitment** is adherence to a failing course of action when a purely objective decision maker would abandon it. This irrational tendency to persist in error is based on a variety of organizational, social, and psychological factors:

        a)   Structural resistance to change in an organization

        b)   Organizational politics

        c)   Organizational culture, e.g., values that stress persistence in the face of obstacles

        d)   Societal approval of those who persevere and overcome obstacles

        e)   Personal desire to avoid the embarrassment of conceding defeat

        f)   Perceived opportunity to reverse the trend of events

        g)   Competitive desire to win

        h)   Attempted justification of prior decisions

3) **Overconfidence** is the common tendency to overestimate the chances of success. It tends, paradoxically, to be directly related to the difficulty of the undertaking.

   a) One explanation for this phenomenon is that overconfidence may be necessary to develop the fortitude to embark on a very difficult course of action.

4) A primary disadvantage of forcing another party to accept terms in a negotiation is that it damages the relationship between the negotiators.

d. The BATNA also helps to define the **bargaining zone**. It is the difference between the BATNAs belonging to each side, i.e., the set of outcomes acceptable to both.

   1) For example, a parent wishes to sell a subsidiary for US $1.5 billion, with a BATNA of US $1.2 billion. A buyer wishes to acquire the subsidiary for US $1 billion, with a BATNA of US $1.3 billion. Hence, negotiation is feasible because a bargaining zone (buyer's BATNA of US $1.3 billion – seller's BATNA of US $1.2 billion) exists.

   2) Negotiation is **not feasible** in the absence of a bargaining zone. In the example above, if the seller's BATNA were US $1.4 billion, negotiation would be fruitless.

   3) Negotiation is **not necessary** if the parties do not disagree. For example, they may have contracted to accept the result of a formal appraisal of the value of something to be bought and sold.

   4) Determining the other side's BATNA may be the most difficult aspect of a negotiation. Each side has an incentive to keep its BATNA confidential.

      a) Thus, the other side's BATNA must be estimated so that, in turn, the negotiating zone may be estimated.

4. The steps to overcoming unexpected resistance from another party are as follows:

   a. Attempt to determine the reason behind the resistance (first step).
   b. Stop the meeting and address the other party's concerns privately.
   c. Restate the negotiator's position regarding the issue.
   d. Research the other party to determine its views and requirements.

Other Negotiation Concepts

5. **Added-value negotiating** was developed by Karl and Steve Albrecht. It is applied when something more than the elements of negotiation described in this subunit is necessary. Its basic concept is that the two sides make **multiple deals** to add value to the process.

   a. Step one is for the parties mutually to **clarify interests**.

      1) These interests may be subjective as well as objective. The purpose is to isolate commonalities.

   b. Step two is to **identify options**.

      1) The purpose is to establish a **marketplace of value**, i.e., the range of values each side can give the other.

   c. Step three is to **design alternative deal packages**.

      1) The distinctive feature of added-value negotiation is that it provides for multiple win-win offers. Each consists of groups of the values identified in step two.

   d. Step four is to **select a deal** after the parties have considered the deal packages designed in step three.

      1) They evaluate each possible deal's **value, balance, and fit**. The mutually acceptable deal is then chosen.

e.   Step five is to **perfect the deal**.

    1)   Details are negotiated, and the deal is put in written form.

    2)   The process creates **relationships** that will benefit later negotiations.

    3)   The keys are openness, flexibility, and mutuality in the quest for a successful exchange of value.

6.   The **principled negotiation method** focuses on basic interests, mutually satisfying options, and fair standards. The following are basic principles:

    a.   Separating the people from the problem
    b.   Focusing on interests, not positions
    c.   Inventing options for mutual gain
    d.   Insisting on using objective criteria

7.   **Distributive bargaining** is a negotiation in zero-sum conditions (i.e., when a negotiation gain by one party is offset by a loss by the other party).

    a.   The negotiator operates with a maximum desired result (target point) and a minimum acceptable result (resistance point) in mind. If the ranges of feasible outcomes (aspiration ranges) overlap, an agreement is possible.

    b.   In **integrative bargaining**, both parties may gain.

8.   Various types of third-party negotiations are available to parties facing disagreement.

    a.   A **mediator** is a neutral third party who facilitates a negotiated solution by using persuasion and offering solutions. However, the mediator has no authority to make a decision.

    b.   An **arbitrator** has the authority to impose an agreement. Arbitration may be requested by the parties or may be imposed by law or by the terms of a contract.

    c.   A **consultant** is skilled in facilitation and communication skills but does not have authority to make a decision. A consultant helps improve relations between the two disagreeing parties but does not offer specific solutions.

    d.   A **conciliator** provides an informal communication link between the two parties but does not have authority to make a decision.

Core Concepts

- Robert Kreitner cites Northwestern University scholars who define negotiation as "a decision-making process among interdependent parties who do not share identical preferences." The parties to the relationship must decide through bargaining what values will be exchanged (given and taken) by each side.

- Two-party and three-party negotiations are common. For example, a two-party negotiation occurs when a person sells his/her car to a used car dealer. An example of a three-party negotiation is a person's sale of stock through a broker.

- Effective negotiation allows the parties to meet their needs and to establish the trust necessary for future bargaining. It emphasizes a win-win attitude. It is cooperative, seeking mutual benefit and satisfaction. In some cultures, however, the dominant approach is competitive. Rewards are given for winning, and punishment is given for losing (win-lose attitude).

- Harvard researchers developed the idea of the best alternative to a negotiated agreement (BATNA), a concept understood by effective negotiators. The BATNA is the acceptable minimum outcome if a negotiator cannot obtain the desired result. Understanding the BATNA helps a negotiator to avoid the following two mistakes: (1) accepting an unfavorable agreement and (2) rejecting a favorable agreement.

- A reasonable BATNA protects against bad decisions caused by the following: (1) framing error (a perceptual problem), (2) escalation of commitment (the adherence to a failing course of action), and (3) overconfidence (the common tendency to overestimate the chances of success).

■   The BATNA also helps define the bargaining zone. It is the difference between the BATNAs belonging to each side, i.e., the set of outcomes acceptable to both. Negotiation is not feasible in the absence of a bargaining zone. It is not necessary if the parties do not disagree.

■   Added-value negotiating was developed by Karl and Steve Albrecht. It is applied when something more than the elements of negotiation described in this subunit is necessary. Its basic concept is that the two sides make multiple deals to add value to the process. The five steps in this kind of negotiation are to (1) clarify interests, (2) identify options, (3) design alternative deal packages, (4) select a deal, and (5) perfect the deal.

Stop and review! You have completed the outline for this subunit. Study multiple-choice questions 13 through 25 beginning on page 240.

QUESTIONS

10.1 Time Management Skills

1. All of the following are skills that managers must focus on when attempting to manage time properly **except**

A.   The ability to focus on results.

B.   Striving to stay busy.

C.   Concentrating time and energy on tasks with the highest payoffs.

D.   The ability to plan, delegate, organize, direct, and control.

Answer (B) is correct. *(Publisher, adapted)*
   REQUIRED: The skill not necessary for effective time management.
   DISCUSSION: To function effectively, managers must learn to manage time properly. The key principle is to focus on results rather than on staying busy. Time management is actually self-management. The skills needed to manage others are the same skills needed to manage oneself. Time management requires self-discipline and control until it becomes an everyday habit.
   Answer (A) is incorrect. The key principle behind effective time management is to focus on results. Answer (C) is incorrect. A manager needs to concentrate time and energy on the tasks with the highest payoffs or the most benefits so that results are optimized. Answer (D) is incorrect. These specific skills are necessary to manage time.

2. Which of the following are common techniques for effective time management?

I.   Finding out how much time is worth
II.   Developing an action plan
III. Learning to say "No"

A.   I only.

B.   I and II only.

C.   II and III only.

D.   I, II, and III.

Answer (D) is correct. *(Publisher, adapted)*
   REQUIRED: The common techniques for effective time management.
   DISCUSSION: For effective time management, there are several techniques that a manager can use. By finding out how much his/her time is worth, a manager can assess whether there is a net benefit or a net loss to the organization when the manager performs a particular duty. Developing an action plan can help manage time because it allows an individual to focus on a single goal. By learning to say "No," managers can avoid performing tasks that are not part of the daily plan, which can be crippling to proper time management.

3. The technique that calls for the manager to concentrate on tasks that are **most** closely related to the manager's strengths is

A.   Keeping an activity log for about a week.

B.   Creating a prioritized to-do list.

C.   Prioritizing work.

D.   Developing an action plan.

Answer (C) is correct. *(Publisher, adapted)*
   REQUIRED: The method that requires an assessment of the tasks that are most closely related to a manager's strengths.
   DISCUSSION: Managers use several common techniques for effective time management. One is prioritizing work. There are three methods that can be employed to prioritize work. The first one is for the manager to concentrate on the things that (s)he enjoys. The second is for the manager to concentrate on tasks most closely related to his/her strengths. The third method is for the manager to determine how (s)he is being evaluated and to prioritize tasks accordingly.
   Answer (A) is incorrect. Keeping a log merely provides an input to the process of setting priorities. Answer (B) is incorrect. Creating a prioritized to-do list calls for the manager to compile a list of all the tasks performed and/or completed during a day ranked according to their importance. Answer (D) is incorrect. Developing an action plan requires listing all the tasks that need to be performed to achieve a goal.

4. After performing an assessment of time worth, the manager of a corporation determined that the net benefit to the organization for performing a particular task is less than the manager's hourly worth to the organization. Which of the following statements is **most** true in relation to this situation?

A. The manager should delegate this task to an assistant whose time is less costly.

B. The manager should continue performing the task because there is no way to change this outcome.

C. If the manager receives a salary raise, the gap between the net benefit and the manager's hourly worth will decrease.

D. The manager should work more hours so that the manager's hourly worth increases.

Answer (A) is correct.   *(Publisher, adapted)*
 REQUIRED: The true statement with regard to finding out how much time is worth.
 DISCUSSION: A manager should calculate how much money (s)he costs the organization each year, including salary, office space, equipment, etc. After adding to that amount the annual expected profit to be generated by the manager, the total should be divided by the annual hours expected to be worked. The result is the manager's hourly worth to the organization. If the net benefit to the organization of the manager's performing a task is less than his/her hourly worth, it should be delegated to an assistant whose time is less costly.
 Answer (B) is incorrect. The manager can correct this inefficiency by delegating this task to an assistant. Answer (C) is incorrect. A raise in the manager's salary will widen the gap between the net benefit and the manager's hourly worth. Answer (D) is incorrect. If the manager works more hours, the manager's hourly worth will decrease.

10.2 Conflict

5. Auditor 1 and Auditor 2 are working on similar projects. After looking at Auditor 2's work, Auditor 1 informs Auditor 2 that Auditor 2's project contains many errors and is not acceptable. Auditor 1 discusses with Auditor 2 ways to improve to prevent the errors from happening again. Auditor 2 acknowledges the mistakes and vows to work harder. Auditor 2 listens to Auditor's 1 suggestions, corrects the errors on the current project, and returns a high-quality project. This is an example of

A. Cooperative conflict.

B. Competitive conflict.

C. Destructive conflict.

D. None of the answers are correct.

Answer (A) is correct.   *(Publisher, adapted)*
 REQUIRED: The example of cooperative conflict.
 DISCUSSION: Auditor 1's conflict with Auditor 2 is productive because dialogue between the two workers is productive. The workers share the same goals for a high-quality project.
 Answer (B) is incorrect. The two employees are not competing with each other. Auditor 1 desires to help with Auditor 2's project. Answer (C) is incorrect. Auditor 1 and Auditor 2 both displayed constructive behavior. Answer (D) is incorrect. The situation is an example of cooperative conflict.

6. Conflict may be

I. Cooperative
II. Competitive

A. I only.

B. II only.

C. Both I and II.

D. Neither I nor II.

Answer (C) is correct.   *(Publisher, adapted)*
 REQUIRED: The accurate description of conflict.
 DISCUSSION: Conflict may be either cooperative or competitive. Cooperative conflict is constructive and competitive conflict is destructive.

7. Which of the following conflict triggers is **best** resolved by reorganization?

A. Scarcity of people, funds, or other resources.

B. Badly defined job descriptions.

C. Failure of communication.

D. Deadlines.

Answer (B) is correct.   *(Publisher, adapted)*
 REQUIRED: The conflict trigger best resolved by reorganization.
 DISCUSSION: Job descriptions are in effect jurisdictional boundaries. If these boundaries are badly designed, the best resolution is to redraw the boundaries (reorganization).
 Answer (A) is incorrect. The scarcity of people, funds, or other resources is best resolved by increasing resources. Answer (C) is incorrect. Failure of communication is best resolved by removing obstacles to effective two-way communication. Answer (D) is incorrect. Deadlines may induce better performance or anger and frustration. Reorganization is not the best solution for conflicts with deadlines.

8. Which of the following conflict resolution techniques places another's needs first?

    A. Accommodation.

    B. Compromise.

    C. Collaboration.

    D. Avoidance.

Answer (A) is correct. *(CIA, adapted)*
    REQUIRED: The conflict resolution technique that places another's needs first.
    DISCUSSION: The goal of accommodation is maintaining harmonious relationships by placing an emphasis on another's needs and concerns.
    Answer (B) is incorrect. Compromise resolves conflict through a process in which each side makes concessions. Answer (C) is incorrect. Collaboration resolves conflict. The parties work together to obtain a solution. Answer (D) is incorrect. Avoidance does not resolve conflict. It is nonaction.

9. Time consumption most likely is a disadvantage when managers address conflict by

    A. Smoothing.

    B. Forcing.

    C. Problem-solving.

    D. Expanding resources.

Answer (C) is correct. *(Publisher, adapted)*
    REQUIRED: The conflict management technique that uses excessive time.
    DISCUSSION: Problem solving is a means of resolving the conflict by confronting it and removing its causes. The emphasis is on facts and solutions, not personalities and assignment of blame. The disadvantage is that problem solving is time consuming.
    Answer (A) is incorrect. Smoothing is a short-term avoidance approach. Answer (B) is incorrect. Forcing occurs when a superior uses his/her formal authority to order a particular outcome. Answer (D) is incorrect. Expanding resources resolves conflicts that result from scarcity.

10. Which of the following are conflict triggers?

    A. Deadlines.

    B. Policies, procedures, rules, or other standards viewed by employees as unfair.

    C. Not meeting expectations.

    D. All of the answers are correct.

Answer (D) is correct. *(Publisher, adapted)*
    REQUIRED: The example(s) of conflict triggers.
    DISCUSSION: Deadlines are conflict triggers because time pressures may induce better performance (constructive) or anger and frustration (destructive). Polices, procedures, rules, or other standards viewed by employees as unfair are conflict triggers and should be changed to avoid competitive conflict if very unpopular. Not meeting expectations is a conflict trigger, but the problem can be avoided through clarifying in advance the expectations employees have about their jobs.

11. Intentional stimulation of conflict can be triggered by

I.   Making changes to the organizational structure

II. Hiring new employees with different values, attitudes, and backgrounds

III. Assigning an employee the role of opposing the majority view

    A. I only.

    B. I, II, and III.

    C. I and III only.

    D. II only.

Answer (B) is correct. *(Publisher, adapted)*
    REQUIRED: The action(s) that cause intentional stimulation of conflict.
    DISCUSSION: Intentional stimulation of conflict is triggered by (1) making changes in the organizational structure; (2) hiring new employees with different values, attitudes, backgrounds, and managerial styles; and (3) assigning an employee to oppose the majority view.
    Answer (A) is incorrect. Hiring new employees with different values, attitudes, and backgrounds and assigning an employee to oppose the majority view are also triggers of intentional stimulation of conflict. Answer (C) is incorrect. Hiring new employees with different values, attitudes, and backgrounds is another trigger of intentional stimulation of conflict. Answer (D) is incorrect. Making changes in the organizational structure and assigning an employee the role of opposing the majority view are additional ways to intentionally stimulate conflict.

12. A manager resolves a conflict between two employees by recommending that concessions to be made by both employees. The two employees agree to the concessions and the conflict is resolved. Both employees gain and lose. Which of the following describes the way the manager addressed the conflict?

    A. Forcing.

    B. Smoothing.

    C. Compromise.

    D. Problem solving.

Answer (C) is correct. *(Publisher, adapted)*
    REQUIRED: The ways in which managers address conflicts.
    DISCUSSION: Compromise involves negotiation by the parties in conflict. The conflict is resolved through a process by which each side makes concessions. Thus, the parties both gain and lose. Because both employees made concessions, the conflict was resolved through compromise.
    Answer (A) is incorrect. Forcing occurs when a superior uses his/her formal authority to order a particular outcome. It does not resolve the conflict. Forcing may intensify it. Answer (B) is incorrect. Smoothing is a short-term avoidance approach. The parties in conflict are asked by management to submerge their differences temporarily until a project is completed. Answer (D) is incorrect. Problem solving is a means of resolving the conflict by confronting it and removing its causes. The emphasis is on facts and solutions, not personalities and assignment of blame.

10.3 Negotiation

13. Which of the following is an example of a two-party negotiation?

    A. A person sells a car to a used car dealer.

    B. A person requests a financial institution to pay another person.

    C. A person sells stock through a broker.

    D. A person sells a house through a real estate agent.

Answer (A) is correct. *(Publisher, adapted)*
    REQUIRED: The true example of a two-party negotiation.
    DISCUSSION: A person's sale of a car to a used car dealer is an example of a two-party negotiation. Only the seller and dealer are involved in the negotiations.
    Answer (B) is incorrect. A person who requests a financial institution to pay another person is engaged in a three-party negotiation. The three parties involved are the person requesting the financial institution to use funds from his/her account to pay another individual, the financial institution responsible for paying the payee, and the person receiving the funds from the financial institution. Answer (C) is incorrect. A person who sells stock through a broker is engaged in a three-party negotiation. The seller, broker, and buyer are involved. Answer (D) is incorrect. Sale of a house through a real estate agent is a three-party negotiation.

14. A reasonable BATNA (best alternative to a negotiated agreement) protects against bad decisions caused by the following:

I.   Framing error
II. Escalation of commitment
III. Overconfidence

    A. I and III only.

    B. I, II, and III.

    C. I only.

    D. II and III only.

Answer (B) is correct. *(Publisher, adapted)*
    REQUIRED: The problems avoided by a reasonable BATNA.
    DISCUSSION: A reasonable BATNA protects against bad decisions caused by the following: framing error, escalation of commitment, and overconfidence. Framing error is a perceptual problem. The presentation or context of information may bias its interpretation and the resulting decision. Escalation of commitment is adherence to a failing course of action when a purely objective decision maker would abandon it. Overconfidence is the common tendency to overestimate the chances of success.
    Answer (A) is incorrect. A reasonable BATNA also protects against escalation of commitment. Answer (C) is incorrect. A reasonable BATNA also protects against escalation of commitment and overconfidence. Answer (D) is incorrect. A reasonable BATNA also protects against framing errors.

15. In regard to effective negotiation, a win-win attitude is characterized by

    A. Seeking mutual benefit and satisfaction.

    B. Cooperative.

    C. It promotes support of, and commitment to, the agreement.

    D. All of the answers are correct.

Answer (D) is correct. *(Publisher, adapted)*
    REQUIRED: The characteristic(s) of a win-win attitude.
    DISCUSSION: In regard to effective negotiation, a win-win attitude is characterized by seeking mutual benefit and satisfaction, being cooperative, and promoting support of, and commitment to, the agreement. In contrast to a win-win attitude, a win-lose attitude is competitive and is a zero-sum game instead of a positive-sum game.
    Answer (A) is incorrect. Cooperation and promoting support and commitment to the agreement are additional characteristics of a win-win attitude. Answer (B) is incorrect. Seeking mutual benefit and satisfaction and supporting and committing to the agreement are characteristics of a win-win attitude. Answer (C) is incorrect. Two additional characteristics of a win-win attitude are seeking mutual benefit and satisfaction and being cooperative.

16. When planning for successful negotiations, the negotiator should

    A. Understand the implications for both sides if the negotiation fails.

    B. Concentrate solely on the issues in the negotiation at hand.

    C. Not deviate from stated positions.

    D. Depend on the initial research prepared for the negotiation.

Answer (A) is correct. *(CIA, adapted)*
    REQUIRED: The necessary action when planning for successful negotiations.
    DISCUSSION: Negotiators should assess the best alternatives for both themselves and the other parties to determine their relative strengths in the negotiation process. If alternatives are not readily available or are unattractive, a party is under additional pressure to make the negotiation work.
    Answer (B) is incorrect. The negotiator should evaluate all alternatives to avoid placing undue pressure on the success of the negotiation. Answer (C) is incorrect. An objective perspective may assist the negotiator in identifying alternatives. Answer (D) is incorrect. Additional research may be required to fully understand the other party's alternatives to negotiation.

17. When negotiating with an analytical personality, the negotiator should

    A. Present facts and precedents in an organized manner.

    B. Push the other party for quick closure of negotiations.

    C. Focus on creating a bond with the other party.

    D. Include unimportant items in the proposal for bargaining.

Answer (A) is correct. *(CIA, adapted)*
    REQUIRED: The necessary action when negotiating with an analytical personality.
    DISCUSSION: An analytical person tends to be drawn to details and swayed by factual information.
    Answer (B) is incorrect. Pushing an analytical person may result in increased resistance. Answer (C) is incorrect. Analytical personalities make decisions based on facts rather than on emotions. Answer (D) is incorrect. The analytical person tends not to enjoy negotiation games as much as other personality types. If the other party believes the negotiator to be deceitful, (s)he may be unwilling to cooperate or may stop negotiations altogether.

18. Which of the following is the acceptable minimum outcome if a negotiator cannot obtain the desired result?

    A. Win-win attitude.

    B. Cooperation.

    C. Best alternative to a negotiated agreement (BATNA).

    D. Win-lose attitude.

Answer (C) is correct. *(Publisher, adapted)*
    REQUIRED: The acceptable minimum outcome if a negotiator cannot obtain the desired result.
    DISCUSSION: BATNA is the acceptable minimum outcome if a negotiator cannot obtain the desired result. The BATNA helps a negotiator to avoid accepting an unfavorable agreement and rejecting a favorable agreement.
    Answer (A) is incorrect. A win-win attitude is cooperative. It is founded on the principle that resources are sufficient for all and a third alternative is preferable. Answer (B) is incorrect. Cooperation is the act of seeking mutual benefit and satisfaction. Answer (D) is incorrect. A win-lose attitude is competitive. It results as a zero-sum game.

19. Understanding the best alternative to a negotiated agreement (BATNA) helps a negotiator to avoid which of the following?

I. Accepting an unfavorable settlement.
II. Rejecting a favorable settlement

    A. I only.

    B. II only.

    C. I and II.

    D. Neither I nor II.

Answer (C) is correct. *(Publisher, adapted)*
    REQUIRED: The mistakes avoided by understanding the BATNA.
    DISCUSSION: Accepting an unfavorable settlement and rejecting a favorable settlement are two mistakes avoided by understanding the BATNA. The BATNA is the acceptable minimum outcome if a negotiator cannot obtain the desired result.
    Answer (A) is incorrect. Rejecting a favorable settlement is avoided by understanding the BATNA. Answer (B) is incorrect. Accepting an unfavorable settlement is avoided by understanding the BATNA. Answer (D) is incorrect. Accepting an unfavorable settlement and rejecting a favorable settlement are avoided by understanding the BATNA.

20. Which of the following is an example of framing error?

I. A job seeker may hope that the attractive appearance of a resume will sway the judgment of a potential employer.

II. A glass still holds 50% of its capacity whether the glass is described as half full or half empty. However, the former (latter) characterization may lead to a more (less) favorable opinion of the content.

    A. I only.

    B. I and II.

    C. II only.

    D. Neither I nor II.

Answer (B) is correct. *(Publisher, adapted)*
    REQUIRED: The example(s) of framing error.
    DISCUSSION: Framing error is a perceptual problem. The presentation or context of information may bias its interpretation and the resulting decision. Thus, favorably (unfavorably) presented information may be viewed more (less) favorably than its merits warrant. Both I and II are examples of framing errors.
    Answer (A) is incorrect. Situation II is also an example of framing error. The favorably (unfavorably) presented information may be viewed more (less) favorably than its merits warrant. Answer (C) is incorrect. Situation I is also a correct example of framing error. Answer (D) is incorrect. Both of the situations listed are examples of framing error since the presentation or context of information may bias its interpretation and the resulting decision.

21. The negotiator, when encountering unexpected resistance from another party, should first

    A. Attempt to determine the reason behind the resistance.

    B. Stop the meeting and address the other party's concerns privately.

    C. Restate the negotiator's position regarding the issue.

    D. Research the other party to determine the party's views and requirements.

Answer (A) is correct. *(CIA, adapted)*
    REQUIRED: The negotiator's actions when encountering unexpected resistance.
    DISCUSSION: The first step in overcoming unexpected resistance is to attempt to determine the reason behind the resistance. Without knowing the reason, the negotiator is unable to counter it effectively. For example, knowing whether the other party is concerned about a major issue or a detail will affect the negotiator's response.
    Answer (B) is incorrect. Generally, a resolution should be attempted at the time. Only if one or both parties to the negotiation need additional time to evaluate new information or calm down should a break be taken. Answer (C) is incorrect. The negotiator should first work with the other party to determine the cause of disagreement. Answer (D) is incorrect. Research regarding the other party should occur prior to the initial negotiation meeting.

22. A parent wishes to sell a subsidiary for US $1.6 billion. A buyer wishes to acquire the subsidiary for US $1.1 billion, with the best alternative to a negotiated agreement (BATNA) of US $1.4 billion. What is an acceptable BATNA for the seller in order for negotiation to be feasible?

    A. US $1.3 billion.

    B. US $1.5 billion.

    C. US $1.7 billion.

    D. US $1.75 billion.

Answer (A) is correct. *(Publisher, adapted)*
    REQUIRED: The acceptable BATNA for the offer to be feasible.
    DISCUSSION: US $1.3 billion is an acceptable BATNA because the BATNA of the buyer is US $1.4 billion. Any amount over US $1.4 billion would cause negotiation not to be feasible.
    Answer (B) is incorrect. US $1.5 billion is higher than the US $1.4 billion BATNA of the buyer. The buyer will not be willing to negotiate with the seller. Answer (C) is incorrect. US $1.7 billion is higher than the buyer's BATNA of US $1.4 billion. Once again, negotiation is not feasible in this situation. Answer (D) is incorrect. US $1.75 billion BATNA is higher than the US $1.4 billion BATNA of the buyer.

23. Two individuals negotiate the details and put a deal in written form. The individuals have developed a good relationship and future negotiations will benefit. Which step of the added-value negotiating process has taken place?

- A. Perfect the deal.
- B. Identify options.
- C. Design alternative deal packages.
- D. Select a deal.

Answer (A) is correct. *(Publisher, adapted)*
REQUIRED: The steps in the added-value negotiation process.
DISCUSSION: The individuals performed step five of added-value negotiation by perfecting the deal. This step is characterized by negotiating details and putting the deal in written form. The process creates relationships that will benefit later negotiations.
Answer (B) is incorrect. The purpose of identifying options is to establish a marketplace of value, i.e., the range of values each side can give the other. Answer (C) is incorrect. Designing alternative deal packages exemplifies the distinctive feature of added-value negotiation that provides for multiple win-win offers. Answer (D) is incorrect. Selecting a deal is completed after the parties have considered the deal packages.

24. Steps in a negotiation include clarifying interests, identifying options, designing alternative deal packages, selecting a deal, and perfecting the deal. The type of negotiation described is

- A. Two-party.
- B. Three-party.
- C. Added-value.
- D. Ineffective.

Answer (C) is correct. *(Publisher, adapted)*
REQUIRED: The type of negotiation.
DISCUSSION: In added-value negotiating, the two sides make multiple deals to add value to the process. Clarifying interests, identifying options, designing alternative deal packages, selecting a deal, and perfecting a deal are all steps in added-value negotiating.
Answer (A) is incorrect. A two-party negotiation occurs between two persons, for example, when a person sells his/her car to a used car dealer. Answer (B) is incorrect. A three-party negotiation occurs between three persons, for example, when a person sells his/her stock through a broker. Answer (D) is incorrect. Added-value negotiating is an example of effective negotiation.

25. What is a primary disadvantage of forcing another party to accept terms in a negotiation?

- A. Damage of the relationship between the negotiators.
- B. Lack of achievement of the negotiator's goals.
- C. Increased time involved in reaching an agreement.
- D. Reduction in internal support for the negotiator's tactics.

Answer (A) is correct. *(CIA, adapted)*
REQUIRED: The primary disadvantage of forcing another party to accept a negotiation's terms.
DISCUSSION: In future negotiations, the opponent will be less likely to work with the negotiator to achieve mutual goals. Negotiations in which one or both parties feel they must win at the expense of the other party ultimately do not build a relationship of trust and cooperation.
Answer (B) is incorrect. The negotiator has achieved the goals of this negotiation. Answer (C) is incorrect. Often a collaborative approach to a negotiation will take longer due to the time taken in understanding the other party's needs and concerns and then resolving the issue to the benefit of both parties. Answer (D) is incorrect. The negotiator's tactics should be supported or condoned, so long as the negotiation resulted in favorable terms for the firm.

Use the additional questions in Gleim *CIA Test Prep* Software to create Test Sessions that emulate Pearson VUE!

APPENDIX A
IIA EXAM CONTENT OUTLINES
AND CROSS-REFERENCES

For your convenience, we have reproduced verbatim The IIA's exam content outlines for this CIA exam part from its website (www.globaliia.org/certification/cia-certification/pages/exam-syllabus.aspx). Note that those levels labeled "proficiency level" mean the candidate should have a thorough understanding and the ability to apply concepts in the topics listed underneath. Those levels labeled "awareness level" mean the candidate must have a grasp of the terminology and fundamentals of the concepts listed underneath. We also have provided cross-references to the study units and subunits in this book that correspond to The IIA's more detailed coverage. If one entry appears above a list, it applies to all items. Please visit The IIA's website for updates and more information about the exam. Rely on the Gleim materials to pass each part of the exam. We have researched and studied The IIA's content outlines as well as questions from prior exams to provide you with an excellent review program.

PART 4 – BUSINESS MANAGEMENT SKILLS

A. **STRATEGIC MANAGEMENT (20 - 30%)** (awareness level)

1. Global analytical techniques

   a. Structural analysis of industries (1.2, 2.4)
   b. Competitive strategies (e.g., Porter's model) (1.1, 1.3, 1.4)
   c. Competitive analysis (2.1, 2.2)
   d. Market signals (2.3)
   e. Industry evolution (2.5)

2. Industry environments (2.4)

   a. Competitive strategies related to:

      1) Fragmented industries (3.1)
      2) Emerging industries (3.2)
      3) Declining industries (3.3)

   b. Competition in global industries (3.4)

      1) Sources/impediments
      2) Evolution of global markets
      3) Strategic alternatives
      4) Trends affecting competition

3. Strategic decisions

   a. Analysis of integration strategies (4.1)
   b. Capacity expansion (4.2)
   c. Entry into new businesses (4.3)

4. Portfolio techniques of competitive analysis (2.2)
5. Product life cycles (2.5)

B. **GLOBAL BUSINESS ENVIRONMENTS (15 - 25%)** (awareness level)

1. Cultural/legal/political environments

   a. Balancing global requirements and local imperatives (5.1)
   b. Global mindsets (personal characteristics/competencies) (5.3)
   c. Sources and methods for managing complexities and contradictions (5.1-5.3)
   d. Managing multicultural teams (5.4)

2.   Economic/financial environments

    a.   Global, multinational, international, and multilocal compared and contrasted (5.1)
    b.   Requirements for entering the global market place (5.1)
    c.   Creating organizational adaptability (5.3)
    d.   Managing training and development (5.4)

C. ORGANIZATIONAL BEHAVIOR (15 - 25%) (awareness level)

1.   Motivation (6.1, 6.2)

    a.   Relevance and implication of various theories
    b.   Impact of job design, rewards, work schedules, etc.

2.   Communication

    a.   The process (6.3, 6.4)
    b.   Organizational dynamics (6.3)
    c.   Impact of computerization (6.5)

3.   Performance (7.1, 7.2)

    a.   Productivity
    b.   Effectiveness

4.   Structure (7.4, 7.5)

    a.   Centralized/decentralized (7.6)
    b.   Departmentalization (7.3)
    c.   New configurations (e.g., hourglass, cluster, network) (7.6)

D. MANAGEMENT SKILLS (20 - 30%) (awareness level)

1.   Group dynamics

    a.   Traits (e.g. cohesiveness, roles, norms, groupthink) (8.1)
    b.   Stages of group development (8.2)
    c.   Organizational politics (8.3)
    d.   Criteria and determinants of effectiveness (8.4)

2.   Team building (8.4)

    a.   Methods used in team building
    b.   Assessing team performance

3.   Leadership skills

    a.   Theories compared/contrasted (9.1, 9.2)
    b.   Leadership grid (topology of leadership styles) (9.2)
    c.   Mentoring (9.2)

4.   Personal time management (10.1)

E. NEGOTIATING (5 - 15%) (awareness level)

1.   Conflict resolution (10.2)

    a.   Competitive/cooperative
    b.   Compromise, forcing, smoothing, etc.

2.   Added-value negotiating (10.3)

    a.   Description
    b.   Specific steps

APPENDIX B
IIA EXAMINATION BIBLIOGRAPHY

The Institute has prepared a listing of references for the CIA exam, reproduced below. These publications have been chosen by the Professional Certifications Department as reasonably representative of the common body of knowledge for internal auditors. However, all of the information in these texts will not be tested. When possible, questions will be written based on the information contained in the suggested reference list. This bibliography for Part 4 is listed to give you an overview of the scope of the exam. The IIA also indicates that the examination scope includes

1. Articles from *Internal Auditor* (The IIA periodical)
2. IIA research reports
3. IIA pronouncements, e.g., The IIA Code of Ethics and SIASs
4. Past published CIA examinations

The IIA bibliography is reproduced for your information only. The texts you will need to acquire (use) to prepare for the CIA exam will depend on many factors, including

1. Innate ability
2. Length of time out of school
3. Thoroughness of your undergraduate education
4. Familiarity with internal auditing due to relevant experience

SUGGESTED REFERENCES FOR PART 4 OF THE CIA EXAM

Part 4: Business Management Skills

Competitive Strategy: Techniques for Analyzing Industries and Competitors, Michael E. Porter, 1998, The Free Press, www.simonandschuster.com.

International Business with Global Resource CD, Powerweb and World Map, 4th Ed., Charles W.L. Hill, 2002, McGraw-Hill/Irwin, www.mhprofessional.com.

International Financial Management, 3rd Ed., Cheol S. Eun, Bruce G. Resnick, and David Percy Rooke, 2003, McGraw-Hill/Irwin, www.mhprofessional.com.

Management, 10th Ed., Robert Kreitner, 2008, Houghton Mifflin Co., www.cengage.com/southwestern/.

Marketing Management, 13th Ed., Philip Kotler, 2008, Prentice Hall, www.mypearsonstore.com.

The Portable MBA, 4th Ed., Robert F. Bruner, Mark R. Eaker, R. Edward Freeman, Robert E. Spekman, Elizabeth Olmsted Teisberg, and S. Venkataraman, 2003, John Wiley & Sons, www.wiley.com.

Getting to Yes: Negotiating Agreement Without Giving In, 2nd Ed., Roger Fisher, William Ury, and Bruce Patton, 1991, Penguin USA, us.penguingroup.com.

Internal Auditing: An Integrated Approach, 2nd Ed., Richard Cascarino and Sandy van Esch, 2006, Juta and Co. Ltd., www.globaliia.org/knowledge/pages/bookstore.aspx.

AVAILABILITY OF PUBLICATIONS

The listing above presents only some of the current technical literature available, and The IIA does not carry all of the reference books. Quantity discounts are provided by The IIA. Request a current catalog by mail, call, or visit www.globaliia.org/knowledge/pages/bookstore.aspx.

The IIARF Bookstore
1650 Bluegrass Lakes Pkwy
Alpharetta, GA 30004-7714
iiapubs@pbd.com
(877) 867-4957 (toll-free) or (770) 280-4183

Contact the publisher directly if you cannot obtain the desired texts from The IIA or your local bookstore. Begin your study program with the Gleim *CIA Review*, which most candidates find sufficient. If you need additional reference material, borrow books from colleagues, professors, or a library.

INDEX

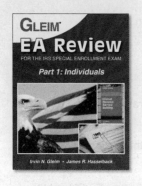

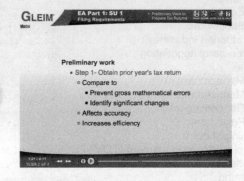
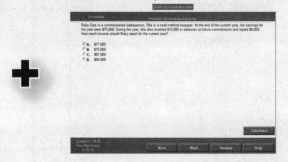
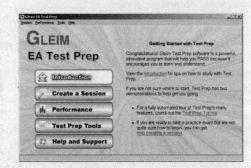

GLEIM CPA REVIEW SYSTEM

All 4 sections, including Gleim Online, Review Books, *Test Prep Software Download*, *Simulation Wizard*, Audio Review, *CPA Review: A System for Success* Booklet, plus bonus Book Bag.

$989.95 x _____ = $_____

Also available by exam section (does not include Book Bag).

GLEIM CMA REVIEW SYSTEM

Includes: Gleim Online, Review Books, *Test Prep Software Download*, Audio Review, *Essay Wizard*, *CMA Review: A System for Success* Booklet, plus bonus Book Bag.

$739.95 x _____ = $_____

Also available by exam part (does not include Book Bag).

GLEIM CIA REVIEW SYSTEM

Includes: Gleim Online, Review Books, *Test Prep Software Download*, Audio Review, *CIA Review: A System for Success* Booklet, plus bonus Book Bag.

$824.95 x _____ = $_____

Also available by exam part (does not include Book Bag).

GLEIM EA REVIEW SYSTEM

Includes: Gleim Online, Review Books, *Test Prep Software Download*, Audio Review, *EA Review: A System for Success* Booklet, plus bonus Book Bag.

$629.95 x _____ = $_____

Also available by exam part (does not include Book Bag).

"THE GLEIM REVIEW SERIES" EXAM QUESTIONS AND EXPLANATIONS

Includes: 5 Books and *Test Prep Software Download*.

$112.25 x _____ = $_____

Also available by part.

GLEIM ONLINE CPE

Try a FREE 4-hour course at gleim.com/cpe
- Easy-to-Complete
- Informative
- Effective

Contact
GLEIM PUBLICATIONS
for further assistance:

gleim.com
800.874.5346
sales@gleim.com

SUBTOTAL $_____

Complete your order on the next page

GLEIM® PUBLICATIONS, INC.

P. O. Box 12848   Gainesville, FL 32604

TOLL FREE:	800.874.5346	Customer service is available (Eastern Time):
LOCAL:	352.375.0772	8:00 a.m. - 7:00 p.m., Mon. - Fri.
FAX:	352.375.6940	9:00 a.m. - 2:00 p.m., Saturday
INTERNET:	gleim.com	Please have your credit card ready,
EMAIL:	sales@gleim.com	or save time by ordering online!

SUBTOTAL (from previous page) $_____
Add applicable sales tax for shipments within Florida. _____
Shipping (nonrefundable) 14.00

TOTAL $_____

Email us for prices/instructions on shipments outside the 48 contiguous states, or simply order online.

NAME (please print) _____

ADDRESS _____ Apt. _____
(street address required for UPS/Federal Express)

CITY _____ STATE _____ ZIP _____

____ MC/VISA/DISC/AMEX ____ Check/M.O. Daytime Telephone (____)_____

Credit Card No. _____ - _____ - _____ - _____

Exp. _____/_____ Signature _____
　　Month / Year

Email address _____

1. We process and ship orders daily, within one business day over 98.8% of the time. Call by 3:00 pm for same day service.
2. Gleim Publications, Inc. guarantees the immediate refund of all resalable texts, unopened and un-downloaded Test Prep Software, and unopened and un-downloaded audios returned within 30 days. Online courses may be canceled within 30 days if no more than the first study unit or lesson has been accessed. In addition, Online CPE courses may be canceled within 30 days if no more than the Introductory Study Questions have been accessed. This policy applies only to products that are purchased directly from Gleim Publications, Inc. No refunds will be provided on opened or downloaded Test Prep Software or audios, partial returns of package sets, or shipping and handling charges. Any freight charges incurred for returned or refused packages will be the purchaser's responsibility.
3. Please PHOTOCOPY this order form for others.
4. No CODs. Orders from individuals must be prepaid.

Subject to change without notice.

02/12

For updates and other important information, visit our website.

GLEIM
KNOWLEDGE
TRANSFER
SYSTEMS®

Share your suggestions on how we can improve *CIA 4*

FEEDBACK

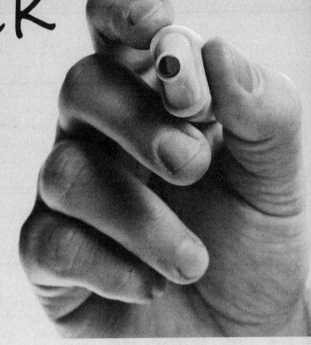

Scan with your mobile

Or go to: www.gleim.com/feedbackCIA4

Success stories!

As I studied and worked through my Gleim materials, it was easy for me to see why Gleim is considered to be a premier provider for CIA Certification learning materials. My background is in IT and I have a BA in Business Administration. However, by using my Gleim materials, I was able to sufficiently refresh my understanding of all processes and also learn many things that I had never been exposed to. Every Gleim employee I have dealt with has always been very courteous, professional, supportive and encouraging along the way, which made the difference for me. To summarize, Gleim has an excellent system in place to learn the materials needed to prepare for and pass the CIA exams.

- Terry Whaley, CIA, CISA, CGEIT, President Heartland-Iowa IIA Chapter

Thanks to Gleim I have passed my CIA Exams. I passed all three (Parts 1, 2, and 3) the first time. You have an excellent self-study system, especially the tests on the computer. Thanks.

- Stef Borghouts, CIA

I took the CIA Part 1 Internal Audit's Role in Governance, Risk Management and Controls exam and I have been informed that I passed. I really appreciate the Gleim education materials, which allowed me to better study and pass the exam. Gleim is part of my success and I will continue to study with the Gleim System. I have to say thank you very much for your support and good service.

- Ahmed Said

The Gleim Online, Audio, Study Guide, and Test Prep software were more than adequate to prepare me for the CIA exams. Despite a heavy work schedule, military deployment, and family challenges I was able to pass all four parts on the first try. I would definitely recommend Gleim to anyone

- Kevin Johnson, CIA